PUDUCHERRY

DEVELOPMENT REPORT

सत्यमेव जयते

PLANNING COMMISSION

GOVERNMENT OF INDIA

Puducherry
Development Report

सत्यमेव जयते

PLANNING COMMISSION
GOVERNMENT OF INDIA
NEW DELHI

Published by

ACADEMIC FOUNDATION
NEW DELHI

First Published in 2010 by

Academic Foundation

4772-73 / 23 Bharat Ram Road, (23 Ansari Road), Darya Ganj, New Delhi - 110 002 (India).
Phones : 23245001 / 02 / 03 / 04. Fax : +91-11-23245005. E-mail : books@academicfoundation.com
www.academicfoundation.com

Published under arrangement with :

Planning Commission,
Government of India,
New Delhi.

Cataloging in Publication Data--DK
Courtesy: D.K. Agencies (P) Ltd. <docinfo@dkagencies.com>

Puducherry development report / Planning Commission, Government of India.
p. cm.
Includes bibliographical references (p.).
ISBN 13: 9788171887842
ISBN 10: 8171887848

1. Pondicherry (India : Union Territory)--Economic policy. 2. Economic development--India--Pondicherry (Union Territory) 3. Rural development--India--Pondicherry (Union Territory) 4. Human services--India--Pondicherry (Union Territory) I. India. Planning Commission.

DDC 338.95486 22

Designed and typeset by Italics India, New Delhi
Printed and bound in India.

Contents

The Core Committee

Member *Planning Commission, New Delhi*	**Chairman**
Adviser (SP-S) *Planning Commission, New Delhi*	**Member**
Planning Secretary *Government of Puducherry, Puducherry*	**Member**
Representatives of Partner Agencies	**Member**

Research Team

1. Dr. G.S. Ganesh Prasad
2. Prof. S. Mohan Kumar
3. Prof. M. Thangaraj
4. Dr. M. Thamizoli
5. Dr. N. Rajasekaran

एम. एस. आहलुवालिया
MONTEK SINGH AHLUWALIA

सत्यमेव जयते

उपाध्यक्ष
योजना आयोग
भारत
DEPUTY CHAIRMAN
PLANNING COMMISSION
INDIA

June 19, 2010

MESSAGE

The Puducherry Development Report is a result of the Planning Commission's initiative to sponsor State Development Reports with much of the work for preparation of the documents being done by reputed national level institutes. The endeavour is to produce quality reference documents on development profiles of individual States and UTs and the possible strategies for accelerating growth and development, and reducing poverty and inequality.

The Puducherry Development Report reviews Puducherry's experience and highlights issues critical for the UT's development in the years ahead. I hope its publication will stimulate debate on growth strategies appropriate for Puducherry. I am sure the roadmap indicated in the Report will stimulate a broader awareness of the critical policy issues, which are being faced by the UT, and will assist Puducherry to move to a higher growth path and achieve all round human and economic development.

(Montek Singh Ahluwalia)

योजना भवन, संसद मार्ग, नई दिल्ली – 110001 दूरभाष : 23096677, 23096688 फैक्स : 23096699
Yojana Bhawan, Parliament Street, New Delhi : 110001 Phones: 23096677, 23096688 Fax : 23096699 E-mail : dch@.nic.in

वी. नारायणसामी
V. NARAYANASAMY

राज्य मंत्री योजना एवं संसदीय कार्य
भारत सरकार
योजना आयोग
योजना भवन, संसद मार्ग,
नई दिल्ली–110 001
MINISTER OF STATE FOR
PLANNING & PARLIAMENTARY AFFAIRS
GOVERNMENT OF INDIA
PLANNING COMMISSION
YOJANA BHAVAN, SANSAD MARG,
NEW DELHI-110 001
TEL: 011-23096561/23096562/23096563
FAX: 011-23096713
E-MAIL: samyselvi@nic.in

MESSAGE

The Planning Commission has taken up the much needed initiative of the preparation of 'Puducherry Development Report' in association with Madras Institute of Development Studies (MIDS), Institute of Finance Management and Research (IFMR) Chennai and M.S. Swaminathan Research Foundation (MSSRF), Chennai. This has been a part of national level exercise, wherein, development reports on each State/UT have been prepared in the Planning Commission.

The Union Territory of Puducherry has been making rapid strides in the realm of development and the support and guidance provided by the Planning Commission, from time to time, have been major contributors in this regard. This initiative of Planning Commission, at this juncture, is therefore, highly commendable. Apart from providing a roadmap for attaining a higher growth trajectory, this report also lucidly analyses the possible areas of focus and development. Though Puducherry UT is one among the best administered States/UTs, their report would further benefit the Government of Puducherry in fine-tuning its planning process.

The in-depth analysis exhibited in the report will act as a ready-reckoner and will be of immense help to all concerned for evolving suitable policies, plans and programmes towards improving the quality of life in Puducherry UT. I compliment the officers and experts concerned in the Planning Commission, Government of Puducherry and other agencies such as MIDS, IFMR, MSSRF etc., for their praiseworthy effort in arriving at such a highly informative 'Puducherry Development Report'

(V. Narayanasamy)

V. VAITHILINGAM
CHIEF MINISTER
GOVERNMENT OF PUDUCHERRY

सत्यमेव जयते

PUDUCHERRY
Date : 04/06/2010

MESSAGE

Planning Commission, as a part of the Central Plan Scheme of 50th year of initiative of planning, has entrusted the task of preparing the SDR for Puducherry with Madras Institute of Development Studies (MIDS). The objective in bringing out the SDR is to provide a quality reference document on development profile and set out strategies for accelerating the growth rate. SDR is aimed to be credible independent document prepared with the assistance of reputed expert national level agencies. The Report is expected to set out the medium term strategies that need to be adopted to bring about the accelerated levels of growth needed to lessen disparities and reduce poverty.

I am happy to note that the SDR prepared by MIDS made analysis among others on Development Strategy and Economic Profile, Fiscal Situation and Policies, Infrastructure Development, Restructuring of Public Sector Undertaking, Governance, etc. I hope that the SDR being the first of its kind in this Union Territory will help the concerned departments and planners in framing suitable and timely policies to accelerate the tempo of economic development, keeping in mind, the target groups and other weaker sections of the society are taken care adequately by ensuring flow of the fruits of development. I am thankful to Planning Commission for having taken the initiative and interest in bringing a Development Report so as to take stock of the situation of the States concerned for further improvement. I congratulate the MIDS and partner institutions for the excellent work done in bringing out a State Development Report for the Union Territory of Puducherry.

V. Vaith
(V. VAITHILINGAM)

Off.: 2333399, 2335530, 2335328, 2335522 Fax: 0413-2333135 Res.: 2227622, 2699489

ARUN MAIRA
MEMBER

Tele.: +91-11-23096750
Fax.: +91-11+23096577
E-mail: arun.maira@nic.in

भारत सरकार
योजना आयोग
योजना भवन
नई दिल्ली–110 001
GOVERNMENT OF INDIA
PLANNING COMMISSION
YOJANA BHAVAN
NEW DELHI-110 001

MESSAGE

The Puducherry State Development Report has been prepared by the Planning Commission with the support of the State Government. The preparation of State Development Reports is an initiative to assess with States the development alternatives available to them keeping in view their financial, human and material resources and felt needs of the people. It is hoped the State Development Report for Puducherry would provide useful inputs to policy makers in the State and Central Government engaged in directing the development process in the State.

The present Report takes stock of the resources available in Puducherry and it may provide a roadmap for achieving a higher level of growth. I hope the Report will be useful for the Government of UT, non-governmental organisations, citizens's groups and other concerned with the formulation and implementation of plans and policies oriented towards achieving a better quality of life for the people of the UT.

I would like to place on record my deep appreciation of the significant contribution to this Report by Dr. Maria Saleth, Director, Madras Institute of Development Studies.

(Arun Maira)

Preface

Madras Institute of Development Studies (MIDS), Chennai was entrusted with the responsibility of preparing the State Development Report of Puducherry during April 2004 under the Central Plan Scheme of '50th Year Initiatives for Planning' which is administered by the Plan Coordination Division in the Planning Commission. The task of MIDS was to coordinate with other partner Institutions, Institute for Financial Management and Research (IFMR) and M.S. Swaminathan Research Foundation (MSSRF).

The Puducherry State Development Report delves into the development of various sectors over the past two decades to understand the development pattern in the state. It looks into the internal integration and social embeddedness among the sectors. Unlike the traditional way of looking at the growth of sectors to assess the development, the report analyses the development pattern, internal integration and the interaction of the economy with the global situation.

Secondary data was collected from the Central Ground Water Board, RBI and NABARD on ground water resources, credit disbursements and GSDP indicators. Detailed discussions were held with the Directors of departments concerned to understand the growth and development over the period in the particular sector. The Director of the Planning and Research Department and the Director of Economics and Statistics Department helped in understanding the macro picture of the economy, temporally and spatially. This assisted us in understanding the different development opportunities available and the social as well as geographical limits to the development of Puducherry. The discussions also dwelt on the development strategies followed over the period and the impact of the programmes on the economic development of the Union Territory.

The cooperation and support from the officials of the Planning Department and the Department of Economics and Statistics, has enabled us to have the privy to published and unpublished data, and information pertaining to various policies and development in Puducherry. In addition, discussions with them transected the development pattern, state policies and development over the period. It also helped in understanding the development strategies followed over the period and the development opportunities available for the future.

Discussions with directors and other department heads of various government departments in Puducherry equipped us with adequate information relating to the development pattern, policy shifts over the period and the internal integration among the departments. We acknowledge the kind cooperation and support received from each of the departments.

We place on record our sincere thanks to the partner institutions, IFMR and MSSRF, for exchanging information and readily accepting the invitations for meetings at periodic intervals to review the progress of the work and bringing consensus in the methodology.

Nevertheless, the views expressed in the report are of the authors, and not of the Institutions to which they belong.

Prof. Padmini Swaminathan

Director

MIDS

Abbreviations

AIDS	Acquired Immune Deficiency Syndrome
AIR	All India Radio
ATM	Automatic Teller Machine
BC	Backward Class
BCG	Bacillus Calmette Guerine (Tuberculosis Vaccination)
BPL	Below Poverty Line
BPO	Business Process Outsourcing
CASIT	Centre for Advanced Studies in Information Technology
CBOs	Community Based Organisations
CHC	Community Health Centres
CMG	Credit Management Group
CMIE	Centre for Monitoring Indian Economy
CSS	Centrally Sponsored Schemes
DHAN	Development of Human Action Network
DIC	District Industries Centre
DIET	District Institute of Educational Training
DPT	Diphtheria Pertussis Tetanus
DRDA	District Rural Development Authority
DT	Diphtheria Tetanus
EPF	Employees Provident Fund
ESI	Employees State Insurance
FFDP	Fish Farmers' Development Programme
GIS	Group Insurance Schemes
GoI	Government of India
GPS	Global Positioning System
GSDP	Gross State Domestic Product
GVA	Gross Value Addition
Ha	Hectare
HCL	Hindustan Computers Ltd
HDI	Human Development Index
HPC	High Power Committee
HUDCO	Housing Development Corporation
HYV	High Yielding Variety
IAF	Indian Air Force
IBM	In-Board Mechanised Boat
ICAR	Indian Council of Agricultural Research
IMA	Indian Medical Association
IMY	Indira Mahila Yojana
INTACH	Indian National Trust for Architectural and Cultural Heritage
IPM	Integrated Pest Management
IQ	Intelligence Quality
IT	Information Technology
JIPMER	Jawaharlal Nehru Institute for Post-Graduate Medical Education and Research
KCC	Kisan Credit Card
Km^2	Square Kilometres
LIC	Life Insurance Corporation
MCM	Million Cubic Metre
m.ha.m	Million Hectare Metres
MLAs	Members of Legislative Assembly
MoU	Memorandum of Understanding
MSSRF	M.S. Swaminathan Research Foundation
MT	Metric Tonnes

NA	Not Available
NABARD	National Bank for Agriculture and Rural Development
NBFC	Non-Banking Financial Company
NGO	Non-Government Organisations
MHRD	Ministry of Human Resource Development
Nos.	Numbers
NSDP	Net State Domestic Product
NTC	National Textile Corporation
OBM	Out-Board Machine Boats
PADCO	Puducherry Adi-dravidar Development Corporation
PAPSCO	Puducherry Agro-Products and Civil Supplies Corporation
PASIC	Puducherry Agro-Services and Investment Corporation
PH	Physically Handicapped
PHC	Primary Health Centre
PIPDIC	Puducherry Industry Promotion, Development and Investment Corporation
PLP	Potential Linked Credit Plan
PMRY	Prime Minister Rozgar Yojana
PMSS	Puducherry Multipurpose Service Society
PPP	Purchasing Power Parity
PRIs	Panchayat Raj Institutions
PSTN	Public Switching Telephone Networks
PSU	Public Sector Undertaking
PTTDC	Puducherry Transport and Tourisms Development Corporation
RBI	Reserve Bank of India
REGP	Rural Employment Guarantee Programme
RIDF	Rural Infrastructure Development Fund
RRB	Regional Rural Bank
SBI	State Bank of India
SC	Scheduled Caste
SCBs	Scheduled Commercial Banks
SEZ	Special Economic Zone
SGSY	Swarnajayanti Gram Swarozgar Yojana
SHG	Self Help Groups
SJSRY	Swarna Jayanti Shaharia Rozgar Yojana
SMEs	Small and Medium-sized Enterprises
SRS	Sample Registration System
SSA	Sarva Shiksha Abhiyan
SSI	Small Scale Industries
SSSBEs	Small Scale Service and Business Enterprises
STD	Sexually Transmitted Disease
TT	Tetanus Toxoid
UCBs	Urban Co-Operatives Banks
UT/UTP	Union Territory–Puducherry
VCRC	Vector Control Research Centre
VRS	Voluntary Retirement Scheme
WAPCOS	Water and Power Consultancy Services

List of Tables, Figures and Annexures

Tables

Figures

Annexures

Executive Summary

The Puducherry State Development Report focuses on the development of various sectors over the past two decades to understand the development pattern in the state. It looks into the internal integration and social embeddedness among the sectors. Unlike the traditional method of looking at the growth of sectors to assess the development, the report analyses the development pattern, internal integration between various sectors, and the interaction of the economy with the global scenario. Internal integration in particular refers to the sectoral and spatial integration of policies and programmes of the state. This assumes significance since large scale inter-sectoral changes are being witnessed in the post-reform period. The exercise specifically looks into the transition from the traditional sectors to the industry and service sector for economic growth of Puducherry.

Puducherry Profile

Puducherry, Karaikal, Mahe, and Yanam merged with Indian Union *de facto* on November 1, 1954. The *de jure* merger took place on August 16, 1962. Since then, Puducherry has witnessed development in most of the sectors. The global public goods like health and education sectors have displayed remarkable strides. Though agriculture has not shown much development in consonance with other sectors, the industries sector and service sectors have been growing exponentially. Infrastructure has been perceptibly well developed to the growing needs of the economy.

Social welfare programmes implemented in the state clearly reiterate the social embeddedness of the development in the economy. In the social sector, all the components have been making exceedingly good progress. Education, both school and higher education, health and social security aspects have been making noticeable progress due to the proactive measures undertaken by the government. The progress in these sectors is made possible by the generous central grants to the level of 'special category states.' The resource base in the state has not been adequately tapped. Though the revenue account now consistently shows a surplus and budget almost balanced, the financial structure does not seem to be healthy due to the overdependence on the centre for grants. Tourism has vast potential to bring in more foreign exchange and revenue to the state. Though concerted efforts are being made to attract tourists, it has not made significant impact in bringing revenues. However, the population depending on the tourism industry has been growing considerably. The decentralisation initiative in conformity with the 73rd and 74th Constitution Amendment needs more attention. The local bodies' election has been conducted after a long gap. Though e-governance initiatives have been taken up proactively, the transparency and information availability questions are not adequately addressed. Nevertheless, the growth and development of the state show signs of optimism.

Demographic and Economic Aspects

The natural resources in Puducherry remain very limited except for the marine resources. Further, the state does not have adequate infrastructure to assimilate the modern technology. There is an urgent need to develop adequate infrastructure for modernising the fisheries sector and exploiting the coastal resources. In the case of water resources too, the integrated water resources management is required to cope with the convergence of rainfall from a bimodal into single season monsoon. The reduction of rainfall in the summers and winters would put tremendous pressure on the groundwater. Hence, there is a necessity to ensure sustainable development and utilisation of groundwater resources and thereby improving the groundwater recharging through efficient rainwater harvesting. The groundwater recharge level is hardly 20 per cent in the alluvial soil. It has to be enhanced substantially to improve the scarce ground water resources. Even the lakes and system tanks have to be maintained with utmost care to harvest the rainwater. Even in the land utilisation, there is an urgent need to control the current fallow and growing barren and uncultivable land. The significant increase in the irrigated area through tubewell source is a real cause for concern for sustainability of ground water resources.

The population growth over the last three decades has been remarkable. A significant transition is taking place in most of the demographic aspects. The decadal growth has come down during the last decade. The sex ratio has become 1001 females to 1000 males. The rural population tends to be only one-third of the total population of the whole Union Territory (UT). In the UT, two regions such as Mahe and Yanam have been declared totally urban areas. Thus, the growing urban population in the UT emphasises the need for developing the urban infrastructure in all the regions. The decline in the rural population also indicates that there is large scale migration of unskilled and semi-skilled labourers to the urban areas. This necessitates enough space to be created to them for alternative livelihood opportunities. Still, the growth of urban population in the Karaikal and Puducherry regions too tends to be very high. The crude birth and death rates indicate that there is a considerably higher birth rate in Puducherry and Yanam. The death rate is noticeably low in the Mahe and other regions. This manifests the ageing of the population. The ageing population has to be provided adequate social security measures to lead a socially respectable life. The increase in life expectancy is noticed in all the regions. The depressed section of the population consists of Scheduled Caste only. It remains to be around 16 per cent. There is no Scheduled Tribe in the whole of UT. The depressed sections namely Scheduled Caste people are increasingly in the Below Poverty Line (BPL) category. Some innovative measures with precise targeting to reach the deserving people should be deigned.

The literacy rate across the region exhibits the total literacy in the Mahe region. The growth of literacy in the UT has been astounding in the successive census period. There is a decreasing trend in infant mortality rates over the years, which is attributed to the efficiency of the health care system of the state. The regular immunisation and other check-ups indicate the improvement in the health parameters in the UT. The Jawaharlal Institute of Post Graduate Medical Education and Research (JIPMER) and the Sri Aurobindo International Institute for Integral Health and Research (SAIIIHR) attract huge medical tourists into the UT. In the poverty level, the urban poverty is very high in the UT. Among the Union Territories, Puducherry has the highest number and proportion of BPL families. This manifests the widespread poverty in the urban areas in the Puducherry regions.

The estimates on GSDP of the Union Territory which was at Rs.418809 lakh at current prices for the year 2001-2002 rose to Rs.503125 lakh for the year 2002-03 and Rs.574632 lakh for the year 2003-04 and Rs.645667 lakh for the year 2004-05 and Rs.719618 lakh for the year 2005-06 respectively, with an increase of 20.13 per cent and 14.21 per cent and 12.36 per cent and 11.85 per cent respectively, over the previous years. The major contributor for the growth in GSDP is the secondary sector especially Manufacturing Registered sector whose gross value addition are supplied by Central Statistical Organisation (CSO) based on the results of Annual Survey of Industries (ASI). As per the ASI results, gross value addition of manufacturing sector rose from Rs.145016 lakh for 2000-01 to Rs.173742 lakh for 2001-02 and Rs.202918 lakh for the year 2002-03 showing an increase of 36.10 per cent, 19.80 per cent and 16.79 per cent respectively, over the previous years. Changes in sectoral contribution reveal that the economy of Puducherry is gradually shifting from agriculture activities to non-agriculture activities.

The growth of the economy is assessed with the help of GSDP across sectors over the period. The proportion of sectoral contribution to the GSDP indicates that the primary sector contribution has declined considerably to the level of some of the developed countries. Even the secondary sector contribution began to decline in the nineties. Only tertiary sector has been growing phenomenally. In the primary sector, contribution of fisheries tends to be higher than the agriculture. Most of the components in the tertiary sector have shown higher growth rates at constant prices. Conversely, there is a negligible growth rate in the old series at constant prices. The growth rate is relatively better in the new series at constant prices.

Similarly, the estimates of per capita income in the recent years have shown significant changes. The estimates of per capita income (NSDP) at current prices increased from Rs. 37,926 in 2001-02 to Rs. 61,064 during 2005-06 indicating improved performance of the economy during the period. The per capita income across other states indicates that there was a decline in the per capita GSDP during the early nineties in the old series. The same is witnessed in Puducherry. The decline in the proportion of contribution of primary sector to the GSDP is a cause for concern to the health of the economy and society. It also provokes the government to provide adequate social risk management measures to rural population.

The employment pattern in Puducherry indicates that there is a perceptible decline in the proportion of agricultural workers whereas the manufacturing and tertiary sectors have registered a noticeable increase. Across the regions, Karaikal region reported a very low proportion of secondary sector workers while Yanam and Mahe found more proportion of workers in fisheries and livestock rearing. The employment in the organised and unorganised sectors insinuates the growth of unorganised sector in the post-reform period. The average number of daily workers in the factories not submitting returns has been leapfrogging year after year. Though the units in the unorganised sector have grown remarkably, the number of persons employed shows signs of decline indicating the 'lean and efficient' policy being adopted in both the organised and unorganised sectors. The unemployment data demonstrates an alarming situation in Puducherry among the educated and uneducated persons. Nearly 15 per cent of the population is in the live register and it keeps increasing at the rate of 1.5 per cent. In comparison with other states, the employment growth rate is apparently progressive due to its proactive measures in the creation of employment to all sections of the society.

Poverty and unemployment are two major issues that need to be given attention in plan schemes. As per the Tenth Plan projections the poverty ratio in Puducherry may reduce from 20.5 per cent (as per the Poverty Live Survey 1999-2000 conducted by the Planning Commission) to 7.7 per cent as against the national average of 27.1 per cent in 1999-2000 to 19.5 per cent by the end of the Tenth Plan. Development of infrastructure facilities would lead to sectoral growth, increase in per capita income and creation of more employment opportunities both under organised as well as unorganised sectors. Special attention needs to be given towards effective implementation of centrally funded rural poverty alleviation programme and urban poverty alleviation programme. Funds available through Lead Bank scheme can be utilised towards implementation of economic development schemes dovetailed with state subsidy for various disadvantaged groups like women, SCs, backward classes and disabled, and promotion of self-employment schemes for educated unemployed youths. Implementation of many welfare schemes would also indirectly contribute towards lifting many poor families above the poverty line by the end of the Eleventh Plan.

The fiscal indicators in Puducherry point to the fiscal discipline in the state. It proclaims the judicious management of resources in the state. Though the tax revenue and non-tax revenue to the GSDP remain low and the surplus in the revenue account is increasingly attributed to the substantial grants-in-aid received by the UT from the Centre. However, unlike other states Puducherry as UT is not eligible for devolution of funds under the Finance Commission award. The grants-in-aid received by the state equals some of the special category states. The growth of cooperative sector manifests the support of the government for cooperative movement to enlist the community participation in the development activities. Certain socially beneficial activities like college, bus service, auto rickshaw pool etc., are seen particularly in Mahe.

Regional Imbalance

An effort has been made to look into the regional imbalances prevailing across the four regions of the Union Territory. The data, wherever available, has been analysed for all the four regions. The regional imbalances are visible and Karaikal emerges relatively as the most backward region within the Union Territory. A note of caution needs to be emphasised here. The backwardness of Karaikal is only with respect to the other Puducherry regions and cannot be compared with other backward regions or districts in either southern states or other states in the country.

Structure and Reforms of Finances

The fiscal deficit, which increased from Rs.81.4 crore in 2000-01 to Rs.146 crore in 2001-02 has since declined to Rs.113 crore in 2002-03. Earlier, emergence of sizeable level of revenue deficit to the extent of Rs.26 crore in 2001-02 has since been reversed. Under the fiscal reforms and budgetary management discipline, steps have been taken to generate revenue surplus in subsequent years. Mobilisation of own resources improved from 55 per cent in 1999-2000 to 62 per cent in 2003-04. There is an increase in actual tax revenue to Rs.353 crore in 2003-04 as compared to tax revenue of Rs.261 crore in 1999-2000. In the coming years, targeting and efficient collection of tax revenue substantially assumes vital importance. Non-tax revenue in the medium-term could increase only marginally and may prove more difficult to step up. As compared to 1999-2000, non-development revenue expenditure increased by 50 per cent in 2003-04, whereas developmental revenue expenditure (excluding electricity) increased by only 33 per cent. Non-development revenue expenditure should not be allowed to grow at a faster pace than development expenditure. Fiscal liabilities increased from Rs.699 crore in 1999-2000 to Rs.1307 crore in 2003-04. The interest rate (10.5 per cent) is much higher than the rate of growth of GSDP (about 6 per cent to 7 per cent per annum) during 2001-2003 indicating poor debt sustainability. The way forward is obviously optimal targeting and efficient collection of revenues, both tax and non-tax, prioritising revenue expenditure, controlling administrative expenditure, curtailing subsidies and following financially prudent capital expenditure programme.

Industrial Development

The large growth rate in the industrial sector between 1995-96 and 2001-02 was due to the significant contribution of the manufacturing sector. Employment in the manufacturing sector significantly increased between 1993-94 and 1999-2000 correspondingly. Exports have shot up from Rs.28 crore in 1989 to Rs.464 crore in 2003 in value terms with chemical and chemical products; leather products, and machinery parts being important items of export in 2003. The industrial policy reforms have been rightly emphasising industrialisation in Puducherry as the state cannot depend on agriculture. Therefore, incentives and concessions continue to play a dominant role in attracting investments in industries in the state.

The large-scale industry (LSI) in Puducherry accounts for more than half of the total investments but the small-scale industry (SSI) sector contributes about 45 per cent of the production value. The LSI and middle-scale industries (MSI) sectors constitute about 27 per cent of the production value each. Even in terms of employment, the SSI employs about two-thirds of the workforce. Puducherry should frame policies to develop it as the IT hardware capital of India. Industrial policies are now oriented to check industrial pollution so that ground water is both conserved and not affected. Therefore, water intensive and chemical industries are now actively discouraged.

Agriculture and Rural Development

The contribution of agriculture to the state income has declined from 11.35 per cent in 1994-95 to 6.12 per cent in 2002-03. Area, production and productivity of crop has declined over a period of time due to the reduction of net area sown, total cropped area and increase of culturable waste and area under wasteland. Consumption of agricultural inputs like fertiliser has increased from 255 kg/ha in 1980-81 to 1305 kg/ha during 2004-05 which leads to unsustainable food production. However, the use of pesticide has reduced from 62 MT in 2001-02 to 43 MT during 2004-05. Increase in the number of implements resulted in fastening the agricultural activity, but could also lead to the problem of unemployment especially during the peak agricultural season like transplanting and harvesting. Failure of monsoon and unavailability of credit at crucial time has left the farmers at risk. Marketing of produce is still difficult to the farmers because of poor road and transport facility and high transportation costs. Another reason for reduced agricultural activity is due to the constraints in labour and reduction in number of cultivators over a period of time. Among the allied activities, in the animal husbandry sector the animal population has decreased substantially in the last two decades. However, the fisheries sector has recorded an impressive growth.

Another important area which needs attention is irrigation, both surface and groundwater. The canal irrigation is limited to the Karaikal region which gets water through the Cauvery river, as per the award of the Cauvery Water Disputes Tribunal. However the cause of concern is in relation to groundwater irrigation. The groundwater potential has reduced over a period of time due to over exploitation, especially by the tubewells. Seawater intrusion into the groundwater aquifers is hindering the agricultural activity.

New schemes have been introduced for conservation of soil and water resources. Since projected water balance is negative, people show interest in goat rearing and fish farming as seen by the increase in number of goats and fish production. Dairy farming activity has decreased because of labour problem. Extension services needs to be strengthened to protect the primary sector activities. Rural development schemes have been introduced by the state government as well as Central government. But the performance has fallen short of targets. Training should be given to the farmers especially farm women, because they play an important role in farm activity. Production, productivity and diversification of crops should be increased to ensure food security but it should be achieved without harming the environment.

Infrastructure

Increasing emphasis is being placed throughout the world on establishing an 'investment friendly' climate. Even in India, states are being ranked according to their investment climate. This ranking is being taken quite seriously by foreign investors especially those who need timely decisions by state level authorities. While infrastructure development is important for creating right investment climate, an equally key component is hastening the process of obtaining clearances for establishing industries. Though Puducherry's industrial policy has emphasised a single window clearance system, in practice this system is not fully operational. While the District Industries Centre is the nodal agency for the single window clearance system, i.e., it is supposed to forward the applications of industrialists to the concerned municipality/commune *panchayats* after getting the necessary clearances, industrialists are still made to approach the various departments concerned to pursue their applications. This is an extremely arduous task as it involves getting an NOC from the Directorate of Industries, approval of the factory layout from the Inspectorate of Factories, site clearance from the Town and Country Planning Department, permission of land conversion from the Agricultural Department, power feasibility certificate from the Electricity Department, building plan approval from the Puducherry Planning Authority, clearance from the Health, Fire Service, and Revenue Departments and licenses if necessary, from the Food and Drugs Administration and Civil Supplies Department.

For all of this to take place, considerable effort will have to be taken to improve the overall efficiency of government departments. While the computerisation of line departments will help to a great extent, equally important is improving the 'friendliness' of both government and public sector employees. Such employees need to undergo training for the necessary attitudinal changes so that they perceive the public as customers. Also, central to creating the right environment is promoting Puducherry as a favoured industrial location. Puducherry needs to much more actively seek out industries to invest in the Union Territory by holding industrial trade fairs, meeting with industrialists on one to one basis, and actively advertising the infrastructural and economic incentives it has to offer. This is all the more important in a situation where states are competing with each other for industrial investment. By attracting a few big industrial houses/ investor groups, Puducherry could lead to substantial spin-off investments in MSI and SSI and also basic infrastructure, which will lead to much more active industrial interest in Puducherry.

Social Sector

Education and health sectors have been making remarkable achievements in the state. The importance for education was prioritised from the date of French arrival. The literacy rate is very close to the Kerala level. It has grown with strides in the last three decades. The growth of enrolment of students, teachers and institutions in both government and private schools remains to be indicative of the sustained proactive efforts undertaken by the government. The student-teacher ratio has been reaching the optimum level of around 20. The student-teacher ratio tends to be low in the private schools. This indicates the quality of education through personal attention to the students. This is one reason for the preference of the private schools. The dropout rates tend to be high among the SCs and BCs at the primary and upper primary level. At the secondary level, the dropout rate is high among girls and upper caste students. This manifests that the upper caste students are invariably able to study at least up to the secondary level but in the case of SCs and BCs the dropouts occur at the primary and upper primary level. Those who cross this milestone are able to pursue their education at higher levels. Thus, proactive measures have to be taken up to arrest the dropout of students from SC and BC categories at the primary and upper primary level. The major reason for this is undoubtedly the repetition. Similarly, the children with special needs have to be taken care at the school level.

Higher education is highly privatised and the department has been making concerted effort to attract more educational tourism and developing huge human resource potential locally to take advantage of the emerging industrialisation and information technology. The student-teacher ratio has been increasing marginally. The decline in girl student-teacher ratio in all the courses indicates the increase in the number of women teachers in higher educational institutions. Barring the law, and arts and science colleges, the student-teacher ratio in all the other courses has been deplorably low indicating the underutilisation of available capacity. This indicates the need for optimum use of available resources. The IT education has been getting impetus since nineties to meet the growing needs of the state and the vision of creating the state as a leading hardware centre in the country.

The health indicators in Puducherry have been far progressive when compared with the national indicators. But within the state, the urban Karaikal region has the highest birth and death rates, whereas IMR is the highest in Puducherry urban region. In the recent release of the Directorate of Health and Family welfare, the doctor and nurse population ratio is not comfortable to meet the requirements. Nevertheless, with the available human resources the state is able to manage the medical and surgical facilities in the medical institutions of the state. In a recent move, the state has passed orders to register the private practitioners, private hospitals and nursing homes, which would be to facilitate a new policy on health that includes the private sector as well.

Under the health services provided by the state in the allopathic treatment, there is a decline in the patients availing the services. Increase in private health services has contributed substantially in balancing the health services provided in Puducherry. There is a steep increase in availing services under homeopathy treatment, which is still limited in the state. The provision of Indian system of medicine and homeopathy could be boosted, to reach more population by adding the facilities in the dispensaries and PHCs.

Lack of good drainage is another possible cause contributing to water-borne diseases. In Puducherry, open drains are prevalent. Closing these drains with a cover could avert the prevalence of diseases. In rural areas, there are reported leaks, incidences of contamination and subsequent infections. Regular IEC activities addressing these issues could avert such incidences.

Under protective social security, the public and private sector undertakings enrol their employees under the EPF and ESI. They avail the benefits under their respective organisation. The unorganised sector in Puducherry has two divisions, one is a society and other is a welfare board. These two divisions have started functioning only in the past few years. Awareness generation among the unorganised sector could promote the outreach in future. The promotional social security is being undertaken by social welfare department, Adi Dravidar welfare department and the department of women and child development in Puducherry. While doing this a special attention needs to be given to women and female children.

Tourism

The establishment of a separate Tourism Development Corporation and Transport service of Puducherry as constituent of it, facilitated the tourism industry by providing innovative tourism products and services. The low cost accommodation through youth hostels, Yatri Niwas accommodation, government guest houses and low cost high quality boarding provided through the *La Caffes* and the Seagull restaurants encouraged the tourists to prefer Puducherry as the favoured destination. The JIPMER and multi-specialty private medical colleges bring in a lot of medical tourists to the state. The government has been increasingly encouraging the private sector to establish tourist resorts and hotels with attractive incentives. All these things boosted up the number of tourists, both domestic and foreign, visiting the state. The concomitant impact is noticed in the number of people depending on the tourism industry. The government has been making huge investments in the development of innovative products and services to the tourists and showcasing it through a fat advertisement budget. However, there is need to showcase the facilities and the tourists attractions in the UT.

Public Sector Units: Restructuring and Reforms

So far PSU reforms in Puducherry have been confined to internal productivity/efficiency measures on a case-by-case basis. In really difficult cases like Anglo-French Textiles, VRS scheme has been attempted in addition to modernisation and rehabilitation. Puducherry government is required to do zero-base budgeting of most of the state PSUs. Puducherry government could possibly emulate Tamil Nadu government and constitute something similar to Raghavan Committee to suggest reforms and restructuring of its PSUs, specifically in terms of disinvestments, spin-off as joint ventures, mergers and phased close down.

Financial Services

The financial sector comprising banking and finance, which was 8 per cent of the service sector at the beginning of economic liberalisation in 1991-92, presently forms 12 per cent. As in other states, the banking sector provides the bulk of credit requirements in the Union Territory of Puducherry also. In Puducherry the annual compound growth rate of bank deposits of Scheduled Commercial Banks was 9.64 per cent in the decade of the nineties which is an indicator of the growth of the financial sector. The rate of growth of loans was 4.55 per cent in the same period indicating much lower level of fund usage and this is again reflected in the marked unsatisfactory level in the C/D ratio throughout the last decade (less than 50 per cent). However, the same has picked up since 2000-01 and has improved to 55 per cent in recent years. There has been no shortage of credit availability from credit institutions in the state.

The Puducherry State Cooperative Bank, which has been in operation for more than four decades, has been through periods of uncertain business. Though it has had negative earnings in the eighties and nineties, it has turned profitable in recent years. The recent surge of failures, all over India, of cooperative banks highlights the need to restructure their regulatory guidelines by RBI, keeping in view their intrinsic character.

NBFCs even in Puducherry cater to a wide range of customised demands for many types of loans. The salient characteristic of NBFCs is their non-formality. Further, documentation for availing of loans is simple in contrast to that in SCBs.

Governance

The democratic decentralisation initiatives in the UT need more attention. The elections to the communes and *panchayats* have been conducted in 2006 after a gap of 38 years. The Conformity Act for the 73rd and 74th Amendments Act has not been passed. Though two Finance Commissions have been appointed and submitted their reports, they are perfunctory in nature and substance. The revenue and expenditure pattern in the communes manifest the huge potential available for generating more resources and spending on development activities. The e-governance initiatives have been commissioned with the help of the IBM company. Already some of the departments have been networked and automated. There is a provision for allotting two per cent of the budget of each department for office automation and e-governance initiatives. The right to information process has been initiated through the publication of Citizens' Charters and installation of kiosks in the department offices. Thus, the government has been increasingly proactive in the e-governance initiatives.

Way Forward

Puducherry as a Model Small State

Puducherry is emerging as a model small state on the national scene, as evident from being judged as the best small state in *India Today*'s annual state survey. Its enormous potential, with per capita income second only to Goa, and literacy rate second only to Kerala, needs to be harnessed in full measure. With much needed provision of maritime port, functional airport and broad gauge rail network, its potential as a prosperous special economic zone and springboard of all-round growth can be realised.

Prospect and Retrospect

A study of the changing composition of GSDP of the state between 1993-94 and 2000-01 shows drastic decline in primary sector, mainly traditional agriculture. There is a redeeming increase in secondary sector, mainly industries. However, as against national and global trend of dominance in recent years (more than 50 per cent share) of tertiary sector, mainly service sector, that of Puducherry has marginally decreased from 48.6 per cent to 44.3 per cent.

It is imperative for Puducherry to take proactive measures for accelerated development of its service sector as its future engine of growth. Both composition change of GSDP in Tamil Nadu between 1993-94 and 1999-2000 (24.3 to 20 per cent in primary, 32.4 to 30 per cent in secondary, and 43.3 to 50 per cent in tertiary sectors) with slant on service sector and all-India level contribution of about 55 per cent of GSDP from service sector emphasise the enormous potential of service sector for economic growth and more importantly employment opportunities.

In primary sector, increasing shift to horticulture, floriculture, inland fisheries and cottage industries should be encouraged. Natural resource-based integrated farming system model with crop diversification and livestock integration need to be promoted. In secondary sector, continued emphasis on small and medium enterprises and small scale service business enterprises would provide gainful employment to urban youth. Water-intensive, power-intensive and polluting units should be discouraged.

Service sector consists of human related services such as health, education, housing and sanitation, and economic related ones such as transport, financial services, hotels and restaurants, and tourism and IT/Software/BPO. Private sector participation in the human related services needs to be increasingly tapped. In economic related services of IT/Software and financial services, major players in these two fields should be actively pursued for extending their activities to Puducherry. Besides heritage and cultural tourism, potential for eco, educational and medical facility tourism should be harnessed.

- The natural resource base in Puducherry has been quite limited. In all the regions, marine resource is the commonly available natural resource and majority of the population is depending on these resources for their livelihood. The government has recognised the significance of fisheries sector to economic development of the UT through implementing various programmes for the growth of the sector. However, major infrastructure development such as fishing harbour, ice plants for preserving fish and market yards needs to be strengthened significantly to harness the full potential of the sector.
- With steep decline in agriculture/primary sector, all steps to accelerate both industrial and service sectors growth is vital for the economy of Puducherry. Industrial policies should facilitate growth of employment-oriented but non-power

and non-water-intensive and non-polluting industries such as computers and IT, engineering and auto items, electronics etc., so that power availability and groundwater are not affected. State should tap public-private partnership mode to provide world-class infrastructure for accelerated growth of industries with increasing slant on exports.

- Taking advantage of the existing state's pro-industry policies, number of integrated post-harvest value addition zones could be identified for the promotion of food processing industries for diverse products.
- In the backdrop of globalisation and free trade, India is one the signatories in Agreement of Agriculture (AoA) under the WTO. In this context, Puducherry agriculture needs to gradually shift to 'demand driven-market oriented' production rather than 'production driven' agriculture. Decline in area under cultivation, stagnant productivity of the major crops, overexploitation of groundwater resources, intensive use of land and high quantity of chemical fertiliser usage, inadequate extension services etc., are the major issues need to be addressed to improve agriculture growth. It is necessary to gradually reorient from traditional crops to horticulture and floriculture arenas.
- It is essential to increase the agricultural production vertically combined with sustainable utilisation of natural resources and available human resources. In order to bring sustainable utilisation of the natural and human resources at the farm and village level, the 'bio-village' concept is proposed. With the increasing water scarcity and changing global trade/policies, there is a need to introduce crop diversification and Integrated Farming System approach.
- The bio-village concept could be integrated with the support of the Department of Agriculture to promote decentralised extension services and horizontal transfer of knowledge. Along with agriculture, allied components like integrated dairy farming and goat farming with maximum forward and backward linkages and scientific management need to be integrated to diversify the income sources and spread the risk. Since the state has more area under paddy and coconut, it is suggested to develop integrated processing facilities in the rural areas to diversify the value addition activities. In paddy, since it occupies more than 86 per cent of the land area, System of Rice Intensification (SRI) method needs to be promoted further.
- There is a need to promote farm-based rainwater harvesting facilities wherever possible, coupled with the practice of water saving irrigation technologies. Also, it is essential to renovate the common water storage systems to augment the underground water table. It needs to be done at the village level and the annual renovation activity needs to be institutionalised through local *panchayats* and involving Uzhavar Udhaviyagams and the groups established in Tank Rehabilitation Programme under a single umbrella.
- As agriculture is moving towards knowledge-based management, it is essential to continuously upgrade the knowledge and skills of farmers by providing training on judicious management of water and chemical inputs especially to farm women and agricultural labourers.
- Puducherry with limited physical resources like land, water, power, and raw materials should focus its attention on providing industrial and social infrastructure. Obviously it needs to significantly improve its accessibility—road, rail, port, airport etc., and also upgrade its present infrastructure base (industrial estates, power, social infrastructure), in order to attract investments in all sectors. State should provide world-class infrastructure for accelerated growth of industries with slant on exports. Tapping public-private partnerships (PPPs) mode for its infrastructure projects should be given top priority.
- The modern ICT supported village level knowledge centres (Uzhavar Udhaviyagams) established have very huge potential to serve the rural community with cost effective manner. They could be promoted to play the role of multipurpose service centres with satellite connectivity.
- Proper guidance and motivation of students and their parents at the doorsteps is very much essential in arresting the problem of school dropouts in Puducherry. Teachers need to be trained accordingly to tackle this problem seriously. Similarly, the children with special needs have to be taken care at the school level.

- The democratisation of access to higher education has to be aimed at through selective targeting in the fees and other facilities to the genuinely deserving people.
- Promotion of health care systems in the identified regions with immediate attention to promote intensive, curative, and preventive measures are required to strengthen the existing medical facilities. The provision of Indian system of medicine and homeopathy could be encouraged, by adding the facilities in the dispensaries and PHCs.
- Innovative methods like telemedicine can be strengthened further and could be expanded with the ICT supported Village Knowledge Centres facilitated by government department, NGOs and managed by community based organisations operating in the villages.
- Even though the increase in the rate of AIDS is not alarming, it is essential to promote intensive and extensive awareness as a preventive measure. New partnership could be facilitated between the IEC divisions of the government with local NGOs, community-based organisations in the field of health for effective dissemination of health related information, generate awareness and conduct appropriate skill and capacity building programmes.
- In order to ensure an effective maternal health care, a comprehensive approach with community participation especially with the involvement of local women groups needs to be promoted. To meet the health concerns, further enhancement of skilled training to the village health guides and trained *dais* need to be provided.
- To enhance the participation of the unorganised labour in the programmes, awareness generation among the poor could be promoted with appropriate methods. Ensuring representation and active participation by the grassroot level SHGs, farmers and labourers' forums would improve the relevance and the quality of the schemes. The programme outreach has to be more vibrant to bring down the families in the BPL list in consonance with the aim of attaining Millennium Development Goals. Also, there is a need to target the subsidies only to the BPL families.
- There is a need to provide better social and institutional support to the aged and the disabled people in the UT. In the case of disabled people, the focus should be promotion of skill and capacity building and appropriate entrepreneurial programmes for the target groups, which could help them to become independent in their life over a period of time. It is vital that more than achieving the set target, the quality and the approach of the programme is more important. This can be achieved through establishing partnerships with appropriate institutions and experienced NGOs in the local areas, both at the designing and implementation stages.
- SHGs, a proven concept for social mobilisation of rural poor can be effectively utilised with the support of the experienced NGOs to mobilise the BPL families and to enhance the outreach of the social security programmes. The other vital factor is to ensure quality delivery of the programme and continuous human resource development for the staff executing the different programmes. Sufficient representation needs to be ensured for women's contribution at various stages of planning and implementation of various social security programmes.
- In order to promote the tourism industry the government could enter into more public–private initiatives. Further policies need to be framed for attracting more private investments in the tourism sector.
- As a result of all the infrastructure development, manpower development, innovative initiatives and incentives to education, the results in the public examination is quite satisfying in the Puducherry, Karaikal, and Mahe regions. In Yanam however, it remains unsatisfactory. Across government and private schools, private schools have produced better results. Hence, there is a compulsion for the department of education to deliver results.
- Lack of good drainage system and drinking water facilities are important causes contributing to water-borne diseases. Regular information, education and communication (IEC) activities addressing these issues and improving the situation with suitable measures could reduce and avert such incidences.
- In the industrial sector, the government's priority should be to operationalise the single window clearance system in such a manner that investing in Puducherry is not a cumbersome process. In

the Tenth Five Year Plan for industries, the government has rightly stressed the need for simplifying procedures. Even if multiple permissions are required, a nodal agency such as the Industries Department can act as the coordinator so that the entrepreneur obtains clearances smoothly from various departments.

- A single window clearance system can only be effective if the process itself is computerised in order to facilitate inter-department transactions. Once this is done, it will be possible for industrialists to pursue their applications online and consequently speed up the process. A redressal cell should also be established so that any unnecessary delays can be expeditiously pursued.
- Promotion of low cost decentralised tiny and cottage, small and medium enterprises with the underlying principles of 'technological demystification' and the appropriate linkages with technical institutions and ensuring forward linkages with the marketing agencies would simultaneously address the critical problem of rural unemployment and income enhancement. The opportunity available is the large number of well mobilised SHGs which could manage particularly small business enterprises tiny and cottage industries.
- Puducherry government needs to have a hard look on most of its PSUs functioning. It would do well to set up, similar to Raghavan Committee constituted a decade back in Tamil Nadu, PSU reforms and restructuring committee to pave the way for various options of disinvestments, spin-offs as joint ventures, mergers and phased closed down of PSUs.
- Corrective steps need to be taken to further improve its credit–deposit ratio significantly to at least 60 per cent, in consultation with all stakeholders—industry, agriculture, service sector, and scheduled banks. Active joint campaign and support by the Government and Scheduled Banks for setting up of small and medium-sized enterprises (SMEs) and small scale service and business enterprises (SSSBEs) would not only improve credit-deposit ratio but also provide significant employment opportunities. With dwindling agriculture sector base, emphasis on tiny and cottage sector and micro finance/SHGs would boost rural economy.
- The outcome of cooperative movement has been significant in all the fields. The investments through the Scheduled Commercial Banks have come down perceptibly in the agriculture sector and other rural development aspects mainly due to the microcredit programmes initiated through both credit cooperatives and non-credit cooperatives. In the recent past, the NGOs have come to play a major role in promoting microcredit among the poor and vulnerable sections of the society. The government needs to provide more incentives to promote the cooperative activities among marginalised people in the UT.
- The state should specially focus on partnership with SHGs, civil society organisations and NGOs to improve the efficiency in the implementation of various development programmes aimed at poverty alleviation.
- The decentralised institutions in the Union Territory need to be strengthened by transferring more powers to these bodies. There is also an urgent need to act upon the recommendations of the State Finance Commission for devolving more finances to the rural and urban local bodies. These institutions may also be provided with more functional autonomy.
- The fiscal situation of the state shows satisfactory fiscal discipline and prudence of the state. Unless the tax base and tax efforts are widened, the over dependence on grant-in-aid from the centre would make the economy and further development unsustainable. Also, there is an urgent need to mobilise more of own tax and non-tax revenues. The transaction cost due to the spread of the regions has to be brought down substantially through more effective e-governance initiatives.
- Taking advantage of the potential growth in GSDP, buoyancy in taxes, lowering of interest rates and tapping of public-private finance initiatives, Puducherry government should follow vigorously prudent medium-term fiscal policy measures. This is imperative as Puducherry is on the anvil of transforming from its current status as Union Territory to a full-fledged state. With the possibility of curtailment of extended loan facilities/borrowings from the Centre, like other states, Puducherry may also have to resort to market borrowings.

Policy Initiatives

There is a need to prioritise the development strategies for the Union Territory. The positive side of development is reflected in performance of social sectors in Puducherry. A number of measures initiated by the state have resulted in improving the various indicators of health and education in particular.

The contribution of primary sector especially agriculture has been dwindling over the years. There is an urgent need to follow the 'knowledge-based farming' with focus on improving the research and extension activities. The secondary and tertiary sectors have been showing increased growth rates and special efforts and support needs to be provided to sustain them in the long run.

There is also an urgent need to focus on the important issue of attaining the statehood. The statehood would result in a decrease in grant-in-aid from the Union government. The state has to make additional efforts to mobilise more resources to meet the deficit. Firstly, there is a need to reduce the subsidies provided in the state. Secondly, the concept of user charges with respect to water and electricity needs to be promoted to mobilise more funds.

Finally there is a need to have an Administrative Reforms Commission to look into the staffing pattern, devolution of more powers to the Collectors and Regional Administrators to make the system more accountable. The state also needs to address the issue of devolution of more functions, functionaries and finances to the newly created panchayati raj institutions.

Introduction

1. Introduction

The experience and knowledge of development in number of countries transpire that development depends on constellation of factors and development knowledge is contingent on the conditions of time and place (WDR, 2000). There is no single overarching policy for development in the complex situations. The states and markets remain to be two of the many partners of development. Hence, deconstructing development for reconstructing would mean identifying the constellation of factors and players, both partners and stakeholders in development.

The significant areas of development at the state level *inter alia* include education, health and capital markets. Improving the quality of life involves better health services, educational services, greater participation in public life, clean environment and so on (WDR, 2000). Institutions of good governance and partnership among all elements of civil society would ascertain consensual, participatory and transparent processes, which are critical for the development. World Bank (2000) observed that 50 years of development experience has yielded four critical lessons.

1) Macroeconomic stability is an essential prerequisite for achieving the growth needed for development.
2) Development must address human needs directly as growth does not trickle down spontaneously.
3) No one policy would trigger development. A comprehensive approach is needed.
4) Institutions matter. Sustained development should be rooted in processes that are socially inclusive and responsive to changing circumstances.

Effective development requires partnership among different layers of government, private sector, donor groups and civil society. As the comprehensive development framework envisages, the effective development refers to growth in human, physical, sectoral, and structural aspects. While the sectoral aspects stress on the importance of crosscutting elements such as coordination, management and maintenance of an effective enabling environment for private business and community institutions, the structural aspects focus on the need for good governance, transparent decision making, effective legal and judicial processes and sound regulatory system. It is also essential to discern what has been the record to date of development and what does the future hold.

The Puducherry State Development Report delves into the development of various sectors over the past two decades to understand the development pattern in the state. It looks into the internal integration and social embeddedness among the sectors. Unlike the conventional way of looking at the growth of sectors to assess the development, the report analyses the development pattern, internal integration and the interaction of the economy with the global situation. It also makes an attempt to deconstruct the constellation of factors that have powerful influence on the development of the economy and the state.

2. Objectives

As all the development reports, the performance of the economy over the period and the future opportunities have been the core focus of the study.

1) Assessing trends and patterns of growth over the period across all the sectors.
2) Understanding the coordination and integration of various sectoral policies to the overall objective of the state.

3) Study the social embeddedness of various policies and programmes implemented in the state and to elucidate the social inclusive nature of the policies.
4) Explore the interaction of the economy to the global situation.
5) Scrutinise the transparency and governance of the state.
6) Appraise the institutions evolved and the social responsiveness of the institutions.
7) Suggest future development opportunities and strategies.

3. Approach

In addition to assessing the trends and patterns of the growth in different sectors, the causality and relations in the pattern have been analysed and interpreted. The field visits to all the regions and case studies of the best practices in various sectors in diverse situations in the state have enriched the interpretation of the growth patterns. The case studies, participant observation, unpublished data from departments concerned in all the regions and secondary data have been used in the study.

Secondary data was collected for all the relevant variables for the last 20 years from 1980-81 to 2000-01. Data on education, per capita income, GSDP, credit status, fisheries production both inland and marine, rainfall across the seasons, state budgetary positions, classification of workforce, employment situation, education, both school and higher education, governance and tourism were collected from the government departments and published sources. Similarly, data on finance, infrastructure, industrial development and reform in the public sector have been collected from various departments after having intensive discussion with the officials of the Directorates. Data have been checked duly after entering in the master sheet and in the computer. In addition, data have been collected from the Central Ground Water Board, RBI, and NABARD on groundwater resources, GSDP indicators and credit disbursements respectively. Data has been presented by regions to understand the regional differences in the UT. Data were also collected from other sources relating to the economy of other states for comparison purposes from *www.Indiastat.com* and CMIE publications.

Detailed discussions with department officials helped in understanding the growth and development over the period in the particular sector. These discussions facilitated the understanding of the internal integration between sectors and social embeddedness of various schemes and policies implemented through different departments and sectors. The discussions with heads of department of fisheries, forestry, and industries have given the big picture of internal integration and social embeddedness of the department policies and programmes. Discussions with the Directors of tourism and local administration department have enriched our understanding of the governance issues and importance given to tourism as a source of revenue to the economy and to the people of the Union Territory. The Directors of the Planning and Research Department and Economics and Statistics have presented the macro picture of the economy temporally and spatially. This also assisted us in understanding the different development opportunities available and the social as well as geographical limits to the development of the Union Territory. The discussions also dwelt on the development strategies followed over the period and the impact of the programmes on the economic development of the Union Territory.

The discussions with the Tourism and Industries departments focused on the interaction of Puducherry economy with the global and national developments. The growth of software and the hardware industries as well as SEZs indicates the interaction and responsiveness of the Puducherry economy to the global changes. The big push approach followed in infrastructure and global public goods like education and health also encourage the medical, educational, and religious tourism into the UT.

For triangulation, the complete data have been given to the Directors of Planning Department and Economics and Statistics. They approved the authenticity of the data. Discussions with them also brought to light some of the policy shifts taken place during certain points of time.

Separate visits were made to the regions like Karaikal, Mahe, and Yanam for understanding the regional differences in the UT and to get the holistic or Whole and Part theory perspective (Durkhiem). It brought to light the differences of opinion between the regions on the resource sharing and importance given to the Puducherry region and the neglect of the other regions. It also enabled to understand the extent of resource-base available and non-plan expenditures allocated at the regions. Hence, integrated approach would be followed to bring out the holistic development strategies for the UT.

4. Limitations

Major limitations include the distance between the regions and cultural diversities in the regions and the assimilation of the culture of the neighbouring states. The four regions are located in a trapezium shape in three states with totally different agro-climatic zones and cultural practices. Karaikal is nearly 135 kms in the southern direction from the headquarters, Mahe is nearly 650 kms in the south west direction, and Yanam is nearly 800 kms in the north eastern direction. Whether it has been making a heavy transaction cost in the effective governance is a veritable question to be answered. The visit of senior staff from the headquarters and vice versa means a huge burden on the exchequer of the UT.

The location of four regions in three culturally diverse states brings in a perceptible heterogeneity among the population of the UT. The variations between the regions on rainfall, cropping pattern, sex ratio, industrial development and livelihood systems have been noticeable in consonance with the encircled states. Thus, the population of the UT has three culturally diverse identities. This has made the limitation on getting the holistic picture of Union Territory and comparability of the regions.

5. Puducherry—Geographical Features

The map of this region presents more or less a flat land. There are no hills or forests in this region. The main soil types in this region are red ferrallitic, black clay and coastal alluvial.

Puducherry is the capital of this Union Territory. It is on the east coast about 162 kms. south of Chennai located on the Coromandel Coast of the Bay of Bengal. The Union Territory of Puducherry comprises of four coastal regions namely Puducherry, Karaikal, Mahe, and Yanam. Puducherry and Karaikal are situated on the East Coasts in Tamil Nadu, Yanam on the East Coast in Andhra Pradesh, and Mahe on the West Coast in Kerala.

Puducherry region is located on the Coromandel Coast between 11°46' and 12°30' of north latitude and between 79°36' and 79°52' of east longitude. Its boundary on the east is the Bay of Bengal and on the other three sides is Cuddalore and Villupuram districts of Tamil Nadu state. This is not a contiguous area but interspersed with some parts of Cuddalore and Villupuram districts of Tamil Nadu state. It presents a picture of scattered parts enclosed within Cuddalore and Villupuram districts. The layout of Puducherry region described above which is located within Tamil Nadu presents a peculiar picture of territorial jurisdiction, perhaps the only one of its kind in the world. The historical reasons, which prompted the French and the British to limit their territories in the intermingling manner, are not known.

Languages and Religion

Main languages spoken in the region are Tamil, Telugu, and Malayalam. English and French are other languages, which are spoken by a considerable number of people. Majority of the people are Hindus. There are quite a good number of Christians and Muslims, very few Jains, Sikhs, and Buddhists.

Puducherry at a Glance

Legendary associations trace the origin of this city to Rishi Agastya, the revered sage of the south. Excavations near Puducherry reveal that a Roman settlement existed here 2000 years ago. Puducherry has been the theatre of many battles in the wars between the British and the French, and was the capital of French India before it attained independence in 1954. Puducherry is famous as a centre chosen by late Sri Aurobindo, revolutionary turned saint, who built his *ashram*, which draws huge crowd of tourists.

The diversity of Puducherry is reflected in the festivals celebrated here. Pongal the harvest festival in January, Bastille Day in July, Sri Aurobindo's birth anniversary on 15 August, Fete de Puducherry on 15-17 August with the brilliantly lit Park monument and of course the standard festivals like Ganesh Puja, Dussehra, Christmas, Diwali etc., have been the attractions to the city. It is a blend of spiritual aura, French colonial heritage, Tamil culture and the cosmopolitan flair of many nationalities in a small but varied town. The inherent ambience of Puducherry, as it is fondly called, becomes most evident in the oldest part of the town, which flanks the seashore boulevard. Colonial buildings, some of which trace back to the 18th century, line along a grid of straight clean streets and house the French Institute, private homes and businesses, and the sprawling premises of the famous Sri Aurobindo Ashram. The visitor is greeted by mellow colours of cream, yellow, pink, and grey with flamboyant bougainvillea bursting over gates and compound walls of cool courtyards.

The region Puducherry, and its main capital Puducherry is situated in south-east India by the Bay of Bengal. The primary occupation of the area is agriculture with some textile, chemical, and electronic industry. The district has a literacy rate of 75 per cent, and a high poverty in rural areas. The district presents more or less a flat land. There are no hills or forests. The main soil types are red ferrallitie black clay and coastal alluvial. There are two main drainage basins, the one of Gingee river which crosses it diagonally from north-west to the south-east, and the other of Pennaiyar which forms the southern border. There is a metre gauge railway line between Villupuram and Puducherry. Puducherry has an important trading port. The principal trade at this port consists mainly of imports of wheat, fertilisers, and cement. Main items of exports include groundnut, rice, fish, hides and skin, handicrafts, etc.

The percentage of cultivable area to total area and percentage of irrigated area to total cultivable area are 78.62 and 54.27 respectively. This region cultivates mainly rice, sugarcane, coconut, betel vines, millets etc. In some parts cotton and also flowers such as jasmine, rose, marigold, etc., are grown. The by-products of foodgrains such as straw etc., are used for feeding the cattle. They also help to produce farmyard manure. There is a cooperative milk supply society and also a dairy. The common species of poultry are fowls and ducks. Cattle shows, calf rallies, milk yield competition and fodder yield competition are held every year.

The Bahour and Oussoudu lakes are the two biggest ones in Puducherry region for fishing purposes. The varieties which appear in fairly large numbers are ribbon fish, sardine and silver belly sharks, etc. The flying fishery, which lasts from May to July, is the most important seasonal fishery of the district. Now these two lakes are being rehabilitated to serve the drinking water requirements of the city and tourism purpose, for most of the agricultural land has been converted to non-agricultural use.

Major industries in the area are Swadeshi Cotton Mills Ltd., Sri Bharathi Mills, and Anglo-French textiles. Small scale industrial units are mainly engaged in the manufacture of furniture, dry cells, cosmetics, steel utensils, cement products, etc. Cottage industrial units include pottery, carpentry, blacksmith, basket making, dying, pipe making, cane works, handmade paper, *agarbathi* making, embroidery, etc.

Karaikal

Karaikal region has an area of 161 sq.kms. out of the 480 sq.kms. of the Union Territory. It is surrounded by the Nagapattinam district of Tamil Nadu. It is about 135 kms from Puducherry in the east coast. The sex ratio is 1023 and the literacy rate is 82.24. Population density is 1060 per sq.km. according to 2001 census.

The district is situated in more or less a flat land. There are no hills or forest in this region. This region consists of almost entirely coastal alluvial soil, which is highly suitable for cultivation of paddy and pulses. The total geographical area of the district is 14035.56 hectares. The percentage of cultivable area to total area and percentage of irrigated area to total cultivable area are 84.92 and 82.81 respectively. Pulses, cotton, chillies, coconuts, ground nuts, vegetables, and sunflower are the other popular items grown in the district.

Karaikal is a good fishing centre with the following ten marine fishing villages spread along the coast. They are Mandabathur, Kalikuppam, Akkampettai, Kottucherrymedu and Kasakudymedu, in Karaikal municipal area, Kilinjalmedu and Karaikalmedu; in Tirumalairayan Pathinam commune, Karakalchery; in Neravy commune, Keezhaiyur Pattincacherry and North Vanjore. Fresh and dry fishes are exported. Good quality conches (conch shells) are also available in the sea of Karaikal.

The only large scale industry in this district is a textile unit, M/s Soundararaja Mills Ltd., located in Nedungadu. Handloom weaving units too are also prevalent. There is an Industrial Training Institute located in Tirumalairayan Pathinam.

Mahe

Mahe, which the natives call 'Mayyazhi', got a place in the geographical map of India after the settlement of the French. Mahe is the smallest pocket of the Union Territory of Puducherry lying at 653 kms. away on the Arabian coast embedded within Kerala between the districts of Kozhikode and Kannur. Mahe was under the French rule for over 233 years. Total geographical area is 9 sq.kms. and the population according to 2001 census is 36,823 with 17,146 males and 19,677 females. The density of population is 4091 per sq.kms. The government staff including the municipality staff are 1856.

This picturesque little area is bounded on the south-west by the Arabian sea, on the north by river Ponniyar and on the other sides by a stretch of calcareous hills of medium height which are linked to the *ghats* by a series of wooden hillocks. The district consists of three entities namely, Mahe town proper, the small enclave of Kallayi, and of Naluthura. Mahe is situated on the Malabar Coast. This district is entirely rain fed and is covered by typical red laterite soil. There is no forest area in this district but large expanse of mangroves is found along the coast line.

The coast line here lies between the richest fishing belt between Ponnani and Mangalore on the west coast. Mahe is at the centre of a prawn chain, which stretches from Quilon to Mangalore. The major marketing centres in and around Mahe are Mahe, Cannanore, Kozhikode, and Tellicherry.

Industrial units have concentration only in Puducherry and Karaikal. The only large scale industry functioning in this district is the Cannanore Spinning and Weaving Mills.

Yanam

Yanam is situated in the east coast of the Indian Peninsula bounded on all sides by the East Godavari district of Andhra Pradesh. It is around 800 kms. away from the Puducherry region. Total geographical area is around 20 sq.kms. While density of population is 1568 per sq.km., sex ratio is 975. Literacy rate remains to be very low among the regions in the UT at 74.16 per cent.

The district lies on the spot where the Coringa river (Atreya) branches off from Gauthami into two parts. It is more or less a flat land. The soil is alluvial type suitable for the cultivation of paddy, tobacco, chilly, etc. The normal rainfall during a year is 1226 mm. The crops of this district are coconut, paddy, *jowar*, *ragi*, pulses, coriander, fenugreek etc. The main fishing units are Gulrimpeta, Agraharam, Kothapeta, Mettakur, Kanakalapeta, Kursampeta, Padvarevupeta, and Sangadirerupeta. The shoe *dhony* (canoe) is the commonest fishing crafts here. *Padona* is another kind of boat in use. The catches consist mainly of mullets, hilsa, prawns, cat fish etc. The major bridge across the river bed has changed the face of trade and economy of the district.

UNION TERRITORY AT A GLANCE

Union Territory Came into Existence	November 1954
Capital	Puducherry
Area (in square km)	492
Population (2001)	9,73,829
Total Number of Districts	4 – Puducherry, Karaikal, Mahe and Yanam
Major Rivers	Gingee, Pennaiyar, Coringa, Godavari, Mahe, Cauvery
Urban/Rural Ratio	2:1
Administrative Language	Tamil, English
Principal Languages	Tamil, Telugu, Malayalam, English, French
Per Capita Income (NSDP) (2001-02)	Rs. 18820/- (Advanced Estimate) (At 1993-94 Prices).
Population Density (2001)	2029/sq.km.
Birth Rate (2000)	17.8/thousand
Death Rate (2000)	6.5/thousand
Literacy Rate (2001)	81.49 per cent
Sex Ratio (2001)	1001 females/1000 males
Major Religions	Hindu (86.16 per cent); Muslim (6.54 per cent); Christian (7.23 per cent); Buddhist (0.01 per cent); Jain (0.06 per cent)
Scheduled Caste/Scheduled Tribe (per cent in Total Population)	16.24 per cent and 0 per cent
Major Source of Income	Agriculture (45 per cent people's occupation)
Major Industries	Textile, Sugar, Beer, Auto parts etc.
Major Tourist Places	Puducherry, Karaikal, Yanam and Mahe
Major Festivals	Maskred, Masimagum, etc.

Source: Statistical Abstract of Puducherry- Various Issues

Reference

World Bank (2000). *World Development Report - 2000, Attacking Poverty*. New York: Oxford University Press.

World Bank (2002). *World Development Report–Building Institutions for Market*. New York: Oxford University Press.

Government of Puducherry, *Annual Statistical Abstract of Puducherry*, Directorate of Economics and Statistics, Various Issues.

Chapter 1

Development Strategy and Economic Profile

1.1 Natural Resources

The natural resources available in the Union Territory include land, water and coastal resources. There is no reserve forest land. Trees and plantations laid along the roads, tanks and parks are treated as forests.

1.1.1 Land Resources

Land use pattern across the regions is presented in Table 1.1. Five years average is computed to avoid the cyclical fluctuations in the utilisation pattern. The land use pattern in Puducherry across regions explicates that the land under non-agricultural use has recorded a consistent increase over the period. This indicates the increase in industrial development, infrastructure build up and extension of residential areas. Among the regions Mahe region displayed a huge difference by doubling the non-agricultural land. This could be due to the declaration of the whole region as urban centre. All other categories of land use such as net sown area, grazing and permanent pasture, current fallow and miscellaneous trees have reported a decline from 1980-81 to 2000-01. Across the regions, net area sown has shown a considerable increase in the 1990-1995 period in the Puducherry region and vice versa in the current fallow. This indicates the good monsoon during the early nineties. This also draws the inference that the decline in net sown area is also partially due to the poor monsoon and the consequent increase in the current fallow. This posits a positive correlation between net sown area and monsoon as well as between net sown area and current fallow. The data also shows that there is an inverse relationship between net sown area and the current fallow in the nineties in the Yanam region. During the late nineties Andhra Pradesh coincidentally received good rains. The barren and uncultivable land displayed a positive change in the 1990s due to the initiatives of the forest department to identify the barren and uncultivable land to acquire it to forest development, for converting the barren and uncultivable land into forest lands through land reclamation activities. This manifests the qualitative change in the land use pattern in Puducherry. Most of the barren and uncultivable lands have been acquired by the forest department to grow forest trees. The social forestry scheme also made use of these lands. The decline in net sown area and fluctuating current fallows remain to be a veritable cause for concern in the emerging situation of over crowding due to various types of migration and tourisms. The grazing and pasture lands are found only in the Karaikal region. The consistent decline in this area indicates the decline in the free grazing area for the livestock and in turn livelihood to the poor landless people. This would precipitate undoubtedly the negative externalities in the quality of life of marginalised and vulnerable sections of the society. Mahe region has shown a fluctuating trend in the area under current fallow while the net area sown has reported a consistent decline. Hence there is perforce a need to improve land use efficiency. Since Mahe has been declared as totally urban inhabitation, the net sown area has been on the decline.

The overall land utilisation pattern in Puducherry as presented in Table 1.2 and Figure 1.1 manifests an ecological imbalance by exhibiting lack of forest area and declining area under miscellaneous trees and grazing and pastures land. The increase in the barren and uncultivable land is an alarming situation in the land scarce region. In addition the trade off between the current fallow and net sown area implies the over dependence on monsoon for the cultivation. The rapid decline in the net sown area and fast growing use of land for non-agriculture purpose foretells a food scarcity situation in the future. Hence, there is an urgent need to attend to the forewarning for ascertaining a better quality life to the future generation.

TABLE 1.1

Land Use Pattern Across Regions

(in hectares)

Land Particulars	*1980-81 to 1984-85*	*1985-86 to 1989-90*	*1990-91 to 1994-95*	*1995-96 to 1999-2000*	*2000-01 to 2002-03*	*Slope**
Geographical Area						
Puducherry	29377	29377	29377	29377	29377	0.0
Karaikal	15338.8	15548.2	16013.4	16199	16199	52.4
Mahe	841	841	846.8	870	870	1.9
Yanam	1968.8	2111.2	2396	2396	2396	25.4
Total	47525.6	47877.4	48633.2	48842	48842	79.7
Agriculture Use (Net sown area)						
Puducherry	·16892.4	15583.8	16225.4	15108.8	14181.7	-125.0
Karaikal	10907.8	9792.8	9737	8656.8	7693.3	-161.8
Mahe	727.2	707.8	671.4	639.6	633.0	-5.6
Yanam	713.2	543.4	530.2	677.4	686.7	1.4
Total	29240.6	26627.8	27164	25082.6	23194.7	-291.0
Non-Agriculture Use						
Puducherry	8103.8	8489.6	8827.4	9547.4	10277.3	115.2
Karaikal	2418.2	3101.8	3751.2	4256.8	4461.3	114.8
Mahe	101.8	111.6	149.8	196.2	203.0	6.3
Yanam	695.8	1141.6	1362	1031.6	1069.0	14.8
Total	11319.6	12844.6	14090.4	15032.0	16010.7	251.2
Barren and Uncultivable land						
Puducherry	78.6	80	87.8	112.0	86.7	1.2
Karaikal	0	0	0	0.0	0.0	0.0
Mahe	1	1	1.2	1.0	1.0	0.0
Yanam	0	0	0	0.0	0.0	0.0
Total	79.6	81	89	113.0	87.7	1.2
Grazing and Permanent Pasture						
Puducherry	0	0	0	0.0	0.0	0.0
Karaikal	65.2	59.8	52	26.0	16.7	-2.8
Mahe	0	0	0	0.0	0.0	0.0
Yanam	0	0	0	0.0	0.0	0.0
Total	65.2	59.8	52	26.0	16.7	-2.8
Miscellaneous Tree						
Puducherry	1914.4	1791.6	208.4	304.2	418.0	-100.3
Karaikal	468.2	467.6	185.2	203.0	181.3	-18.5
Mahe	2.8	2.4	1.8	1.8	3.3	0.0
Yanam	6.4	6	65.6	309.2	364.3	21.9
Total	2391.8	2267.6	461	818.2	967.0	-96.9
Current Fallow land						
Puducherry	1245.8	1496.6	1238.8	1258.2	1044.0	-13.1
Karaikal	392.6	1209.2	895	789.8	760.0	7.9
Mahe	2.6	5.6	5.4	7.0	2.7	0.1
Yanam	75.2	85.8	53.6	30.0	30.7	-3.2
Total	1716.2	2797.2	2192.8	2085.0	1837.3	-8.3

Note: * indicates the slope of the linear regression line through the given data points.
Source: Various issues of *Statistical Abstracts*, Puducherry.

TABLE 1.2

Land Use Pattern

(in per cent)

Land Particulars	*1980-81 to 1984-85*	*1985-86 to 1989-90*	*1990-91 to 1994-95*	*1995-96 to 1999-2000*	*2000-01 to 2002-03*	*Slope**
Agriculture Use (Net sown area)	61.53	55.62	55.85	51.35	47.49	-0.52
Non-Agriculture Use	23.82	26.83	28.97	30.78	32.78	0.37
Current Fallow Land	3.61	5.84	4.51	4.27	3.76	-0.02
Miscellaneous Tree	5.03	4.74	0.95	1.68	1.98	-0.17
Barren and Uncultivable Lands	0.17	0.17	0.18	0.23	0.18	0.00
Grazing and Permanent Pasture	0.14	0.12	0.11	0.05	0.03	0.00

Note: * indicates the slope of the linear regression line through the given data points.
Source: Various issues of *Statistical Abstracts*, Puducherry.

FIGURE 1.1

Land Use Pattern in Puducherry

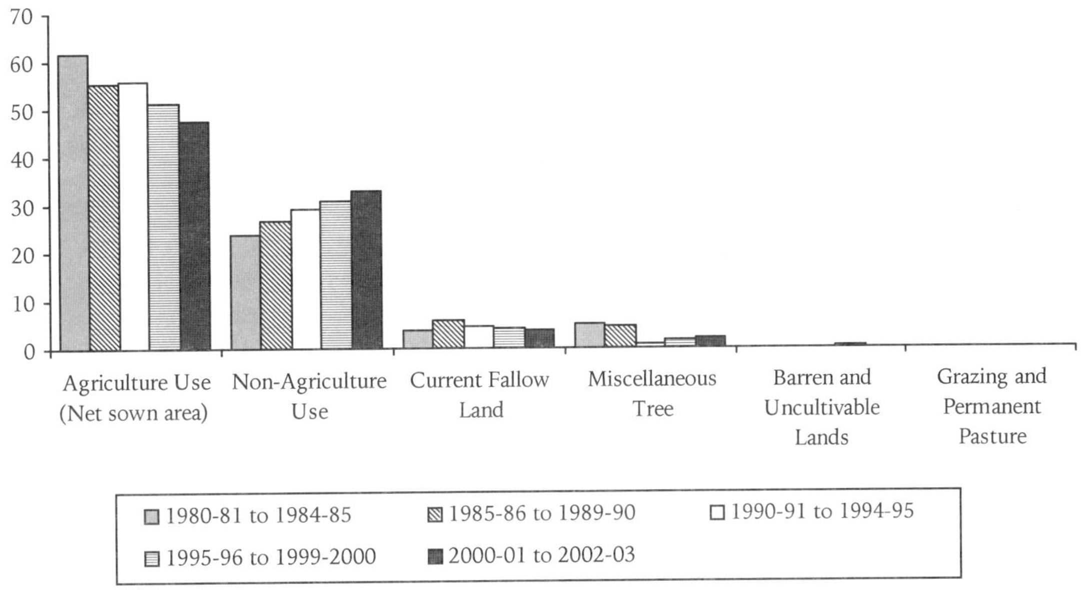

1.1.2 Water Resources

The rainfall remains to be scanty in all the regions except Mahe in Puducherry Union Territory. As all the three regions namely, Puducherry, Karaikal and Yanam are located in the lower riparian areas, water becomes a scarce commodity for both drinking and irrigation purposes. Quality of ground water is also deteriorating due to industrial waste. Seawater intrusion is happening but under strict control. In the Puducherry region, pathogens in the groundwater are very less but it is very high in Karaikal region. Immunity to contaminated water is higher in the Karaikal region. Totally 84 major tanks with 46.4 MCM capacity and 140 small tanks are there in the UT. Usteri lake is being converted into drinking water source. Similar initiative is being undertaken in utilising Bahoor lake water for drinking purpose, as this would reduce the dependence on ground water. Another thing to note is that most of the agriculture land under Bahoor lake has been shifted for non-agricultural use. The feeder canal *voodu* for Usteri lake is being rehabilitated to improve the rainwater harvest. This would reduce the pressure on groundwater exploitation in Puducherry region and in turn arrest the sea water intrusion.

Percolation rate is hardly 8 to 12 per cent due to silt formation in the tanks and rivers. The ideal is around 18 to 20 per cent. Return circulation is around 30 per cent. Sometimes it is up to 45 per cent but natural barriers to percolation are relatively higher in Puducherry. In the groundwater recharging, Puducherry is in the dark category (above 100 per cent exploitation of groundwater recharged). Malattar, Gingee, Sankaraparani, Pennar, and Sunnar rivers are the major water sources. In Kalapet and Auroville, watershed and water harvest structures have been developed. Rooftop water harvest, rehabilitation of tanks and reviving tank feeder canals have been the priority areas to recharge the groundwater and to harvest the rainwater. European Union has funded the rehabilitation of all the 84 tanks. World Bank Phase II project for tank rehabilitation is also being implemented. Unfortunately the key for success of all these initiatives lies in the hands of rain god. The pattern of monsoon over the years has been analysed to understand the water availability across the regions and possible actions to challenge the situation.

Table 1.3 explicates that while the Puducherry and Karaikal regions have their major share of rainfall during the north east monsoon, Mahe and Yanam regions get their major share of rainfall during the south west monsoon. There is a notable shift in the rainfall pattern in the Yanam region. There is a consistent decline in the share of south west monsoon and a perceptible increase in the north east monsoon rainfall. In comparison with other regions, Yanam has the advantage of equal distribution of rainfall during the major monsoons. This indicates the water availability for longer period. The drastic decline in the winter rainfall and summer rainfall over the period signifies the relevance and necessity of the water resource management and rainwater harvest for making the water

TABLE 1.3

Distribution of Rainfall

Across Seasons	*Actual Rainfall in mm*					*Rainfall in per cent*				
	1980-81 to 1984-85	*1985-86 to 1989-90*	*1990-91 to 1994-95*	*1995-96 to 1999-00*	*2000-01 to 2002-03*	*1980-81 to 1984-85*	*1985-86 to 1989-90*	*1990-91 to 1994-95*	*1995-96 to 1999-00*	*2000-01 to 2002-03*
South West Monsoon (June to September)										
Puducherry	350	344	406	483	297	29.99	28.86	30.37	27.85	30.97
Karaikal	278	233	249	314	250	21.43	16.26	19.12	19.47	20.68
Mahe	3380	2485	2672	2581	1924	83.05	79.20	80.41	82.05	65.79
Yanam	757	732	613	869	463	69.16	56.44	45.51	56.02	50.13
North East Monsoon (October to December)										
Puducherry	665	719	837	1124	566	57.04	60.35	62.59	64.84	58.92
Karaikal	849	1005	943	1168	787	65.43	70.03	72.28	72.49	65.14
Mahe	407	323	405	405	560	9.99	10.29	12.18	12.86	19.15
Yanam	274	337	629	613	355	25.04	25.99	46.74	39.52	38.46
Winter (January to February)										
Puducherry	102	53.4	37.4	55	64	8.77	4.48	2.80	3.16	6.63
Karaikal	122	87.8	53.6	85	118	9.37	6.12	4.11	5.30	9.76
Mahe	17.4	30.4	0	9	24	0.43	0.97	0.00	0.29	0.82
Yanam	32.6	56	14.6	42	26	2.98	4.32	1.08	2.68	2.82
Summer (March to May)										
Puducherry	49	75.2	56.8	72	33	4.20	6.31	4.25	4.14	3.47
Karaikal	49	109	58.6	44	53	3.77	7.58	4.49	2.73	4.41
Mahe	266	299	246	151	417	6.53	9.54	7.41	4.79	14.25
Yanam	31	172	89.8	28	79	2.83	13.26	6.67	1.78	8.60
Total										
Puducherry	1166	1191	1338	1733	960	100	100	100	100	100
Karaikal	1298	1435	1305	1611	1209	100	100	100	100	100
Mahe	4070	3138	3323	3146	2925	100	100	100	100	100
Yanam	1095	1297	1347	1551	923	100	100	100	100	100

Source: Various issues of *Statistical Abstract*, Puducherry.

available for longer period. The declining summer and winter rainfall portends an alarming water scarcity situation for both ground and surface water during the summer seasons. The convergence of rainfall during one monsoon also elucidates the need for integrated water management practices to ensure adequate potable water to the growing urban population in the Puducherry.

The deviation from normal rainfall during the four monsoon periods over the years has been analysed to understand the shift in rainfall pattern over the years. Table 1.4 indicates that there is a decline in the rainfall over the years in Mahe whereas all the other regions have reported a marginal increase. In the winter and summer rains, there has been a noticeable deviation in the rainfall in all the regions. This transpires that there has been a general dearth of rainfall for nearly six months in all the regions. Hence, there is an urgent need to take note of this to ensure drinking water supply to the people during the six months by creating adequate infrastructure. Even during the north east and south west monsoons, though there are perceptible deviations from the normal rainfall over the years, there is no major shift in the overall rainfall.

The integrated water management practice necessitates the identification of the interest and influence of all the primary, secondary and key stakeholders in water management. The participation of all stakeholders could be ensured through forming various people's organisation and community based organisations (CBOs). State Social Advisory Board in Puducherry organised the programmes and 65 water user associations have been formed. Water management training with demonstration is being given to the members of the association. Environment and

TABLE 1.4

Deviation of Actual Rainfall from the Normal Rainfall

(in per cent)

Regions	*Normal Rainfall*	*1980-81 to 1984-85*	*1985-86 to 1989-90*	*1990-91 to 1994-95*	*1995-96 to 1999-2000*	*2000-01 to 2002-03*	*Slope**
South West Monsoon (June to September)							
Puducherry	379	-7.65	-9.23	7.12	27.34	-21.55	0.40
Karaikal	259	7.34	-10.04	-3.86	21.08	-3.47	0.28
Mahe	2730	23.81	-8.97	-2.12	-5.44	-29.51	-2.18
Yanam	678	11.65	7.96	-9.59	28.14	-31.76	-1.25
North East Monsoon (October to December)							
Puducherry	849	-21.67	-15.31	-1.41	32.34	-33.37	0.81
Karaikal	993	-14.5	1.21	-5.04	17.58	-20.71	0.25
Mahe	367	10.9	-11.99	10.35	10.25	52.59	2.12
Yanam	450	-39.11	-25.11	39.78	36.22	-21.11	2.46
Winter (January to February)							
Puducherry	46	121.74	16.09	-18.7	19.13	38.41	-3.87
Karaikal	66	84.85	33.03	-18.79	29.39	78.79	-0.72
Mahe	10	74	204	-100	-8.00	140.00	-2.61
Yanam	27	20.74	107.41	-45.93	54.07	-3.70	-2.11
Summer (March to May)							
Puducherry	64	-23.44	17.5	-11.25	12.19	-47.92	-0.92
Karaikal	63	-22.22	73.02	-6.98	-30.16	-15.34	-1.96
Mahe	280	-5	6.79	-12.14	-46.14	48.81	0.81
Yanam	71	-56.34	142.25	26.48	-61.13	11.74	-1.57
Total							
Puducherry	1338	-12.86	-10.99	0	29.51	-28.25	0.45
Karaikal	1388	-6.48	3.39	-5.98	16.04	-12.92	0.10
Mahe	3387	20.17	-7.35	-1.89	-7.12	-13.64	-1.47
Yanam	1226	-10.69	5.79	9.87	26.51	-24.71	0.07

*Note:** indicates the slope of the linear regression line through the given data points on annual basis.
Source: Various issues of *Statistical Abstract*, Puducherry.

community sanitation works are also undertaken through these people's organisations and CBOs. Politicians and government officials interaction is cordial as there is very less power conflict. On the contrary, village conflicts tend to be hibernating and even a spark can lead to major conflict.

The net irrigated area across various sources illustrated in Table 1.5 and Figure 1.2 indicates that the canals and

TABLE 1.5

Net Irrigated Area by Sources

(in hectares)

Source of Irrigation	*1980-81 to 1984-85*	*1985-86 to 1989-90*	*1990-91 to 1994-95*	*1995-96 to 1999-2000*	*2000-01 to 2002-03*	*Slope**
Canals	10753.6	9329.3	9059.2	8295.4	7467	-164.20
Tanks	1168.8	73.5	23.8	0	0	-54.17
Tubewells	13273.8	13490.5	13785.4	13471	12794.7	-17.60
Ordinary wells	1.2	0.8	0	0	0	-0.07
Others sources	184.2	160.5	97.4	68.8	57	-7.59
Total	25381.6	23054.5	22965.8	21835.2	20318.7	-243.63

Note: * indicates the slope of the linear regression line through the given data points on annual basis.
Source: Various issues of *Statistical Abstract*, Puducherry.

tank irrigation in the UT has been losing its relevance. The tubewells became increasingly prominent sources of irrigation in the UT. Nearly two-thirds of the area irrigated remains to be under groundwater sources. The ordinary (open or surface) wells became non-viable due to the worsening water table situation in the regions. The declining area irrigated more than once and gross sown area also indicates the fall in the cropping intensity (Table 1.6). The combined effect of low cropping intensity and declining net sown area would create an unfavourable terms of trade in agriculture and food insecurity. This could be one of the reasons for the increasing urban population. Unless some deliberate intervention is initiated to arrest the situation, it would lead to migration of semi-skilled labourers to urban areas and the resultant social problems.

In Puducherry, water is shared on the basis of 80:4:16 among agricultural use, industries and domestic use. The international standard is 69:23:8. WAPCOS study observed that total groundwater availability was estimated to be 85 MCM but requirement is assessed to be 134.5 MCM (Table 1.7). The annual recharge is estimated to be 85 per cent. A detailed study conducted by state government water unit in 1989 assessed that there is around 20 per cent rainfall percolation in alluvial sand, which covered 80 per cent of the area in the Puducherry state. This transpires the state of alarm in groundwater situation.

FIGURE 1.2

Irrigation Pattern by Sources

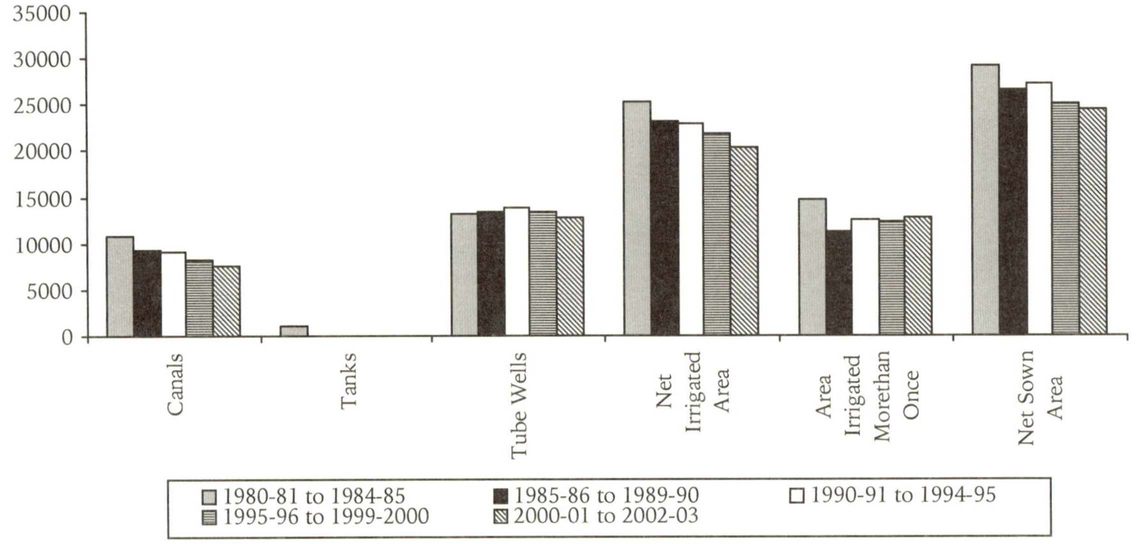

TABLE 1.6

Land Use in Agriculture

(in hectares)

Utilisation Pattern	*1980-81 to 1984-85*	*1985-86 to 1989-90*	*1990-91 to 1994-95*	*1995-96 to 1999-2000*	*2000-01 to 2002-03*	*Slope**
Net Sown Area	29234.0	26627.8	27164.0	25073	24330.0	-246.26
Area Sown More than Once	19230.0	15639.6	18448.8	18583.5	18510.8	31.29
Gross Sown Area	48464.0	42867.4	45612.8	43583.8	43277	-212.57
Net Irrigated Area	25381.6	23054.5	22965.8	21835.2	20318.7	-243.63
Area Irrigated More than Once	14613.8	11275.0	12537.6	12334	12683.3	-65.66
Gross Irrigated Area	39995.8	34327.0	35503.4	34169.2	33002	-309.25

Note: * indicates the slope of the linear regression line through the given data points on annual basis.

Source: Various issues of *Statistical Abstract*, Puducherry.

TABLE 1.7

Groundwater Potential

	Units	*Puducherry*	*Karaikal*	*Total*
Replenishable Groundwater Resource	m.ha.m/yr	0.01454	0.00291	0.01746
Provision for Domestic Industrial and other Uses	m.ha.m/yr	0.00218	0.00044	0.00262
Available Groundwater Resource for Irrigation in Net terms	m.ha.m/yr	0.01236	0.00248	0.01484
Utilizable Groundwater Resource for irrigation in Net terms	m.ha.m/yr	0.01112	0.00223	0.01335
Gross Draft Estimated on Pro rata basis	m.ha.m/yr	0.01324	0.00321	0.01645
Net Draft	m.ha.m/yr	0.00927	0.00225	0.01152
Balance Groundwwater Resource for future use in net terms	m.ha.m/yr	0.00309	0.00023	0.00332
Level of Groundwater Development	per cent	75	90.77	77.63

Source: WAPCOS and Groundwater Department, Puducherry.

1.1.3 Coastal Resources

Another major natural resource in Puducherry is coastal resources. It has a coastal line of 45 kms. Both in-shore and in-land water fishing are practised in 27 and 23 hamlets respectively. The number of people involved in both the practices is 38711 and 6957 respectively, in 2001 Census. In the financial year 2002-03, Rs.6.7 crore has been spent by the Fisheries Department. In the year 2004-05, it has increased to Rs.8 crore. Nine major schemes are being implemented to enhance the fisheries production, welfare of the fisher folk and women members of the fisher folk. Till the 10th Plan, there were 17 schemes. Now some of them are merged. The welfare schemes subsume lean season support, Group Insurance Scheme (GIS) for active fisher women and cash award to meritorious students from fishing community. Under Janasree Beema Yojana, the active fisher women are covered under LIC's GIS policy on the basis of the premium contribution ratio of 40:10:50 from state government, people and LIC itself respectively.

Similarly incentives are also given to improve fish production by providing subsidised catamaran, OBM/IBM and dugout canoes. In addition, huge capital investment on infrastructure development was also done. It includes GPS, eco-sounder and integrated fish finders. As a result, Puducherry and Karaikal regions have registered a twofold increase in the production of marine fishing while Mahe and Yanam displayed a moderate increase.

The fish production over the period across regions is displayed in Table 1.8. Overall production of marine fish has also doubled since eighties. Similarly, inland fishing has also shown noticeable increase in the eighties. It has increased manifolds in the Puducherry and Karaikal regions. In Yanam region, there is a mixed trend due to its drought prone nature and rain fed condition. When the monsoon is good, the inland fish harvest is phenomenally higher in Yanam. In Mahe, there is no inland fishing as the total area is as small as 9 sq. km. In the nineties, Karaikal region displayed a noticeable increase in the inland fishing.

In the 1990s prawns also began to form a major part in the fish production. The inland prawn cultivation has begun to decline due to environmental consciousness of the people and pressure from environmental activists. On the contrary, the marine prawn harvest has not shown a perceptible change. In the marine prawn harvest too, Karaikal contributes more than half of the total production. Thus, in the coastal resources, Karaikal plays a vital role in both marine and inland fishing. Karaikal economy is largely dependent on coastal resources.

Tsunami has overturned the whole coastal economy and the livelihood of the people depending on the coastal resources. The damage caused to the coastal resources and human lives in Karaikal and Puducherry regions has been a mind boggling one. This exhibits the vulnerability of the people depending on coastal resources. This envisages that adequate preventive measures should be made to circumvent this type of natural disasters like constructing rainbow arc walls and growing thick mangroves in the coastal areas, for the regions with thick mangroves and casuarinas got less affected during the tsunami. Hence, coastal areas and resources have to be maintained and protected on priority basis. Huge infrastructure has to be developed in the coastal areas as the economy and people dependent on coastal resources remain sizeable.

TABLE 1.8

Fish Production Across Regions

	1980-81 to 1984-85	*1985-86 to 1989-90*	*1990-91 to 1994-95*	*1995-96 to 1999-2000*	*2000-01 to 2002-03*
Inland Harvest (in Tonnes)					
Puducherry	2541.2	5862.4	7584.8	10586.0	12182.9
Karaikal	3086.8	10399.6	15607.2	18762.8	23855.8
Mahe	0	0	0	0	0
Yanam	5569.6	5533.4	11870	11697.0	11161.3
Total	11197.6	21795.4	35062	41045.8	47200.0
Marine Harvest (in Tonnes)					
Puducherry	132671	197178	280622	165771.8	189820.3
Karaikal	**	**	**	55891.6	148158.3
Mahe	11740.4	8428.6	29850.4	53434.7	32870.0
Yanam	16264.2	26818	38928	27434.6	24667.3
Total	160676	232425	349400	302532.7	395516.0
Prawns					
Inland Harvest (in Tonnes)					
Puducherry	NA*	NA	NA	126.3	140.3
Karaikal	NA	NA	NA	356.7	425.3
Mahe	NA	NA	NA	0.0	0.0
Yanam	NA	NA	NA	1017.8	0.0
Total	NA	NA	NA	1500.8	565.7
Marine Harvest (in Tonnes)					
Puducherry	NA	NA	NA	10166.0	12878.7
Karaikal	NA	NA	NA	28951.1	26046.0
Mahe	NA	NA	NA	2608.6	2878.7
Yanam	NA	NA	NA	2013.4	1850.7
Total	NA	NA	NA	43739.1	43654.0

Note:* Data Not Available.
** Puducherry figures include Karaikal also.
Source: Various issues of *Statistical Abstract*, Puducherry.

The fisheries department has focused more on the production in the eighties. In the nineties, the emphasis is increasingly on the welfare of the fisherfolk through the various welfare schemes implemented by the Central and state governments. This indicates the social embeddedness of the programmes designed by the government. Now it is time to equip the establishment to be prepared for facing the natural disasters and unforeseen contingencies with a well designed warning systems and relief packages.

1.1.4 Forest Resources

Puducherry does not have any declared forest land but the trees and plantations laid along the roads, tanks and coastal areas are treated as forest land. According to forest department, area under forest in government land is 52.14 ha, other government land 534.64 ha and non-government land 82.52 ha. Totally 669.36 ha forest land is there in forest department records. Social forestry area comes to 346.55 ha. Mangroves area in Yanam region is 449.2 ha.

Forest department was established in 1997 only. In 2003 (31st March) only, a separate department was created. Till then, it was working as a constituent of agriculture department. An Expert Committee was constituted to identify the forest land in the state. GIS data was used in the identification. The Eco Watch Group underscores that 33 per cent of the total geographical area should be under forest. Some initiatives are being taken to improve the forest area. Tree cutting permission is restricted to public places. The forest department has identified certain areas to enlist the participation of diverse stakeholders for developing forest in the UT.

1. SHGs in the maintenance of seed and nurseries.
2. Planting fruit yielding trees like tamarinds, *jamoons*, etc., along the side of the roads with SHGs having the usufruct rights.

3. Chunnambar river bank—tourism and forest department linkage is planned.
4. Acquisition of private land for forest particularly the NTC land is in progress.

Thus, forest department has become an important player to bring qualitative changes in the environment of the State.

The forest department is responsible for implementing the provisions of forest and wild life laws in Puducherry. It includes preventive and punitive action against poaching of wild animals, illicit trade in wild animals and articles derived from wild animals and unlawful trade in forest produce from neighbouring states. To achieve its goal, the department is implementing three schemes:

- Social forestry
- Forestry extension and implementation of improved technologies
- Preservation, conservation, protection and development of forest wildlife.

To abate pollution, industries are forced to plant trees in their premises for a clean green environment.

Joint Forest Management

The objectives of JFM is to involve local people in taking up afforestation projects in government waste lands, community lands, temple lands and any other land owned by government like canals, tanks, etc., and share with them the sustainable benefits from the forests so created. The unit of management under JFM is an entire village.

Coastal Shelter Belt

In the entire coast line of Karaikal and Puducherry the plantation work was taken up with the involvement of Coastal Fishermen Communities. Total area covered as on December 2005 by plantation was 78.16 hectares.

The Ariankuppam and Thengaithittu mangroves are situated in the backwaters of Ariankuppam river in the revenue villages of Ariankuppam, Murungapakkam and Thengaithittu. The vegetation is dominated by *avicennia* species and *suaeda* species. The growth of mangrove species is in the form of small thickets scattered over Ariankuppam backwater from Thengaithettu to Veerampattinam.

In Yanam region, the mangrove swamps are found in Island No. 1, 2, 3, and 4 to an extent of 449 hectares. Action is being taken to declare this forest area as protected area as there were many reported cases of illicit liquor preparation and sale. The Forest Survey of India has been requested to demarcate the area so that a comprehensive proposal could be sent to the government for notification.

1.2 Human Resources

1.2.1 Demographic Aspects

According to 2001 population census, the population of the Puducherry Union Territory was 9.74 lakh with the sex ratio of 1001 females per thousand males. Table 1.9 presents the population across the regions in the rural and urban areas in Puducherry for the last three censuses. While the population in the rural areas reported a marginal increase during the last three censuses, the urban areas displayed a quantum jump in the population growth during the same period. It has more than doubled. This indicates the urban growth in the UT.

Amazingly, two-thirds of the population in Puducherry lives in urban areas in the 2001 census. In the 1981 census, it was 2.8 lakh rural and 3.1 lakh urban population. In the 1991 census, it was 2.9 and 5.1 lakh respectively. In the 1991 census itself, Mahe was declared to be a total urban region. Hence, the increase in the urban population during the 2001 census manifests the movement of people from rural to urban areas in addition to normal decadal growth of population. While rural population was 2.8, 2.9, and 3.2 lakh during the last three censuses, the urban population grew in strides with 3.1, 5.1, and 6.4 lakh respectively. This manifests the growth of urban area and necessity of improving urban infrastructures to meet the needs of the growing urban population. Across the regions, Yanam and Mahe are totally urban regions. In addition, the migration from the neighbouring states to Puducherry has been sizeable due to the social security system available and the opportunities for alternative livelihood systems. The other two regions have been reporting consistently higher growth rate of urban population in the subsequent censuses from 1981. Across gender, it has not shown any noticeable shift though the difference in the ratio is noticeably high in Karaikal and Mahe regions. Female-male ratio is more than 1000 from 1981 census onwards in the Karaikal and Mahe regions. In the 2001 census the ratio is 1001 in the entire Puducherry indicating more female population than male.

1.2.2 Population Growth Rate

The decadal growth rate was significantly higher from 1971 to 1991 census (Table 1.10). In the 2001 census, it has got stabilised below the national average decadal growth rate. Across the regions, the decadal growth rate is

TABLE 1.9

Rural and Urban Population by Sex across Regions

Region		1981 Male	1981 Female	1981 Total	1991 Male	1991 Female	1991 Total	2001 Male	2001 Female	2001 Total
Puducherry	Rural	99044	93953	192997	105842	101059	206901	115982	113307	229289
	Per cent	43.82	43.02	43.43	34.18	33.84	34.01	31.40	30.98	31.20
	Urban	126997	124423	251420	203859	197578	401437	253336	252379	505715
	Per cent	56.18	56.98	56.57	65.82	66.16	65.99	68.60	69.02	68.80
Karaikal	Rural	38089	38513	76602	41757	42142	83899	47604	48703	96307
	Per cent	64.17	63.51	63.83	57.55	57.61	57.58	56.43	56.45	56.44
	Urban	21272	22130	43408	30800	31004	61804	36761	37572	74333
	Per cent	35.83	36.49	36.17	42.45	42.39	42.42	43.57	43.55	43.56
Mahe	Rural	8789	10036	18825	0	0	0	0	0	0
	Per cent	66.28	66.23	66.25	0.00	0.00	0.00	0.00	0.00	0.00
	Urban	4471	5117	9588	15516	17931	33447	17416	19677	36823
	Per cent	33.72	33.77	33.75	100.00	100.00	100.00	100.00	100.00	100.00
Yanam	Rural	0	0	0	0	0	0	0	0	0
	Per cent	0.00	0.00	0.00	0.00	0.00	0.00	0.00	0.00	0.00
	Urban	5893	5738	11631	10307	9990	20297	15876	15486	31362
	Per cent	100.00	100.00	100.00	100.00	100.00	100.00	100.00	100.00	100.00
Total	Rural	145992	142502	288424	147599	143201	290800	163563	162010	325596
	Per cent	47.92	47.51	47.72	36.17	35.83	36.00	33.61	33.26	33.43
	Urban	158639	157408	316047	260482	256503	516985	323119	325114	648233
	Per cent	52.08	52.49	52.28	63.83	64.17	64.00	66.39	66.74	66.57

Source: Census data.

considerably higher in the Yanam region from 1971 onwards. This could be attributed to the large-scale migration from Andhra Pradesh to this region due to certain favourable economic conditions and government policies. The growth is perceptibly low in the Mahe and Karaikal regions. Puducherry region has reported relatively higher decadal growth from the 1961 census onwards. This is increasingly due to higher rate of migration than higher birth rate.

TABLE 1.10

Decadal Growth Rate across Regions

Region	Population 2001 Persons	Population 2001 Males	Population 2001 Females	Decadal Growth Rate 1981-1991	Decadal Growth Rate 1991-2001
Puducherry	735,004	369,318	365,686	36.88	20.82
Karaikal	170,640	84,365	86,275	21.41	17.11
Mahe	36,823	17,146	19,677	17.72	10.09
Yanam	31,362	15,876	15,486	74.51	54.52
Total	973,829	486,705	487,124	33.64	20.56

Source: 2001 Census Handbook.

The sex ratio across the regions as presented in Table 1.11 shows a marginal increase in all the regions. Across the regions, Mahe displays a very high sex ratio indicating a marginal decline in the 2001 census. Karaikal is slowly catching up with the Mahe sex ratio. All the other regions, registered a considerable increase in the sex ratio during the 2001 census. In the case of density too, all the regions disclosed a considerable increase in the density during the 2001.

TABLE 1.11

Sex Ratio and Density of Population across the Regions

Union Territory/ Region	Sex Ratio 1991	Sex Ratio 2001	Density 1991	Density 2001
Puducherry	964	990	2098	2534
Karaikal	1008	1023	905	1060
Mahe	1156	1148	3716	4091
Yanam	969	975	1015	1568
Total (UT)	979	1001	1683	2029

Source: 2001 Census Hand Book.

The density of population has reported a consistent increase in all the regions in the state. Even across the rural and urban areas too, Table 1.12 explicates that there has been a considerable increase. This reiterates the increase in population both in rural and urban areas. In the state, it has almost doubled from 1229 per km^2 to 2029 between 1981 and 2001 censuses. The growth in density of population has been remarkable in Yanam region where it has increased from 381 per km^2 to 1568 km^2. It has quadrupled in the last three decades. This indicates a warning signal to arrest the growth of population particularly due to migration.

In comparison with neighbouring states, Puducherry has registered a very high growth in the density of population throughout the 20th century (Table 1.13). Though it could be attributed to the more urban nature and small size of the UT, it is still a cause for concern. It could throw a heavy weight on the existing assets and real estate to jack up its value.

1.2.3 *Crude Birth Rate and Death Rate*

The crude birth rate and death rate for the last ten years from 1991 to 2001 indicate the better life expectancy rate and health parameters (Figure 1.3). The live birth rates have declined from 45 per thousand population to 33 in 1998 but it began to increase marginally from 1999 onwards. The death rate has declined substantially from 10.5 in 1991 to 7.7 in 2000.

FIGURE 1.3

Birth and Death Rates in Puducherry

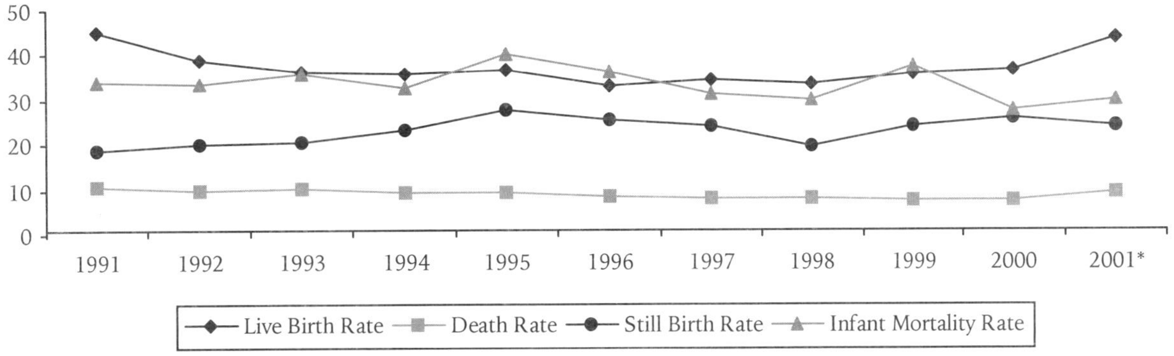

TABLE 1.12

Density of Population across Regions

(per sq.km.)

Regions	1981			1991			2001		
	Rural	Urban	Total	Rural	Urban	Total	Rural	Urban	Total
Puducherry	793	5075	1517	916	5971	2076	-	-	2534
Karaikal	543	2285	2285	672	1757	911	-	-	1060
Mahe	3157	6267	3157	0	3716	3716	0	4091	4091
Yanam	0	30	381	0	677	677	0	1568	1568
Total (UT)	736	3158	1229	829	3656	1642	-	-	2029

Source: Census data.

TABLE 1.13

Density of Population in the Neighbouring States

(per sq.km.)

States/UTs	1901	1911	1921	1931	1941	1951	1961	1971	1981	1991	2001
Puducherry	501	523	496	526	579	645	750	959	1229	1683	2029
Tamil Nadu	148	161	166	180	202	232	259	317	372	429	478
Andhra Pradesh	69	78	78	88	99	113	131	158	195	242	275
Kerala	165	184	201	245	284	349	435	549	655	749	819
India	77	82	81	90	103	117	142	177	216	267	324

Source: Census data.

This manifests the improvement in health and life expectancy. Across the regions the birth rate has declined remarkably in the Mahe region. High birth rate could be noticed in Puducherry region. The death rate is also very high in Puducherry region. The birth rate has been frog-leaping in the Yanam region. Surprisingly, the higher still birth rate and infant mortality rates exhibit a disturbing situation. Both the rates tend to increase over the period. The higher still birth rate could be attributed to the female foeticide since the developments in the medical field like scanning would help the couple to identify the sex of the baby. This has been a common practice in the female infanticide regions in Tamil Nadu like Madurai, Salem, and Dharmapuri. Similarly, the higher infant mortality rates raise an alarm over the prevalence of female infanticide in the region.

1.2.4 Weaker Sections

The population of scheduled castes forms nearly 16 per cent of the total population in the UT. Table 1.14 presents the population of scheduled castes across regions for the last three censuses. It has recorded a marginal growth over the last three censuses from 15.99 to 16.45 per cent. Across the regions, Karaikal region has registered a considerable increase in the proportion of scheduled caste population. All the other regions have displayed a negative growth rate in the proportion of scheduled caste population. Yanam has the highest proportion of the scheduled caste population among the regions, but it has noticed a decline in the proportion over the period. Across the rural and urban areas, majority of the scheduled caste population continues to live in rural areas. In Karaikal region, the scheduled caste population reported an increase in both the rural and urban areas. There is no scheduled tribe population in Puducherry.

1.2.5 Fertility Rate

Across the religious communities, Hindus form around 80 per cent of the population. The decadal growth rate of Hindus comes to 34.56 per cent. Christians occupy the second place but their decadal growth rate is 16.93 during the 1981-1991 censuses. The decadal growth rate among Muslims was 44.2. This indicates that the reduction of decadal growth rate in the UT is mainly because of the lower fertility rate among some sections of the society.

1.3 Human Development Indices

The Human Development Index (HDI) measures literacy, education, life expectancy, poverty, and other factors. It is a standard means of measuring well-being. The HDI measures the average achievements in three basic dimensions of human development:

1. A long and healthy life, as measured by life expectancy at birth.
2. Knowledge, as measured by the adult literacy rate (with two-thirds weight) and the combined primary, secondary and tertiary gross enrolment ratio (with one-third weight).
3. A decent standard of living, as measured by GDP per capita.

1.3.1 Literacy

In the literacy rate, Puducherry has displayed a consistent growth from 37.43 per cent in 1961 census to 81.49 per cent in the 2001 census. Across the regions, literacy level is perceptibly high in the Mahe region. The astounding progress in the literacy in the region is because of the geographical influence of Kerala. Interestingly there is a convergence in the literacy between male and female in the Mahe region. Even in the

TABLE 1.14

Population of Scheduled Castes across Regions

(in per cent)

Regions	*1981*			*1991*			*2001*		
	Total	*Rural*	*Urban*	*Total*	*Rural*	*Urban*	*Total*	*Rural*	*Urban*
Puducherry	16.66	23.82	11.16	16.65	28.33	10.64	16.19	27.18	10.67
Karaikal	16.65	21.58	7.97	17.72	22.79	10.83	18.07	23.22	11.4
Mahe	0.26	0.17	0.43	0.37	0	0.37	0.32	0	0.32
Yanam	21.9	—	21.9	19.9	0	19.9	18.48	0	18.48
Total (UT)	15.99	21.68	10.79	16.25	26.73	10.36	16.45	28.84	10.83

Source: Census Data.

TABLE 1.15

Literacy Rate across Regions

Regions	*1981*						*1991*						*2001*					
	Rural			*Urban*			*Rural*			*Urban*			*Rural*			*Urban*		
	Total	*Male*	*Female*	*Total*	*Male*	*Female*	*Total*	*Male*	*Female*	*Total*	*Male*	*FeMale*	*Total*	*Male*	*Female*	*Total*	*Male*	*Female*
Puducherry UT	47.98	59.39	36.30	63.04	71.77	54.23	65.36	76.44	53.96	79.88	87.70	71.98	74.28	83.87	64.63	85.05	91.4	78.78
Puducherry	43.54	55.76	30.66	63.26	72.30	54.02	61.63	73.32	49.39	79.20	87.50	70.64	71.41	81.72	60.87	85.11	92.87	78.38
Karaikal	52.80	64.42	41.31	62.85	71.87	54.17	74.45	84.29	64.76	77.57	86.08	69.19	81.07	89.07	73.29	83.76	90.50	77.20
Mahe	73.94	78.50	69.96	74.45	77.07	72.15	0.00	0.00	0.00	94.10	96.91	91.73	0.00	0.00	0.00	95.78	97.59	94.23
Yanam	0.00	0.00	0.00	49.57	55.90	43.08	0.00	0.00	0.00	76.86	82.38	71.19	0	0	0	74.16	79.11	69.07

Source: Census Data.

other regions there is a move towards convergence between sex and even rural-urban literacy levels. While it has come down from 25 per cent to 20 per cent in the Puducherry region, the difference between the male and female in the rural areas in Karaikal declined from 23 per cent to 16 per cent (Table 1.15). Thus, there is a decline in the gender disparity in the education.

1.3.2 Life Expectancy

The life expectancy in Puducherry has improved substantially due to an integrated health measure undertaken from the child to the old age health treatments. JIPMER, being one of the premier medical centres in India, caters to the health requirements of the UT and attracts a huge number of medical tourists to the place. The integrated health practices with the coordination of JIPMER ascertain the effectiveness and efficiency in the outcome. This could be noticed in the vital statistics.

Table 1.16 presents the birth, death and infant mortality rate in the state for the last ten years. This indicates that there is considerable decline in the birth rate and death rate in the UT. Birth rate has remained at around 45 during the 1991 to 2002 period and the death rate has declined from 10 to 9.5 during the same period. This manifests the decline in fertility rate in the region. The decline in the death rate also expounds the astounding progress in the health parameters. Surprisingly, increasing still birth rate contradicts the progress in the other parameters. Similarly the slow or negligible decline and fluctuations in the infant mortality rate is a veritable cause for concern. It foreshadows the prevalence of infant mortality in the region. The infant mortality data across sex also tilts the scale in favour of this. An in-depth analysis of the demographic aspects would throw more light on this aspect.

TABLE 1.16

Vital Statistics on Birth, Death and Infant Mortality

Year	*Live Birth Rate*	*Death Rate*	*Still Birth Rate*	*Infant Mortality Rate*
1991	45.0	10.5	18.6	33.9
1992	38.7	9.9	20.2	33.4
1993	36.0	10.1	20.5	35.9
1994	35.5	9.3	23.0	32.8
1995	36.5	9.4	27.8	40.1
1996	33.2	8.3	25.6	36.0
1997	34.3	7.9	23.9	31.1
1998	33.4	8.0	19.7	29.8
1999	35.7	7.5	24.3	37.6
2000	36.7	7.7	25.9	27.6
2001	43.9	9.4	24.2	29.8
2002	45.2	9.5	25.2	NA

Source: Vital Statistics, Local Administration Department, Puducherry.

The achievements in the immunisation as presented in Table 1.17 vividly delineate the total immunisation given to all the children in the region. In the immunisation of polio, DPT and TT achievements indicate the near total achievement in the initial stage basic vaccines to the babies. Even in other vaccines the achievement indicates the cooperation of the people and the interest of the officials concerned. This achievement in immunisation proclaims the improvement in the health parameters and the health consciousness of the people in the region. This leads to the improvement in the life expectancy. This has been substantiated by the death across age.

1.3.3 Poverty Levels

In Puducherry, the urban poverty remains to be higher than the rural poverty. This could be attributed to the higher urban population which is nearly two-thirds of the total population. In addition, most of the new entrants are migrants seeking employment and livelihood in a new environment. Naturally this would lead to transient poverty due to change in environment.

TABLE 1.17

Achievement in Immunisation Programme

Sl. No.	Year	TT (P.W)	DPT	Polio	BCG	Measles	DT [5]	TT [10]
1.	1994-95	19092	19202	19419	20162	17602	17576	20914
2.	1995-96	17624	18875	18895	23665	15876	26806	18060
3.	1996-97	19265	18465	18435	30290	15810	18250	19470
4.	1997-98	16625	17011	17011	36412	15213	15885	18043
5.	1998-99	19308	19584	19584	30164	19110	16742	19745
6.	1999-2000	19519	18103	18103	32068	16245	24555	28502
7.	2000-01	19551	19062	19062	32853	18601	17899	21146
8.	2001-02	19682	19201	19201	33307	17581	19468	21238

Source: Local Administration Department, Puducherry.

Table 1.18 presents the number of BPL families over the three points of time. This indicates that there is considerable growth in the number of families below poverty line in the communes of Puducherry region. In Mahe region it has registered a notable decline in the number of BPL families. Karaikal and Yanam regions reported a marginal increase in the number of families. The proportion of SC families to the total BPL families comes to 35.66 per cent. This indicates the poverty situation among the SC population which needs the support of the government to cope with the nascent situations and structural changes due to economic reforms and liberalisation. Better targeting and arresting the pilferage should be the key word for reaching the deserving people.

TABLE 1.18

DRDA Survey of BPL Families, 1997

Name of the Block	Year 1986	Year 1992	Year 1997	SC in 1997
Ariankuppam	13,730	14,374	18,308	7,750
Oulgaret	4,613	8,337	10,793	2,551
Villinaur	11,539	12,772	18,509	6,913
Karaikal	13,050	13,050	13,160	4,740
Mahe	1,779	1,779	248	3
Yanam	2,160	2,160	2,244	605
Total	46,871	52,472	63,262	22,562

Source: DRDA Survey Report.

Poverty levels across the states as illustrated in Table 1.19 explicate that the poverty in urban areas tend to be higher than rural poverty in all the southern states including Puducherry. Poverty level tends to be higher in the North-eastern states and Eastern states. Among the UTs, the poverty level in both rural and urban areas tends to be noticeably higher in Puducherry. This could be due to large scale migration from the neighbouring

TABLE 1.19

Number and Percentage of Population Below Poverty Line by States,1999-2000

Sl. No.	State/UT	Rural		Urban		Combined	
		No. of Persons (Lakh)	%	No. of Persons (Lakh)	%	No. of Persons (Lakh)	%
1.	Andhra Pradesh	58.13	11.05	60.88	26.63	119.01	15.77
2.	Arunachal Pradesh	3.80	40.04	0.18	7.47	3.98	33.47
3.	Assam	92.17	40.04	2.38	7.47	94.55	36.09
4.	Bihar	376.51	44.30	49.13	32.91	425.64	42.60
5.	Goa	0.11	1.35	0.59	7.52	0.70	4.40
6.	Gujarat	39.80	13.17	28.09	15.59	67.89	14.07
7.	Haryana	11.94	8.27	5.39	9.99	17.34	8.74
8.	Himachal Pradesh	4.84	7.94	0.29	4.63	5.12	7.63
9.	Jammu and Kashmir	2.97	3.97	0.49	1.98	3.46	3.48
10.	Karnataka	59.91	17.38	44.49	25.25	104.40	20.04
11.	Kerala	20.97	9.38	20.07	20.27	41.04	12.72
12.	Madhya Pradesh	217.32	37.06	81.22	38.44	298.54	37.43
13.	Maharashtra	125.12	23.72	102.87	26.81	227.99	25.02
14.	Manipur	6.53	40.04	0.66	7.47	7.19	28.54
15.	Meghalaya	7.89	40.04	0.34	7.47	8.23	33.87
16.	Mizoram	1.40	40.04	0.45	7.47	1.86	19.47
17.	Nagaland	5.21	40.04	0.28	7.47	5.49	32.67
18.	Orissa	143.69	48.01	25.40	42.83	169.09	47.15
19.	Punjab	10.20	6.35	4.29	5.75	14.49	6.16
20.	Rajasthan	55.06	13.74	26.78	19.85	81.83	15.28
21.	Sikkim	2.00	40.04	0.04	7.47	2.05	36.55
22.	Tamil Nadu	80.51	20.55	49.97	22.11	130.43	21.12
23.	Tripura	12.53	40.04	0.49	7.47	13.02	34.44
24.	Uttar Pradesh	412.01	31.22	117.88	30.89	529.89	31.15
25.	West Bengal	180.11	31.85	33.38	14.86	213.49	27.02
26.	A. and N. Islands	0.58	20.55	0.24	22.11	0.82	20.99
27.	Chandigarh	0.06	5.75	0.45	5.75	0.51	5.75
28.	Dadra and N. Haveli	0.30	17.57	0.03	13.52	0.33	17.14
29.	Daman and Diu	0.01	1.35	0.05	7.52	0.06	4.44
30.	Delhi	0.07	0.40	11.42	9.42	11.49	8.23
31.	Lakshadweep	0.03	9.38	0.08	20.27	0.11	15.60
32.	Puducherry	0.64	20.55	1.77	22.11	2.41	21.67
	All India	**1932.43**	**27.09**	**670.07**	**23.62**	**2602.50**	**26.10**

Source: Indiastat.com

states and the declining importance to agriculture. The contribution of agriculture sector as a whole has come down deplorably in Puducherry region in the nineties. This could be one of the reasons for the disturbance in the livelihood system of the rural people. Since majority of them are unskilled and semi-skilled, they encounter a hostile territory in the urban areas and end up in transient poverty till they find some entry point to the alternative livelihood system. To overcome these social risks, the coping and mitigating mechanisms have to be provided to the rural people through diverse skill development opportunities and resources to develop income generating activities. Hence, a comprehensive social risk management programme is essential to ensure alternative livelihood opportunities to the rural people.

The following three tables (1.20, 1.21 and 1.22) present an interesting picture of poverty trend over the period in all the southern states and all India. This indicates that Puducherry has the highest poverty level among the southern states ironically. The poverty level in Kerala has come down drastically from the highest among the southern states to lowest since 1973-74. Tamil Nadu, Karnataka, and Puducherry sail more or less in the same boat. Another interesting thing to note is that in the urban poverty Andhra Pradesh has displayed very high proportions whereas Kerala and Andhra Pradesh reported a very low rural poverty. This shows that urban poverty situation is relatively better in Puducherry and Tamil Nadu in comparison with other states. This vividly manifests that rural poverty has to be sincerely attended to reduce the pressure on urban areas and infrastructure in Puducherry and Tamil Nadu too. In turn it reduces the urban transient poverty.

TABLE 1.20

Poverty Levels across Southern States

(in percentage)

State/UT	*1999-2000*	*1993-94*	*1987-88*	*1982-83*	*1977-78*	*1973-74*
Andhra Pradesh	15.77	22.19	25.66	28.91	39.31	48.86
Karnataka	20.04	33.16	37.53	38.24	48.78	54.47
Kerala	12.72	25.43	31.79	40.42	52.22	59.79
Tamil Nadu	21.12	35.03	43.39	51.66	54.79	54.94
Puducherry	21.67	37.40	41.46	50.06	53.25	53.82
All India	**26.10**	**35.97**	**38.86**	**44.48**	**51.32**	**54.88**

Source: Planning Commission, Government of India.

TABLE 1.21

Rural Poverty Levels across Southern States

(in percentage)

State/UT	*1999-2000*	*1993-94*	*1987-88*	*1982-83*	*1977-78*	*1973-74*
Andhra Pradesh	11.05	15.92	20.92	26.53	38.11	48.41
Karnataka	17.38	29.88	32.82	36.33	48.18	55.14
Kerala	9.38	25.76	29.10	39.03	51.48	59.19
Tamil Nadu	20.55	32.48	45.80	53.99	57.68	57.43
Puducherry	20.55	32.48	45.80	53.99	57.68	57.43
All India	**27.09**	**32.27**	**39.09**	**45.65**	**53.07**	**56.44**

Source: Planning Commission, Government of India.

TABLE 1.22

Urban Poverty Levels across Southern States

(in percentage)

State/UT	*1999-2000*	*1993-94*	*1987-88*	*1982-83*	*1977-78*	*1973-74*
Andhara Pradesh	26.63	38.33	40.11	36.30	43.55	50.61
Karnataka	25.25	40.14	48.42	42.82	50.36	52.53
Kerala	20.27	24.55	40.33	45.68	55.82	62.74
Tamil Nadu	22.11	39.77	38.64	46.96	48.69	49.40
Puducherry	22.11	39.77	38.64	46.96	48.69	49.40
All India	**23.62**	**32.36**	**38.20**	**40.79**	**45.24**	**49.01**

Source: Planning Commission, Government of India.

1.3.4 HDI across States

HDI figures for rural, urban, combined and the gender disparity index have been taken from the Human Development Report 2001. HDI ranks for rural area as given in Table 1.23 indicate that Puducherry stands next to Kerala among the states and UTs but in the urban areas it is pushed to the 13th place. In the combined HDI rank it comes in the 6th place. This indicates that the quality of life in the urban areas in Puducherry remains to be deplorably low. In both the rural and urban areas, Bihar ranks almost last in the HDI ranking. Most of the UTs come within the first ten. This could be due to the small size and homogeneity in the population. Most of the large states rank low due to its diversity in culture and heterogeneity in the population.

In the gender disparity index too, Puducherry ranks fifth among the states and UTs in India. It attests to the gender equality in the region. In the gender ranking too, Bihar ranks last in the list of states and UTs. Even the high ranking of HDI in Kerala could be, *inter alia,* due to its small size and homogeneity in the culture and population. This draws the inference that the small size of the state and homogeneous culture among its population would ascertain better quality of life to its people and gender equity among its population.

1.4 State Domestic Product

1.4.1 Growth of GSDP

In the Gross State Domestic Product at current prices as illustrated in Table 1.24, the contribution of primary sector has drastically come down to 5.63 per cent in 2001-2002. Even the secondary sector also experienced a considerable decline in its share to GSDP from 54.27 per cent in 1980-81 to 32.03 per cent in 1995-96. Then onwards it started registering a marginal increase to reach 51.22 per cent share in 2001-02. The tertiary sector has displayed a remarkable increase in its share. In the early 90s, tertiary sector contributed nearly half of the GSDP in Puducherry. This indicates that the service sector is going to play a major role in the economy of Puducherry in the years to come.

TABLE 1.23

State-wise Human Development Index, 2001

States/UTs	*Rural*		*Urban*		*Combined*		*Gender Disparity Index*	
	Value	*Rank*	*Value*	*Rank*	*Value*	*Rank*	*Value*	*Rank*
Andhra Pradesh	0.344	23	0.473	29	0.377	23	0.801	23
Arunachal Pradesh	0.300	28	0.572	15	0.328	29	0.776	18
Assam	0.326	26	0.555	19	0.348	26	0.575	30
Bihar	0.286	30	0.460	31	0.308	32	0.469	32
Goa	0.534	3	0.658	3	0.575	4	0.775	13
Gujarat	0.380	18	0.532	23	0.431	17	0.714	22
Haryana	0.409	15	0.562	17	0.443	16	0.714	17
Himachal Pradesh	0.442	12	0.700	1	0.469	13	0.858	4
Jammu and Kashmir	0.364	22	0.575	14	0.402	21	0.740	25
Karnataka	0.367	21	0.523	24	0.412	19	0.753	11
Kerala	0.576	1	0.628	9	0.591	3	0.825	2
Madhya Pradesh	0.282	32	0.491	28	0.328	30	0.662	28
Maharashtra	0.403	16	0.548	21	0.452	15	0.793	15
Manipur	0.503	7	0.618	12	0.536	9	0.815	3
Meghalaya	0.332	24	0.624	10	0.365	24	0.807	12
Mizoram	0.464	10	0.648	5	0.548	7	0.770	6
Nagaland	0.442	13	0.633	7	0.486	11	0.729	21
Orissa	0.328	25	0.469	30	0.345	28	0.639	27
Punjab	0.447	11	0.566	16	0.475	12	0.710	19
Rajasthan	0.298	29	0.492	27	0.347	27	0.692	16
Sikkim	0.398	17	0.618	11	0.425	18	0.647	20
Tamil Nadu	0.421	14	0.560	18	0.466	14	0.813	9
Tripura	0.368	20	0.551	20	0.389	22	0.531	29
Uttar Pradesh	0.284	31	0.444	32	0.314	31	0.520	31
West Bengal	0.370	19	0.511	26	0.404	20	0.631	26
Andaman and Nicobar Islands	0.528	5	0.653	4	0.574	5	0.857	1
Chandigarh	0.501	8	0.694	2	0.674	1	0.764	7
Dadra and Nagar Haveli	0.310	27	0.519	25	0.361	25	0.832	14
Daman and Diu	0.492	9	0.629	8	0.544	8	0.714	8
Delhi	0.53	4	0.635	6	0.624	2	0.690	10
Lakshadweep	0.52	6	0.545	22	0.532	10	0.680	24
Puducherry	0.556	2	0.591	13	0.571	6	0.783	5
India	0.340		0.511		0.381		0.676	

Source: National Human Development Report 2001, Planning Commission, Government of India.

TABLE 1.24

Contribution of Major Sectors to GSDP at Current Prices

Years	*Primary Sector*	*Secondary Sector*	*Tertiary Sector*
Old Series			
1980-81	18.61	54.27	27.12
1981-82	17.77	52.83	29.41
1982-83	15.59	54.00	30.41
1983-84	14.86	53.42	31.72
1984-85	15.59	51.56	32.85
1985-86	17.60	48.63	33.77
1986-87	16.71	48.95	34.34
1987-88	16.08	46.91	37.01
1988-89	16.79	45.93	36.62
1989-90	15.09	44.85	36.60
1990-91	16.74	41.85	38.04
1991-92	17.99	37.57	40.95
1992-93	20.00	37.02	42.99
New Series			
1993-94	16.38	34.34	49.28
1994-95	17.34	33.09	49.56
1995-96	14.47	32.03	53.51
1996-97	9.54	43.06	47.40
1997-98	6.71	50.21	43.08
1998-99	7.11	49.03	43.86
1999-2000	7.84	44.98	47.18
2000-01	6.42	50.24	43.34
2001-02	5.63	51.22	43.15

Source: State Domestic Products, Directorate of Economics and Statistics, Puducherry.

Table 1.25 (Figures 1.4 and 1.5) presents the average proportion for the five years from 1980-81. This attests to the fact that the late nineties have brought noticeable changes in the importance of different sectors to the economy. The service sector began to play an important role in the economy after the introduction of economic reforms and liberalisation.

TABLE 1.25

Contribution of Different Sectors to the GSDP at Current Prices

Years	*Primary Sector*	*Secondary Sector*	*Tertiary Sector*
Old Series			
1980-81 to 1984-85	16.48	53.21	30.30
1985-86 to 1989-90	16.46	47.05	35.67
1990-91 to 1992-93	18.24	38.81	40.66
New Series			
1993-94 to 1997-98	12.89	38.55	48.57
1998-99 to 2001-02	6.75	48.87	44.38

Source: State Domestic Products, Directorate of Economics and Statistics, Puducherry.

FIGURE 1.4

Major Sectoral Contribution to GSDP–Current Prices

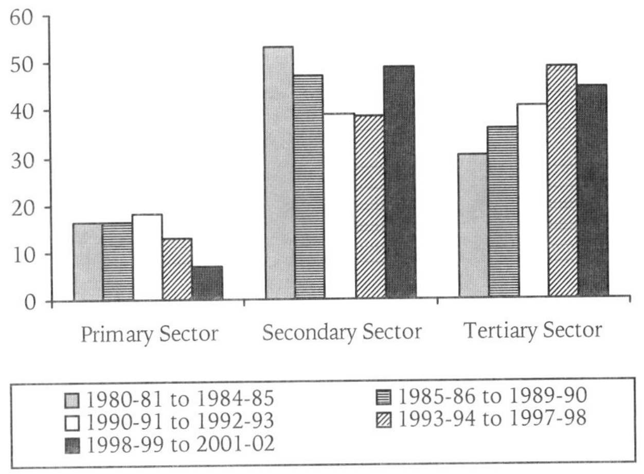

FIGURE 1.5

Major Sectoral Contribution to GSDP–Current Prices

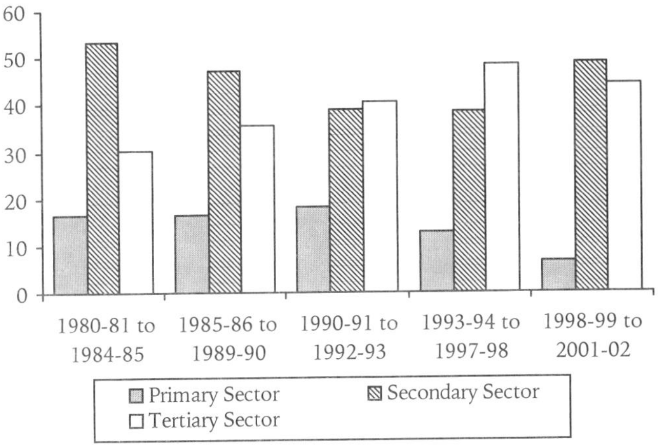

1.4.2 Sectoral Composition of GSDP

The proportion of contribution across the major components in the three sectors has been presented in Table 1.26. Across the sectors, all the components in the primary sector such as agriculture, forestry, and fishing have reported a noticeable decline in their share to GSDP. Though in absolute terms, it has shown a manifold increase, the decline in their share to GSDP indicates the spectacular growth in other sectors. In the secondary sector, registered manufacturing sector exhibited a remarkable growth from 11.97 in 1980-81 to 41.26 in the year 2001-02. This indicates the health of the economy. Surprisingly, discussions with the officials concerned and people transected that most of the manufacturing units in reality remain as assembling units for major multinationals and other industrial giants in India. The

TABLE 1.26

Contribution of Major Sectors to GSDP at Current Prices

	Old Series (1980-81 base)			New Series (1993-94 base)	
	1980-81 to 1984-85	*1985-86 to 1989-90*	*1990-91 to 1992-93*	*1993-94 to 1997-98*	*1998-99 to 2001-02*
Primary Sector	16.48	14.25	18.24	12.89	6.75
Agriculture and animal husbandry	9.01	26.48	2.97	6.46	2.70
Forestry and logging	0.00	21.35	0.00	0.64	0.22
Fishing	5.01	3.25	2.60	4.16	1.80
Mining quarrying	0.00	0.00	0.00	0.00	0.00
Secondary sector	53.21	43.52	38.81	38.55	48.87
Manufacturing industries					
1) Registered	10.13	16.57	8.40	21.88	26.97
2) Unregistered	5.73	4.35	2.16	6.02	4.21
Construction	31.21	9.02	9.57	3.64	1.67
Electricity, power, water supply	-0.14	0.26	0.06	0.55	0.37
Tertiary Sector	30.30	42.39	40.66	48.57	44.38
Railways	0.01	0.01	0.01	0.02	0.01
Transport by other means and storage	3.84	2.16	2.33	1.69	1.64
Communication	0.35	0.37	0.26	0.48	0.46
Trade, hotels, restaurants	5.28	7.66	2.45	12.40	10.96
Banking and insurance	1.51	2.14	1.92	3.20	1.83
Real estate ownership of dwelling and business services	2.20	4.49	1.32	9.20	4.58
Public administration	5.04	3.31	2.10	4.25	2.95
Other services	5.70	4.90	2.64	7.79	4.58
Total	**100**	**100**	**100**	**100**	**100**

Source: State Domestic Products, Directorate of Economics and Statistics, Puducherry.

unregistered manufacturing sector has stabilised around 6 per cent share to the overall GSDP. The major loser in the secondary sector is construction. It lost its significance in the Puducherry economy. It declined from 31.21 per cent share in the GSDP in 1980-81 to 9.57 per cent in 1992-93 in the old series and subsequently to 1.67 per cent in 2001-02 (in the new series). This manifests that the growth of Puducherry economy is stabilised to a certain extent and any further growth in the population would jack up the real estate business by enhancing the value of dwelling units. This is visible in the real estate component in the tertiary sector.

In the tertiary sector, the trade, hotels and restaurants component has exhibited a considerable increase till 1999-2000. Then it declined marginally. This could be due to the implementation of uniform floor rate tax which has made the commodities dearer on par with neighbouring states. Similar to trade, the real estate business component has multiplied manifold in the old and the new series. The major contributing variants for this trend include the educational migration, medical migration, in-migration for employment and the developments in the manufacturing sector. All the other variants in the tertiary sector like transport, banking, public administration and other services maintained more or less similar positions with minor fluctuations in the early nineties. This transpires that the macro level policies influence the economy with immediate effect. Thus, the external environment plays a vital role in the economy of Puducherry.

Similar to sectoral differences at current prices, the sectoral difference in the constant prices also exhibits similar proportions in most of the components (Tables 1.27 and 1.28). On the contrary it makes a significant difference in the growth rates. Thus, it indicates that growth rates in real term are negligible.

TABLE 1.27

Contribution of Major Sectors to GSDP at Current Prices

Years	*Primary Sector*	*Secondary Sector*	*Tertiary Sector*
1980-81 to 1984-85	16.71	55.43	27.85
1985-86 to 1989-90	14.78	56.04	29.18
1990-91 to 1992-93	14.80	51.22	33.98
1993-94 to 1997-98	14.47	35.53	50.00
1998-99 to 2001-02	7.50	49.32	43.18

Source: State Domestic Products, Directorate of Economics and Statistics, Puducherry.

TABLE 1.28

Contribution of Different Sectors to the GSDP at Constant Prices

Components in the Sectors	*Old Series*			*New Series*	
	1980-81 to 1984-85	*1985-86 to 1989-90*	*1990-91 to 1992-93*	*1993-94 to 1997-98*	*1998-99 to 2001-02*
Primary Sector	**16.71**	**14.78**	**14.80**	**14.47**	**7.50**
Agriculture and animal husbandry	10.64	8.23	8.20	8.43	4.31
Forestry and logging	0.00	0.00	0.00	0.88	0.37
Fishing	6.08	6.54	6.60	5.15	2.82
Secondary Sector	**55.43**	**56.04**	**51.22**	**35.53**	**49.32**
Registered manufacturing	11.26	13.70	23.49	23.96	40.88
Unregistered manufacturing	6.17	6.30	4.36	8.62	6.99
Construction	40.02	38.31	26.13	4.83	2.62
Electricity, power, water supply	-2.01	-2.26	-2.76	-1.87	-1.17
Tertiary Sector	**27.85**	**29.18**	**33.98**	**50.00**	**43.18**
Railways	0.01	0.00	0.01	0.01	0.01
Transport by other means and storage	3.66	4.65	5.44	1.11	2.05
Communication	0.32	0.32	0.52	0.46	0.61
Trade, hotels, restaurants	6.65	6.33	6.68	16.41	18.14
Banking and insurance	1.91	2.80	5.55	4.35	3.01
Real estate ownership of dwelling and business Services	2.25	2.63	2.97	11.96	7.23
Public administration	5.99	5.77	5.43	5.10	4.49
Other services	7.06	6.69	7.39	10.60	7.64
Total	**100.00**	**100.00**	**100.00**	**100.00**	**100.00**

Source: State Domestic Products, Directorate of Economics and Statistics, Puducherry.

1.4.3 Growth Rates of GSDP

The analysis of growth rates as presented in Table 1.29 also reinforces the results of the sectoral composition. Across the sectors, trade, real estate and registered manufacturing variants have displayed scintillating growth rates. The other sectors have disclosed a very marginal increase over the period. All the growth rates were highly significant and the R^2 is also close to one in all the variables, save constructions. Though the current prices present the actual improvement in the economy without adjusting to the inflation, it is close to reality in the economy as a whole. To find the growth in real terms, the GSDP components at constant prices is also analysed.

The growth rates of GSDP at constant prices from 1980-81 to 1993-94 at 1980-81 prices and 1994-95 to 2001-02 at 1993-94 prices have been calculated to understand the real change in GSDP adjusted to inflation. Astonishingly, the secondary and tertiary sectors have shown respectable growth rates in the old series (1980-81 to 1993-94) but in the new series (1994-95 to 2001-02) all the sectors have registered a very negligible growth rate (Table 1.30). Between 1980-81 to 1992-93, agriculture in the primary sector and construction in the secondary sector have indicated negative growth. Fisheries in the primary sector registered manufacturing in the secondary sector and banking in the tertiary sector have displayed high growth rates in their respective sectors. In the tertiary sector, transport, communication, and real estate business have reported considerably higher growth rates. This transpires the real development opportunities available in the liberalised situation. This indicates that communication, transport and real estate business have very good scope to flourish in the future and contribute to the Puducherry economy. In the 1993-94 to 2001-02 period, all the components in all the three sectors have displayed very negligible growth rates. This could be because of the higher base but interestingly no variant has reported negative sign.

Though in the current prices most of the variants of GSDP have exhibited closer to double-digit growth rates,

TABLE 1.29

Growth Rates of GSDP by Sectors at Current Prices

(per cent)

Sectors	With Constant		Without Constant	
	1980-81 to 1992-93	1993- 94 to 2001-02	1980-81 to 1992-93	1993-94 to 2001-02
Primary	12.49*	4.69**	100.14*	54.07*
Agriculture	-0.51	-0.18	84.31*	49.55*
Forestry	0.00	-3.66**	0.00	36.55*
Fishing	4.80*	0.91	82.10*	47.30*
Secondary	8.82*	25.40*	110.78*	62.74*
Manufacturing registered	9.38*	24.51*	92.19*	59.53*
Manufacturing unregistered	2.48	12.75*	81.92*	50.96*
Construction	-1.85	1.83*	98.43*	46.81*
Electricity	0.00	8.94*	0.00	37.59*
Tertiary	15.33*	17.20*	108.74*	63.08*
Railways	0.00	-0.70*	0.00	17.11*
Transport	6.64*	16.71*	79.98*	44.89*
Communication	7.66*	17.74*	53.92*	38.02*
Trade and Hotels	3.53*	15.55*	81.37*	55.51*
Banking and Insurance	13.84*	6.94*	74.02*	46.85*
Real Estate and business services	6.24*	4.95*	73.50*	52.18*
Public administration	2.76*	10.05*	80.57*	48.87*
Other services	3.45*	7.11*	82.11*	51.70*
Total	12.01*	19.30*	119.84*	67.28*

Note: * indicates one per cent level significance and
** denotes the five per cent level significance.

Source: State Domestic Products, Directorate of Economics and Statistics, Puducherry.

TABLE 1.30

Growth Rates of GSDP by Sectors at Constant Prices

(per cent)

Sectors	With Constant		Without Constant	
	1980-81 to 1992-93	1993-94 to 2001-02	1980-81 to 1992-93	1993-94 to 2001-02
Primary	1.54	0.04	90.99*	52.62*
Agriculture	-0.51	-0.18	84.31*	49.55*
Forestry	0	-3.66**	0	36.55*
Fishing	4.8*	0.91	82.1*	47.3*
Secondary	2.67	20.33	105.42*	61.17*
Manufacturing registered	9.38*	24.51*	92.19*	59.53*
Manufacturing unregistered	2.48	12.75*	81.92*	50.96*
Construction	-1.85	1.83**	98.43*	46.81*
Electricity	0	8.94*	0	37.59*
Tertiary	5.23*	10.6*	99.29*	61.01*
Railways	0	-0.7	0	17.11*
Transport	6.64*	16.71*	79.98*	44.89*
Communication	7.66*	17.74*	53.92*	38.02*
Trade and Hotels	3.53*	15.55*	81.37*	55.51*
Banking and Insurance	13.84*	6.94*	74.02*	46.85*
Real Estate and business services	6.24*	4.95*	73.5*	52.18*
Public administration	2.76*	10.05*	80.57*	48.87*
Other services	3.45*	7.11*	82.11*	51.7*
Total	3.33*	13.6*	112.3*	65.51*

Note: * indicates one per cent level significance and
** denotes the five per cent level significance.

Source: State Domestic Products, Directorate of Economics and Statistics, Puducherry.

the constant prices GSDP reveal a pessimistic picture of liberalisation and its much acclaimed growth and development. Interestingly in the percentage distribution, it has not shown much difference between current prices and constant price GSDP shares. This manifests the internal integration between sectors and its response to global policy changes.

1.4.4 Per Capita GSDP

The per capita income at current prices as given in Table 1.31 has increased from Rs.2794 in 1980-81 to Rs.10849 (in the old series) in 1995-96 but at the new series the same was Rs. 12202. In the new series with 1993-94 base, it has galloped from Rs.9781 in 1993-94 to Rs.29383 in 1999-2000 and to Rs.37696 in 2001-02. On the contrary, in the constant prices it has moved from Rs.2794 in 1980-81 in the old series to Rs.2424 in 1992-1993. In the new series it has increased from Rs.9781 in 1993-94 to Rs.19374 in 1999-2000 and subsequently to Rs.2296 in 2001-02. This indicates that in the old series, the per capita income has not disclosed any considerable increase but in the new series it has reported noticeable increase. This necessitates a closer look at the measurement and the macroeconomic stabilisation problems (higher inflation rate etc.) for the growth rates of GSDP variants in constant prices have not shown much change in the new series period.

Table 1.32 indicates the growth rate of per capita in the old and the new series at current and constant prices. The per capita income across states at constant prices is presented in Table 1.33. It indicates that the increase in the per capita during the new series is perceptibly higher

TABLE 1.31

Per Capita Income Over the Period

Years	*Current Prices*	*Constant Prices*
1980-81	2794	2794
1981-82	3039	2758
1982-83	3325	2898
1983-84	3715	2847
1984-85	4118	2923
1985-86	4475	2976
1986-87	4897	3067
1987-88	5140	3003
1988-89	5785	3055
1989-90	6231	3100
1990-91	6683	3183
1991-92	7129	2883
1992-93	7584	2434
1993-94	9781	9781
1994-95	10997	9661
1995-96	12202	9889
1996-97	18631	13512
1997-98	25720	17402
1998-99	28768	19279
1999-2000	29383	19374
2000-01	35190	22252
2001-02	37696	22926
Growth rate	12.72	11.77

Source: State Domestic Products, Directorate of Economics and Statistics, Puducherry.

TABLE 1.32

Growth Rate of Per Capita Income

Prices	*Old Series*	*New Series*	*Overall*
Current	8.47	18.46	12.72
Constant	0.07	12.68	11.77

Source: State Domestic Products, Directorate of Economics and Statistics, Puducherry.

in comparison with the old series. During the old series period, the per capita income at constant prices reported a decline during the early nineties. This could mean that the economic boom brought about by reforms was not visible in reality. Across the states, Puducherry has reported a decline during the early nineties cohort. In the other cohorts of new series, it has reported astounding progress in majority of the states.

The growth rates across southern states indicate that Karnataka and Puducherry are the major beneficiaries of economic reforms (Table 1.34). Though Tamil Nadu has also reported a relatively higher growth rate, it is closer to the pre-reform period growth rate or old series growth rate. Thus, Puducherry growth rate is noticeably higher in the new series. Among the southern states, Kerala has exhibited a very low growth rate during the old and new series. Across the states, Puducherry reported a striking performance during the nineties.

1.5 Employment Characteristics

The employment characteristics across sectors have been analysed with the help of Census data and the State Government Official data from the Employment Exchange Office published at the Statistical Abstract by the Directorate of Economics and Statistics.

1.5.1 Workers in Census Data

The Census data for the three points of time from 1981 to 2001 explicates that there is a considerable mobility in the labour force from one sector to another. Table 1.35 indicates that the proportion of agricultural workers has been on the decline. Registered manufacturing sector has shown a marginal increase. In the tertiary sector, the proportion of workers in the trade, hotels and restaurants, and other services tend to be more than other sectors in Puducherry. This manifests that the semi-skilled and unskilled workers from agriculture find some opportunities in the tertiary sectors. At present in Puducherry nearly 50 per cent of the workers count on tertiary sector for their livelihood. Across regions, agriculture sector engages more workers as agricultural labourers in the Karaikal region. More workers are involved in the fishing and livestock related activities in the Mahe and Yanam regions. In the manufacturing sector, Puducherry and Yanam regions engage higher proportion of workers. Karaikal is reporting very low proportion of workers in the secondary sector. It manifests that the natural advantages it has inherited have not been optimally utilised. It could be because of poor infrastructure facilities created. Nearly two-thirds of the workers are involved in the service sector occupations in the Mahe region. Since this is a small region with very limited scope for huge infrastructure development and raw material availability, the other sectors are not able to progress at the desirable levels. This manifests the diversities between the regions and its impact on the employment opportunities. While Karaikal has the advantage of primary sector development, Yanam and Puducherry regions have the infrastructure and natural advantage for promoting the manufacturing sector. Since Mahe is too small to have primary or secondary sector development, the advantages over the tertiary sector

TABLE 1.33

Per Capita GSDP across States at Constant Prices

	Old Series with 1980-81 Prices			*New Series with 1993-94 Price*	
	1980-81 to 1984-85	*1985-86 to 1989-90*	*1990-91 to 1995-96**	*1993-94 to 1996-97***	*1997-98 to 1999-2000*
Andhra Pradesh	1523.40	1867.80	2206.83	7928.00	8926.67
Arunachal Pradesh	1766.80	2263.20	3243.17	8710.75	8622.33
Assam	1408.00	1489.80	1575.00	6465.25	5748.33
Bihar	975.20	1106.60	1059.67	3102.25	3197.00
Jharkand	0.00	0.00	0.00	5924.75	7411.33
Goa	3149.40	3661.60	5398.50	18037.50	23776.67
Gujarat	2133.60	2365.80	3017.50	11546.50	13414.33
Haryana	2449.60	2994.00	3548.67	11703.25	12808.33
Himachal Pradesh	1696.00	1960.80	2324.83	8575.00	10261.67
Jammu Kashmir	1792.20	1735.60	1850.00	6768.00	7269.33
Karnataka	1624.40	1858.80	2338.67	8323.25	10292.33
Kerala	1468.20	1552.20	2004.83	8547.25	9625.33
Madhya Pradesh	1372.00	1447.00	1708.67	6753.25	7723.33
Chhattisgarh	0.00	0.00	0.00	6528.00	6791.67
Maharashtra	2498.60	2900.60	3971.67	12756.50	14492.33
Manipur	1482.20	1649.80	1887.17	5695.25	6467.33
Meghalaya	1368.00	1469.00	1712.67	6994.25	8451.00
Mizoram	0.00	0.00	0.00	0.00	0.00
Nagaland	1606.80	1859.40	1398.50	9566.25	9377.00
Orissa	1303.60	1513.00	1524.33	4981.75	5529.33
Punjab	2886.40	3443.40	3968.17	12876.75	14263.00
Rajasthan	1337.40	1513.60	1920.50	7098.50	8602.67
Sikkim	1721.80	2606.80	1715.33	7633.00	9680.33
Tamil Nadu	1609.00	1982.00	2618.50	9871.00	11656.00
Tripura	1283.40	1402.00	1797.00	5711.00	7397.00
Uttar Pradesh	1323.20	1477.40	1635.83	5308.75	5542.00
Uttaranchal	0.00	0.00	0.00	7264.75	7362.00
West Bengal	1791.20	2012.00	2405.17	7305.50	8847.33
Andaman and Nicobar	2547.20	2702.00	2925.00	15658.25	15381.67
Chandigarh	0.00	0.00	0.00	22040.25	26543.00
Delhi	4219.00	5003.60	6168.50	19471.50	23734.67
Puducherry	2844.00	3040.20	2836.00	10710.75	18685.00
All India	0.00	0.00	0.00	8314.00	9655.00

Note: * Data relates to the old series with 1980-81 as base.
** Data relates to the new series with 1993-94 as the base.

Source: *RBI Bulletin*, Various issues.

TABLE 1.34

Growth Rate of GSDP across States in the Southern Region

States	*Old Series*	*New Series*
Andhra Pradesh	3.50	3.86
Karnataka	3.59	5.86
Kerala	2.99	3.67
Tamil Nadu	4.68	4.74
Puducherry	-0.09	14.28

Source: *RBI Bulletin*, Various issues.

TABLE 1.35

Distribution of Workers across Different Categories and Regions

	Puducherry			*Karaikal*			*Mahe*			*Yanam*			*Total*		
	Male	*Female*	*Total*	*Male*	*Female*	*Total*	*Male*	*Female*	*Total*	*Male*	*Female*	*Total*	*Male*	*Female*	*Total*
Cultivators															
1981	11278	732	12010	3099	272	3371	65	9	74	382	4	386	14824	1017	15841
1991	11913	1932	13845	3456	222	3678	85	20	105	326	5	331	15780	2179	17959
2001	9409	1102	10511	1974	199	2173	14	1	15	254	5	259	11651	1307	12958
Agricultural labourers															
1981	24229	14243	38472	10569	3582	14151	323	177	500	812	579	1391	35933	18581	54514
1991	35057	22707	57764	12130	5156	17286	365	117	482	1061	610	1671	48613	28590	77203
2001	36631	22963	59594	9089	3858	12947	132	43	175	1474	394	1868	47326	27258	74584
Household Industries- Manufacturing, Processing, Services and repairs															
1981	2401	950	3351	266	134	400	4130	675	4805	1737	277	2014	8534	2036	10570
1991	1211	543	1754	98	56	154	78	51	129	64	25	89	1451	675	2126
2001	2988	2380	5368	399	332	731	43	21	64	193	48	241	3623	2781	6404
Other workers															
1981	65812	9267	75079	14889	2091	16980	4130	675	4805	1737	277	2014	86568	12310	98878
1991	35397	12232	47629	6691	2001	8692	1508	796	2304	969	307	1276	44565	15336	59901
2001	196177	45717	241894	30032	5817	35849	6899	1267	8166	6042	888	6930	239150	53689	292839
Marginal workers															
1981	2466	3929	6395	578	3265	3843	182	72	254	13	78	91	3239	7344	10583
1991	1365	2413	3778	169	1014	1183	244	97	341	25	87	112	1803	3611	5414
2001	13465	11823	25288	2988	2874	5862	598	290	888	352	259	611	17403	15246	32649
Non-workers															
1981	119855	189255	309110	29966	51299	81265	8447	14140	22587	2892	4787	7679	161160	259481	420641
1991	151951	250044	401995	35442	63625	99067	9412	16643	26055	4973	8481	13454	201778	338793	540571
2001	228291	403399	631690	40005	73224	113229	9467	18053	27520	7578	13907	21485	285341	508583	793924

Source: Various Censuses Data, Puducherry.

due to its proximity to Kerala and Karnataka could be harvested.

1.5.2 *Employment in the Organised and Unorganised Sectors*

The employment pattern in the organised and unorganised sectors reveals the flip side of the economic reforms and liberalisation. Table 1.36 explicates that the employment opportunities remain constant in the post-reform period whereas in the daily wages category it is galloping in the subsequent years of reforms. It increased tenfold from 1991 to 2003 (2225 to 23885). The number of factories submitting returns also reported a considerable decline in the post-reform period though the number of working factories displayed a noticeable increase. This indicates that liberalisation and economic reforms increasingly facilitated the growth of unorganised sector and unorganised labour force. Though the unorganised labour provides an enabling atmosphere for private investments, it should not lead to unbridled exploitation of labour at the hands of profit motivated entrepreneurs.

The number of commercial establishments and the number of people employed in these as illustrated in Table 1.37 reveal the remarkable growth of the unorganised sector units like shops, commercial establishments, hotels and theatres in Puducherry. The number of people employed per shop has increased over the period from 1.12 to 1.5. In the case of commercial establishments, it has declined marginally from around

TABLE 1.36

Workers Employed in Organised and Unorganised Sectors

Year	*No. of Working Factories*	*Factories Submitting Returns*	*Percentage of Factories Submitting Returns*	*No. of Workers in Factories Submitted Returns*	*Percentage of Workers in Factories Submitting Returns*	*Workers in Factories not Submitting Returns*	*Percentage of Workers in Factories not Submitting Returns*	*Average Daily No. of Workers Employed*
1980	621	406	65.38	14496	93.58	955	6.16	15491
1981	687	453	65.94	14526	89.74	1660	10.26	16186
1982	658	486	73.86	15220	93.00	1146	7.00	16366
1983	737	521	70.69	10173	59.12	7038	40.90	17207
1984	749	271	36.18	10145	57.25	7576	42.75	17721
1985	800	393	49.13	10873	60.42	7124	39.58	17997
1986	815	469	57.55	15149	89.17	1840	10.83	16989
1987	861	539	62.60	16558	88.18	2220	11.82	18778
1988	948	580	61.18	15617	84.23	2925	15.77	18542
1989	1027	665	64.75	17353	88.58	2238	11.42	19591
1990	1103	739	67.00	19621	89.95	2193	10.05	21814
1991	1144	783	68.44	20784	90.33	2225	9.67	23009
1992	1219	467	38.31	17045	70.83	7015	29.15	24064
1993	1179	380	32.23	17723	66.51	8924	33.49	26647
1994	1174	468	39.86	22662	77.78	6473	22.22	29135
1995	1315	397	30.19	21086	62.85	12463	37.15	33549
1996	1416	482	34.04	28104	69.21	12500	30.79	40604
1997	1444	506	35.04	26681	60.50	17417	39.50	44098
1998	1557	408	26.20	25839	54.03	21982	45.97	47821
1999	1553	449	28.91	27844	55.76	22087	44.24	49931
2000	1752	416	23.74	28671	55.72	22785	44.28	51376
2001	1869	500	26.75	28651	53.46	24938	46.54	53589
2002	1284	461	35.90	28380	51.55	26678	48.45	55058
2003	1421	599	42.15	31415	56.81	23885	43.19	55300

Source: Various Issues of *Abstract of Statistics*, Puducherry.

TABLE 1.37

Employment in Shops and Commercial Establishments

Years	*Shops*		*Commercial Establishment*		*Cinema theatres, Hotels and Restaurant*		*Total Establishment*	
	Numbers	*Number of Persons Employed*	*Numbers*	*Number of Persons Employed*	*Numbers*	*Number of Persons Employed*	*Numbers*	*Number of Persons Employed*
1980 to 1984	6848.2	8107	609.2	2315.4	828.4	3784	8291.8	14202.4
1985 to 1989	10005	9959.4	907.2	2945.2	1090.8	4446.2	12003	17350.8
1990 to 1994	13023.2	13420.8	1217.6	3689.2	1430.4	5223.6	15670	22015
1995 to 2000	13313.7	16991	1690.8	5443.6	1384.7	5878.2	16389	28562
2001 to 2003	16012.0	23116.0	2018.7	7001.0	1602.0	6485.3	19632.7	36602.3

Source: Various issues of *Abstract of Statistics*, Puducherry.

3.8 to 3.5 between 1980-81 and 2000-2003. In the theatres and hotels category also, the number of persons employed has declined from 5.3 to 4.2 during the same period. On the whole, it has made negligible changes in the number of workers per establishments. This indicates that there is a noticeable decline in the number of people employed in the establishments. This reiterates that in line with the structural adjustment policies and changing management paradigms, the lean and efficient perspective has been brought into the unorganised sector too.

The employment pattern in the public sector shows that the Central and state governments began to downsize from the 1995-96 period whereas the quasi government and local bodies tend to remain constant or show a marginal increase. This reiterates the conditionalities of the structural adjustment programme that while state and Central governments should reduce their role to monitor level, decentralised governance should be promoted by establishing appropriate institutions of local self-governance. The employment pattern in various public sector wings reinforces the sincere application of the conditionality. Table 1.38 (Figure 1.6) manifests that the proportion of employees in the quasi government has been on the rise from the nineties whereas the proportion in the state and Central government employees began to show signs of fluctuation and decline. On the contrary, the proportion of employees in the local bodies began to increase from the 1993-94 period. This insinuates that the 73rd and 74th Amendments of the Constitution have made some inroads in the administration though the Conformity Act for these Amendments has not been made. Now after 38 years, elections to local bodies have been conducted in June 2006. Now the employees in the local bodies may increase. The increase in the proportion of quasi government employees and the local bodies employees expounds the sincerity of the government to decentralise power in the state.

TABLE 1.38

Distribution of Employees in Government

Years	Central Government	State Government	Quasi Government	Local Bodies	Total	Percentage of Employees to the Total: Central Government	State Government	Quasi Government	Local Bodies
1980-81	2209	17969	6568	1416	28162	7.84	63.81	23.32	5.03
1981-82	4001	18524	6743	1409	30677	13.04	60.38	21.98	4.59
1982-83	4228	19665	6816	1512	32221	13.12	61.03	21.15	4.69
1983-84	4255	20197	6956	1576	32984	12.90	61.23	21.09	4.78
1984-85	4264	20189	7047	1618	33118	12.88	60.96	21.28	4.89
1985-86	4307	22612	7150	1577	35646	12.08	63.43	20.06	4.42
1986-87	4465	20343	13010	1600	39418	11.33	51.61	33.01	4.06
1987-88	4473	20556	13231	1789	40049	11.17	51.33	33.04	4.47
1988-89	4762	22502	12372	1756	41392	11.50	54.36	29.89	4.24
1989-90	4766	24146	11278	1928	42118	11.32	57.33	26.78	4.58
1990-91	4854	24999	11278	1984	43115	11.26	57.98	26.16	4.60
1991-92	4813	25505	11128	1965	43411	11.09	58.75	25.63	4.53
1992-93	4848	25814	11444	2040	44146	10.98	58.47	25.92	4.62
1993-94	4910	25613	11558	2090	44171	11.12	57.99	26.17	4.73
1994-95	4885	25778	11247	2090	44000	11.10	58.59	25.56	4.75
1995-96	4865	25761	11163	2090	43879	11.09	58.71	25.44	4.76
1996-97	5098	21360	11875	2104	40437	12.61	52.82	29.37	5.20
1997-98	4657	20450	13476	1994	40577	11.48	50.40	33.21	4.91
1998-99	2215	16616	12536	1956	33323	6.65	49.86	37.62	5.87
1999-2000	5018	21017	9818	706	36559	13.73	57.49	26.86	1.93
2000-01	2718	7919	8360	1217	20214	13.45	39.18	41.36	6.02
2001-02	5605	17169	10820	2247	35841	15.64	47.90	30.19	6.27
2002-03	5253	26665	8235	2713	42866	12.25	62.21	19.21	6.33
2003-04	NA	NA	NA	NA	NA	NA	NA	NA	NA
2004-05	5166	27527	8220	2663	43576	11.86	63.17	18.86	6.11

Note: NA: Data Not Available.

Source: Various issues of *Abstract of Statistics*, Puducherry.

FIGURE 1.6

Employment Pattern in the Government of Puducherry

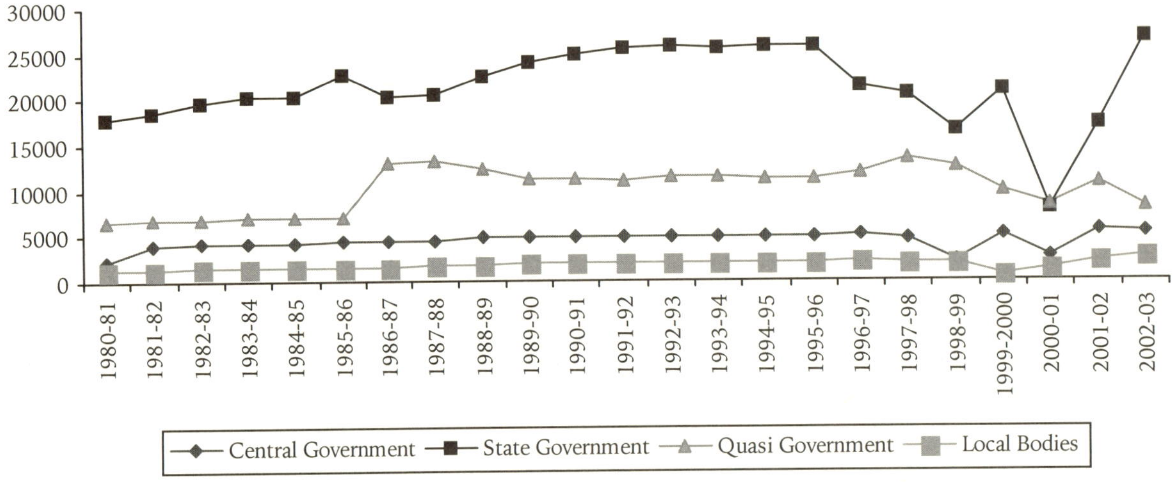

1.5.3 Unemployment Rates

The unemployment rates and educated unemployment rates have been analysed with the help of Employment Exchange Office data. Table 1.39 shows that total number of persons in the live register is 166770 (2003) out of the total population of 973829 in 2001 census. This explicates that nearly 17 per cent of the people remains to be in the live register aspiring to get placement through the Employment Exchange Office. Out of this the educated persons come to 90294. It comes to around 10 per cent of the total population. The output from the educational institutions in the year 2000-01 was 18057. It comes to nearly two per cent of the population. Out of this, 6354 persons enrol in the live register. This transpires two things vividly at once. Less than 50 per cent of the educated youth only register with the Employment Exchange Office and as a result the actual unemployment rate could be considerably higher than in the live register. On the contrary, this could also mean the sizeable 'outside the state' students enrolling in Puducherry for the private institutions of higher education attract large number of students from other states. Interestingly, the change from the previous year in both the number of persons in live register and educated person tend to have a pattern with minor fluctuations. This constantly growing number in the live register is a veritable cause for concern. Since the public sector has breezed almost the appointment of additional positions, creation of alternative employment opportunities becomes highly essential to provide employment to educated and uneducated persons before it worsens.

TABLE 1.39

Number of Persons in the Live Register and Placement Effected

Years	*Total Persons in Live Register*	*No. of Fresh Registration*	*No. of Vacancies Notified*	*Percentage of Vacancies Notified to Persons in Live Register*	*No. of Placement Effected*	*Percentage of Placement Effected to Total Vacancies Notified*
1981	39873	8110	1859	4.66	471	22.9
1982	43826	10602	1886	4.30	874	46.3
1983	50332	10071	1575	3.13	758	48.1
1984	57789	12911	1961	3.39	769	39.2
1985	69144	13265	2326	3.36	399	17.2
1986	78552	11578	1595	2.03	315	19.7
1987	88238	9217	2371	2.69	354	14.9
1988	98078	11764	2650	2.70	747	28.2
1989	108600	12829	4005	3.69	1309	32.7
1990	117942	13965	1790	1.52	303	16.93
1991	121013	12574	2072	1.71	177	8.54
1992	129715	10971	2183	1.68	331	15.16
1993	132392	11846	2126	1.61	264	12.42
1994	140713	12535	2407	1.71	297	12.34
1995	147171	13312	1858	1.26	387	21
1996	150024	13615	1873	1.25	111	6
1997	138649	11413	2303	1.66	161	7
1998	146979	11946	1958	1.33	123	6.28
1999	126192	12891	2083	1.65	208	9.99
2000	130663	14721	1222	0.94	209	17.1
2001	132288	1625	2211	1.67	202	9.14
2002	142172	9884	2032	1.43	1083	53.29
2003	166770	24598	1573	0.94	376	23.90

Source: Various issues of *Abstract of Statistics*, Puducherry.

The employment effected over the period remains to be low in comparison with the number of fresh registration. Table 1.40 discloses that in the eighties, it has come down to 1-2 per cent of the fresh registration. The difference between the vacancies notified and the placement effected also tends to lower considerably in the subsequent years. This manifests the alarming state of vacant positions and unemployment situation in the union territory.

Thus, the unemployment situation remains to be alarming. Unless concerted efforts are made to generate employment to the educated youth, it would bring down the total factor productivity in the economy. This would also question the social embeddedness of the economic policies and the social inclusion in the development programmes. It also implies that people should diversify their skills and livelihood sources instead of waiting for the placement in government jobs. Though people are learning to live with the situation by developing skills and giving utmost importance to quality education, the sudden structural changes brought by the globalisation has plunged the people into insecure labour market.

The growth of employment from 1982-83 to 1999-2000 on the basis of gender across states is presented in Table 1.41. The growth rates of employment in the nineties across states have been noticeably low in comparison with the eighties. The growth rate of women employment tends to be negative in some states. Though the gender equality is increasingly emphasised in the government policies, negative employment growth for women throws a challenge to the government. Among the states Nagaland has shown very high growth rate during both the periods. Most of the UTs displayed reasonably high growth rates during these periods. In the growth rate of employment in both the points of time, Puducherry has reported a comparatively higher employment in both male

TABLE 1.40

Progress on Live Register of Employment and Output of Education Institution

Years	*Total No. of Persons in the Live Register*	*Change Compared to Previous Year*	*No. of Educated Person on the Live Register*	*Output of Educational Institution*	*Percentage of Additional People Enrolled Every Year*	*Percentage of Educated Person in Live Register*	*Percentage of Additional Educational Output to Total in Live Register*
1980-81	39873	4592	23097	4688	11.52	57.93	11.76
1981-82	43826	3953	27562	4806	9.02	62.89	10.97
1982-83	50332	6506	30224	4830	12.93	60.05	9.60
1983-84	57789	7457	33771	5061	12.90	58.44	8.76
1984-85	69144	11355	37661	5828	16.42	54.47	8.43
1985-86	78552	9408	42550	6043	11.98	54.17	7.69
1986-87	88238	9686	49465	6492	10.98	56.06	7.36
1987-88	98078	9840	55312	6938	10.03	56.40	7.07
1988-89	108600	10522	60345	6874	9.69	55.57	6.33
1989-90	117942	9342	66387	7564	7.92	56.29	6.41
1990-91	121013	3071	69590	8119	2.54	57.51	6.71
1991-92	129715	8702	78407	9942	6.71	60.45	7.66
1992-93	132392	2677	76466	11206	2.02	57.76	8.46
1993-94	140713	8321	83437	11531	5.91	59.30	8.19
1994-95	147171	6458	88408	11924	4.39	60.07	8.10
1995-96	150024	2853	89790	12020	1.90	59.85	8.01
1996-97	138649	11375	78347	12919	8.20	56.51	9.32
1997-98	146979	8330	73040	15462	5.67	49.69	10.52
1998-99	126192	20787	94991	16341	16.47	75.27	12.95
1999-2000	130663	4471	90294	18057	3.42	69.10	13.82
2000-01	132288	1625	91783	NA	1.23	69.38	NA
2001-02	142172	9884	105040	NA	6.95	73.88	NA
2002-03	166770	24598	145261	NA	14.75	87.10	NA

Source: Various issues of *Abstract of Statistics*, Puducherry.

TABLE 1.41

State-wise Growth in Employment

(Per cent per annum)

States/UTs	1983 to 1993-94			1993-94 to 1999-2000		
	Male	Female	Persons	Male	Female	Persons
Andhra Pradesh	2.1	2.7	2.4	1.6	0.3	1.1
Arunachal Pradesh	-	-	-	0.5	-0.7	0
Assam	1.3	3.2	1.6	2.5	2.3	2.5
Bihar	1.8	-1.7	0.9	2.3	3	2.5
Goa	1.7	-3	0.1	2.6	-4.1	0.8
Gujarat	2.4	1.6	2.1	2.1	2.2	2.1
Haryana	2.5	4.7	3.1	1.9	-3.1	0.6
Himachal Pradesh	2.8	3	2.9	1.4	1.5	1.4
Jammu and Kashmir	1.7	5.9	2.9	2.2	-1.2	1.1
Karnataka	2.2	2.4	2.3	2	0.8	1.6
Kerala	2	-1.2	0.9	1.6	1.4	1.6
Madhya Pradesh	2.4	1.7	2.2	1.9	1.5	1.8
Maharashtra	2.1	2.3	2.2	1.8	-0.2	1
Manipur	3.6	2.9	3.3	3.2	-0.3	2
Meghalaya	3.1	4	3.5	2.3	3	2.6
Mizoram	3.1	20.5	6.3	2.9	5.9	4
Nagaland	19.7	34.5	22.4	4.6	15.9	8.6
Orissa	1.8	2.9	2.1	1.5	1	1.3
Punjab	1.8	-1.4	1	1.5	6.1	2.6
Rajasthan	2.6	2.4	2.5	2.2	0.5	1.5
Sikkim	2.9	0.6	2.3	1.4	9.1	3.4
Tamil Nadu	1.6	2	1.8	1.4	-0.3	0.8
Tripura	3.3	10.4	4.3	2.7	-5.5	1.4
Uttar Pradesh	2.3	1.1	2	1.8	1.4	1.7
West Bengal	2.4	2.1	2.4	1.6	-0.8	1.1
Andaman and Nicobar Islands	3.9	12.9	6.1	2.4	-8	-0.7
Chandigarh	3.7	5	3.9	2.5	-1.1	1.8
Dadra and Nagar Haveli	4.5	3.4	4	3.5	-2	1.2
Daman and Diu	4.2	-2.7	1.8	4.8	7	5.4
Delhi	4.1	3.2	3.9	2.7	4.2	2.9
Lakshadweep	-	-	-	3.8	11	5.2
Puducherry	3.4	1.4	2.8	3.5	3	3.4
India	2.2	1.7	2.1	1.9	0.9	1.6

Source: Indiastat.com

and female employment among the states and UTs. This heralds the growth of tertiary sector in the Puducherry though there is a huge difference between the vacancies notified and employment effected in the government sector. Particularly while the growing unorganised sector is able to absorb the unskilled labourers, the growing manufacturing sector and mushrooming service sector units are able to absorb the professionally qualified youth. Thus, the employment rate has been on the rise for both the male and female.

1.6 Financial Resources

1.6.1 Growth of Revenue and Expenditure

In the budgetary resources, major portion of the resources comes in the form of grants-in-aid from the Union government. It forms around 55 per cent of the total revenue receipts. This proportion is close to the grants-in-aid received by some of the Special Category States. Own tax revenue comes to around 40 per cent and the rest is the non-tax revenue. In the nineties, the central transfers grew at the rate of 9.03 per cent annual growth rate whereas the own tax revenue is growing at 6.88 per cent. Table 1.42 presents the average revenue and expenditures for the last four quinquenniums. It indicates that the proportion of tax revenue to total revenue has been on the decline over the period from 67 per cent to 57 per cent during the last 20 years whereas proportion of the non-tax revenue has displayed a perceptible increase (Figure 1.7). Even in the expenditure, the plan expenditure reported a considerable decline in the late eighties and nineties. In the late nineties, it began to improve substantially again. This indicates the need for plan investments due to the nascent structural changes in the region as a result of globalisation measures.

The major contributors of the own tax revenue include state excise and sales tax. The sales tax contribution to revenue pool grows at faster rate than the state excise collection. The overall higher growth of own tax revenue collection indicates the huge potential available in Puducherry for expanding the tax base and the rate. Sources of non-tax revenue remain limited to interest receipts and dividends, cost recoveries on services provided, license fees and fines. Since Puducherry does not have State Electricity Board, revenue account includes the payments received and expenditure incurred by State Electricity Board as non-tax revenue and expenditure incurred in the economic services. Actually speaking, these are not government revenue receipts and

TABLE 1.42

Details of Revenue and Expenditure in the Revenue Account

Details	*1981-82 to 1985-86*	*1986-87 to 1990-91*	*1991-92 to 1995-96*	*1996-97 to 1999-2000*	*2000-01 to 2004-05*
Tax revenue	2266.55	5108.35	11590.40	22166.30	27260.35
Non-tax revenue	1076.30	2966.63	8997.67	16269.04	34196.16
Total revenue	3342.85	8074.98	20588.07	38435.34	61456.51
% of tax to total revenue	67.80	63.26	56.30	57.67	44.87
% of non-tax to total revenue	32.20	36.74	43.70	42.33	55.13
Plan and CSS expenditure	2447.99	3956.94	6962.09	22964.44	31222.99
Non-plan expenditure	4773.67	10633.26	24093.30	53051.98	86490.40
Total expenditure	7221.67	14590.20	31055.38	76016.42	117713.39
% of plan expenditure	33.90	27.12	22.42	30.21	26.52
% of non-plan expenditure	66.10	72.88	77.58	69.79	73.48

Source: Various issues of *Abstract of Statistics*, Puducherry.

FIGURE 1.7

Revenue and Expenditure Pattern in Puducherry (in Per cent)

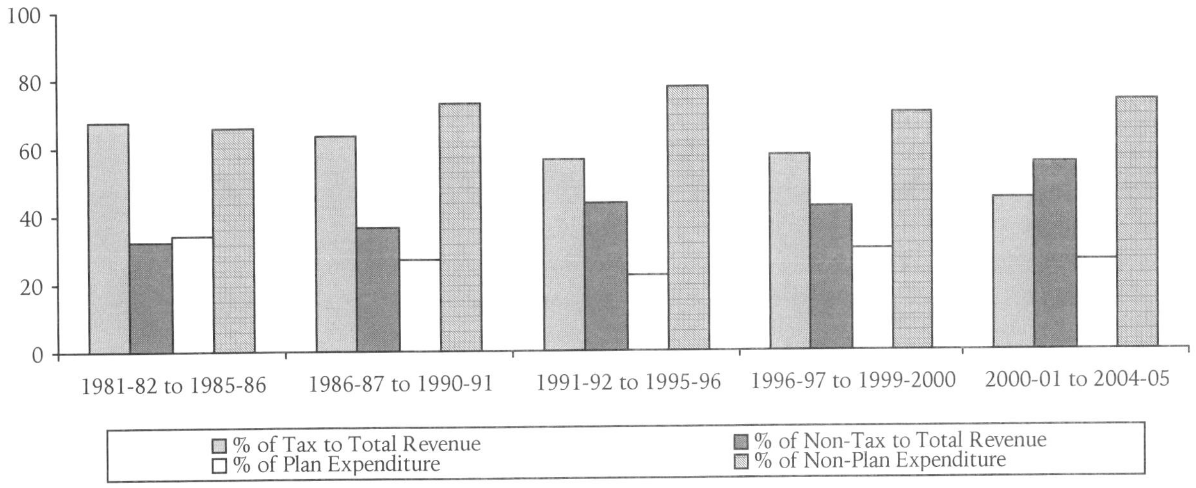

expenditures. The grants-in-aid received by the Puducherry government come in the form of resource transfers from the Home Ministry, not as a share in central taxes. Per capita transfer to Puducherry in 1998-99 was Rs.3304, ranks second after Arunachal Pradesh.

1.6.2 Fiscal Finance Components and GSDP

Table 1.43 presents the ratio of budget components to the GSDP. The proportion of grants-in-aid to total revenue comes to around 40 to 50 per cent over the period. The expenditure-GSDP ratio began to dwindle in the later part of the nineties. It declined to 32.09 per cent in 1999-2000 from 49.51 per cent in 1995-96. This sudden fall in the ratio was due to remarkable increase in GSDP. In the expenditure stream, nearly 75 per cent of the budget resources are earmarked for development expenditure. In this too, major part is allocated for social and community services. This manifests the social embeddedness of the government policies and programmes. Though economic services also seem to be large, it is because of the inclusion of the electricity expenditure. The consistent increase in the expenditure to local bodies and other PRIs reiterates the government's commitment to the democratic decentralisation. The revenue expenditure grows at a lesser pace than the revenue receipts. The budget deficit remains to be very negligible over the period. In the late nineties it has been declining and in the late nineties it has produced surplus budget. This indicates the financial discipline in the state.

1.6.3 Fiscal Imbalances

The difference between revenue receipts and expenditure has been reflected in the different types of deficit. Revenue deficit was noticed in a couple of years in the beginning of the eighties and nineties. During all the other years there was a surplus budget in the revenue account. Fiscal deficit has been on the rise in the nineties due to huge capital investments in infrastructure in water, power and minerals. In the overall budget, there was surplus budget for a few years. The budget deficit hovers around less than one per cent of GSDP. Last five years have been consistently surplus budget years. This indicates the sound financial position of the state.

Table 1.44 presents the deficits in the budget for the last two decades to the GSDP. This explicates that the revenue account is producing substantial surplus in the consecutive budgets. This surplus enables the government to make huge capital investments in plan expenditure.

TABLE 1.43

Details of the Budget Indicators to GSDP Over the Years

(in percentage)

Years	*Grants-in-aid to the Total Revenue*	*Grants-in-aid to the to GSDP*	*Tax Revenue to GSDP*	*Non-Tax Revenue to GSDP*	*Total Revenue to GSDP*	*Revenue Expenditure to GSDP*	*Capital Receipts to GSDP*	*Expenditure on Capital Receipts*	*Total Expenditure to GSDP*	*Total Deficit to GSDP*
1981-82	17.87	3.25	10.90	4.06	14.96	20.95	5.49	5.56	26.51	-2.80
1982-83	37.17	7.80	8.69	4.50	13.19	21.60	6.36	6.34	27.93	-0.58
1983-84	39.16	9.06	9.46	4.62	14.08	21.44	5.86	5.75	27.19	1.82
1984-85	41.86	9.58	8.90	4.41	13.30	23.13	6.82	6.99	30.12	-0.42
1985-86	55.84	16.89	8.95	4.41	13.36	29.89	9.67	9.73	39.62	0.31
1986-87	53.30	16.15	9.23	4.93	14.15	29.74	7.45	7.64	37.39	0.37
1987-88	47.96	16.19	11.53	6.04	17.57	33.66	7.24	7.45	41.11	-0.11
1988-89	46.46	15.56	11.42	6.52	17.94	33.45	7.19	8.02	41.47	-0.78
1989-90	44.18	15.56	12.54	7.12	19.66	34.60	6.94	7.16	41.77	-0.39
1990-91	42.69	16.29	13.22	8.65	21.87	38.32	8.89	9.20	47.52	-0.47
1991-92	42.57	17.28	13.98	9.33	23.31	40.81	9.51	9.58	50.39	-0.30
1992-93	39.22	16.85	14.51	11.61	26.12	41.91	9.33	9.55	51.46	0.84
1993-94	36.76	13.87	13.04	10.81	23.86	37.77	10.29	10.20	47.97	0.04
1994-95	37.43	15.02	13.94	11.18	25.11	37.77	7.20	9.74	47.50	-0.17
1995-96	36.93	15.62	15.14	11.53	26.67	39.28	6.64	10.23	49.51	-0.58
1996-97	36.07	10.84	11.52	7.69	19.21	27.17	4.72	7.27	34.44	0.33
1997-98	43.46	11.14	8.88	5.61	14.49	24.00	3.74	5.46	29.46	-0.09
1998-99	46.89	13.09	8.40	6.42	14.82	25.73	4.42	6.27	32.00	0.33
1999-2000	45.41	12.77	8.35	7.00	15.36	27.11	4.29	4.98	32.09	0.33

Source: Various issues of *Abstract of Statistics*, Puducherry.

This is obvious in the infrastructural development of the region.

The huge deficit in the capital account intimates the size of capital investment. The capital receipts of the state declined in the nineties due to the surplus generated in the revenue account. This reinforces the capital investments made in the region and a fixed capital expenditure incurred in the UT. The overall budget deficit to GSDP remains to be appreciably low. This also reiterates the fiscal discipline in the region.

TABLE 1.44

Fiscal Imbalances in the Budget to the GSDP Ratio

	1981-82 to 1985-86	*1986-87- to 1990-91*	*1991-92 to 1995-96*	*1996-97 to 1999-2000*	*2000-01 to 2001-02*
Revenue deficit	-0.11	0.23	1.23	1.93	0.05
Capital account deficit	-0.03	-0.35	-1.27	-1.70	0.17
Budget deficit	-0.34	-0.28	-0.03	0.23	0.22

Source: Various issues of *Abstract of Statistics*, Puducherry.

1.7 Investment Activity

1.7.1 Industrial Investment

Industrial investment across different scale industries for the last two decades has been collected from the Department of Industries Centre (DIC). Table 1.45 shows that there has been a consistent increase in the number of units across all categories of industries. The growth is noticeably higher from the beginning of the second half of nineties. This could be attributed to the obvious reason of economic reforms. The employment generation has also been huge. The large-scale units create at least 60 to 90 jobs per unit. The medium scale units create at least 40 jobs per unit. The small units also generate around 10 jobs per unit. The investment per unit has increased noticeably in the nineties. The capital-output ratio is close to one in both medium and small scale units. In the case of large scale units it is close to 3. Though it manifests the scale advantage of large units in the efficiency and effectiveness in utilising resources, in a labour abundant country the social embeddedness of the units has to get the priority for the wholesome development of the economy.

1.7.2 Banking and Non-banking Finance

The agricultural credit has been growing in a perceptibly good tempo in the nineties from 29.42 crore in 1990-91 to 116.6 crore in 1997-98. Since then it showed signs of decline. This indicates the increasingly growing demand for agricultural credit in the nineties. Agricultural credit comprised of both direct and indirect finances. The indirect finance is hardly two to three per cent of the total credit. In the early nineties, it was around 5 per cent. The direct finance is provided by the formal institutions. There were 86 branches of 32 commercial banks operating in the territory as of March 2004. In addition to the commercial bank branches, 53 primary agricultural cooperative societies and Puducherry Cooperative Central Land Development Bank with one branch at Karaikal extend agricultural credit to the farmers. Still there was a perceptible gap between the availability and demand for credit in some sectors of agriculture. In the case of crop loans, around 75 to 80 per cent of the credit needs of the farmers are met through formal financial institutions. Now the microfinance mobilised through SHGs promoted by the NGOs like DHAN, MSSRF, PMSSS, Mangalam Society, and so on have made available substantial credit for agricultural

TABLE 1.45

Investment Growth in Industries over the Period

Year	*Large Scale Industries*				*Medium Scale Industries*				*Small Scale Industries*			
	Units	*Invest-ment*	*Annual Production*	*Employ-ment*	*Units*	*Inves-ment*	*Annual Production*	*Employ-ment*	*Units*	*Invest-ment*	*Annual Production*	*Employ-ment*
Up to 1984	9	15782.41	64937.19	11519	11	1868.68	3317.68	773	1948	3841.68	24809.10	16311
1984-85 to 88-89	4	5454.82	3601.14	746	31	4991.79	13600.24	2830	1363	2387.87	25594.58	9914
1989-90 to 1993-94	10	31663.45	9007.19	1545	18	5151.23	7554.48	1174	1526	3120.90	40091.82	12003
1994-95 to 1998-99	14	17235.24	52932.00	1690	51	19100.06	147806.40	2184	1179	14980.55	163611.83	11266
1999-2000 to 2003-04	28	37870.25	196009.95	1967	36	8155.94	138285.45	1638	1112	20405.65	274956.30	10281
1984-85 to 2003-04	56	92223.76	261550.28	5948	136	37399.02	307246.57	7826	5180	40894.97	504254.53	43464
Total	65	108006.17	326487.47	17467	147	39267.70	310564.25	8599	7128	44736.65	529063.63	59775

Source: Department of Industries and Commerce Document.

activities through their members and CBOs. Many other NGOs also linked their SHGs with scheduled commercial banks for savings and credit purposes. Now a large number of SHGs have been credit linked with the commercial banks to avail loans for starting micro enterprises and agricultural activities through deliberate policy initiatives. This facilitated the marginalised people with no access to credit to acquire loans and advances from formal financial institutions with low rate of interest through peer group collateral.

Tables 1.46 and 1.47 present the number of accounts in the scheduled commercial banks (SCBs) and the

TABLE 1.46

Distribution of Scheduled Commercial Bank Loans across Sectors on the Basis of Number of Accounts

(in percentage)

	1994-95	*1995-96*	*1996-97*	*1997-98*	*1998-99*	*1999-2000*	*2000-01*
Total bank credit (in Rs.)	**98125**	**89222**	**91431**	**87587**	**94897**	**93268**	**87903**
Direct finance	**99.49**	**99.87**	**99.90**	**99.95**	**99.73**	**99.52**	**99.83**
Indirect finance	**0.51**	**0.13**	**0.10**	**0.05**	**0.27**	**0.48**	**0.17**
Agriculture	40.66	50.30	49.97	51.77	30.05	33.42	28.41
Industries	3.24	3.03	3.38	3.22	6.85	7.38	5.23
Mining and quarrying	0.02	0.01	0.01	0.01	0.00	0.00	0.00
Manufacturing and processing	3.17	2.96	3.32	3.15	6.72	7.32	4.52
Food mfg and process	0.22	0.23	0.19	0.11	0.21	0.61	0.14
Rice, flour and *dal* mills	0.05	0.04	0.04	0.03	0.11	0.51	0.03
Sugar	0.00	0.00	0.00	0.00	0.01	0.01	0.00
Edible oils and *vanaspati*	0.04	0.03	0.04	0.03	0.03	0.03	0.03
Other food industries	0.12	0.15	0.11	0.05	0.07	0.07	0.08
Beverages and tobacco	0.01	0.02	0.01	0.00	0.02	0.03	0.03
Textiles	0.09	0.11	0.10	0.09	0.08	0.09	0.10
Cotton textiles	0.06	0.06	0.03	0.03	0.04	0.04	0.05
Other textiles	0.04	0.05	0.07	0.05	0.04	0.05	0.05
Paper products and printing	0.14	0.14	0.13	0.15	0.13	0.14	0.10
Leather and leather products	0.03	0.04	0.03	0.03	0.03	0.03	0.02
Rubber and rubber products	0.06	0.06	0.05	0.03	0.03	0.04	0.04
Chemical and chemical products	0.25	0.30	0.31	0.24	0.24	0.35	0.27
Heavy industrial chemical	0.04	0.04	0.04	0.02	0.01	0.01	0.01
Fertilisers	0.00	0.00	0.00	0.00	0.00	0.00	0.00
Drugs and pharmaceuticals	0.04	0.05	0.03	0.01	0.03	0.06	0.06
Other chemicals	0.17	0.20	0.24	0.20	0.20	0.28	0.20
Petroleum, coal and nuclear fuel	0.01	0.01	0.00	0.00	0.00	0.01	0.00
Cement and cement products	0.00	0.01	0.00	0.00	0.01	0.01	0.01
Basic metals and metal products	0.13	0.15	0.16	0.11	0.11	0.14	0.11
Iron and steel	0.05	0.06	0.05	0.02	0.01	0.02	0.03
Non-ferrous metals	0.01	0.01	0.01	0.01	0.00	0.00	0.00
Other metal products	0.08	0.08	0.10	0.08	0.09	0.12	0.08
Engineering	0.14	0.15	0.17	0.26	0.24	0.57	0.59
Heavy and light engineering	0.07	0.06	0.05	0.05	0.04	0.11	0.09
Electrical machinery and goods	0.03	0.04	0.05	0.04	0.15	0.39	0.45
Electronic machinery and goods	0.04	0.05	0.06	0.16	0.05	0.07	0.05
Vehicles, parts and equipment	0.03	0.05	0.04	0.04	0.05	0.07	0.05
Other industries	2.05	1.71	2.13	2.08	5.57	5.24	3.06
Electricity, gas and water	0.01	0.01	0.01	0.01	0.00	0.00	0.02
Gas and water	0.01	0.01	0.01	0.00	0.00	0.00	0.02
Construction	0.05	0.06	0.05	0.06	0.13	0.05	0.69
Transport operation	1.16	1.01	1.12	1.26	0.73	0.65	0.56
Professional and other services	5.65	4.80	3.86	2.44	2.34	2.66	3.05
Personal loans	16.33	17.87	21.80	22.80	35.46	38.90	44.30
Loans for consumer durables	1.86	2.51	2.71	3.32	3.44	5.65	6.27
Loans for housing	1.52	1.74	1.75	1.82	2.00	4.50	5.13
Other personal loans	12.95	13.62	17.35	17.66	30.02	28.75	32.89
Trade	14.10	9.83	9.37	9.94	8.71	9.36	12.15
Wholesale trade	0.36	0.23	0.57	0.66	1.01	0.45	0.66
Retail trade	13.74	9.61	8.80	9.28	7.70	8.90	11.49
Finance	0.02	0.01	0.01	0.01	0.04	0.05	0.03
Miscellaneous	18.84	13.15	10.48	8.56	15.81	7.58	6.28
Artisans and village industries	0.28	0.31	0.79	0.48	0.91	2.30	0.40
Other small scale industries	2.23	2.02	1.88	1.88	2.95	3.70	2.32

Source: CMIE, Economic Indicators, 2004.

TABLE 1.47

Distribution of Credit across Different Sectors

(in percentage)

	1994-95	*1995-96*	*1996-97*	*1997-98*	*1998-99*	*1999-2000*	*2000-01*
Total bank credit	**308.2**	**371.9**	**446**	**470.7**	**472.7**	**540.8**	**575**
Direct finance	**91.97**	**94.09**	**98.35**	**97.08**	**94.80**	**96.97**	**97.57**
Indirect finance	**8.03**	**5.91**	**1.65**	**2.92**	**4.99**	**3.03**	**2.43**
Agriculture	11.71	12.75	21.75	24.77	10.18	9.15	9.32
Industries	48.73	50.01	46.14	41.19	41.15	42.05	40.26
Mining and quarrying	0.58	0.05	0.07	0.06	0.00	0.02	0.05
Manufacturing and processing	47.76	49.56	45.02	40.73	39.62	41.57	39.72
Food mfg and process	8.27	5.46	1.50	0.83	5.31	9.50	8.00
Rice, flour and *dal* mills	0.97	0.27	0.49	0.28	0.87	3.03	1.79
Sugar	4.19	3.82	0.00	0.00	3.51	4.72	4.61
Edible oils and *vanaspati*	*2.30*	*0.65*	*0.58*	*0.30*	*0.34*	*0.70*	*0.52*
Other food industries	0.81	0.73	0.45	0.25	0.61	1.05	1.08
Beverages and tobacco	0.32	0.51	0.16	0.02	0.08	1.68	2.26
Textiles	15.35	16.97	13.16	9.09	6.75	5.71	5.23
Cotton textiles	14.34	13.74	9.82	7.35	4.76	3.64	4.03
Jute textiles	0.00	0.00	0.09	0.08	0.08	0.09	0.02
Other textiles	1.01	3.23	3.27	1.66	1.93	1.98	1.18
Paper products and printing	1.91	1.72	2.44	3.27	3.30	1.79	1.53
Leather and leather products	1.62	1.83	0.63	0.34	1.50	0.35	0.33
Rubber and rubber products	0.68	0.65	0.63	0.38	0.47	0.67	0.61
Chemical and chemical products	4.87	6.78	9.24	7.58	8.86	9.93	7.29
Heavy industrial chemical	1.82	3.33	4.22	3.12	2.79	2.22	0.37
Fertilisers	0.00	0.00	0.04	0.02	0.04	0.04	0.03
Drugs and pharmaceuticals	0.62	1.13	1.48	0.98	0.83	1.41	1.15
Other chemicals	2.43	2.31	3.52	3.46	5.23	6.27	5.74
Petroleum, coal and nuclear fuel	0.13	0.11	0.00	0.02	0.11	0.39	0.37
Cement and cement products	0.03	0.03	0.02	0.08	0.02	0.02	0.02
Basic metals and metal products	3.15	2.77	2.98	1.13	1.71	2.68	3.48
Iron and steel	2.40	1.86	1.28	0.40	0.23	0.83	1.20
Non-ferrous metals	0.16	0.27	0.70	0.04	0.85	0.24	0.37
Other metal products	0.55	0.65	1.01	0.68	0.66	1.63	1.91
Engineering	2.21	1.45	2.65	8.07	7.57	4.01	2.57
Heavy and light engineering	1.52	0.70	1.05	2.49	0.74	1.66	0.56
Electrical machinery and goods	0.29	0.40	0.63	3.48	2.88	1.22	0.89
Electronic machinery and goods	0.39	0.32	0.99	2.10	3.96	1.11	1.15
Vehicles, parts and equipments	0.68	0.35	0.49	0.30	0.28	0.17	0.12
Other industries	8.60	11.00	11.12	9.60	3.66	4.68	7.91
Electricity, gas and water	0.10	0.08	0.85	0.08	0.17	0.13	0.21
Gas and water	0.10	0.08	0.04	0.06	0.17	0.13	0.21
Construction	0.29	0.32	0.25	0.32	1.33	0.31	0.28
Transport operation	1.72	1.40	1.39	1.27	0.97	0.92	0.82
Professional and other services	4.15	3.12	3.32	2.72	3.77	3.40	4.17
Personal loans	13.98	16.99	11.86	11.43	21.41	21.63	22.99
Loans for consumer durables	0.49	0.67	0.63	0.76	1.12	2.13	2.42
Loans for housing	5.71	6.13	3.52	2.87	7.59	5.45	6.17
Other personal loans	7.79	10.19	7.71	7.78	12.69	14.07	14.42
Trade	11.36	8.85	9.08	11.94	14.11	13.39	16.28
Wholesale trade	2.27	1.69	2.47	2.32	4.23	3.20	4.02
Retail trade	9.09	7.15	6.61	9.62	9.88	0.94	12.26
Finance	0.55	1.18	1.57	1.53	0.19	0.20	0.49
Miscellaneous	7.79	5.70	4.91	5.16	8.27	9.26	5.69
Artisans and village industries	0.10	0.11	0.49	0.25	0.40	0.54	0.16
Other small scale industries	11.49	13.53	10.81	10.54	10.49	10.98	10.09

Source: CMIE, Economic Indicators, 2004.

amount outstanding in SCBs in Puducherry. Though there is a marginal decline in the number of accounts in the nineties, the total bank credit amount tends to go up steadfastly. This indicates the increase in the size of loans taken from the formal sources. In the case of agricultural credit there has been a considerable decline in both the number of accounts and amount. However, the decline is relatively less in the amount indicating the increase in the size of loan taken for agriculture. Another important reason for the decline in agricultural credit is the mushrooming of microfinance institutions in the villages with the support of NGOs and other civil society organisations. In the case of industries both the number and size of credit has increased manifold. All categories of industries have registered a noticeable increase in the number and size of the credit. The textile sector has been sliding back in both these parameters indicating the sliding back of the textile sector itself in Puducherry. Chemical industries also take advantage of the banking finance available in the UT though chemical industries are facing challenges from the environment department. The service sector is taking advantage of the banking finance in the UT. All the components in the service sector are increasing their number of accounts and their size of credit in the SCBs. In line with the importance of this sector in the economy, huge investment is also taking place with the support of the SCBs. The impact of this is noticed in the share of this sector in the GSDP.

1.7.3 Cooperative Sector

A separate Cooperative Act was formulated by the Cooperative Department, Puducherry in 1972, and enacted various rules there under in 1973. It regulates the functioning of various types of cooperative societies in the Union Territory. At the same time it contributed enormously to promote the cooperative movement in the UT. This made the provision for a number of incentives to the members of cooperative societies. The growth of cooperative societies in the credit and non-credit categories has been phenomenal. The contribution of cooperative societies to the economic development and social risk management has been noticeable. Though the number of societies keeps increasing, the membership has started dwindling in the nineties. The prevalence of more number of non-credit societies indicates the development of civil society in the regions. Particularly in Mahe, the prevalence of cooperative societies has been widespread over all sectors and among people from all walks of life.

Table 1.48 indicates the spread of cooperative movement and its significance in the economy of Puducherry. The number and size of the sector is huge enough to equal the revenue budget of the state. Till 1999, more than 50 per cent of the whole population had membership in one or other cooperative societies. This manifests that practically all the adult population irrespective of gender had membership in cooperative societies. This indicates that there has been a remarkable increase in associational life and civil society. Even the deposits and borrowings in the cooperative societies show that sizeable borrowings and investments are done through the societies. Deposits have been growing at a greater speed. The decline in the membership and working capital in the year 2000 is a disturbing trend for the cooperative sector as a whole.

The spread of cooperative society has been so intense that in Mahe there is a Bus User's Cooperative Society, which has purchased two buses and operating them

TABLE 1.48

Growth of Cooperative Sector

Item	*Units*	*1999*	*2000*	*2003*
Number of societies	Nos.	462	464	491
Membership	Nos.	553195	475218	399843
Working capital	Rs. in lakh	38231.18	30058.49	81621.32
Share capital paid	Rs. in lakh	6293.70	6185.53	12744.09
Reserve and other funds	Rs. in lakh	5939.82	5485.16	57201.94
Borrowings	Rs. in lakh	10214.70	6442.81	110534.00
Deposits	Rs. in lakh	14939.21	19422.43	294560.50
Debentures of land development bank	Rs. in lakh	657.83	649.37	Nil
Number of societies per lakh of population		49	49	50
Number of members of societies	Per lakh inhabitants	58970	49720	41037
Average working capital per head of population	In Rs.	4075	3145	8377

Source: Bureau of Economics and Statistics, Government of Puducherry.

profitably. Similarly there are a number of auto owner's cooperative societies which have provided loans to the members to purchase autos from the working capital and deposits. One of the contributing factors for the proliferation of cooperative societies is the sizeable working capital provided by the cooperatives department in the initial stages and the constant monitoring of the functioning of the societies including the regular meetings and recovery status. The recovery rate has been quite high in the societies. This shows the credit worthiness of the members. This also indicates the burgeoning associational life and civil society in the Union Territory.

1.8 Development Opportunities and Strategies

The natural resources in the UT remain very limited. The only exception is the coastal resources. It also doesn't have adequate infrastructure to absorb the modern technology. There is an urgent need to develop adequate infrastructure for modernising the fisheries sector and exploiting the coastal resources.

In the case of water resources too, the integrated water resources management is required to cope with the convergence of rainfall. The reduction of rainfall in the summer and winter would put tremendous pressure on the groundwater. Hence, there is a necessity of sustainable development of groundwater resources and improving the recharging. The groundwater recharge level is hardly 20 per cent in the alluvial soil. It has to be enhanced substantially to improve the groundwater resources. Even the lakes and system tanks have to be maintained with utmost care to harvest the rainwater. Even in the land utilisation, there is an urgent need to control the current fallow and growing barren and uncultivable land. The significant increase in the irrigated area through tubewell source is real cause for concern for sustainability of groundwater resources. Forest development should take priority in the government programme to improve the environment quality and sustainability. A minimum 20 per cent of the geographical area should be devoted for forests and mangroves to maintain ecological balance and biodiversity.

The population growth over the last three decades has been remarkable. A demographic transition is taking place in most of the regions. The decadal growth has come down during the last decade. The sex ratio has become 1001 females to 1000 males. The rural population tends to be only one-third of the total population of the whole UT. In the UT, two regions such as Mahe and Yanam have been declared totally urban areas. Still the growth of urban population in the Karaikal and Puducherry regions too tends to be very high. The crude birth rate and death rates indicate that there is considerably higher birth rate in Puducherry and Yanam. The death rate is noticeably low in Mahe and other regions. This manifests the ageing of the population. The increase in life expectancy is noticed in all the regions. The weaker section population consists of scheduled caste population only. It also remains to be around 16 per cent only. There is no scheduled tribe population in the whole UT. The fertility rate is also remarkably low in the region.

Thus, the growing urban population in the UT indicates the need for developing the urban infrastructure in the regions. The decline in the rural population also indicates that there is large scale migration of unskilled and semi-skilled labourers to the urban areas and enough space has to be created to them to have alternative livelihood opportunities. The ageing population has to be provided adequate social security measures to lead a socially respectable life. The weaker sections particularly scheduled caste people are increasingly in the BPL category. Some innovative measures with precise targeting to reach the deserving aged people and marginalised sections of the society should be designed.

The growth of literacy in the UT has been astounding in the successive census periods. The infant mortality rate and reported cases of still birth forewarns the prevalence of infanticide or foeticide in the region. The regular immunisation and other checkups indicate the improvement in the health parameters in the UT. The JIPMER and the Aurobindo attract huge medical tourists into the UT. In the poverty level, the urban poverty is very high in the UT. Among the Union Territories, Puducherry has the highest number and proportion of BPL families. This manifests the widespread poverty in the urban areas in the Puducherry regions.

The growth of the economy is assessed with the help of GSDP across sectors over the period. The proportion of contribution of the sectors to the GSDP indicates that the primary sector contribution has declined considerably to the level of some of the developed countries. Even the secondary sector contribution began to decline in the nineties. Only tertiary sector has been growing phenomenally. In the primary sector, contribution of fisheries tends to be higher than the agriculture. This reinforces the argument for higher investment in infrastructure to the sector. In the growth rates, most of the departments in the tertiary sector have shown higher growth rates at current prices. Conversely, there is a negligible growth rate in the old series at constant prices.

The growth rate is relatively better in the new series at constant prices. The per capita income across states also indicates that there was a decline in the per capita GSDP during the early nineties in the old series. The decline in the proportion of contribution of primary sector is a cause for concern to the health of the economy and society since there is a sizeable population still depending on agriculture for their livelihood in the rural areas. It also provokes the government to provide adequate social risk management measures.

The employment pattern in the Puducherry indicates that there is a perceptible decline in the proportion of agricultural workers whereas the manufacturing and tertiary sectors have registered a noticeable increase. Across the regions, Karaikal region reported a very low proportion of secondary sector workers while Yanam and Mahe found more proportion of workers in fisheries and livestock rearing. The employment in the organised and unorganised sectors insinuates the growth of unorganised sector in the post-reform period. The average number of daily workers in the factories not submitting returns has been leapfrogging year after year. Though the units in the unorganised sector have grown remarkably, the number of persons employed per unit shows signs of decline indicating the lean and efficient policy being adopted in both the organised and unorganised sectors. The unemployment data demonstrates a distressing situation in the Puducherry among the educated and uneducated persons. Nearly 15 per cent of the population is in the live register and it keeps growing at the rate of 1.5 per cent. In comparison with other states, the employment growth rate is appreciably progressive due to its proactive measures in the creation of employment to all sections of the society.

The fiscal indicators in the Puducherry extol the fiscal discipline in the state. It proclaims the judicious management of fiscal resources in the state. Though the tax revenue and non-tax revenue to the GSDP remain very low, the surplus in the revenue account is increasingly attributed to the huge grants-in-aid received by the UT. The grants-in-aid received by the state equals some of the Special Category States. This is also because of the poor resource base in the state. Tax effort should be enhanced and tax base widened to improve the proportion of own tax revenue.

The industrial growth in the UT has been consistent over the years. In the second half of the nineties, there has been a considerable jump in the number and size of industrial development. Though SCBs play a vital role in the industrial investments, credit needs of agriculture and other unorganised sector are being met by the cooperative sector and the SHGs. The growth of civil society and associational life in the UT has been perceptibly satisfying.

The outcome of cooperative movement has been noticeable in all the fields. The investments through the scheduled commercial banks have come down perceptibly in the agriculture sector and other rural development aspects due to the microcredit programmes initiated through both credit cooperatives and non-credit cooperatives. Of late, the NGOs have come to play a major role in promoting microcredit among the poor and vulnerable sections of the society. The government also provides innumerable incentives to promote the cooperative activities among marginalised people in the UT. Though it is increasingly visible in the Mahe region, the reasons for the lesser spread of cooperative exercise in other regions have to be identified and attended to on priority as it is quite promising for the development of the marginalised people.

Taking on the advantage of existing state's pro-industry policies, a number of integrated post-harvest value addition zones could be identified for the promotion of food processing industries for diverse products.

The modern ICT supported village level knowledge centres (Uzhavar Udaviyagams) established have very huge potentials to serve the rural community with cost effective manner. They could be promoted to play the role of multipurpose service centres with satellite connectivity.

1.9 Case Study

Sustainable Economic and Regional Development: A Study of Auroville

Aurovilians work at the small and medium levels in the primary, secondary and tertiary sectors. They continue to work, as they have from Auroville's inception, in primary industry: farming and forestry.

Overtime, Auroville has seen the addition of manufacturing and service units.

The Auroville Handbook lists 100 enterprises, some of which provide services to Aurovilians. Others, however, make leather products, garments, jewellery, dolls, processed foods and water, handicrafts, bed/chair/table covers, handmade cards, wooden bowls, quilted products, sleeping and sitting hammocks, cloth bags, incense and aromatics, photo frames, lampshades, paper and paper products, postcards, Indian and fusion music cassettes and CDs, pottery and ceramics. Many of these products are world class at Indian prices.

Some of the enterprises are engaged in particularly natural and eco-friendly activities. Examples:

- grow and market organic cashews.
- produce spirulina, tofu, tempeh and cheeses.
- make jams, marmalades, peanut butter, pickles, *chutneys*, mustard and more.
- produce pure and naturally dyed garments and do research in this field.

Land and Water Management

This entails care for sustainable environment and the bioregion, including soil and water conservation, biopest control, afforestation, organic agriculture and organic food processing.

Afforestation

This activity has seen the planting of two million trees in an integrated soil/water conservation programme.

- Palmyra in Aurobrindavan, a Centre for Sustainable Ecological Land Use and Rural Development:
  - coordinates soil/water management (60 check dams to date) and afforestation, working with people in surrounding villages,
  - maintains a nursery, mainly of timber trees for agro-forestry, and
  - rehabilitates ancient irrigation tanks.
- Pitchadikulam Bio-Resource Centre and Shakti Nursery work in biodiversity and traditional medicinal plant knowledge,
- The Village Action Group acts as liaison and spreads awareness, and
- The Forest Group coordinates these activities.

Water Conservation activities include

- Afforestation.
- Raised bunds or earth embankments to prevent run-off.
- Drip irrigation and sprinklers.
- Research to distill sea water by evaporation, making it suitable for irrigation and domestic purposes.
- Recycling waste water for irrigation through lagooning in 24 ponds containing filters and plants.
- Screening a video in Tamil for local farmers on managing salt water intrusion in workshops to explain the causes of this cause of widespread infertility of large areas.

Ecological Agriculture seeks to heal and nourish the earth naturally.

- Palmyra in Aurobrindavan does research into biological pest control.
- Agricultural Renewal in India for a Sustainable Environment (ARISE), in Aurobrindavan, propagates organic farming, organising workshops and training.
- Auroville Health Centre promotes biodynamic agriculture among village farmers makes organic compost.
- The Farm Group coordinates these activities.

Auroville gives training in:

- Afforestation and soil conservation.
- Agro-forestry, organic farming, permaculture.

Nature Sanctuaries

Auroville Herbarium has a duplicate herbarium for consultation, 4000 sheets of specimens, most from local tropical dry evergreen forest as well as the Andaman and Nicobar Islands.

Pitchandiukulm Bio-Resource Centre teaches and trains on the protection, propagation and use of medicinal plants. One of 19 medicinal plant conservation parks in southern India (together with the Auroville Herbarium), it has:

- A 70 acre self-generating forest sanctuary containing 800 species, half being medicinal.
- Photos of 200 local medicinal plants and a seed propagation nursery serving as a gene bank for endangered medicinal plants.
- Actively engaged in restoring the Tropical Dry Evergreen Forest (TDEF) through educating local populations in sustainable forest management.
- Implementing programmes to re-establish and maintain healthy ecosystems throughout the bioregion
- A concentrated herbal garden with 100 species to supply herbal practitioners.

Renewable Energy

Auroville is the biggest concentration of alternative and appropriate energy systems in India.

The Centre for Scientific Research (CSR) is working on solar curing chambers for ferrocement prefabricated elements, solar concentrators, and solar thermal collectors. Various units produce solar lanterns, electronic components for solar systems and solar cookers. CSR has also worked with other Indian organisations to establish a solar power plant for the lighting at Matrimandir and a thermal concentrator.

Biogas – mainly methane from organic fermentation; used for cooking on biomass stoves.

CSR, which leads in using ferrocement for biogas systems, and has improved the design of the biomass stove. Cynergy, a CSR sub-unit has done a feasibility study of biomass gasifiers that convert wood or agricultural waste into the cheapest available clean fuel for internal combustion engines or gas turbines and is considering the possible use of industrial and other wastes as fuel for gasifiers.

Appropriate Building Technology

Auroville is working on cost effective building technology (including training courses) in:

- Ferrocement, which uses cement and steel in an efficient, cost-effective and easily learned manner.
- Unfired Earth Technology, in which compressed earth blocks can be made on site with a made-in-Auroville manual press using about a quarter of the energy required to fire bricks. The Visitors Centre, the Solar Kitchen and Pitanga are products of this technology.
- Equipment for earth construction.
- Prefabricated ferrocement elements (roof channels, doors, wall modules, water tanks, latrines, biogas plants) for construction.

References

Government of Puducherry, *Annual Statistical Abstract of Puducherry*, Directorate of Economics and Statistics, Various Issues.

Government of Puducherry, *Groundwater Situation in Puducherry*, WAPCOS and Groundwater Department.

Government of Puducherry (2003). *Pondicherry Vision 2020*. Madras School of Economics, 2003.

Government of India, *District Census Handbook*, Census Department—1981, 1981 and 2001.

Government of India, National Human Development Report, Planning Commission, New Delhi.

Reserve Bank of India, *RBI Bulletin*. Bombay: RBI Publications.

CMIE (2004). *Economic Indicators*. Bombay: CMIE Publications.

Government of Puducherry, *Vital Statistics*, Local Administration Department, Puducherry.

Chapter 2

Fiscal Situation and Policies

2.1 Overview

Reserve Bank of India's Annual Report (2002-03) has observed:

> It is increasingly recognised that it is the State Finances where the Government Sector's interface with the people is most significant. Issues in the reform of fiscal policy in the States have a direct bearing on quality of life.

According to earlier research studies in the Reserve Bank, the factors responsible for the disparity in the growth rates of receipts and expenditures and the consequent widening of the fiscal gap of state governments include: (i) a growing interest burden, (ii) increasing pension liabilities, (iii) large administrative expenditure, (iv) losses incurred by State Public Sector Undertakings, (v) inappropriate user charges, and (vi) deceleration in central transfers. The fiscal stress, in turn, has seriously constrained the states' ability to discharge their primary responsibility of social and economic infrastructures. Resurfacing of revenue deficit last year in respect of Puducherry needs to be tackled seriously.

Against the above backdrop, the Union Territory of Puducherry was till recently in an advantageous fiscal position as under:

1. Since 1995-96 and till date Puducherry continues to have a much higher (per capita GSDP) and faster growing economy (GSDP) with potential tax base than other states, particularly in the south. Extent to which the economic base has been tapped to yield tax and non-tax revenues and also user charges in the past and scope for the same in future is worth exploring, particularly on non-tax revenues and user charges.
2. Central transfers constitutes about 60 per cent of its revenue receipts (excludes electricity related receipts) and has one of the highest per capita transfers from the Centre almost on par with Special Category States. Obviously Central transfers cover not only the amount in lieu of devolution of funds under Finance Commission (not available to Puducherry as Union Territory) but also the facility of interest roll over in grants-in-aid, electricity charges deficit, etc.

   In addition Central loans and grants-in-aid not only take care of its capital expenditure (plan and non-plan) but also annual principal instalment due. Thus, debt servicing in both interest and instalment accounts is also taken care of by the Central transfers. This reduces the necessity for Puducherry government to tap its economic base (GSDP) efficiently and effectively for resource mobilisation in terms of tax resources and more importantly non-tax revenues and user charges.
3. For Puducherry, the proportion of development expenditures in revenue expenditures is fairly and consistently high (since 1990-91) in the range of 65 per cent to 68 per cent. Generally, a healthy and commendable fiscal policy has a bearing on quality of life. However, the major slant on social services (65 per cent of development expenditure) as against economic services (excluding electricity related expenditure) may not be sustainable in the long run. Despite increasing administrative costs (including pension) and debt servicing costs, Puducherry has maintained its thrust on development expenditure (65 per cent to 68 per cent), as against Tamil Nadu (61 per cent), Kerala (61 per cent), Punjab (47 per cent), and Goa (53 per cent). All India states' average is less than 55 per cent on this score.
4. The percentage of plan expenditure to total expenditure in Puducherry, slipped from about 30

per cent in the eighties to 22.5 per cent in first half of the nineties. It then improved to 30 per cent in the latter half of the nineties. In the subsequent three years 2000-01, 2001-02 and 2002-03, the per cent of plan expenditure to total expenditure is still hovering around 30 per cent.

The consolidated Budget of Puducherry from 1990-91 to 2002-03 is given in Table 2.1. Salient aspects of the Table are as under:

(i) Total revenue receipts to GSDP (including grants-in-aid from the Centre) which was about 23 per cent in 1990-91 increased to 26 per cent in 1995-96 and has now slipped to less than 20 per cent from 1998-99 onwards. The fall, though mainly due to fast rise in GSDP of Puducherry after 1995-96, also indicates scope for future resource mobilisation in terms of not only tax revenues but also more importantly non-tax revenues and user charges.

(ii) Total revenue expenditure to GSDP, which was around 21 per cent in 1990-91, increased to 23 per cent by 1995-96 and has slipped to about 20 per cent and less from 1998-99 onwards.

(iii) For reasons explained earlier, possibility of revenue deficit should not normally arise in respect of Puducherry with its interest roll over as well as electricity charges deficit cover under grants-in-aid. However, it is noteworthy that fiscal deficit as per cent of GSDP has come down significantly after 1995-96 from around 3.5 per cent to 4.5 per cent during 1990-91 to 1995-96 to less than 2.0 per cent in 1998-99. Subsequently, it has increased to a level of 2.5 per cent to 3.5 per cent during 1999-2000, 2000-01, 2001-02 and 2002-03.

(iv) During nineties, there was no revenue deficit except for an insignificant amount (less than Rs.1 crore) in 1990-91. Revenue deficit surfaced again

TABLE 2.1

Consolidated Budget—From 1990-91 to 2002-03

(Rs. in lakh)

Details	*1990-91*	*1995-96*	*1998-99*	*1999-2000*	*2000-01*	*2001-02*	*2002-03*
Total Revenues*	16304 (22.46)	34219 (25.92)	58836 (19.73)	67517 (21.65)	70794 (18.73)	79135 (19)	79755 (18.01)
Total Revenue Expenditures**	16393 (22.57)	30992 (23.47)	52985 (17.77)	64326 (20.62)	68028 (18)	81748 (19.62)	76337 (17.24)
Revenue Deficit (-) or Surplus (+)*	-89 -(0.12)	3227 (2.44)	5851 (1.96)	3191 (1.02)	2766 (0.73)	(-)2613 -(0.63)	3418 (0.77)
Capital Receipts (Excluding net borrowing):							
Recoveries of Loans and Advances	181 (0.25)	398 (0.30)	831 (0.28)	378 (0.12)	545 (0.14)	625 (0.15)	588 (0.13)
Total Capital Receipts	181 (0.25)	398 (0.30)	831 (0.28)	378 (0.12)	545 (0.14)	625 (0.15)	588 (0.13)
Capital Expenditures:							
(i) On Services	3050 (4.20)	7561 (5.73)	10995 (3.69)	10306 (3.30)	10185 (2.7)	11925 (2.87)	14751 (3.33)
(ii) Loans and Advances	316 (0.44)	963 (0.73)	1117 (0.38)	934 (0.3)	1267 (0.36)	732 (0.18)	543 (0.12)
Total Capital Expenditures (i+ii)	3366 (4.64)	8524 (6.5)	12112 (4.06)	11240 (3.60)	11452 (3.03)	12657 (3.04)	15294 (3.45)
Total Receipts@*	16485 (22.71)	34617 (26.22)	59667 (20.01)	67895 (21.77)	71339 (18.87)	79760 (19.14)	80343 (18.14)
Total Expenditures@*	19759 (27.22)	39516 (29.93)	65097 (21.82)	75566 (24.24)	79480 (21.02)	94405 (22.66)	91631 (20.7)
Total Deficit (-) or Surplus (+) @*	-3274 -(4.5)	-4899 -(3.7)	-5430 -(1.82)	-7671 -(2.5)	-8141 -(2.15)	-14645 -(3.51)	-11288 -(2.55)
GSDP	72,600	132038	298202	311921	378065	416672	442807

Note: Figures in parentheses indicate as percentages of GSDP.

@ - There may be (minor) differences in the total figures due to rounding up.

* - Figures exclude the contribution of electricity department from both revenue receipts and revenue expenditures.

** - Revenue expenditure includes power subsidy.

Source: Annual Financial Statement of the Union Territory of Puducherry (Various Years) and CSO, Government of India, (1999, 2000) diskettes.

in 2001-02 (Rs.26 crore). Since then the trend has been reversed to be one of revenue surplus.

With respect to scope for improvement on points (i) and (ii) above, comparison with other states indicate:

(a) Revenue receipts constitute practically 98.5 per cent of total receipts in Puducherry as against 75 per cent in Tamil Nadu. Obviously there is significant scope for improvement on capital receipts account.

(b) Own revenues to GSDP in Puducherry is 8.1 per cent in 1998-99 as against 9.5 per cent, 9.3 per cent, 9.2 per cent, and 8.3 per cent in neighbouring states of Andhra Pradesh, Karnataka, Tamil Nadu and Kerala respectively. Within own revenues, with tax revenues of 7.7 per cent of GSDP Puducherry stands third and on non-tax revenues almost last among all the states (0.4 per cent of GSDP).

Thanks to a booming economic base and even now significant central transfers (on per capita basis on par with many of the special category states), Puducherry is ensured to be financially in a sound position. If it wants to be self-reliant, then it has to exploit its non-tax potential besides tax potential. Further if it wants developmental measures/expenditure to be sustainable, then greater emphasis should gradually shift to Economic Services with appropriate user charges.

If we exclude energy/electricity related receipts and expenditure (except for power subsidy), then composition of revenue receipts in terms of tax, non-tax (excluding power charges) and Grant-in-aid receipts as well as total expenditure in terms of development expenditure (social, economic and other services) and non-development expenditure and its trend analysis over the years (1990-1991, 1995-96, 1998-99, 1999-2000, 2000-01, 2001-02, 2002-03 and 2003-04) are as follows:

With respect to revenue receipt, the pattern which emerges from a study of Table 2.2 is as follows:

(i) Till 1995-96, tax revenue and grants-in-aid were more or less of same magnitude. Major dependence on grants-in-aid started in 1998-99 and continues to be.

(ii) During the nineties (1990-91 to 1999-2000), tax revenue, non-tax revenue, and grants-in-aid

TABLE 2.2

Revenue Account: Receipts and Expenditure

(Rs. in lakh)

	Details	*1990-91*	*1995-96*	*1998-99*	*1999-2000*	*2000-01*	*2001-02*	*2002-03*	*2003-04*
1.	Tax Revenue	7044	16252	22498	26059	29185	26859	27638	35277
2.	Non-Tax Revenue*	580	1199	1288	1616	1635	2107	2397	2404
3.	Grants-in-Aids	8680	16768	35050	39842	39974	50169	49720	49542
I.	Revenue Receipts	16304	34219	58836	67517	70794	79135	79755	87223
	Development Expenditure								
1.	Social Services	7606	14793	24641	30278	31771	31920	36107	41113
2.	Economic Services**	4098	6475	10191	14163	15202	27287	15037	15704
3.	Others (Grants)	117	469	719	282	202	238	259	287
II.	(a) Development Expenditure	11821	21737	35551	44723	47175	59445	51403	57104
	Non-Development Expenditure								
1.	Organs of State	166	545	748	914	940	1041	952	1118
2.	Fiscal Services	166	459	761	838	900	933	982	1119
3.	Interest and Debt Services	1698	4246	7826	7453	8640	10099	11559	13451
4.	Administrative Services	1730	2667	4226	5086	5615	5527	5679	6519
5.	Pension and Misc.	772	1338	3873	5312	4758	4703	5762	7232
II.	(b) Non-Development Expenditure	4532	9255	17434	19603	20853	22303	24934	29439
	II (a) + II (b). Revenue Expenditure	16353	30992	52985	64326	68028	81748	76337	86543
	Revenue Deficit/Surplus [I – II(a) – II(b)]	-49	3227	5851	3191	2766	-2613	3418	680

Note: * excludes electricity receipts.

** includes power subsidy.

Source: Government of Puducherry Budget documents.

increased nearly four-fold, nearly three-fold and more than four-fold respectively. From 2000-01 onwards to 2003-04 both tax revenues and non-tax revenues are more or less stagnant at Rs.290 to Rs.310 crore and Rs.21 to 23 crore respectively. It is a quantum jump of Rs.100 crore in grants-in-aids from Rs.400 crore in 2000-01 to Rs.500 crore and thereafter is now the main plank for revenue receipts.

With respect to development revenue expenditure, the picture that emerges is that:

(i) Except for the year 2001-02, development expenditure in social services has been at double the level as that of economic services ever since 1990-91 and till date. Mainly because of power subsidy/deficit of Rs.127 crore in 2001-02, as against normal annual power subsidy of Rs.35 crore, revenue expenditure in that year on economic services was within the same range as that of social services.

(ii) Grant to Local Bodies/*Panchayats* and others which was Rs.5 to 7 crore during 1995 to 1999 is now at a low level of Rs.2½ to 3 crore annually from 2001-02 onwards.

(iii) During nineties, both development and non-development revenue expenditure increased four-folds. As compared 1999-2000, we find that from 2000-01 till 2003-04, there is only 33 per cent increase in development revenue expenditure while non-development component has increased by 50 per cent in the same time window.

In short stagnancy in own revenues after 2000-01 and steep increase in non-development revenue expenditures has resulted in revenue deficit surfacing again which was non-existent in the nineties (except for small revenue deficit of less than Rs.1 crore in 1990-91).

A revisit to the factors identified by RBI's study of fiscal stress on state finances, in the context of Puducherry is as under:

a. Growing Interest Burden

Interest constituted around 38 per cent of non-development revenue expenditure during nineties. Since 2000-01, it forms about 45 per cent, thus putting pressure on growth in revenue surplus. In 2002-03, revenue deficit was avoided by drastically curtailing development expenditure in economic services. Till 2000-01, interest was one-fifth (20 per cent) of grants-in-aid and subsequently increased from 26 per cent to 27 per cent (more than one-fourth). It is partly because interest burden is mounting and mainly because grants-in-aid appear to be frozen around Rs.500 crore during the last three years.

b. Increasing Pension Liabilities

Annual pension liabilities which were less than Rs.50 crore in 2000-01 have increased by 50 per cent to Rs.73 crore in the last 3 or 4 years.

c. Large Administrative Expenses

If one excludes interest payments from non-development expenditure/general services, we find that administrative and allied expenses constitute 18 per cent of revenue expenditure. During the period 2002-03 and 2003-04, expenditure on organs of the state and administrative services has shot up by nearly 20 per cent. Besides galloping interest burden, this spurt in administration related expenditure has resulted in squeeze on revenue surplus in 2003-04. Further Fifth Pay Commission recommendations introduced after 1998 has resulted in increasing salaries, pension liabilities and large administrative expenses. Therefore, government needs to be prudent in hiring additional staff in future.

d. Losses Incurred by State PSUs

Most of the PSUs are making losses being unable to compete in the market. They are primarily spinning mills, distilleries and sugar mills. Radical measures are needed including disinvestments/privatisation to reverse the negative returns of 8 per cent to 10 per cent on share capital employed in State PSUs.

e. Inappropriate User Change

The proportion of revenue from economic services has declined from 23.5 per cent in 1990-91 (it was 35.1 per cent in 1985-86) to 16.9 per cent in 1999-2000 and to 16 per cent by 2003-04. It is seen that revenue contribution of almost all economic services except non-ferrous mining has declined. The possibility of raising fees and service charges in real terms i.e., at least above the inflation rate needs to be explored.

f. Deceleration in Central Transfers

As indicated earlier, after the quantum jump in grants-in-aid from Rs.400 crore in 1999-2000 and 2000-01 to Rs.500 crore in 2001-02, the same appears to have been frozen at Rs.500 crore during the last three years.

The way forward to improve the fiscal situation of Puducherry and attendant policy measures necessary for the same could emerge from the following three analyses:

a. Comparison of recent trends in fiscal position with that of the best year namely 1998-99.

b. Outside-in view in terms of comparison of composition of revenue receipts and revenue expenditure of other normal states with that of Puducherry.

c. Critical examination of each of the following nine aspects:

   i. Revenue receipts, own tax revenues and Central transfers.

   ii. Own non-tax revenues.

   iii. Composition of revenue expenditure and capital receipts and expenditure.

   iv. Subsidies and losses of PSUs.

   v. Borrowings, outstanding liabilities, interest burden and sustainability of public debt.

   vi. Fiscal deficit and budgetary problems.

   vii. Finances of urban local bodies and PRIs.

   viii. Annual plans, plan and non-plan outlay composition and regional balance.

   ix. Taxation and levy powers, also tax buoyancy and efforts to tap the same.

Each of the above nine aspects are examined in subsequent nine sub-sectors.

In terms of healthy fiscal position of Puducherry, the year 1998-99 has been marked by:

i. Revenue surplus to the extent of 10 per cent revenue receipts available for capital expenditure. In absolute terms also high level of revenue surplus ever achieved (Rs.5851 lakh).

ii. Own revenues well in excess of non-development revenue expenditure i.e., part of own revenue also available for social and economic services.

iii. Relatively high level of capital receipts ever achieved in terms of recovery of loans and advances (Rs.831 lakh) as compared to subsequent years.

iv. Relatively low level of fiscal deficit i.e., only 1.8 per cent of GSDP.

v. Power subsidy was less than Rs.20 crore as compared to annual power subsidy of Rs.35 crore during subsequent years.

vi. Own tax revenues was 8.1 per cent of GSDP.

The one non-redeeming feature was the high level of non-development expenditure (33 per cent) accommodated at the expense of developmental outlays, mainly economics services (19 per cent) and partly social services (46.5 per cent).

In contrast to 1998-99, during recent years:

i. Revenue deficit has surfaced again.

ii. Own revenue receipts barely cover non-development expenditure. Therefore, social services and economic services are totally dependent on grants-in-aid and borrowings.

iii. Capital receipts in terms of recoveries of loans and advances has declined even in absolute terms to around Rs.600 lakh from Rs.831 lakh in 1998-99.

iv. Fiscal deficit as per cent of GSDP has doubled from around 1.8 per cent to 3.5 per cent.

v. Annual power subsidy is now in the range of Rs.35 crore.

vi. Own tax revenue is now around 7.2 per cent to 7.3 per cent of GSDP i.e., tax levy and efforts have slackened in the recent years. Further non-tax revenue is stagnant.

Further the non-redeeming feature is high level of non-development expenditure (32.7 per cent) being accommodated at the expense of mainly economics services (21.3 per cent) and partly social services (45.7 per cent).

Based on the RBI study of Budgets of States, the composition of revenue receipts and revenue expenditures of selected states is indicated in Table 2.3.

The above study shows that for most of the normal states in terms of revenue receipts:

i) Own tax revenue is in the range of 50 per cent to 60 per cent whereas for Puducherry it is around 40 per cent.

ii) Own non-tax revenue is in the range of 10 per cent to 20 per cent whereas for Puducherry it is 2 per cent to 3 per cent only.

iii) Transfer from Centre for normal developed states is 30 to 40 per cent, whereas for Puducherry it is 60 per cent almost, like special category states.

The study also shows that for most of the normal states in terms of revenue expenditure:

i. General services is 30 to 35 per cent similar to Puducherry.

TABLE 2.3

Composition of Revenue Receipts and Revenue Expenditures for Selected States in India (1998-99)

States	*Composition of Revenue Receipts (per cent)*				*Composition of Revenue Expenditures (per cent)*		
	Own Tax Revenue	*Own Non-Tax Revenue*	*Total Own Revenue*	*Transfers from the Centre @*	*General Services*	*Economic Services*	*Social Services*
(1)	(2)	(3)	(4)	(5)	(6)	(7)	(8)
Andhra Pradesh	55.8	13.0	68.8	31.2	33.2	24.3	41.6
Arunachal Pradesh	1.2	7.0	8.2	91.8	31.0	37.5	31.5
Assam	21.8	10.0	31.8	68.2	36.1	19.3	44.4
Bihar	28.8	12.4	41.2	58.8	43.5	10.4	36.0
Delhi	84.4	5.1	89.5	10.5	24.6	8.4	64.6
Goa	31.1	56.7	87.8	12.2	46.7	25.2	28.0
Gujarat	59.8	21.7	81.5	18.5	30.5	34.3	34.8
Haryana	56.9	27.7	84.6	15.4	39.6	30.7	29.7
Himachal Pradesh	24.7	8.9	33.6	66.4	32.6	29.0	37.9
Karnataka	61.8	13.1	74.9	25.1	33.2	26.8	37.4
Kerala	64.6	7.7	72.3	27.7	38.3	24.8	36.3
Madhya Pradesh	45.0	15.7	60.7	39.3	33.5	24.3	39.2
Maharashtra	65.3	16.4	81.7	18.2	41.4	21.2	36.7
Manipur	3.4	3.5	6.9	93.1	36.9	24.1	39.0
Meghalaya	10.6	6.2	16.8	83.2	34.4	28.8	36.8
Orissa	32.7	12.2	44.9	55.1	40.4	19.3	39.9
Puducherry	38.2	2.2	40.4	59.6	34.1	16.2	48.3
Punjab	56.7	26.2	82.9	17.1	52.4	15.3	31.5
Rajasthan	45.9	15.8	61.7	38.3	39.4	17.8	42.5
Sikkim	2.0	70.9	72.9	27.2	75.4	10.4	14.2
Tamil Nadu	67.5	8.1	75.6	24.4	33.2	20.8	40.1
Tripura	6.6	3.5	10.1	89.8	34.8	25.9	38.2
Uttar Pradesh	45.5	8.5	54.0	46.0	44.1	18.5	34.1
West Bengal	50.9	4.1	55.0	45.0	41.2	17.7	39.6

Note: @ Transfers include the share in central taxes and the grants-in-aid.

Source: Computed from RBI (2000). *State Finances-a Study of Budgets of 2000-01.*

ii. Economic services is 25 per cent to 35 per cent whereas for Puducherry it is considerably less at 16 per cent.

iii. Social services is around 35 per cent whereas for Puducherry it is nearly 50 per cent.

With central transfers almost frozen at the level of Rs.500 crore, tapping own tax revenues vigorously, augmenting non-tax revenues substantially and according equal emphasis to developmental activities of economic services and social services appear to be the rough contours of the road map to improve the fiscal situation of Puducherry to a healthy state on the revenue account side. Increasing emphasis should be on improving per cent of plan expenditure to total expenditure. Curtailing non-developmental expenditure needs to be taken up seriously. Zero-base budgeting of all on-going activities/ schemes is called for.

Though debt swap could improve debt servicing to some extent, permanent solution is only through ensuring much higher level of interest, dividend and profits and capital receipts. Capital receipts have come down from Rs.831 lakh in 1998-99 to Rs.575 lakh in 2003-04. Interest receipts increased from Rs.260 lakh in 1998-99 to Rs.435 lakh in 2003-04. As against this, interest payments have increased from Rs.7825 lakh in 1998-99 to Rs.13451 lakh in 2003-04 and so also principal/capital repayment from Rs.4680 lakh in 1998-99 to Rs.6935 lakh in 2003-04. Policy measures to mitigate and resolve this acute problem are necessary to ensure debt servicing sans debt trap.

The way forward is obviously optimal targeting and efficient collection of revenues, both tax and non-tax, prioritising revenue expenditure, controlling administrative expenditure, curtailing subsidies and following financially prudent capital expenditure programme. With the same in view, subsequent sub chapters critically examines the nine relevant aspects [c (i) to (ix) indicated above].

Taking advantage of the potential growth in GSDP, buoyancy in taxes, lowering of interest rates and private finance initiative, Puducherry government should initiate prudent medium-term fiscal policy measures. This is imperative as Puducherry is on the anvil of transforming from its current status as Union Territory to a full fledged state.

2.2 Revenue Receipts, Own Tax Revenues and Central Transfers

A study of the composition of revenue receipts (includes electricity receipts) in 1990-91, 1995-96 and year-wise from 1998-99 onwards till 2003-04 (Table 2.4) shows the following trends:

1. While non-tax revenue per cent is stagnating, even tax revenue per cent in the recent past has declined. Therefore per cent of own revenues to total revenue expenditure has declined from the peak of 68 per cent in 1995-96 to 62.4 per cent in 2003-04.
2. Reliance on grants-in-aid from the Centre (about 42 per cent of revenue receipts) enables Puducherry both to meet the non-plan revenue gap and to rollover the annual debt servicing. Interest servicing now constitutes one-fifth of grant-in-aid.

Interest payments (Rs.100.99 crore) during 2001-02 formed 9.2 per cent of revenue expenditure of Rs.1098.72 crore (including power charge cost charges of about Rs. 408.70 crore) as against 8.8 per cent and 9.4 per cent during previous two years respectively. In fact if power charge receipts are set off against power purchase cost and allied expenses, then the base of revenue expenditure would be reduced and consequently interest charges as per cent of such adjusted revenue expenditure works out as 11.6 per cent, 12.3 per cent, and 14.6 per cent in 1999-2000, 2000-01 and 2001-02 respectively. Similarly, interest charges as per cent of adjusted revenues receipts (power receipts not considered) stands at 11 per cent, 12.5 per cent, and 12.8 per cent in 1999-2000, 2000-01 and 2001-02 respectively. In 2002-03, interest payment accounted for 10.1 per cent and 15 per cent of revenue expenses with and without power charges. During 2003-04 interest payment increased further to 10.4 per cent of revenue expenditure.

TABLE 2.4

Revenue Receipts and Expenditure

(Rs. in crore)

Year	*Tax Revenue*	*Non-Tax Revenue*	*Grant-in-Aid from Centre*	*Revenue Receipts*	*Revenue Expenditure*	*Percentage of Own Revenue to Rev. Exp.*	*Interest Rollover in Grant-in-Aid (per cent of Rev. Exp.)*
1990-91	70.44 (34.6)	46.08 (22.7)	86.79 (42.7)	203.31	204.21	57.1	NA
1995-96	162.52 (35.8)	123.84 (27.3)	167.68 (36.9)	454/-4	421.76	67.9	42.46 (10.0)
1998-99	224.98 (30.1)	171.97 (23.0)	350.50 (46.9)	747.45	688.94	57.6	78.25 (11.3)
1999-2000	260.59 (29.7)	218.47 (24.9)	398.42 (45.4)	877.49	845.58	56.6	74.53 (8.8)
2000-01	291.85 (30.84)	255.12 (26.92)	399.74 (42.24)	946.73	919.07	57.76	86.40 (9.4)
2001-02	268.59 (25.04)	302.31 (28.18)	501.69 (46.78)	1072.59	1098.72	51.96	100.99 (9.2)
2002-03	276.38 (23.3)	411.90 (34.8)	497.20 (41.9)	1185.49	1151.31	59.8	115.59 (10.1)
2003-04	352.77 (27.08)	454.34 (34.88)	495.42 (38.04)	1202.52	1293.61	62.39	134.51 (10.4)

Note: Figures in brackets indicate per cent.
Source: Government of Puducherry Budget documents.

At present Puducherry's entire capital expenditure is met through Central loans with attendant debt servicing burden. As UT, it is obtaining plan assistance in the form of two-thirds as grant and one-third as loan. If it is considered as 'normal' state on attaining statehood, then loan proportion would increase to 70 per cent and grants reduce to 30 per cent i.e., practically adverse reversal of grant to loan ratio. Consequently debt-servicing burden is bound to lead to debt trap.

Grants-in-Aid in 2001-02, 2002-03 and 2003-04 constitutes 47 per cent, 42 per cent, and 41 per cent respectively, of the revenue receipts. Therefore, grants-in-aid would continue to constitute just less than 45 per cent of revenue receipts in the years to come, particularly as local ST revenue is expected to be less buoyant with introduction of uniform sales tax rate (with CST emerging as preferred option for inter state trade and commerce) and advent of VAT regime. Further interest payments are likely to constitute one-quarter of the grants-in-aid in the years to come. It was 21.4 per cent in 2000-01, and 20.2 per cent in 2001-02, 23 per cent in 2002-03, and 27 per cent in 2003-04.

The annual growth rates in tax revenue, non-tax revenue and grants-in-aid for the period 1995-96 to 1999-2000 (five years) are as under:

Sl. No.	Item	Factor (5 years)	Per cent Growth Rate*
1.	Tax Revenue	260.59/162.52	12.5
2.	Non-Tax Revenue**	218.47/123.84	15.25
3.	Grants-in-Aid	398.42/167.68	24.15

Note: * During 1995-2000 period, annual growth rate of tax revenues and grants-in-aid was both in double digit. In contrast it is only about 5 per cent during 1999-2004 period.

** Power charge receipts are the main item and the only growth item.

The annual growth rates in tax revenue, non-tax revenue and grants-in-aid for the five year period from 1999-2000 to 2003-04 are given below:

Sl. No.	Item	Factor (5 years)	per cent Growth Rate*
1.	Tax Revenue	309.00/260.59	4.35
2.	Non-Tax Revenue**	416.00/218.47	17.40
3.	Grants-in-Aid	499.55/398.42	5.82

Note: * During 1995-2000 period, annual growth rate of tax revenues and grants-in-aid was both in double digit. In contrast it is only about 5 per cent during 1999-2004 period.

** Power charge receipts are the main item and the only growth item.

Trends in current revenue of Puducherry during nineties and subsequent during 2000-2004 after excluding electricity related receipts are as given in Table 2.5.

TABLE 2.5

Trends in Current Revenues (Excluding Electricity Receipts from Non-Tax Revenues)

(Rs. in lakh)

Year	Own Tax Revenue	Own Non-Tax Revenue	Grants-in-Aid	Total Current Revenue	Per Capita Current Revenue (Rs.)
1985-86	2749 (33.1)	362 (4.4)	5189 (62.5)	8300 (100.0)	1209
1990-91	7044 (43.2)	581 (3.6)	8678 (53.2)	16304 (100.0)	2045
1991-92	8224 (43.1)	703 (3.7)	10165 (53.2)	19092 (100.0)	2313
1992-93	9418 (44.5)	795 (3.8)	10937 (51.7)	21151 (100.0)	2472
1993-94	10817 (46.4)	1006 (4.3)	11501 (49.3)	23324 (100.0)	2630
1994-95	13241 (46.7)	855 (3.0)	14271 (50.3)	28366 (100.0)	3088
1995-96	16252 (47.5)	1199 (3.50)	16768 (49)	34219 (100.0)	3597
1996-97	19248 (49.7)	1410 (3.6)	18106 (46.7)	38764 (100.0)	3931
1997-98	20860 (43.4)	1045 (2.2)	26174 (54.4)	48078 (100.0)	4597
1998-99	22498 (38.2)	1288 (2.2)	35050 (59.6)	58836 (100.0)	5546
1999-2000	26059 (38.6)	1615 (2.4)	39843 (59.0)	67516 (100.0)	6752
2000-01	29186 (41.23)	1634 (2.31)	39974 (56.47)	70794 (100.0)	7080
2001-02	26859 (33.94)	2107 (2.66)	50169 (63.4)	79135 (100.0)	7914
2002-03	27638 (34.65)	2397 (3.01)	49720 (62.34)	79756 (100.0)	7976
2003-04	35277 (40.44)	2404 (2.76)	49542 (56.82)	87233 (100.0)	8723

TABLE 2.5A

Annual Growth Rates (Current Prices)

1991-92 to 1995-96	15.0	10.8	12.5	14.5
1995-96 to 1999-00	12.0	7.5	21.5	17.0
1999-2000 to 2003-04	4.3	6.5	6.0	5.0

Source: *Annual Financial Statement of the Union Territory of Puducherry* (Various Years).

Overall revenue annual growth rate of well above 15 per cent in nineties has slid to five per cent in recent years, mainly because of decline in own tax revenues and near freezing of central transfers in recent years.

A study of the composition of tax revenues trends shows heavy reliance on sales tax, which constituted half the tax revenue in 1990-91 and practically two-thirds from 1998-99 onwards (Table 2.6).

TABLE 2.6

Tax Revenues

(Rs. in crore)

Year	*Sales Tax*	*State Excise*	*Stamps and Reg. and Land Revenue*	*Tax on Vehicles, Other Commodities*	*Total Tax Revenue*
1985-86	11.80 (42.9)	12.00 (43.7)	1.61 (5.9)	1.86 (6.8)	27.49 (100)
1990-91	36.47 (51.8)	24.85 (35.3)	5.03 (7.1)	3.5 (5)	70.44 (100)
1995-96	102.31 (63)	36.70 (22.6)	11.32 (7.0)	11.78 (7.3)	162.52 (100)
1998-99	148.63 (66.1)	51.93 (23.1)	8.02 (3.6)	15.61 (6.9)	224.98 (100)
1999-2000	171.42 (65.8)	61.00 (23.4)	10.35 (3.9)	17.83 (6.9)	260.60 (100)
2000-01	193.50 (66.3)	66.18 (22.7)	12.60 (4.3)	19.58 (6.7)	291.86 (100)
2001-02	160.42 (59.72)	76.13 (28.33)	13.31 (4.95)	18.73 (7.00)	268.59 (100)
2002-03	150.09 (54.3)	87.70 (31.7)	16.43 (5.9)	22.16 (8.1)	276.38 (100)
2003-04	203.19 (57.60)	105.66 (29.55)	20.57 (5.83)	23.35 (6.62)	352.77 (100)

Source: Government of Puducherry Budget documents.

The growth rates of tax revenue sources for the recent five years with the trends during the seventies, eighties and nineties indicates that state excise revenue has practically become stagnant in recent years. There was a significant dip of 20 per cent in sales tax revenue during 2000-01 and 2002-03. However, in recent years it has picked up and bounced back to 2000-01 level of Rs.180 to 190 crore. Earlier two years dip in sales tax is attributable to uniform flow rate (UFR) in sales tax introduced as per instructions of the Central government.

Years	*Growth Rate*	
	Sales Tax	*State Excise*
1970-1980	11.87	7.65
1980-1990	10.72	1.03
1990-91 to 1999-2000	16.5	10.5
1999-2000 to 2003-04	1.2	9.8

Consequent to introduction of UFR in local sales tax, 10 per cent annual growth seen in the nineties, has now tapered down to 1 per cent. Centre is expected to come forward to release the CST collection (Rs.70 to 80 crore annually) to Puducherry to augment its sales tax revenue. Annual growth rate of 10.5 per cent in state excise in nineties has now declined to 9.8 per cent per annum in recent years.

The tax revenue of Puducherry is mainly from the five sources of: (i) sales tax (ii) state excise (iii) land revenue (iv) stamp duty and registration fees and (v) taxes on vehicles. Puducherry can tap about 19 sources of taxes as indicated in the list II of the Seventh Schedule. It should not limit itself to exploiting only the above five taxes, with major slant on the first two sources i.e., sales tax and state excise.

With central transfer stagnating at around Rs.500 crore, besides pressing for release of CST collections by Centre, Puducherry should both widen its sources of tax revenue and also optimally target sales tax and state excise and efficiently collect the same.

2.3 Own Non-Tax Revenues (Excluding Electricity-Related Receipts)

The non-tax revenue comprises:

(i) interest and dividends;

(ii) service charges for general services (such as police, public works and other administrative services) rendered by the government;

(iii) fees, sales proceeds, fines, etc., received by the government for social services (such as education, health, family welfare, water supply, sanitation, and urban development); and

(iv) economic services (power, union minor irrigation, crop husbandry, and fisheries).

Interstate comparison reveals that Puducherry ranks at the top both in terms of per capita revenue receipts (with grants-in-aid from the Centre as a major component) and per capita expenditure. However, the revenue gap defined as shortfall in own revenues (excluding electricity-related receipts) as percentage of total revenue expenditure is quite high about 40 per cent. While there is scope for improvements in tax revenue efforts, the revenue gap to be bridged effectively also requires augmenting non-tax revenue potential of the state. During recent years (2001-2002 to 2003-04) non-tax revenue is stagnating around Rs.21 crore to Rs.23 crore.

It may be of interest to note that while in per capita own tax revenue Puducherry is among the top three or four states, in terms of per capita non-tax revenue it is at the bottom. The share of non-tax revenue receipts (excluding electricity receipts) declined from 4.46 per cent in 1985-86 to 3.6 per cent in 1990-91 and further to 2.2 per cent in 1998-99. It was 2.4 per cent, 2.3 per cent, 2.7 per cent, 3.0 per cent, and 2.5 per cent during 1999-2000, 2000-01, 2001-02, 2002-03, and 2003-04 respectively.

Notwithstanding the fact that non-tax revenues cannot increase as fast as tax revenues, augmentation of non-tax revenues should be considered as an equally important own means of raising financial resources of Puducherry. The changing pattern of non-tax revenues during 1990-91 to 2003-04 is evident from Table 2.7.

It may be noted that for the above analysis electricity receipts are excluded (since Puducherry unlike other states does not have SEB of its own, consequently power charges are reflected in its Budget). It is seen that revenue receipts from economic services has declined from 23.5 per cent in 1990-91 to 16.9 per cent in 1999-2000 and further to 16.0 per cent by 2003-04. Further share of almost all economic services i.e., crop husbandry, animal husbandry, ports and lights, have declined except for non-ferrous mining.

The proportion of general services' contribution earlier steady around 27 per cent or 28 per cent in nineties, has now declined to 20 per cent in 2003-04. On the other hand proportion of contribution by social services has increased over the period from 27 per cent in 1990-91 to 43 per cent by 1999-2000 and now in 2003-2004 it is 44.3 per cent. Main reason for the same is contribution by medical, health and family welfare services. Further major slant in development expenditure is for social services as compared to economic services.

Among economic services, power sector is in fact subsidised to the extent of Rs.30 crore to Rs.35 crore (except for 1995-96) and therefore a financial burden on its budget. Further, in spite of increasing investments in PSUs, receipts of interest, dividends and profits had

TABLE 2.7

Pattern of Non-Tax Revenues (Percentage Shares)

(Rs. in lakh)

Details	*1990-91*	*1995-96*	*1998-99*	*1999-2000*	*2000-01*	*2001-02*	*2002-03*	*2003-04*
Non-Tax Revenue: Total	581 (100.0)	979* (100)	1287 (100.0)	1615 (100.0)	1635 (100)	2107 (100)	2397 (100)	2404 (100)
i) Interest Receipts, Dividends and Profits (Rs. lakh)	118 (20.2)	149 (15.2)	259 (20.1)	222 (13.8)	215 (13.2)	418 (19.8)	512 (21.3)	450 (18.7)
ii) Other Non-Tax Revenue (Rs. lakh)	464 (79.8)	830 (84.8)	1029 (79.9)	1394 (86.2)	1420 (86.9)	1689 (80.1)	1885 (78.7)	1954 (81.3)
General Services	29.5	27.7	33.0	26.7	29.3	21.5	21.7	20.8
Police	0.3	2.0	5.1	2.7	3.1	2.1	1.9	2.0
Stationery and Printing	3.1	2.8	1.8	1.1	2.1	1.0	1.1	1.7
Public Works	4.2	7.3	12.2	5.6	6.3	6.4	5.3	5.9
Other Administrative Services	9.0	16.0	5.8	9.6	6.0	4.8	6.4	6.7
Others	12.8	0.3	8.1	7.7	11.8	7.2	7.0	4.5
Social Service	26.8	38.5	30.5	42.7	38.5	37.5	41.7	47.1
Education, Sports, Art and Culture	4.0	9.1	2.2	5.0	3.7	1.6	5.3	4.3
Medical, Health and Family Welfare	8.0	10.2	13.0	17.7	18.3	15.9	14.9	22.7
Water Supply and Sanitation	10.1	10.6	10.1	9.2	10.0	10.4	11.3	9.6
Housing and Urban Development	2.4	4.8	3.4	8.7	4.2	7.2	5.0	4.6
Others	2.2	3.7	1.8	2.1	2.3	2.4	5.2	5.9
Economic Services	23.5	18.5	16.3	16.9	19.0	21.2	15.3	13.4
Crop Husbandry	5.0	3.6	2.7	2.7	3.9	1.8	1.2	1.4
Animal Husbandry	1.2	1.3	0.9	0.6	0.8	0.7	0.8	0.6
Fisheries	1.2	1.1	1.1	1.8	1.0	0.7	0.8	0.6
Cooperation	1.0	1.0	1.5	0.8	1.1	0.5	0.7	0.6
Other Rural Devt. Programmes	0.1	0.1	0.1	0.1	2.2	3.7	3.4	0.6
Major, Medium and Minor Irrigation	1.1	1.1	1.1	1.8	1.4	0.6	0.8	0.9
Non-ferrous Mining and Metallurgical	0.0	0.2	0.8	1.3	1.2	1.2	0.3	1.3
Ports and Light Houses	3.2	1.7	1.4	0.5	1.0	1.5	1.5	2.3
Roads and Bridges	5.7	2.9	2.3	3.1	3.6	4.6	0.9	1.6
Tourism	1.1	1.2	0.8	0.7	0.7	0.8	1.0	1.4
Others	3.4	3.7	2.9	2.7	2.1	5.1	3.9	2.1

Note: * excludes profit/surplus of Rs.221 lakh in electricity/power related activity. In other years power subsidy was provided.

Source: Computed using data from *Annual Financial Statement of the Union Territory of Puducherry* (Various Years).

declined in proportion from 20 per cent in 1990-91 to 14 per cent in 1999-2000 and then increased to 20.72 per cent by 2003-04.

Interest receipts increased from Rs.260 lakh in 1998-99 to Rs.435 lakh in 2003-04. As against this, interest payments have increased from Rs.7825 lakh (30 times of Rs.260 lakh) in 1998-99 to Rs.13451 lakh (31 times of Rs.435 lakh) in 2003-04. Therefore, interest receipts are insignificant as compared to interest payments since 1998-1999. Even during 1995-96 interest receipts and payments were Rs.149 lakh and Rs.4246 lakh about 28 times of Rs.149 lakh. This gap in interest receipts and payments need to be scaled down in the medium-term through both debt swap (taking advantage of declining interest rates) and better investment/resource allocation to revenue yielding activities. A re-look on investments in state PSUs is necessary, including measures for disinvestments.

2.4 Composition of Revenue Expenditure and Capital Receipts and Expenditure

2.4.1 Revenue Expenditure

An analysis of percentage composition of revenue expenditure (including electricity related expenditure), shows stagnancy for social services, slightly declining trend for economic services (mainly power payments) and slight upward trend for general services (Table 2.8).

TABLE 2.8

Composition of Revenue Expenditure

(Rs. in crore)

Year	General Services	Social Services	Economic Services*	Grants	Total Rev. Exp.
1985-86	16.24 (17.7)	41.17 (44.8)	33.92 (37.0)	0.48 (0.5)	91.81 (100)
1990-91	45.66 (22.4)	76.06 (37.2)	81.32 (39.8)	1.17 (.6)	204.21 (100)
1995-96	92.55 (21.9)	147.93 (35.1)	176.60 (41.9)	4.69 (1.1)	421.76 (100)
1998-99	174.34 (25.3)	246.41 (35.8)	261.00 (37.9)	7.19 (1.0)	688.94 (100)
1999-2000	196.02 (23.2)	302.78 (35.8)	343.95 (40.7)	2.82 (0.3)	845.58 (100)
2000-01	208.52 (22.7)	317.71 (34.6)	390.81 (42.6)	2.02 (0.25)	919.06 (100)
2001-02	223.02 (20.2)	319.20 (29.2)	554.11 (50.3)	2.38 (0.21)	1098.72 (100)
2002-03	249.34 (21.66)	361.07 (31.37)	538.30 (46.77)	2.59 (0.22)	1151.31 (100)
2003-04	294.74 (22.86)	413.18 (32.05)	587.51 (45.57)	2.87 (0.22)	1289.30 (100)

Note: * includes electricity related revenue expenditure.
Source: Government of Puducherry Budget documents.

Earlier in the eighties it was social services (42 per cent), which had the edge over economic services (34 per cent). In the nineties, economic services (mainly power payments) constituted the main revenue expenditure item (about 41 per cent), followed by social services (35 per cent) and general services (24 per cent). It may be appropriate to look at the growth rate of revenue disbursement items in the past decades and more importantly in the recent five years. The scorching growth rates in nineties have come down significantly (includes electricity related expenditure) during last five years as under:

Growth Rate of Revenue Disbursement Items

Year	Growth Rate		
	General Services	Social Services	Economic Services
1970-1980	5.5	7.41	6.88
1980-1990	11.8	9.99	12.74
1990-91 to 1999-2000	16.3	15.5	16.0*
1999-2000 to 2003-04	10.0	7.8	13.0*

Note: * Mainly due to power payments.

If one excludes, electricity related expenditure from economic services (except for power subsidy) then pattern of revenue expenditure over the years among general services, social services and economic services is shown in Table 2.9.

During the period 1990-91 to 1999-2000, revenue expenditure has increased four-fold. Development expenditure constituted about 70 per cent of total revenue expenditure from 1990-91 to 1999-2000. Social services expenditure continued to dominate about 47 per cent share of revenue expenditure in the nineties. Economic services expenditure declined from 25 per cent in 1990-91 to 22.3 per cent in 1999-2000. During the same period non-development expenditure increased from 27.9 per cent to 30.5 per cent.

During the period 2000-01 to 2003-04, development expenditure has slipped from 69.3 per cent to 67.3 per cent. During this period social services outlay has slightly declined from 46.7 per cent to 45.7 per cent of revenue expenditure. Economic services have also shown decline from 22.3 per cent in 2000-01 to 21.3 per cent in 2003-2004. It may be noted that power subsidy expenditure has been included in the above table for analysis. Non-development expenditure has increased from 30.7 per cent to 32.7 per cent during this period i.e., by 2 per cent at the expense 1 per cent of revenue expenditure each in social service and economic services. 2001-02 appears to

TABLE 2.9

Composition of Revenue Expenditures (Excludes Electricity Related Expenditure Except Power Subsidy) (Percentage Shares)

Details	*1990-91*	*1995-96*	*1998-99*	*1999-2000*	*2000-01*	*2001-02*	*2002-03*	*2003-04*
Revenue Disbursements (in Rs. lakh)	16393	30992	52985	64326	68028	81748	76337	90330
1. Development expenditures	72.1	70.1	67.0	69.5	69.3	72.7	67.3	67.3
a) Social Services	46.4	47.7	46.5	47.0	46.7	39.0	47.3	45.7
b) Economic Services	25.0	20.9	19.2	22.3	22.3	33.4	19.7	21.3
c) Grants-in-aid and contributions	0.7	1.5	1.3	0.4	0.3	0.3	0.3	0.3
2. Non-Development Expenditures	27.9	29.9	33.0	30.5	30.7	27.3	32.7	32.7

Source: Computed using data from *Annual Financial Statement of the Union Territory of Puducherry* (Various Years).

be an odd year in which revenue expenditure on social services decreased to 39 per cent (from normal level of 46 per cent to 47 per cent) and that of economic services increased to 33.4 per cent (from normal level of 21 per cent to 22 per cent). The reason for high increase in economic services in 2001-02 is because of high level of power subsidy/deficit of Rs.127 crore (normal annual level is Rs.30 to Rs.35 crore only).

2.4.2 Capital Receipts and Expenditure

The trends of capital receipts (practically central loans/ public debts) and capital expenditure and its deficit/ surplus of Puducherry are indicated in Table 2.10.

TABLE 2.10

Capital Receipts and Expenditure

(Rs. in crore)

Year	*Capital Receipts (Public Debts Components)*	*Capital Exp. (Public Debt Repayment)*	*Deficit/ Surplus*
1990-91	47.39 (45.3)	49.02 (24.56)	(1.63)
1995-96	71.31 (67.3)	109.81 (24.56)	(38.5)
1998-99	118.35 (110.0)	167.93 (46.8)	(49.58)
1999-2000	133.88 (130.3)	155.41 (43.0)	(21.53)
2000-01	160.84 (155.4)	170.65 (48.26)	(9.81)
2001-02	199.59 (193.4)	180.65 (54.08)	+18.94
2002-03	229.97 (230)	214.41 (61.47)	+15.56
2003-04	268.40 (233.6)	220.76 (69.33)	+47.64

Note: Figures in brackets indicate percentage.

Source: Government of Puducherry Budget documents.

For all practical purposes, capital receipts are central loans/public debt only. Public debt/central loans repayment constituted about 30 per cent of capital expenditure.

The composition of capital disbursement reveals that economic services accounts for just less than half of the same, followed by central loans/public debt repayment (25 per cent) and with significantly less capital outlay for social services (Table 2.11).

TABLE 2.11

Composition of Capital Disbursement

(Rs. in crore)

Year	*General Services*	*Social Services*	*Economic Services*	*Public Debts*	*Loans*	*Total*
1990-91	0.81 (1.7)	6.33 (13.0)	23.36 (47.5)	15.36 (31.3)	3.16 (6.5)	49.02 (100)
1995-96	2.98 (2.7)	9.67 (8.8)	62.97 (67.3)	24.57 (22.4)	9.63 (9.8)	109.81 (100)
1998-99	6.65 (4.1)	17.34 (10.3)	85.96 (51.0)	46.8 (27.9)	11.17 (6.6)	167.93 (100)
1999-2000	7.63 (4.9)	24.84 (16.07)	70.59 (45.4)	43.00 (27.6)	9.34 (6.0)	155.40 (100)
2000-01	9.38 (5.5)	24.36 (14.3)	74.12 (44.0)	48.26 (28.3)	14.54 (8.5)	170.65 (100)
2001-02	14.57 (8.05)	22.23 (11.95)	82.45 (46.4)	54.08 (29.6)	7.32 (4.0)	180.65 (100)
2002-03	20.13 (9.39)	39.68 (18.51)	87.69 (40.9)	61.47 (28.7)	5.43 (2.53)	214.41 (100)
2003-04	11.09 (5.02)	43.78 (19.83)	91.62 (41.54)	69.33 (31.41)	4.94 (2.23)	220.75 (100)

Note: Figures in brackets is per cent.

Source: Government of Puducherry Budget documents.

As compared to own revenue receipts of Rs.33000 lakh in 2003-04 and own capital receipts (excludes net borrowing) in terms of recoveries of loans and advances of Rs.575 lakh in 2003-04 i.e., own total receipts of

Rs.33575 lakh, own capital receipts constitute only 1.7 per cent. Further own capital receipts of Rs.5.75 crore are not even sufficient to meet one-tenth of principal debt repayment of Rs.69.35 crore in 2003-04. A re-look at capital expenditure programme is essential.

2.5 Subsides and Losses of State PSUs

2.5.1 Subsidies

Direct subsidies to the various sectors from the state budget for the nine years 1995-96 to 2003-04 are shown in Table 2.12.

TABLE 2.12

Details of Subsidies to Various Sectors

(Rs. in crore)

Name of Sector	*1995-96*	*1996-97*	*1997-98*	*1998-99*	*1999-2000*	*2000-01*	*2001-02*	*2002-03*	*2003-04*
Housing	0.36	0.34	0.21	0.14	0.15	0.62	0.82	0.90	1.34
Welfare of SC/ST	0.17	0.20	0.15	0.20	0.35	0.20	0.75	1.05	2.77
Animal Husbandry	0.21	0.53	0.02	0.13	0.28	0.30	0.24	0.87	1.50
Fisheries	0.72	1.90	1.19	1.11	1.35	1.44	0.29	1.01	0.76
Energy	0.39	0.20	0.15	0.27	0.15	0.43	-	-	-
Industries		4.70	2.62	0.45	0.60	-	-	0.06	0.30
Total	1.85	7.87	4.34	2.30	2.88	2.99	2.09	3.89	6.67

Source: Government of Puducherry Budget documents.

Direct subsidies earlier around Rs.8 crore in 1996-97, is now around the level of Rs.4 crore in recent years. Housing, welfare of SC/ST, animal husbandry and fisheries account for Rs.1 crore each approximately per year.

It is the indirect subsidies, which are of much higher order arising out of:

i) Revenue deficit of Rs.30 crore per year under revenue receipts and expenditure on purchase and sale of energy.

Rs. in crore

Year	*1998-99*	*1999-2000*	*2000-01*	*2001-02*	*2002-03*	*2003-04*
Deficit	10.0	32.0	31.0	127.0	20.0	29.00

ii) Losses of State PSUs covered in 2.5.2 below.

2.5.2 Losses of State PSUs

An issue of important consideration in Puducherry, as in other states, is the health of public sector units (PSUs). Puducherry has a number of public sector industrial units primarily, spinning mills, distilleries, and sugar mills. These units were established both as a means to stimulate growth and to generate employment in the Union Territory. In addition to these government-owned units, there are a number of other autonomous government bodies in which the government has invested significantly such as PIPDIC and PASIC. These PSUs are not production-oriented in the same way as the industrial units but still demand considerable investment from the government.

The need for sustaining the PSUs as in the current fashion requires a relook. Details with regard to profits/losses of select PSUs (mostly government corporations) as given in the Report of the CAG of India (2003) are shown in Table 2.13.

TABLE 2.13

Financial Status of Select Public Sector Units

(Rs. in lakh)

Name of PSU	*Net Profit (+) / Loss (-)*	*Share Capital*
PASIC	+ 37.41	550
PAPSCO	- 139.55	425
Puducherry Distilleries	+ 217.71	645
PIPDIC	+427.33	3550
PELECON	+4.09	10
Puducherry Textile Corporation Ltd.	-2443.60	7250
Puducherry Adi-Dravidar Development Corporation Ltd.	-53.52	175
Puducherry Tourism and Transport Development Corporation Ltd.	- 239.80	360
Puducherry Power Corporation Ltd.	+834.49	9950
Total	- 1,355.44	22915

Source: Report of the CAG of India (2003).

Cooperative sector PSUs such as the Puducherry Co-operative Sugar Mill and the Puducherry Co-operative Spinning Mill have intermittently been making profit. However, public sector companies like Swadeshi Cotton Mills, Anglo French Textiles, and Shri Bharathi Mills have been continuously running at substantial loss.

The recent position during 2005-06 for some of the PSUs are indicated below (Rs. in lakh):

1. PSUs which have since been making profits

No.	Corporation	Net Profit	Share Capital
1.	Puducherry Textile Corporation	2583	23000
2.	PAPSCO	17.4	899.8

2. PSUs which are continuing to make profits

No.	Corporation	Net Profit	Share Capital
1.	Puducherry Distilleries Ltd.	237.3	845.0
2.	PIPDIC	473.0	4040.0
3.	Power Corporation Ltd.	889.4	1330.4

3. PSUs which have since been able to reduce the magnitude of their losses relative to their share capital

No.	Corporation	Net Profit	Share Capital
1.	Puducherry Adi-Dravidar Development Corporation	98.3	311.4
2.	Puducherry Road Transport Corporation	65.0	1996.2

2.6 Borrowings, Outstanding Liabilities, Interest Burden and Sustainability of Public Debt

Puducherry as UT borrows from the Centre only under Non-Plan, Plan and CSS schemes besides raising small savings (Table 2.14).

TABLE 2.14

Borrowings from Central Government

(Rs. in crore)

Year	Non-Plan	Plan	CSS	Small Savings	Total
1995-96	23.92	38.59	-	4.82	67.33
1996-97	25.47	38.59	0.04	9.68	73.78
1997-98	33.30	42.45	0.01	9.18	84.94
1998-99	45.67	57.38	0.03	6.95	110.03
1999-2000	46.64	61.74	0.04	18.62	127.04
2000-01	55.07	60.72	0.11	39.50	155.40
2001-02	54.75	54.94	-	83.65	193.34
2002-03	60.61	65.30	0.55	103.51	229.97
2003-04	68.0	69.0	0.57	126.0	263.57

Source: Government of Puducherry Budget document.

From 2000-01 onwards, Puducherry has started relying heavily on high cost and medium-term maturity small savings scheme. It is almost at the same level (above Rs.100 crore) of that of annual central loans (plan and non-plan). The move by the Centre to allow NCT of Delhi and UTs to tap market borrowings directly under the aegis of RBI is yet to be given effect in respect of Puducherry.

Two Tables 2.15(A) and 2.15(B) compare the level of debt servicing, both in terms of principal and interest on various components of central loans during the two periods 1996-97 to 1999-2000 and 2000-01 to 2003-04.

During the time window 1996-2000, both annual principal instalment and interest servicing have doubled. In comparison to position during 1999-2000, annual principal instalment is 1.5 times and annual interest burden 1.9 times in 2003-04. Obviously interest burden is on higher side and calls for debt swap [Tables 2.15(C) and 2.15(D)].

TABLE 2.15(A)

Debt Servicing Profile on Central Loans from 1995-96 to 1999-2000

		1996-97		1997-98		1998-99		1999-2000	
	Categoryof Loans	Principal	Interest	Principal	Interest	Principal	Interest	Principal	Interest
1.	Non-plan Scheme	8,98,92,145	11,50,22,582	9,12,64,286	16,92,12,627	18,66,68,861	25,77,95,815	16,64,42,855,	27,34,87,069
2.	UT Plan Scheme	14,38,52,437	27,42,06,625	14,65,74,300	35,01,61,256	28,04,62,300	52,27,85,756	26,26,00,700	46,97,73,527
3.	Central Plan Scheme	35,000	9,450	35,000	7,088	35,000	4,725	35,000	2,363
4.	Centrally Sponsored Plan Scheme	6,80,244	21,94,691	8,13,994	21,32,573	9,15,240	20,63,758	9,22,073	20,16,530
	Total	23,44,59,826	39,14,33,348	23,86,87,580	52,15,13,544	46,80,81,401	78,26,50,054	43,00,00,628	74,52,79,489

Source: Government of Puducherry Budget documents.

TABLE 2.15(B)

Debt Servicing Profile on Central Loans from 2000-01 to 2004-05

Category of Loans	2000-01 Principal	2000-01 Interest	2001-02 Principal	2001-02 Interest	2002-03 Principal	2002-03 Interest	2003-04 Principal	2003-04 Interest
1. Non-plan Scheme	19,41,52,135	33,50,71,181	22,21,47,847	43,93,51,081	27,23,30,712	55,48,49,296	32,06,49,275	70,66,89,986
2. UT Plan Scheme	28,72,25,000	52,34,76,898	31,71,05,736	56,84,49,487	33,94,60,000	59,91,72,702	36,44,10,000	63,54,66,775
3. Central Plan Scheme	-	-	95,500	1,04,852	-	-	-	-
4. Centrally Sponsored Plan Scheme	11,94,794	19,73,120	14,89,215	19,88,584	29,06,870	18,41,618	82,43,849	29,17,664
Total	48,25,71,929	86,05,21,199	54,08,38,298	1,00,98,94,004	61,46,97,582	1,15,58,63,616	69,33,03,124	1,34,50,74,425

Source: Government of Puducherry Budget documents.

TABLE 2.15(C)

Outstanding Balance of Loans Received from Central Government as on 31/3/2000

No	Category-wise of Loan	Outstanding Balance (Rs.)
1.	Non-plan Scheme	262,58,85,724
2.	Plan Scheme	433,85,20,736
3.	Central Plan Scheme	95,500
4.	Centrally Sponsored Plan Scheme	1,90,33,228

Source: Government of Puducherry Budget documents.

TABLE 2.15(D)

Outstanding Balance of Loans from Central Government as on 31/3/2004

No	Category-wise of Loan	Outstanding Balance (Rs.)
1	Non-plan Scheme	7,65,15,05,755
2	Plan Sscheme	5,45,99,20,000
3	Central Plan Scheme	—
4	Centrally Sponsored Plan Scheme	1,17,35,000

Source: Government of Puducherry Budget documents.

During the period 2000-2004, public debt (central loans) has increased by Rs.842 crore and with principal repayments of Rs.234 crore (rolling adjustment), the net public debt has nearly doubled from Rs.699 crore to Rs.1307 i.e., by Rs.608 crore. Average annual interest burden of 10 per cent in 2000 has increased to 10.5 per cent by 2004. Debt swap may mitigate the same.

2.7 Fiscal Deficit and Budgetary Problems

Fiscal deficit problem of Puducherry in recent years is compounded with the emergence of revenue deficit. Main budgetary problems of the state arise from:

a) Own revenue receipts, particularly tax revenues, barely covers non-development expenditure. Non-tax revenue (excluding electricity receipts) constitutes hardly 6 per cent of own revenue receipts. Therefore, the state has to depend on grant-in-aid from the Centre for developmental expenditure. Freezing of grant-in-aid at Rs.500 crore (40 per cent of revenue receipts) during last three years, coupled with stagnant non-tax revenue and a mere Rs.18 crore increase in tax revenue between 2000-01 (Rs.291.85 crore) and 2003-04 (Rs.309.00 crore) has seen the surfacing of revenue deficit.

b) Capital receipts have come down from Rs.831 lakh in 1998-99 to Rs.575 lakh in 2003-04. Further annual interest receipts are insignificant (3 per cent) as compared to annual interest payments. Effective interest rate on outstanding liabilities has increased from 10 per cent to 13.5 per cent p.a. during last four years.

c) Overemphasis on social developmental schemes (consumption related) at the expense of economic services/schemes (productive).

d) Large annual outlays on loss making PSUs without economic purpose.

e) Mounting administrative and pension related expenditure.

Under fiscal reforms and budgetary management requirement, the state should:

i) Aim for optimal tapping and efficient collection of revenues, both tax and non-tax; prioritise revenue expenditure with slant on economically sensible developmental expenditure; control administrative/non-developmental expenditure.

ii) Curtail subsidies and follow financially prudent capital investment in schemes and PSUs.

iii) Though debt swap could improve debt servicing to some extent, emphasis should be equally on ensuring higher level of interest, dividends, profits, capital receipts and user charges i.e., adequate returns on investments.

iv) A re-look of over relying on small savings scheme loans.

v) Reforms and restructuring of PSUs in real sense, including disinvestments, spinning off as joint ventures and hard decisions on closures of PSUs which have turned white elephants i.e., they do not even produce goods and services efficiently and economically leave alone generate surplus/ profit.

Unless above measures are undertaken, revenue deficit would hover around 1 per cent to 1.5 per cent of GSDP and fiscal deficit 4 per cent to 5 per cent of GSDP as per current indications for UT of Puducherry.

2.8 Finances of Urban Local Bodies and Commune *Panchayats*

In Puducherry, there are 5 municipalities and 10 Commune *Panchayats*. At present about Rs.7 crore is paid by the state to the various local bodies by way of their share on stamps and registration fees.

In the context of 73rd and 74th Amendments, the Constitution has prescribed transfer of certain powers statutorily to the Urban and Rural Local Bodies. This has to be done by amending the Puducherry Municipalities Act and Puducherry Village and Commune Panchayat Act, which is expected to take more time. Meanwhile, Second State Finance Commission has recommended that a grant to the extent of 4 per cent of own tax revenue i.e., about Rs.13 crore be made available. To start with additional grants-in-aid at least to the extent of Rs.10 crore over and above Rs.7 crore in lieu of stamps and registration fees was made available. In neighboring southern states additional grants-in-aid to municipalities and *panchayats* is to the extent of 8 per cent of own state revenues as against 4 per cent proposed in Puducherry.

In the municipal fund is constituted of the following sources of revenue:

- Tax Revenue: Income from property tax, entertainment tax, profession tax, advertisement tax, duty on transfer of properties, and duty on toddy trees.
- Non-Tax Revenue: License fee, bus stand parking fee, income from leasing of fruits of trees and fishing rights, income from land properties, etc.
- Grants-in-Aid and loan from government: The Government at present contributes every year non-statutory grants for undertaking departmental works to provide civic amenities. Loan is also provided for remunerative enterprises/activities.

The Commune *Panchayat* fund constitutes tax revenue, non-tax revenue, statutory grants and non-statutory grants and loans. Tax revenues cover entertainment tax, local cess and surcharge, cinematography tax, taxes and duties leviable by village *panchayats*. Non-tax revenues constitutes of market fees, license fees, income from ferries and fisheries.

The statutory grants from government covers local cess surcharge matching grants and local roads, maintenance grants. Government also contributes every year to the funds of commune *panchayat* by way of non-statutory grants and loans for undertaking various departmental works and remunerative enterprises.

Annual Plan 2005-06 of Puducherry earmarks Rs.9.95 crore as financial assistance to municipalities for construction and improvement of buildings and Rs.5 crore for sanitation, solid and liquid waste management. Thus plan grant is Rs.15 crore and non-plan grant about Rs.7 crore. In addition, MLA local area development outlay of Rs.12 crore is also provided in Annual Plan 2005-06.

2.9 Annual Plans, Plan and Non-Plan Composition and Regional Balance

2.9.1 Plan and Non-Plan Outlay Composition

The plan expenditure as percentage of total expenditure slipped from 34 per cent in the first half of the eighties to 27 per cent in the second half of the

TABLE 2.16

Plan and Non-Plan Outlay Composition

(Rs. in crore)

Year	*Plan Expenditure*	*Total Expenditure*	*Per cent*
2001-02	280.20	991.70	28.2
2001-02	305.00	1101.10	27.7
2002-03	419.00	1304.00	32.2
2003-04	400.00	1359.50	31.5

Source: Government of Puducherry Budget documents.

eighties. It further declined to 22.5 per cent in the first half of the nineties but subsequently bounced back to 30 per cent in the latter half of nineties. Plan expenditure outlay as per cent of total expenditure outlay during subsequent four years indicates slight improvement only (Table 2.16).

In comparison to 1999-2000, developmental revenue expenditure in 2003-04 increased by 33 per cent whereas non-development expenditure has increased by 50 per cent.

2.9.2 Regional Balance

Till recently, the entire UT of Puducherry is treated as single revenue district with only one IAS Collector. However, for the purpose of development planning each region is treated as a separate unit due to peculiar geographical position of Karaikal, Mahe, and Yanam. Schemes are formulated to ensure balanced development in all the four regions, with outlays broadly on the basis of regional composition of population. Separate meetings are held in the three outlaying regions and proposals included in respective Annual Plans.

Only recently, Karaikal has also been made a revenue district under a separate IAS Collector.

The regional budgeted and revised outlay for Annual Plans of 2004-05 and 2005-06 are indicated in Table 2.17.

TABLE 2.17

Annual Regional Plans

(Rs. in lakh)

Region	*2004-05*		*2005-06*	
	Budgeted Outlay	*Per cent*	*Budgeted Outlay*	*Per cent*
Puducherry	36,207	78.6	85,297	77.6
Karaikal	6,901	15.0	16,919	15.4
Mahe	1,445	3.1	3,681	3.3
Yanam	1,547	3.3	4,103	3.7
Total	46,100	100.00	1,10,000	100.00

TABLE 2.17 (contd..)

In terms of composition of population, the regional position is as follows:

	Per cent
Puducherry	75.5
Karaikal	17.5
Mahe	4.0
Yanam	3.0
Total	100.00

Source: Government of Puducherry Budget documents.

2.10 Taxation and Levy Powers, also Tax Buoyancy

The tax revenue of Puducherry is mainly from the five sources of: (i) sales tax; (ii) state excise; (iii) land revenue; (iv) stamp duty and registration fees; and (v) taxes on vehicles. It can tap about 19 sources of taxes as indicated in the List II of Seventh Schedule. It should not limit itself to exploiting only the above five taxes, further with major slant only on the first two sources i.e., sales tax and state excise.

With introduction of uniform floor rate in sales tax, there was a dip in sales tax for a few years. However, now the Centre has come forward to transfer Rs.70 crore to Rs.80 crore annually of the CST, for which Union Territory is not eligible, to compensate Puducherry for the same. The annual growth rate of local sales tax during the nineties was around 15 per cent to 16 per cent. After the year 2000-01 the annual growth of local sales tax till 2003-04 is insignificant. During the last two years, state excise is stagnating at Rs.87 crore to 88 crore. Further non-tax revenue (other than electricity revenue) is also stagnating at Rs.21 crore to 23 crore.

With annual central transfer pegged at around Rs.500 crore besides pressing for CST collection from centre, Puducherry should:

i. Widen its sources of tax revenue, beyond the already chosen five.

ii. Vigorously tap sales tax and state excise and efficiently collect the same.

iii. Bridge the gap (Rs.35 crore) between electricity receipts and expenditure by revising electricity tariff, which is much lower than its neighbour Tamil Nadu.

iv. Explore possibility of luxury tax and service tax.

During the last two decades, annual growth rates and buoyancy of taxes in Puducherry are as follows:

	Tax Buoyancy	*Growth Rate*
During eighties	13.5 per cent	1.4
During nineties	12 per cent	1.1

After the introduction of uniform floor rate of sales tax, tax revenues dipped in Puducherry after 2000-01. Possibly earlier tax buoyancy was due to diversion of trade.

2.11 Summary

Taking advantage of the potential growth in GSDP, buoyancy in taxes, lowering of interest rates and tapping of public-private finance initiatives, Puducherry government should initiate prudent medium-term fiscal policy measures. This is imperative as Puducherry is on the anvil of transforming from its current status as Union Territory to a full-fledged state.

References

Government of Puducherry (2003). *Pondicherry Vision 2020*. Madras School of Economics.

Annual Financial Statement of the Union Territory of Puducherry (Various Years) and CSO, Government of India, (1999, 2000) diskettes.

RBI (2000). *State Finances-a Study of Budgets of 2000-01*.

Report of the CAG of India (2003).

Government of Puducherry Budget documents.

Chapter 3

Industrial Growth

3.1 Introduction

Puducherry is not rich in natural resources, which could have provided the Union Territory a comparative advantage in specific industries. Its attraction to investors however has been in terms of easy availability of land, water, labour, and power, and in terms of incentives, concessions and tax holidays. Over the last couple of decades, the Union Territory has built up infrastructure which has served as a basis for industrial growth. Infrastructure needs to be strengthened to aid growth in the future.

The growth of the secondary sector in general and the manufacturing industry specifically has been well over 37.5 per cent and 19.03 per cent between 1990-91 and 1994-95 respectively. In the period 1995-96 to 2001-02 they have grown at a rate of about 46 per cent and 34 per cent respectively (Table 3.1). Both the contribution of the secondary sector and the manufacturing sector has significantly contributed to Puducherry's growth. Employment in this sector has grown at a rate of about 7 per cent per annum between 1993-94 and 1999-2000.

TABLE 3.1

Contribution of Secondary Sector to the GSDP at Current Prices

Years	*Secondary Sector*
1980-81 to 1984-85	53.21
1985-86 to 1989-90	47.05
1990-91 to 1994-95	37.05
1995-96 to 2001-02	45.82

Source: CSO, Diskette data for GSDP 1993-2003.

3.2 Puducherry Industrial Economy—Pattern, Growth and Export Potential

Industrial development in Puducherry has been a thrust for the government for some time now. Industrial development was targeted as a thrust area as early as the Second Five Year Plan (1956-57 to 1960-61). The idea of industrial estates was floated at this time and the first industrial estate was operational by the Third Five Year Plan (1961-62 to 1965-66). During the Fourth Five Year Plan (1969-70 to 1973-74), both public and private investment in industry was emphasised. Puducherry attracted industry through subsidies for power, 'efficient' labour and various incentives and concessions.

The Puducherry Industrial Promotion and Development Corporation (PIPDIC) has been the nodal agency involved in infrastructure development and financial assistance and is the lynchpin behind industrial growth in the Union Territory. PIPDIC is responsible for much of the industrial development and the growth centres in Karaikal and the IT Park and the Electronic Park at Thirubuvanai. It also operates refinance schemes of IDBI and SIDBI.

3.2.1 Growth in Industrial Sector

An analysis of the last two periods namely 1990-91 to 1994-95 and 1995-96 to 2001-02 when the secondary sectors' contribution to the GSDP has increased by almost 9 per cent reveals interesting changes in the components contribution. Manufacturing registered has significantly increased its contribution from almost 19 per cent to 34 per cent; a jump of 15 per cent, while the share of construction has come down from almost 12 per cent to almost 5 per cent (Table 3.2). The above analysis is based at current prices. A corresponding table at constant prices is shown in Table 3.3.

TABLE 3.2

Contributions of the Various Components of the Secondary Sector at Current Prices

Years	1980-81 to 1984-85	1985-86 to 1989-90	1990-91 to 1994-95	1995-96 to 2001-02
Secondary Sector	53.21	47.05	37.05	45.82
Manufacturing Registered	10.97	11.13	19.03	33.89
Manufacturing Unregistered	7.09	7.40	6.01	6.93
Construction	35.11	28.46	12.03	4.85
Electricity, Power, and Water Supply	0.04	0.06	-0.02	0.16

Source: CSO, Diskette data for GSDP for 1993-2003.

TABLE 3.3

Contributions of the Various Components of the Secondary Sector at Constant Prices

Components in the Sectors	1980-81 to 1984-85	1985-86 to 1989-90	1990-91 to 1992-93	1993-94 to 1997-98	1998-99 to 2001-02
Secondary Sector	55.43	56.04	51.22	35.53	49.32
Registered Manufacturing	11.26	13.70	23.49	23.96	40.88
Unregistered Manufacturing	6.17	6.30	4.36	8.62	6.99
Construction	40.02	38.31	26.13	4.83	2.62
Electricity, Power, Water Supply	-2.01	-2.26	-2.76	-1.87	-1.17

Source: CSO, Diskette data for GSDP for 1993-2003.

3.2.2 Contribution to GSDP

The large growth rates in the industrial sector between 1995-96 and 2002-03 meant that the contribution of industry to total GSDP increased significantly. As we can see from Table 3.4 in absolute terms the secondary sector's contribution grew from Rs. 33946 lakh in 1995-1996 to Rs. 168368 lakh in 2002-03 at constant prices. In percentage terms, the industrial sector contribution increased from 31.51 per cent to 57.30 per cent at constant prices. This increase was mostly due to the growth in the manufacturing sector.

3.2.3 Employment

Employment in the secondary sector increased from 30,786 in 1971 to 55,132 in 1991, an almost two-fold increase. As can be seen from Table 3.5, much of the increase can be accounted for due to growth of employment in the manufacturing sector, which increased from 25,243 in 1971 to 41,248 in 1991. Percentage-wise, however, the share of manufacturing to total secondary sector employment actually decreased from 82 per cent in 1971 to 75.14 per cent in 1991. Construction on the other hand, increased from 14.48 per cent to 20.15 per cent during the same period.

Between 1993-94 and 1999-2000 the employment in the manufacturing sector shot up due to a large increase in the manufacturing sector and construction too. In relative terms the contribution of the manufacturing sectors' share has risen to 37.44 per cent.

3.2.4 Exports

Exports in 2003 has picked up in value terms. In 1989 exports was only Rs. 28 crore (mostly of manufactured goods), in 1997-98 it went up to Rs. 320 crore and in 2003 to Rs.464 crore, an increase of 45 per cent since 1997-98 in value terms. As Table 3.6 illustrates chemicals and chemical products accounted for Rs. 121 crore, leather products for Rs. 82 crore, machinery parts for Rs.80 crore and metal parts for Rs. 67 crore are leading product exporters. The exports of the different categories of industries are shown in Table 3.7. Exports in 2004-05 have doubled to that of 1998-99.

TABLE 3.4

Contribution of Industrial Sector to Total GSDP in New Series (at Constant Prices)

(Rs. in lakh)

Item	1995-96	1996-97	1997-98	1998-99	1999-2000	2000-01	2001-02	2002-03
Manufacturing - Registered	20048	44874	78403	83897	79682	103100	112222	145073
Manufacturing - Unregistered	7973	12826	13825	13418	13510	14698	15175	16239
Construction	5112	5223	5330	5922	6125	5401	5484	5610
Electricity, Gas and, Water Supply	812	855	674	1182	1255	1314	1396	1495
Secondary Sector Total	33946	63778	98232	104419	100571	124512	134277	168417
Percentage Contribution of Industrial Sector to Total GSDP	31.51	45.60	54.60	51.61	48.30	51.43	52.51	57.30

Source: CSO, Diskette data for GSDP for 1993-2003.

TABLE 3.5

Employment in the Secondary Sector

Item	1971	1981	1991	1993-94	1999-2000
Manufacturing	25243 (82.00)	32852 (80.54)	41428 (75.14)	55677 (65.09)	94392 (69.19)
Electricity, Gas, and Water Supply	1086 (3.53)	1375 (3.37)	2596 (4.71)	4416 (5.16)	4141 (3.03)
Construction	4457 (14.48)	6562 (16.09)	11108 (20.15)	25450 (29.75)	37917 (27.79)
Secondary Sector Total	30786 (100)	40789 (100)	55132 (100)	85543 (100)	136450 (100)
Per cent to Total Employment	21.83	23.54	21.06	27.60	37.44

Source: Census of India, Puducherry Series.

TABLE 3.6

Export Performance - 2003

Item	Rs. in crore
Chemical and Chemical Products	121
Leather Products	82
Machinery Parts	80
Metal Parts	67
Non-metallic Mineral Products	58
Cotton Textiles and Garments	34
Rubber and Plastics	15
Paper Products	7
Total	464

Source: Government of Puducherry, Industries Department.

TABLE 3.7

Exports from SSI, MSI and LSI

(*Rs. in crore*)

	1998-99	1999-2000	2000-01	2001-02	2002-03	2003-04	2004-05
SSI	140	78	117	57	75	154	136
MSI	125	101	103	120	209	175	219
LSI	64	128	67	143	181	200	246
Total	330	307	286	320	465	529	601

Source: Government of Puducherry, Industries Department.

Compounded annual growth rate of exports during the period 1998-99 to 2004-05 is about 9 per cent.

3.3 Impact of WTO

Puducherry must develop its industrial potential keeping in mind WTO. Economic liberalisation and the opening up of the economy to foreign trade and capital inflows will require industry to become more competitive because of greater competition. Not only tariffs will be reduced but also new environmental and labour standards will come into effect. Industry must ready itself for these new challenges which in turn will offer greater export potential as foreign markets will be more readily accessible if international standards are adhered to judiciously.

The government of Puducherry must play a proactive role with regard to WTO. A WTO cell may be created with the necessary expertise to aid industry in finding new markets. This cell should have a close working relationship with industry so that exchange of ideas is a two way process.

This vision for the industrial sector will help Puducherry to fulfill the goals of its industrial policy. The vision is also aimed at employment creation and environmental sustainability. On the one hand, emphasis has been placed on promoting industries such as leather industry which have good employment potential. On the other hand, emphasis has also been placed on promoting industries which are less polluting and to reward industries, which meet environmental standards.

3.4 Industrial Policy Reforms

The industrial sector occupies a prominent position in the economy of the Union Territory of Puducherry. The main focus of the Union Territory has consistently been on developing a strong industrial sector, as it cannot depend on agriculture alone for its development. The significant contribution of the industrial sector is reflected in its growing share in the state income, which was 44.29 per cent in 2000-01.

The main objectives of the industrial policy are:

- To promote sustainable industrialisation in the Union Territory of Puducherry.
- To gainfully utilise the human resource of the territory and maximise employment.
- To improve the standard of living and quality of life of the people.
- To conserve the environment of Puducherry for sustained and rapid industrial growth.
- To participate in the globalisation of the economy with greater exports and imaginative imports.
- To take advantage of the special features of Puducherry including its heritage and culture.
- To ensure balanced industrial development in all the regions of the Union Territory.

3.4.1 Incentives and Concessions

We have often heard it said that many industries came to establish themselves in Puducherry because of low sales tax rates that had been maintained by the government there. It is further stated that since Puducherry has had to adopt uniform floor rates for sales tax in accordance with an all-states agreement, the advantage of low rates has gone, many industries are closing down and consequently there is not much prospect of future industrial growth. While low rates of local sales tax would have some advantage, since Puducherry comprises a small territory, in many industries local sales tax would have constituted only a small share. However, low local sales tax rates would also help to some extent inter-state sales because CST has a ceiling of 4 per cent. The five-year income tax holiday given to industries in Puducherry must have been of much greater help. We find from data made available to us that the process of industrial growth is continuing. There is a case, therefore, for urging the Central government to continue the tax holiday for income tax for another period of ten years. It is also necessary to phase out CST as early as possible as they work against the interests of small and not highly industrial states like Puducherry. Meanwhile, Puducherry should bring down its CST rate to an average of 1 per cent.

3.4.2 Role of Government

Creating the right environment must be part of a wider strategy to redefine the roles of the public and private sector. In addition to this, however, the government has a few other important tasks. The government can play an important role in enhancing the efficiency of labour. In the past, many companies came to Puducherry because of cheap and skilled labour. Today, however, labour has become more of a constraint and many companies are recruiting their workforce from outside the Union Territory. This is not beneficial to the Union Territory in the sense that unemployment rates are increasing steadily. As there are a number of industrial training institutes (ITIs) in Puducherry run by the government, a concerted effort should be made to provide skills which are in demand. The government needs to liaise with industries much more actively so as to assess what their labour requirements are and then provide the necessary skills to those undergoing training. PIPDIC has an important role to play in terms of liaison. To date, PIPDIC has been largely responsible for setting up industrial estates and growth centres and offering a range of subsidies and incentives to industry. It should, however, also assume a much more active liaison role between the government and industry. This should be of a two way nature. PIPDIC should become a channel through which industrialists can air their concerns and at the same time it can offer consultancy services to industrialists.

The government also has certain regulatory functions it needs to fulfill. The most important of these is zoning. As Puducherry is actively attempting to promote an industrialisation policy which is sustainable, it must ensure that industries do not crop up in an unregulated manner. While the government should not discourage entrepreneurs from investing in the Union Territory by enforcing cumbersome rules and regulations with regard to converting land for industrial purposes, it must also not encourage or permit haphazard growth. Zones classified as 'industrial areas' have already been earmarked by the government and industrial activity should be confined to these zones. Equally important is that the government enforces pollution norms and encourages industry to establish individual and common effluent treatment plants. In the process of redefining the role of the government, the government will have to address the issue of PSUs. As illustrated above, most of the PSUs are running at a loss and placing a huge burden on the exchequer. There are difficult issues involved in resolving the crisis which exists in most PSUs. On the one hand, a closure of these units would result in significant employment loss. On the other hand, they cannot be kept open merely for this reason given the huge losses they are incurring. The government has suggested that some of these units be modernised, namely, Anglo-French Textiles and Puducherry Distilleries Ltd. While this needs to be explored, privatisation cannot be totally ruled out. The Puducherry government must set up a Disinvestment Commission to look into the possibility of allowing private investors to takeover these companies. The status of the different projects is enclosed in the Annexure to the chapter.

Alongside exploring the possibilities of disinvestment, the government must more actively pursue Voluntary Retirement Schemes (VRS). In the case of Anglo-French Textiles, the company has already sent a proposal for a new VRS with an enhanced VRS package for approval for closing down the weaving department and the financial commitment required on the part of the government. Similar options need to be explored in the other PSUs.

3.5 Competitive Classification of Industries

3.5.1 Number, Types and Location of Industries as on 2004

According to the government records there are 7340 industries in the Union Territory in 2004. Out of this, 65 are large scale, 147 medium scale and 7128 small scale. The total employment in these industries was 85841 out of which 59775 are in the small scale sector. Total investment in industrial units in Puducherry in 2004 is Rs. 19201.1 million, more than half of it going to large scale units. Production value is Rs. 116611.5 crore, the SSI sector contributing about 45 per cent of the production value and the LSI and the MSI contributing about 27 per cent production value each (Table 3.8).

TABLE 3.8

Industrial Units, 2004

Item	*LSI*	*MSI*	*SSI*	*Total*
Units (Nos.)	65	147	7128	7340
Investment (Rs. in million)	10800.6	3926.8	4473.7	19201.1
Employment (Nos.)	17467	8599	59775	85841
Production (Rs. crore)	32648.7	31056.4	52906.4	116611.5

Source: Government of Puducherry, Industries Department.

3.5.2 *Large, Medium and Small Scale Industries in Puducherry*

The types of industries prevalent in Puducherry in 2003 are listed in Table 3.9. Chemicals and chemical products is the largest category comprising 21.7 per cent of the total industrial units, followed by food products (12 per cent), metal products (11.5 per cent), cotton products (11.3), and leather, rubber, plastic products (10 per cent). Most of the industries in all the sub-sectors are small scale in nature. As per location, 80 per cent of these industries are in Puducherry region. An overview of industries in Puducherry is shown in Table 3.9.

TABLE 3.9

Large, Medium and Small Scale Industries as on October 2003

Categories	*LSI*	*MSI*	*SSI*	*Total*	*Per cent to Total*
Food products	5	12	850	867	12.0
Cotton products	7	7	801	815	11.3
Wood products	-	-	455	455	6.3
Paper products	4	7	404	415	5.7
Leather, Rubber, Plastic products	8	31	684	723	10.0
Chemical and Chemical products	19	27	1525	1571	21.7
Non-metallic Mineral products	6	5	288	299	4.1
Metal products	2	18	814	834	11.5
Machinery products	7	27	587	621	8.6
Miscellaneous products	-	-	196	196	2.7
Personal Services	3	8	184	195	2.7
Repairing Servicing	-	-	246	246	3.4
Total	61	142	7034	7237	100.0

Source: Government of Puducherry, Industries Department.

Table 3.10 also shows Puducherry's growth in industries in the large, medium and small scale units. The dominance of the growth of the small scale industries in terms of number of units, investment, annual production as well as employment is evident from the table.

A region-wise growth in industralisation is depicted in Table 3.11 and 3.12. Production in terms of value, investment and the number of units set-up in Puducherry from 2000-01 to 2002-03 is shown in Table 3.13. It shows significant growth both in employment and production. However, the increase in the number of units and

TABLE 3.10

Flow of Investments and Employment

Industry Type	*1990-91*	*1997-98*	*1998-99*	*1999-2000*	*2002-03*	*2003-04*	*2004-05*	*CAGR [12 yr] per cent*
No. of SSIs	3883	5726	6014	6199	7031	7126	182	5.2
No. of MSIs	53	93	113	115	142	147	10	8.9
No. of LSIs	29.28	76.04	300.84	108.02	125.43	389.59	137.59	24.1
Investment (Rs.crore)	464.75	785.41	1086.25	1194.27	1530.52	1920.11	2057.11	12.5
Employment	48166	67066	71955	74597	82790	85841	88275	4.9

Source: Government of Puducherry, Industries Department.

TABLE 3.11

Industries Region-wise Break-up

No.	Items/Details	Units	2004-05 Region-wise Puducherry	Karaikal	Mahe	Yanam	State
1.	No. of Small Scale Industries	No	5914	879	245	270	7308
2.	No. of Medium Scale Industries	No	147	4	0	8	159
3.	No. of Large Scale Industries	No	56	10	1	3	70
4.	Investment	Rs. lakh	154170	42269	765	8903	206107
5.	Production	Rs. lakh	1148170	69976	7734	49181	1275061
6.	Sugar Factories	No.	2	-	-	-	2
7.	Textile Mills	No.	5	2	1	-	8

Source: Puducherry at a glance 2005.

TABLE 3.12

Region-wise Large Scale, Medium Scale and Small Scale Industries

No.	Region/State		1992-93	1993-94	1994-95	1995-96	1996-97	1997-98	1998-99	1999-2000	2000-01	2001-02	2002-03
1	2		3	4	5	6	7	8	9	10	11	12	13
1.	Puducherry												
		LSI	2	1	0	0	1	1	10	3	1	4	7
		MSI	1	2	12	7	9	5	18	4	12	3	7
		SSI	282	251	265	215	78	191	248	144	196	116	263
2.	Karaikal												
		LSI	2	0	0	0	0	1	0	1	0	0	1
		MSI	0	1	0	0	0	0	0	0	0	0	0
		SSI	29	10	19	33	8	23	26	23	22	12	15
3.	Mahe												
		LSI	0	0	0	0	0	0	0	0	0	0	0
		MSI	0	0	0	0	0	0	0	0	0	0	0
		SSI	6	6	6	7	3	9	5	14	7	5	4
4.	Yanam												
		LSI	0	0	0	0	1	0	0	0	0	0	1
		MSI	0	0	0	0	0	0	0	0	0	0	0
		SSI	7	5	11	9	3	11	9	4	14	13	10
5.	State												
		LSI	4	1	0	0	2	2	10	4	1	4	9
		MSI	1	3	12	7	9	5	18	4	12	3	7
		SSI	324	272	301	264	92	234	288	185	239	146	292

Source: Government of Puducherry, Industries Department.

TABLE 3.13

Production and Employment of Manufacturing Industries

No.	Items	2000-01	2001-02	2002-03
(1)	(2)	(3)	(4)	(5)
1	Number of Units	6608	6762	7070
2	Total Employment	77341	79232	82843
3	Total Investment (Rs. in lakh)	142951	150470	163113
4	Total Production (Rs. in lakh)	767091	89400	1035601

Source: Government of Puducherry, Industries Department.

TABLE 3.14

Number of Small, Medium and Large Scale Industries and Labourers and Workers registered under Factories Act, 1948

No.	Items	2000-01	2001-02	2002-03
(1)	(2)	(3)	(4)	(5)
1.	Small Scale Industries	6438	6584	6876
2.	Medium Scale Industries	127	132	139
3.	Large Scale Industries	43	46	55
4.	Total Factories (1+2+3)	6608	6762	7070
5.	Workers	77341	79232	82843

Source: Government of Puducherry, Industries Department.

investments is not very high. Table 3.14 shows industrialisation in the various categories of industries from 2000-01 to 2002-03. Puducherry's basic growth comes from SSI.

3.6 Hardware Capital of India

Puducherry has been labelled the IT hardware capital of India, recently due to the governments IT policy which is comprehensive and provides a blueprint for planning and implementation. The main features of the policy are:

- To provide the common man easy access to information in all spheres of life.
- To make the government machinery citizen friendly by facilitating transparency, efficiency and quick decision making in the administration.
- To impart IT training in order to increase IT literacy and creation of trained manpower.
- To create a healthy investment environment and encourage and accelerate the growth of IT-related industries with attractive policies.
- To establish a good information and communication infrastructure.
- To create an organisational structure to achieve the above objectives by 2005.

The IT policy has been framed under two categories namely, the short-term (3 years) and the long-term (5 years), in view of the high rate of obsolescence in the information technology sector.

A number of realisable goals of IT policy need to be used as benchmarks as identified in the draft plan 2005-2006. They are:

- Developing the infrastructure, which is needed to attract IT industries to Puducherry.
- Promoting the IT industry (especially the IT-enabled industries) as a major actor in the economy.
- Introducing e-governance and ensuring that all departments completely switch over to e-governance.
- Encouraging the growth of IT-education centres (both public and private), which impart high-quality (and updated) education.

3.7 Development of Small Enterprises

The growth of small scale enterprises in Puducherry has to be divided into three segments, the first segment is the pre-merger period, the second is the post-merger period but before economic liberalisation and the third being after economic liberalisation. Only in the post merger period and before economic liberalisation the industrial growth was significant because of the following reasons:

- The Central Investment subsidy to the tune of 25 per cent on the fixed assets (with monetary ceiling of 25 per cent) was in existence unto December 1989, which was a real boost to the new industries.
- The existence of Power subsidy to a tune of 33.3 per cent maximum was another thrust for the industrialists to set-up their new ventures in Puducherry.
- The various sales tax incentives namely sales tax holiday, lesser tax on raw material purchase etc., that made the Puducherry origin industries price competitive with others.

After economic liberalisation (1991), the Government decided to withdraw the subsidy incentives to various industries. Thus the Central investment subsidy was withdrawn and the power subsidy was also forced to be withdrawn due to heavy financial burden to the exchequer. This has hampered the growth of industries. The momentum of the growth was hardly sustained by income tax holiday and by sales tax incentive.

3.8 Industrial Pollution

Surface water and groundwater have been affected by industrial pollution. The Mettupalayam industrial estate has contaminated the surrounding groundwater with heavy metals, salts and fluoride. Two borewells have been closed since they were found unfit for drinking and new ones were drilled. Groundwater in Pillayarkuppam—Kirumambakkam has also been contaminated with heavy metals.

Thus industrial pollution from estates and other locations has begun to affect the quality of air, water and land and therefore the quality of life of the surrounding region. Regulatory measures have to be implemented to ensure proper environmental management. Either individual or common effluent treatment plants may be needed. Further growth of industries should take into account the environmental consequences, particularly the use of water as well as the potential for pollution of the air or water or disposal of hazardous wastes. Environmental friendly industries can be encouraged in Puducherry. Maintenance of existing industrial estates needs to be given priority too. The disposal of toxic wastes is also a matter of concern, following the surreptitious dumping of toxic wastes in Ousteri tank in 1993. Location of disposal of the same needs to be identified to ensure that these wastes are disposed in an environmentally sound manner.

3.9 Villages and Small Enterprise Sector

Khadi and Village Industries continue to be relevant even in the midst of highly competitive phase of industrial growth. These industries would receive the support of the government in the interest of thrift and dignity of manual labour and for the protection of rural artisans. Puducherry *Khadi* and Village Industries Board has been further activated to play an important role in promoting these industries to generate more employment in rural areas.

Women, handicapped persons and old people would be given higher priority in taking up *Khadi* and Village Industries. Women organisations like Maathar Sangam, will be encouraged to work for *Khadi* and Village Industries.

Progress of *Khadi* and Village industries produce has been phenomenal. The same is indicated in Table 3.15.

3.10 Small and Tiny Enterprises

The small scale industrial sector has emerged as a dynamic and vibrant sector of the economy of the Union Territory. The Government of India has already de-licensed this sector. In tune with policy, the Union Territory Administration has further simplified to promote the small and tiny enterprises.

Service sub-sector is a fast growing area and there is a need to give due importance to it in view of its recognised potential for generating employment. Hence, all industry-related service and business enterprises are recognised as Small Scale Industries and their investment ceilings will correspond to those of tiny enterprises.

A greater degree of awareness to produce goods and services conforming to national and international standards would be created among the Small Scale Sector.

The aim of District Industries Centre is in:

In development of industries

- To develop the small scale industries and cottage Industries in the Union Territory of Puducherry.

TABLE 3.15

Progress of *Khadi* and Village Industries: Production

Sl. No.	*Items/ Unit*	*1992-93*	*1993-94*	*1994-95*	*1995-96*	*1996-97*	*1997-98*	*1998-99*	*1999-2000*	*2000-01*	*2001-02*	*2002-03*
1	*2*	*3*	*4*	*5*	*6*	*7*	*8*	*9*	*10*	*11*	*12*	*13*
1	Cotton *Khadi**	52262	43978	39082	40211	25144	16631	16281	17825	19010	6507	18582
2	Silk *Khadi**	1034	721	1361	1292	696	515	546	738	2210	194	1249
3	Polyester *Khadi**	22350	67420	103345	66395	136440	138950	143455	120525	0.00	0.00	0.00
4	*Khadi* Hands+	943610	749184	610950	550342	798538	563770	642165	850335	976000	800712	963247
5	Brush#	1.21	1.27	2.52	1.54	1.48	0.56	1.30	1.49	2.82	1.94	3.40
6	Leather Goods#	3.25	3.55	3.11	4.30	1.08	1.51	3.57	1.82	2.01	1.42	1.59
7	Kutir Soap#	0.91	1.55	2.33	2.24	0.19	0.42	4.60	1.80	1.74	3.64	4.21
8	CandB Unit#	0.81	2.01	1.66	1.35	5.12	0.45	0.77	0.82	3.14	10.71	6.96
9	Handmade Paper#	0.04	0.45	0.00	0.00	0.04	0.31	1.70	0.54	0.49	1.17	0.76
10	Readymade Garments	0.00	0.00	0.00	0.00	0.00	0.00	0.00	0.00	0.00	1.76	0.65
11	*Agarbathi*	0.00	0.00	0.00	0.00	0.00	0.00	0.00	0.00	0.00	0.20	0.51
12	Korai Mat	0.00	0.00	0.00	0.00	0.00	0.00	0.00	0.00	0.00	0.10	0.03

Note: * Metres
\+ Nos
\# Rs. Lakh

Source: Government of Puducherry, Industries Department.

- To develop the human skill needed for the above industries by sending the youth to industries to gain experience by working in the plant itself.
- To bring the modern techniques developed to the knowledge of industrialists, entrepreneurs and to their representatives.

In development of handicrafts

- To revive the vanishing handicrafts.
- To increase the number of artisans by giving training and to boost their livelihood.
- To develop new techniques in handicrafts in the territory.
- To enhance sale of handicraft articles.

In development of *khadi* and village industries

- To arrange for grant-in-aid for the development of *khadi* and village industries through Puducherry *Khadi* and Village Industries Board.

In development of coir

- To develop the coir based industries.

In marketing and publicity

- To arrange for exhibition/publicity for sales of products manufactured in the Union Territory.

In implementing centrally sponsored schemes

- To implement the welfare schemes on self-employment introduced by the Central government.

The physical and financial progress of the various plan schemes in Puducherry is enclosed in Annexure A-3.1. The current progress is satisfactory in most of the schemes.

3.11 Summary

With dwindling agriculture/primary sector, all steps to accelerate industrial growth is vital for the economy of Puducherry. Industrial policies should facilitate growth of employment-oriented but non-power-intensive and non-polluting industries such as computers and IT, engineering items, electronics etc., so that power availability and groundwater are not affected. State should tap public-private partnership mode to provide world-class infrastructure for accelerated growth of industries with increasing slant on exports.

References

CSO, Diskette data for GSDP, 1993-2003.

Census of India, Puducherry Series.

Government of Puducherry, Industries Department.

Puducherry at a Glance 2005.

Government of Puducherry (2003). *Pondicherry Vision 2020*. Madras School of Economics.

ANNEXURE A-3.1

FINANCIAL PROGRESS

No.	Name of the Scheme	Date of Approval	Project	Central Release	Release by State/Other	Total Expenditure Agencies	Status of UC	Status Progress Report
1.	Electronic Park, Thirubuvanai	1991-92	4.00 crore	Nil	3.84	4.11	Furnished	Total area is 52.00 acres. All development works, namely, road, drain, laying of water supply line, sewerage line works were completed. Regarding construction of one more RBF building work order issued on 23.2.2006 tendered amount of Rs. 81.00 lakh. Work is under progress. Out of 131 plots, 116 plots were allotted. 15 plots are vacant at present.
2.	Growth Centre	1997	31.00 crore	6.50 crore	8.35 crore	14.40 crore	Furnished	Development works namely, Package I and II under Phase I-A have been completed.
3.	Special Economic Zone	23.11.2004 (In principle)	283.17 crore	Nil	11.11 crore	10.33 crore	Required UC issued to Government	A State SEZ Policy is notified.
4.	Information Technology Park	1999	-	-	5.25 crore	1.65 crore	Furnished	18 Acres of land at Puducherry Engineering College campus was taken possession from Education Department in the First Phase. Guest House building was purchased for Rs. 55.00 lakh and converted as 16 modules/built up space. 13 modules have been allotted and 3 modules are vacant at present. Satellite Earth station has been set up at cost of about Rs. 2.49 crore. It is proposed to implement the Phase-II at cost of Rs. 43.986 crore towards construction of multistoried building at a cost of Rs. 10.50 crore).

(Contd....)

(...contd...)

No.	Name of the Scheme	Date of Approval	Project	Central Release	Release by State/Other	Total Expenditure Agencies	Status of UC	Status Progress Report
5.	Integrated Infrastructure Development		6.65 crore	Nil	1.85 crore	3.87 crore	Furnished	Total extent is 65 acres. An amount of Rs. 2.41 crore has been paid by PIPDIC to Revenue Dept. towards compensation on 20.4.2004. First instance Topographic survey work was taken up through M/s. Geo-Gird Systems, Chennai on 19.12.2005. Recently Government of India has cancelled IID project, vide Lr. No. 18(47)/2000-IID dt.10.4.06 of the O/o. The Development Commissioner, SSI, Ministry of SSI. Hence, land is to be transferred to SEZ.
6.	Aside							
a.	Export Facilitation	2.8.2004	1.25 crore		—	0.02 lakh	Being sent	Revised Building Plan prepared.
b.	Establishment of Call Centre and Business Process Outsourcing Centre	2.8.2004	—	Rs. 3.00 crore released during the year 2002-03 and Rs. 1.50 crore released during the year 2003-04	—	—	—	
c.	Construction of one No, of flatted shed at Electronic Park at Thirubuvanai	2.8.2004	0.75 crore		—	—	—	Completed.
d.	Construction of boundary wall at IT Park, Pillaichavady	2.8.2004	0.15 crore		—	—	—	Completed.

PHYSICAL PROGRESS

No.	Name of the Scheme	Date of Approval	Land Acquired	Plots/ Sheds Developed	Plots/ Sheds Allotted	No. of Units Established	Capital Invested by Units	Employment Generated	Remarks
1.	Electronic Park Thirubuvanai	1991-92	52 acres	131	116	116			
2.	Growth Centre	1997	596.41 acres	74	15	1	25 lakh	15 persons	Development works namely, Package I and II under phase I-A have been completed. The remaining Package-III, IV and V are yet to be taken up.
3.	Special Economic Zone	23.11.2004 (In Principle)		-	-	-	-	-	Land acquisition completed.
4.	Information Technology Park	1999	18 acres	27 modules	24 modules	14			—

(Contd....)

(...contd...)

No.	Name of the Scheme	Date of Approval	Land Acquired	Plots/ Sheds Developed	Plots/ Sheds Allotted	No. of Units Established	Capital Invested by Units	Employment Generated	Remarks
5.	Integrated Infrastructure Development	—	65 acres	Note developed	Not applicable	Not applicable	Not applicable	Not applicable	—
6.	Aside								
a.	Export Facilitation Counter	2.8.2004	—		—	—	—	—	Revised Building Plan prepared.
b.	Establishment of Call Centre and Business Process Outsourcing Centre	2.8.2004	—	Rs. 3.00 crore Released during the year 2002-03 and Rs.1.50 crore released during the year 2003-04	—	—	—	—	
c.	Construction of one no. of flatted shed at Electronic Park at Thirubuvanai	2.8.2004	—		-	-	-	-	Completed.
d.	Construction of boundary wall at IT Park, Pillaichavady	2.8.2004	—		—	—	—	—	Completed.

OUTCOME BUDGET (Rs. in lakh)

No.	Name of the Scheme/ Programme	Objective/Outcome	Outlay 2006-07 (Rs.in lakh)	Quantifiable Deliverables	Processes/ Timelines	Remarks/Risk Factors
1.	Training	214.24				
	a) In-Plant Training	Under the programme, training is given with a stipend @ Rs. 750/- Rs.1500/- and Rs.2000/- p.m. according to their qualification for a period of one year to the unemployed youths of UT of Puducherry to make them to acquire better skill in the different trades of industrial activities so as to start eight their own industries or to get employment in established industries Rs. 200 will be paid to industrial units towards raw materials wastage per trainee per month.	154.08	It is proposed to train 950 candidates	1 year	i) The SISI, Chennai has evaluated that about 50 per cent of the people trained under this scheme have got employed. ii) In order to make the scheme more employment-oriented, it is proposed to introduce new and need based trades into the scheme.
	b) Vocational Training	This scheme has been introduced in the year 2004-05 for the first time with the approval of the Government. Under the scheme, training is given with a stipend @ Rs.750 and Rs. 1500 p.m. according to their qualification for a period of 6 months in certain trades such as, tailoring, beauty parlour, and jute bag making, etc., which are more relevant to the rural/village women to get self-employment and to provide opportunity to create additional	55.04	500 candidates are proposed to give training	6 months	--

(Contd....)

(...contd...)

No.	Name of the Scheme/ Programme	Objective/Outcome	Outlay 2006-07 (Rs.in lakh)	Quantifiable Deliverables	Processes/ Timelines	Remarks/Risk Factors
		income resources. The response for this trade is mainly from women especially hailing rural areas. During the training period Rs. 450 will be paid per trainee per month to the trainer for honorarium and wastage of raw materials. In addition, rent subsidy will be paid to the trainer @ Rs. 500 per month per unit.				
	c) Advanced/ High Skilled Training	i) This training programme has been introduced in the year 2005-06 for the first time. Under the scheme, training is given with a stipend of Rs. 1500 and Rs. 2000 p.m. according to their qualification to the candidates who have completed the basic training interested for advance training in their trade or the candidates who are willing to undergo some special high skilled training are to be sponsored to the relevant reputed units in the neighbouring states so as to develop their skills for making them to start their own ventures or to get suitable better employment opportunity. ii) Under the scheme, travelling allowances are given to the trainees, i.e., one time to and fro expenses restricted to II Class trainee are, course fees/ honorarium and accommodation charges are also given to the trainer/instruction as per their norms.	15.88	100 Nos. candiates will be trained	Period of training may vary depends upon the courses offered.	--
	d) Entrepreneurship Development Programme	i) To develop entrepreneurship skill, training is given under Entrepreneurship Development Programme (EDP) for setting up of their projects. Prospective trainees will be recommended to the banks for availing loan.	1.97	It is proposed to conduct 6 EDPS	Period each EDP is week/ 2 weeks	i) Focus will be on self-employment oriented activities in demand ii) It is proposed to give importance to Women Group Oriented activities. iii) Credit schemes like PMRY will be linked.
	e) Grant-in-aid to Puducherry Management and Productivity Council (For conducting Management Training and Administration)	Under the scheme, management training is being given at 90 per cent subsidised rate to the Entrepreneurs/Industrialists/ their representatives in the various disciplines namely, Financial Management, Marketing Management, Quality Control and Productivity Management, etc., to run their units successfully through PMPC.	12.50	450 candidates are proposed to be given training	Period of each programme is one day	--
2.	Motivation of SC/ST/Women Entrepreneur to Start Industries	Various kinds of subsidies are being provided in order to encourage entrepreneurs/ industrialists to start industries in this UT of Puducherry	100.00	30 Units	Based on the availability of funds	—

(Contd....)

(...contd...)

No.	Name of the Scheme/ Programme	Objective/Outcome	Outlay 2006-07 (Rs.in lakh)	Quantifiable Deliverables	Processes/ Timelines	Remarks/Risk Factors
3.	Development of Handicrafts	i) To revive the vanishing crafts. ii) To restore the traditional handicrafts. iii) To develop the skill and livelihood of rural unemployed youth.	112.87	628	1 Year	—
4.	Development of *Khadi* and Village Industries Board	i) To promote and develop the *Khadi* and Village Industries Programmes/activities with a view to create rural employment. ii) To achieve the above object, the said scheme is continued to give grant to PKVIB to meet out its administrative expenses during X plan period, besides grant of sales rebate.	400.00	—	—	—
5.	Development of Coir Industries	i) To develop coir and coir based industries.	16.65	210	1 Year	—
6.	Fiscal Assistance to new Industries	Grant of subsidy to IT and Thrust area industries	25.00	10 Units	Based on the availability of funds	---
7.	Marketing and Publicity	i) To promote sale of products of small scale industries cottage and tiny sector products. ii) Marketing is the greatest problem for the cottage and tiny units become sick due to the marketing problem. Sales rebate of 15 per cent was given for sales or products through recognised emporia during the past plan periods in addition to the exhibition being conducted by the District Industries Centre in Puducherry and other States. District Industries Centre has been participating in exhibitions being held in other cities like Madras, Bangalore and India International Trade Fair, New Delhi etc. These exhibitions serve as an effective tool for promotion and sale of cottage and tiny and small scale industries sector products. Hence, this scheme has to be continued during X Plan Period also.	93.00	190 Units	1 Year	—
8.	Share capital assistance to Public Sector Corporation (PIPDIC and PDL)	Share capital assistance will be provided to PIPDIC and Puducherry Distilleries Ltd.	100.00	—	Based on the availability of funds	Financial Assistance for IT Park
9.	Development of Infrastructure for Industrial Development	To foster industrial growth in the Union Territory of Puducherry and to provide improved infrastructure to facilitate the entrepreneurs to set up their industries in the Union Territory of Puducherry.	3890-00	—	Based on the availability of funds	Financial Assistance for SEZ and Integrated Infrastructure Development.

(Contd....)

(...contd...)

No.	*Name of the Scheme/ Programme*	*Objective/Outcome*	*Outlay 2006-07 (Rs.in lakh)*	*Quantifiable Deliverables*	*Processes/ Timelines*	*Remarks/Risk Factors*
10.	District Industries Centre	The Scheme District Industries Centre is meant to provide all services and support required by the small entrepreneurs such as identification of suitable schemes preparation of feasibility reports, credit facilities and inputs for marketing and extension services at one place for setting up of small and village industries. District Industries centre assists all small scale, medium and large industries in obtaining various clearances and licence under Single Window System and also implements self-employment schemes like PMRY. To attend the above activities and to provide continued systematic service, it is proposed to continue this plan schemes 'District Industries Centre' during the 10th Five Year Plan (2002-2007) period.	28.00	—	—	Meeting the salaries of staff and office expenses.
11.	Assistance for Restructuring of AFT of PTC Ltd.	To provide financial assistance to Government owned AFT to modernise its spinning, weaving and processing facilities to increase productivity and to sustain its competitive strength.	1700.00	—	—	—
12.	Share capital Assistance to Swadeshee-Bharathee Textiles Mills Ltd	To provide financial assistance to Government owned Swadeshee-Bharathee Textiles Mills Ltd. For its spinning, weaving and processing facilities to increase productivity and to sustain is competitive strength.	500.00	—	—	—
13.	Incentives for Pollution Control Equipments and Energy Saving Devices	i) To encourage the entrepreneurs to install pollution control equipment in their units, so as to promote and maintain clean and pollution free environment in the Union Territory of Puducherry. ii) To encourage the entrepreneur to install energy saving devices and to use alternative sources of energy in lieu of petroleum and electricity. iii) To conduct carrying capacity study on the establishment of industrial units through professional agencies.	0.01 (token provision)	—	—	
14.	Strengthening of Directorate of Industries	Meeting the salaries of staff and office expenses.	20.23	—	—	—

Chapter 4

Agriculture and Rural Development

4.1 Agriculture

4.1.1 Introduction

The Union Territory of Puducherry is a group of four isolated regions (Puducherry, Karaikal, Mahe, and Yanam) scattered over different agro-climatic zones. Agriculture is one of the dominant sectors of the state and contributes less than 10 per cent of GSDP, varying between 4 to 8 per cent for the last 20 years. The share of agriculture in providing employment has been stagnant. It is one of the densely populated regions (2029 per sq.km.) of India (324 per sq.km.). About 50 per cent of the people live in rural area mainly depending on agriculture and another 20 per cent indirectly depend on agriculture. This implies that dependence on agriculture is higher without any perceptible increase in production. Few of the selected indicators of progress in agriculture are given in Table 4.1.

The land spread of the region is almost flat, characterised by deep red and alluvial soils of relatively good fertility levels. It is characterised by bimodal distribution of rainfall with an annual average of 1396.3mm. Mahe region receives the highest amount of rainfall (3070 mm) followed by Puducherry (1427mm), Karaikal (1230 mm), and Yanam (1200 mm). Nearly 83

TABLE 4.1

Indicators of Agricultural Growth

Indicator	*1980-81*	*1990-91*	*2000-01*	*2001-02*	*2002-03*
Rice Production (MT)	78654	58819	61012	66868	57514
Rice Productivity (kg/ha)	2479.48	2363.25	2334.32	2555	2530
Total Cereals Production(MT)	90273	60406	61905	67547	-
Total Cereals Productivity (kg/ha)	2529.01	2283.45	2343.02	-	-
Total Pulses Production (MT)	3137	2405	4034	463	618
Total Pulses Productivity (kg/ha)	475.95	490.02	679.35	-	-
Total Oil Seeds Production (MT)	4504	4146	2605	-	-
Total Oil Seeds Productivity (kg/ha)	1204.6	1460.89	2526.67	-	-
Nutrient (NPK) use (kg/ha) #	255.2	465.4	545.4	-	-
Gross Cropped Area Irrigated (ha)	42005	33527	34146	33633	31227
Gross Cropped Area (ha)	53981	43738	43277	39592	36382
Net Cropped Area (ha)	29908	27294	24330	23686	21568
Cropping/Intensity (%)	180.49	160.25	177.88	-	-
Total Cultivator (in number)	15841	17959	10,900	-	-
Total Agricultural Labour (in number)	54514	77203	72,251	-	-
% of Total Cultivator to Total Workers	9.14	6.86	3.2	-	-
% of Total Agricultural Labour to Total Workers	31.47	29.49	21.1	-	-

Note: # for the year 1980-1982, 1989-1991, and 1998-2000 respectively.
* for the year 1982, 1997, and 2000 respectively.

Source: Directorate of Economics and Statistics, Puducherry.

per cent of the area is irrigated by various sources like wells, canals, tubewells and tanks. Out of the total geographical area of 48,842 ha, net sown area is around 24,330 ha during 2000-01 with the per capita land availability of around 0.05 ha. Cropping intensity is about 178 per cent as against 133 per cent at all India level and is next only to Punjab (180 per cent). There is no natural reserve forest and the territory is fully developed for human habitation.

The four regions of the Union Territory lie in the east and west coasts, with a coastline of 45 km. and 675 sq.km. of inshore water, supplemented by 1347 ha of inland water and 800 ha of brackish water. The state has good potential for fisheries. As per the 2003 census, the total livestock population was 1,58,305 of which 49.3 per cent was cattle followed by 30 per cent of goats, 2.5 per cent of buffaloes, and 1.6 per cent of sheep. Growth rate in agricultural production and productivity is stagnant or negative, with degradation of natural resource base. The production pattern and trade needs are to be reoriented through small and marginal farmer friendly policies and programmes to meet the upcoming pressure of globalisation and free trade.

4.1.2 *Economy and Agriculture*

Even though the contribution of agriculture and animal husbandry is increasing in terms of quantity from 1997 onwards, its share to the total income is declining. Table 4.2 shows that share of agriculture and animal husbandry sector to state income sharply declined from 11.35 per cent in 1994-95 to 6.12 per cent in 2002-03. The decline in the share of agricultural sector to state income was more pronounced during 1997-98 as compared to rest of the years. It indicates decline in the growth of agricultural sector in spite of the efforts taken through government interventions and policies.

TABLE 4.2

Contribution of Agriculture and Animal Husbandry to State's Total Income

(Rs. in lakh)

Year	*Agriculture and Animal Husbandry*	*Contribution to State's Income(%)*
1994-95	12795	11.35
1999-2000	13386	4.12
2002-03	26115	6.12

Source: Directorate of Economics and Statistics, Puducherry.

The reduction in the contribution of agriculture to state income was synchronised with reduction in the percentage of agricultural workers to the total workers in the state (Table 4.3). It is important to note that the total agricultural worker population declined from 95,162 persons (36.35 per cent) in 1991 to 59,546 persons (17.39 per cent) in 2001. In spite of the increase in population, the sharp decline in the total agricultural workers which includes cultivators also, indicates de-peasantisation process.

According to 1991 census the primary sector, agriculture and allied activities provided about 39.2 per cent of employment to main workers, among which women had the major share of 54 per cent followed by 35 per cent by men (Table 4.4).

4.1.3 *Land Use Pattern*

The total geographical area of the state is 48,651 ha during 2003-04, of which area under forest is nil. The indicators of land use show the negative progress of growth in agriculture. Land used for non-agricultural purposes,

TABLE 4.3

Population by Employment Status (Percentage to Total Population)

Puducherry	*1991 Census*			*2001 Census*		
	Persons	*Males*	*Females*	*Persons*	*Males*	*Females*
Main Workers (%)	32.4	50.1	14.3	32.57	50.35	14.80
Marginal Workers (%)	0.7	0.4	0.9	2.60	2.77	2.43
Non-Workers (%)	66.9	49.4	84.8	64.83	46.88	82.77
Population (in number)	807,785	408,081	399,704	974345	486961	487384
Total Agricultural Workers (cultivators and agricultural labourers) in number	95,162			59,546		
Percentage of Agricultural Workers to Total Workers	36.35			17.39		

Source: Census of India 1991, 2001 and Season and Crop Report, Puducherry.

TABLE 4.4

Employment by Major Sectors (Percentage to Total Main Workers)

Sector	1991 Census		
	Person	Male	Female
Agriculture and Allied	39.2	35	54
Mining and Quarry	0.1	0.2	0.0
Primary Sector	39.3	35.2	54
Manufacturing	15.7	18	7.9
Construction	4.2	4.9	2.1
Secondary Sector	19.9	22.9	9.0
Trade and Commerce	14.7	16.2	9.2
Transport, Storage and Communication	3.2	4.1	0.1
Other Service	22.9	21.8	26.8
Tertiary Sector	40.8	42.1	36.1

Source: Census of India 1991 and 2001.

fallow land and uncultivable waste are increasing. During the last 20 years, area put to non-agricultural use increased from 11,211 ha in 1980-81 to 17,125 ha to 2003-04 and other fallow land from 352 ha in 1980-81 to 2360 ha in 2003-04. Area under permanent pastures and grazing land and miscellaneous trees and groves has come down during the last 20 years. It indirectly indicates the reduction in the common property resources. But area under cultivable waste increased from 1418 ha in 1980-81 to 3996 ha in 2003-04 and started to decline during the last three years. The net area sown had also decreased from 29,908 ha in 1980-81 to 20,647 ha in 2003-04. Area sown more than once had also decreased from 24,073 ha to 16,736 ha during the corresponding period. Similarly gross cropped area and area under irrigation also showed a decreasing trend. It was 53,981 ha in 1980-81 and 37,383 ha in 2003-2004. Cropping intensity was fluctuating around 160-180 per cent. However percentage of gross area irrigated to the gross cultivated area increased from 77.8 to 84, which indicates the intensive use of groundwater for cultivation (Table 4.5).

4.1.4 Land Holdings

The agrarian structure of the state underwent a drastic change. Since 1980-81 there is a significant increase in number of holdings as well as area operated by marginal farmers which clearly indicates the fragmentation of land holdings. There is a slight decline in number and area operated by small farmers. This shows that a number of small farmers have become marginal farmers due to progressive subdivision under the law of inheritance. There was a slight decline in both the number and area of

TABLE 4.5

Land Use Pattern

(in hectares)

Land Use Pattern	1980-81	1990-91	2000-01	2003-04
Total Geographical Area (ha)	46822	48581	48842	48651*
Forest	-	-	-	-
Barren and Uncultivable Land (ha)	82	80	113	70
Land put to Non-Agricultural Uses (ha)	11211	14057	15498	17125
Permanent Pasture and Grazing Lands (ha)	73	59	18	-
Land under Miscellaneous Tree Crops and Groves (ha)	2379	369	821	1097
Cultivable Waste land(ha)	1418	1815	4089	3996
Other Fallows (ha)	352	1903	3024	2360
Current Fallows (ha)	1399	3004	950	3356
Net Area Sown (ha)	29908	27294	24329	20647
Area Sown more than once (ha)	24073	16444	18948	16736
Gross Cropped Area (ha)	53981	43738	43277	37383
Cropping Intensity (%)	180.49	160.25	177.88	181.0
Gross Irrigated Area(ha)	42005	33527	34146	31436
Gross Irrigated Area to Gross Cropped Area (%)	77.8	76.6	78.9	84.0

Note: * Revenue records.
Source: Directorate of Economics and Statistics, Puducherry.

TABLE 4.6

Number and Area of Operational Holdings

Class (ha)	1980-81		1990-91		1995-96		2000-01	
	Number	Area(ha)	Number	Area(ha)	Number	Area(ha)	Number	Area(ha)
Marginal (< 1.0)	24466	8320	26096	9299	26500	9615	81019	9133
Small (1.0-2.0)	5014	7046	5011	7105	4419	6499	4054	5758
Semi Medium (2.0-4.0)	2722	7452	2587	7035	2195	6157	1908	5236
Medium (4.0-10.0)	1329	7791	1076	6212	893	5293	750	4263
Large Farmers (>10)	252	4364	205	3627	1216	2353	105	2048
All Size of Holdings	33783	34973	34975	33278	35223	29917	87836	26438

Source: Directorate of Economics and Statistics, Puducherry.

semi-medium, medium and big farmers. The average size of the holdings has decreased from 1.03 ha in 1980-81 to 0.88 ha in 1995-96 (Table 4.6).

Therefore, much attention is needed for development of marginal and small farmers. Both the number of holdings and area under semi-medium, medium and large farmers had declined, of which the decline is higher among medium and big farmers. Nearly 90 per cent of the holdings in the state operate less than two ha, which occupies nearly 54 per cent of the cultivated area. Around 10 per cent of the holders operate nearly 46 per cent of the cultivated area. It indicates the huge variation in the land holding pattern. The agricultural extension services need to refocus the strategies and approaches to cater to the needs of small and marginal farmers. Considering the inadequate asset level of these categories of farmers, appropriate multiple livelihood options have to be designed to enhance the coping strategies.

4.1.5 *Landless Agricultural Labour and Distribution*

Comparing the state as a whole, the agricultural labourers increased from 9.0 per cent in 1981 to 9.5 per cent in 1991 but during 2001 it declined to 7.4 per cent. In the same period number of cultivators also declined (Table 4.7). This may be due to the fact that there might have been a shift from agricultural occupation to non-agricultural occupation.

Involvement of women in agriculture has increased from 2,99,910 persons in 1980-81 to 3,99,704 persons in 1990-91 (Table 4.8). The percentage of women cultivators to women workers was 3.07 per cent in 1980-81 and it increased to 3.80 per cent in 1990-91. Percentage of female agricultural labour to total female workers was 56.6 per cent in 1980-81 and it decreased to 49.89 per cent in 1990-91. It is essential to enhance the skill and knowledge of the women farmers to reduce drudgery and improve their skill to tackle with the changing agro economy and trades. Agricultural labour force among the working force is a major category but so far any formal skill building programmes were implemented. It is also worth to note that no organised institutional mechanism is available, hence there is a need to establish a training centre/programme to cater the needs of the women agricultural labourers.

TABLE 4.7

Number of Agricultural Labourers

Year	Region	No. of Agricultural Labourers		
		Men	Women	Total
1980	Puducherry	24229 (10.7)	14243 (6.5)	38472 (8.7)
	Karaikal	10569 (17.8)	3582 (5.9)	14151 (11.8)
	Mahe	323 (2.4)	177 (1.2)	500 (1.8)
	Yanam	812 (13.8)	579 (10.1)	1391 (11.9)
	Total	35933 (11.8)	18581 (6.2)	54514 (9.0)
1990	Puducherry	35057 (11.3)	22707 (7.6)	57764 (9.5)
	Karaikal	12130 (16.7)	5156 (7.0)	17286 (11.9)
	Mahe	365 (2.4)	117 (0.7)	482 (1.4)
	Yanam	1061 (10.3)	610 (6.1)	1671 (8.2)
	Total	48613 (11.9)	28590 (7.2)	77203 (9.6)
2001	Total	41990 (8.6)	30105 (6.2)	72095 (7.4)

Note: Figures in bracket indicate percentages to the total.

Source: Directorate of Economics and Statistics, Puducherry.

TABLE 4.8

Women in Agriculture

Details	1980-81			1990-91			2000-01		
	Distribution of Workers	% to Total Main Workers Women	% to Total Main Workers	Distribution of Workers	% to Total Workers Women	% to Total Workers	Distribution of Workers	% to Total Workers Women	% to Total Workers
Female Population	299910	-	-	399704	-	-	487384	-	-
Total Main Worker Females	33085	-	19.10	57300	-	21.89	72162	-	22.73
Women in Agriculture									
As Cultivators	1017	3.07	0.59	2179	3.80	0.83	1102	1.52	0.35
As Agricultural Labourers	18581	56.6	10.73	28590	49.89	10.92	22963	31.82	7.23
Allied Activities	-	-	-	164	0.29	0.06	913	1.26	0.29
Total Main Workers	173247	-	-	261800	-	-	317367	-	-

Source: Directorate of Economics and Statistics, Puducherry.

4.1.6 Wages for Agricultural Labourers

The wage rate has increased steadily over the years. The increase is higher for ploughmen as compared to all other workers. This could be seen from the Table 4.9.

TABLE 4.9

Wage Rate of Different Workers

(in Rs.)

Categories	1980-1982		1989-1991		1998-2000	
	Men	Women	Men	Women	Men	Women
Plough Men	8.06	-	39.7	-	122.1	-
Sowers and Transplanter	-	3.2	-	12.5	-	34.5
Reapers and Harvester	7.2	6.5	16.5	15.1	38.2	38.2
Weeders	-	2.8	-	10.7	-	31.4
Other Agricultural Labour	7.1	-	23.9	-	66.3	-
Carpenter	11.8	-	44.3	-	116.1	-
Blacksmith	9.3	-	26.6	-	66.8	-

Source: Directorate of Economics and Statistics, Puducherry.

4.1.7 Cropping Pattern

Puducherry has a heterogeneous cropping pattern covering crops such as rice, groundnut, sugarcane, pulses, tapioca, fruits, vegetables, etc., whereas a homogeneous cropping pattern of rice followed by pulses is common in Karaikal region. Mahe region is characterised by plantation crops and Yanam is dominated by rice in both irrigated and rain fed systems.

TABLE 4.10

Area under Major Crops

(in ha.)

Crops	1980-81	1990-91	2000-01	2002-03
Rice	31722 (58.77)	24889 (56.90)	26137 (60.39)	24142 (66.36)
Total Cereals	35695 (66.13)	25732 (58.83)	26421 (61.05)	24469 (67.26)
Total Pulses	6591 (12.21)	4908 (11.22)	5938 (13.72)	1918 (5.27)
Groundnut	2983 (5.53)	2372 (5.42)	1175 (2.72)	1278 (3.51)
Gingelly	756 (1.40)	466 (1.07)	124 (0.29)	423 (1.16)
Sugarcane	1853 (3.43)	2829 (6.47)	2464 (5.69)	2330 (6.40)
Cotton	826 (1.53)	1062 (2.43)	452 (1.04)	314 (0.86)
Total Cropped Area	53981	43738	43277	36382
Cropping Intensity (%)	180.49	160.25	177.88	—

Note: Figure within ( ) are percentage to the total cropped area.

Source: *Season and Crop Reports* (various issues) of Puducherry.

The area of major crops is shown in Table 4.10. Rice is the principal crop and it occupies a major share of 66.36 per cent to the total cropped area in 2002-03. Among regions, Puducherry had the highest area under rice followed by Karaikal, Yanam, and Mahe. Even though both area under rice as well as total cropped area showed decreasing trend, the percentage area under rice to total cropped area has shown increasing trend from 58.77 per cent in 1980-81 to 66.36 per cent in 2002-03. The intensive mono cropping of rice without crop rotation is the predominant cropping system in the paddy fields and this has led to serious environmental and production consequences such as:

- Resurgence of pests and dominance of selected weed species as a consequence increased use of pesticides without considering the economic threshold level.
- Overexploitation of underground water.
- Destruction of soil physical properties and restricted nutrient use from the narrow root zone, due to puddling.
- Unbalanced application of chemical fertilisers without much use of organic manures leading to changes in the soil fertility status, especially micronutrients, causing ecological problems to both soil and water resources and affecting the flora and fauna diversity.

Area under total pulses was declining. The percentage share of area under total pulses was 12.21 per cent in 1980-81 and it decreased to 5.27 per cent in 2002-03. Area under pulses, especially green gram and black gram is higher in Karaikal compared to all regions. In Puducherry region a steep decline was observed under green gram and black gram. In Yanam region, area under green gram had increased while the area under black gram had declined. Area under groundnut was decreasing. It declined from 5.53 per cent in 1980-81 to 3.51 per cent of the total cropped area in 2002-03. Puducherry region had the highest area under the crop but it showed nearly 50 per cent decline over the years. In Karaikal and Yanam also, a decreasing trend was seen and there was no reported area under groundnut in Mahe region. The total area under gingelly is also showing a decreasing trend. The increase in the area under paddy is at the cost of pulses and oilseeds.

Sugarcane is one of the important commercial crops and the area under this crop is increasing from 3.43 per cent in 1980-81 to 6.40 per cent in 2002-03. Puducherry has the highest area followed by Karaikal. Cotton is another important commercial crop. But the area under cotton has decreased from 1.53 per cent in 1980-81 to 0.86 per cent of the total cropped area in 2002-03. Puducherry had the highest area under cotton followed by Karaikal and there was no reported area in Mahe and Yanam. Change in cropping pattern was mainly due to increase in the input cost, especially for pest management in cotton. In the case of sugarcane, sugar mills are providing package of support with buy back arrangements at a pre-fixed procurement price. This helps the farmers to reduce the market risk.

Rice occupies more than 60 per cent of the cropped area and commercial crops like sugarcane and cotton occupy about 10 per cent of the area. Rice requires nearly 1400 mm of water and in Puducherry much of the paddy cultivation depends on groundwater. Thus there is a need to introduce alternate crops with low water requirement to reduce the overexploitation of groundwater resources. Considering the geographical location, there is a good scope to introduce commercial floriculture with jasmine and crossandra and horticultural crops especially vegetables with market links and assured procurement price.

4.1.8 Horticulture

Horticulture is a major sector with commercial potential. Horticultural crops have higher calorific value compared to agricultural produce per unit of consumption. They are rich in vitamins and minerals and they have an important part in balanced diet for the human beings. These crops have another advantage of consuming less amount of water to produce one unit of output. Crop diversification can be effectively done by using horticultural crops as they can be good alternatives for the low value crops. Area and production of chillies declined over a period of time. Black pepper is an important spice and area under the crop is almost stagnant. Area under tamarind and tapioca is declining. Area under coriander has also declined. Betel nut also showed a declining trend in area (Table 4.11).

TABLE 4.11

Area under Horticultural Crops

(in hectares)

Crops	*1980-81*	*1990-91*	*2000-01*	*2001-02*	*2002-03*
Chillies	117	44	9	6	15
Black Pepper	13	12	12	12	12
Tamarind	73	67	63	71	71
Coriander	29	9	1	2	5
Betelnuts	70	67	65	65	64
Plantain	223	218	239	225	274
Mangoes	251	225	221	219	206
Cashewnuts	367	232	202	191	184
Onion	22	11	13	16	3
Tapioca	752	709	342	464	437

Source: Directorate of Economics and Statistics, Puducherry.

it is essential to bring crop diversification and balance in the cropping system for sustainable management of the natural resources especially water and soil. There is a need to invest in post-harvest processing, infrastructural facilities and market opportunities whenever new cropping pattern is introduced.

4.1.9 Productivity

Productivity of major crops have shown an increasing trend except paddy and cotton which decreased to 2322.9 and 837.9 kg/ha during 1998-2000 from 2525.9 and 1720.4 kg/ha in 1980-1982, respectively. Productivity of all other crops like cereals, oilseeds, pulses, and sugarcane increased. In spite of the higher use of fertilisers and improved technologies the yield in paddy and cotton had shown a decline which necessitates the need to closely study the farming system and develop sustainable production strategies (Table 4.12).

TABLE 4.12

Productivity of Principal Crops

(kg/ha)

Principal Crop	*1980-1982*	*1989-1991*	*1998-2000*	*2000-01*	*2001-02*	*2002-03*
Rice	2525.9	2386.9	2322.9	2491	2555	2530
Total Pulses	424.2	597.6	630.9	596	261	302
Total Oilseeds	1193.4	1494.1	2258.2	1181	1038	1111
Sugarcane	82849.6	87361.6	85196.6	81336	93251	89991.2
Cotton	1720.4	1101.4	837.9	865	877	885

Source: Directorate of Economics and Statistics, Puducherry.

TABLE 4.13

Annual Compound Growth Rate: Area, Production and Productivity

Crop	*Area*		*Production*		*Productivity*	
	1980-1982	*1989-1991*	*1998-2000*	*2000-01*	*2001-02*	*2002-03*
Paddy	- 2.31	0.22	-3.05	0.10	-0.76	-0.12
Green Gram	2.89	4.05	6.64	5.73	3.65	1.62
Black Gram	-6.31	0.16	-2.29	4.74	4.29	4.57
Total Pulses	-2.52	1.47	1.17	4.98	3.78	3.47
Groundnut	-1.63	-9.26	0.62	-4.21	2.28	5.56
Sugarcane	0.41	-0.11	1.86	-0.74	1.44	-0.63
Cotton	4.96	-10.33	2.21	-11.24	-2.62	-1.02

Source: Directorate of Economics and Statistics, Puducherry.

The estimates of growth rates showed the percentage change in area, production and productivity over a period of time. As shown in Table 4.13 negative growth rate was observed in area, production and productivity of paddy. Though the area under paddy attained a positive growth rate of around 0.22 per cent, the productivity recorded a negative growth rate of 0.12 per cent. Hence the positive gains in production (0.10 per cent) were attributed to expansion of area. But in sugarcane, area, production and productivity showed negative growth rate since 1990s. In groundnut, area and production had negative growth rates but the productivity had shown a positive growth rate. In cotton, all the three, area, production and productivity had negative growth rate.

It may be concluded, that the area and production have shown negative growth rate for major crops, except paddy and pulses. And productivity has shown negative growth rate except for groundnut and pulses. Technology transfer and availability of inputs such as quality seeds and irrigation plays major role in deciding the productivity of crops. These areas need grater attention apart from market facilities with better remunerative prices.

TABLE 4.14

Commercialisation of Agriculture

(in ha.)

Year	*Total Food Crops*		*Total Non-food Crops*		*Gross Cropped Area*
	Area	*Percentage*	*Area*	*Percentage*	
1980-81	46606	86.34	7375	13.66	53981
1990-91	35172	80.42	8566	19.58	43738
2000-01	36389	84.08	6888	15.92	43277
2003-04	31699	84.80	5684	15.20	37383

Note: Percentage to Gross Cropped Area.

Source: Season and Crop Reports (various issues) of Puducherry.

Share of food crops and non-food crops to the gross cropped area are shown in Table 4.14. In Puducherry the share of area under food crops to the gross cropped area declined slightly from 86.34 per cent in 1980-81 to 84.80 per cent in 2003-04 and share of non-food crops to gross cropped area slightly increased from 13.66 per cent in 1980-81 to 15.20 per cent in 2003-04. There was only a marginal shift from food crops to non-food crops from 1980-81 to 2003-04, which indicates the lack of commercialisation in agriculture.

There is a need to promote commercialisation of agriculture with suitable farming systems that promote sustainable agro-ecosystem. Also, the higher proportion of food crops indicates the subsistent nature of farming. In the context of globalisation and liberalisation, it is essential to focus on high value crops with suitable value addition and innovative market links. In order to bring the economy of scale it is essential to develop grassroot governance and local institutions through Uzhavar Udaviyagams which would facilitate group farming/ cooperative farming with market-based crop planning approaches. Planned market-oriented production system should be promoted at regional level with Decision Support Systems (like allocation of area, linking subsidy in a comprehensive manner etc.) through cooperative or group farming approaches.

4.1.10 Irrigation

Irrigation plays a vital role in production and productivity of the crops. In Puducherry nearly 90 per cent of the net-cropped area is under irrigation. The major source of irrigation is groundwater in Puducherry and canal irrigation in Karaikal and Yanam regions.

TABLE 4.15

Area Irrigated by Sources

(in ha.)

Sources	*1980-81*	*1990-91*	*2000-01*	*2003-04*
Net Area Irrigated by Canals	10960	8979	8133	316
Net Area Irrigated by Tanks	0	0	0	0
Net Area Irrigated by Tubewells	14897	13353	13196	15026
Net Area Irrigated by Other Sources	189	103	61	2002
Total	26046	22435	21390	17344
% of Net Area Irrigated to Net Area Sown	87.1	82.2	87.9	84.0
Area Irrigated more than once in the Same Year	15956	11090	12756	14092
Total Irrigated Area (Gross)	42005	33525	34146	31436
% of Total Irrigated Area (Gross) to Total Sown Area	77.8	77	78.9	84.1

Source: Directorate of Economics and Statistics, Puducherry.

Total area irrigated in 1980-81 was 26046 ha. It declined to 17344 ha in 2003-04 (Table 4.15). The percentage of net area irrigated to net sown area showed slight decline from 87.1 per cent in 1980-81 to 84.0 per cent in 2003-04. Among the sources, net area irrigated by tubewells is largely followed by canals and other sources. Net area irrigated by tubewells increased from 14897 ha in 1980-81 to 15026 ha in 2003-04. Net area irrigated by canals declined from 10960 ha in 1980-81 to 8133 ha in 2000-01. It declined further to 316 ha in 2003-04. It is evident that the area under surface water sources like canal irrigation has declined and there was no area under tank irrigation. Increase in the area under tubewell irrigation indicates overexploitation of groundwater. The groundwater management studies carried out in Puducherry region have pointed out that there was a fast decline of water level due to overexploitation. Government of Puducherry has initiated tank rehabilitation programme in eight irrigation tanks with the main objective of sustaining agricultural production by tapping surface water with a consequent replenishment to the aquifers system. It is essential to promote mandatory rainwater harvesting system to recharge the underground water especially in village ponds. Under Tank Rehabilitation Programme 84 village level Water Users Associations have been in operation and it is suggested to establish a functional linkage with Uzavar Udhaviyagams and facilitate water literacy.

4.1.11 Soil Management

The soil type in the state is dominated by black clay soil followed by sand and silty clay. The intensive monoculture of paddy has led to the changes in the soil organic carbon status which has come down from 0.48 in 1980 to 0.32 per cent in 2003-04. It indirectly indicates the reduced soil biological activity, and water and nutrient holding capacity. Also, the continuous use of high dose of chemical fertilisers (NPK) has led to micronutrient deficiencies in large areas. Repeated paddy cultivation for the long period has changed the soil physical properties, creating hardpan and sub-soil compaction. This would make the land unfit for cultivation in the long run. Also, care should be taken to arrest or reduce the damage due to soil salinity. Season and field-based soil testing coupled with balanced application of organic and inorganic fertilisers and inclusion of pulse crops in crop rotation would help to save the soils from degradation.

4.1.12 Agricultural Inputs

Modern agricultural development revolves around the use of a variety of inputs in the form of improved seeds (high yielding varieties) and agro chemicals, which includes fertilisers, pesticides and fungicides. These inputs play a vital role in increasing production and productivity.

Fertilisers: Fertiliser consumption per hectare increased from 255.2 kg/ha in 1980-81 to 1305 kg/ha in 2004-05 inspite of decline in net sown area during the corresponding period. The use of nitrogenous fertiliser showed a continuous increase over the years, which might be due to subsides given to the nitrogenous fertilisers. Similarly use of phosphotic and potassium fertiliser showed steady increase over a period of 20 years;

however, in the case of potassic fertilisers, the rate of increase was less between 1990 and 2004.

TABLE 4.16

Consumption of Fertilisers

(kg/ha)

Year	*1980-81*	*1989-90*	*2001-02*	*2004-05*
Nitrogen	148.6	233.1	37	711
Phosphorus	40.1	93.6	59	313
Potassium	66.5	138.7	134	281
Total	255.2	465.4	230	1305

Source: Department of Agriculture, Puducherry.

Table 4.16 shows the excessive application of fertilisers even though soil fertility status is fairly good in Puducherry. The 2004-05 data shows that 1305 kg of fertiliser was used per ha. This excessive use does not help to get additional increase in yield; on the contrary, it affects the soil qualities, beneficial microbial loads and leads to severe micronutrient deficiencies especially when it is not accompanied by adequate application of organic manure. Further the unused nutrients after the crop uptake contaminate water bodies and affect the entire agro ecology. Thus, necessary sensitisation and capacity building programmes need to be imparted on proper nutrient management. Awareness to use more organic inputs need to be done by effectively using the Training and Visit System for improved soil health.

During 2004-05, only 42 MT of biofertiliser was supplied to the farmers, but the state has the potential to use up to 80 MT considering its net sown area. The use of biofertilisers and organic manures needs to be promoted in an integrated manner to gain the benefits of biofertiliser application (Table 4.17).

TABLE 4.17

Distribution of Biofertilisers

(in million tonnes)

Year	*Biofertiliser Distributed*
2003-04	42
2004-05	42

Source: Department of Agriculture, Puducherry.

Pesticides: Pesticide consumption is shown in Table 4.18, which indicates the declining use over the years. In 2000-01 it was 62 MT and it was reduced to 43 MT in 2004-05.

TABLE 4.18

Pesticide Consumption

(in million tonnes)

Year	*Pesticide in Tech Grade*
2000-01	62
2001-02	58
2002-03	52
2003-04	46
2004-05	43

Source: Department of Agriculture, Puducherry.

High yielding varieties: The details of area under high yielding varieties are furnished in Table 4.19. Area covered under high yielding varieties was 27,171 ha as against the target of 24,900 ha in 1998-99, which shows an achievement of 109.12 per cent above the target. The achievement was 97.39 per cent in 1999-2000 and 102.82 per cent during the year 2000-01.

TABLE 4.19

Area under High Yielding Varieties

(in hectares)

Year	*Targeted Area*	*Achievement*
1998-99	24900	27171
1999-2000	27300	26588
2000-01	27300	28070
2001-02	27300	28167
2002-03	27000	23981
2003-04	26000	22671
2004-05	26000	24290
2005-06	25000	23639

Source: Directorate of agriculture, Puducherry.

4.1.13 Farm Mechanisation

Number of manually operated seed cum fertiliser drills, sprayers and dusters had increased over the period of time. Manual drawn levelers increased from 77 to 1203. The implements that give employment opportunities like wooden plough, wetland puddler and animal cart have decreased. This indicates that reduced manpower involvement in production, especially in rural areas, where majority of the population depends on agriculture for their livelihood. Power operated sprayers increased over the years which indicate the wide use of pesticides. Moreover, all power operated implements like power tillers, agricultural tractors, mould board ploughs, disc harrows, levelers, trailers and power-operated thresher increased. Increase in number of implements showed (Table 4.20) the degree of mechanisation. On an average there was one tractor for every 70 ha of gross cultivated area, which is higher than the all India average of 66 ha. Considering the decrease in the labour force, it is essential to improve the appropriate farm tools and machineries. Care should be taken to ensure that the proposed interventions address the need of small and marginal farmer, without eliminating the opportunities available for the agricultural labour force.

TABLE 4.20

Farm Mechanisation

Implements	*Year*	
	1982	*1997*
Manually operated		
a. Seed cum Fertiliser Drill	1	6
b. Sprayer and Duster	634	808
Animal Operated Implements		
a. Wooden Plough	13402	2173
b. Steel Plough		
b1. Soil Stirring	912	1286
b2. Soil Turning	18	818
c. Seed cum Fertiliser Drill	-	5
d. Seed Drill	-	10
e. Leveler	77	1203
f. Wet Land Puddler	624	301
g. Animal Cart	3424	1353
Plant Protection Equipment Engines etc.		
a. Power Operated Sprayer Duster	105	182
b. Electric Pump Set	4199	2065
Tractor and Other Power Operated Implements		
a. Agricultural Power Tillers	9	92
b. Agricultural Tractors	289	483
c. Mould Board Plough	-	315
d. Disc Harrow	-	286
e. Seed cum Fertiliser Drill	-	14
f. Leveler	4	171
g. Trailers	158	191
Power Operated Rice Thresher	9	22

Source: Directorate of Economics and Statistics, Puducherry.

4.14 Government Schemes in Agricultural Development

Tables 4.21 and 4.22 show the expenditure on various schemes in agriculture. The total expenditure has increased from Rs. 1673.67 lakh in 2002-03 to Rs. 2326.34 lakh in 2004-05. The agricultural college and KVK have received a major share followed by crop production technology, development of horticultural crops, promotion of agricultural mechanisation, and development of infrastructure for agricultural marketing.

TABLE 4.21

Agricultural Development Schemes

(Rs. in lakh)

Name of the Scheme	*Actual Expenditure*		
	2002-03	*2003-04*	*2004-05*
CROP HUSBANDRY			
Crop Production Technology	370.00	356.34	419.22
Integrated Programme for Seed Promotion and Certification	35.52	66.69	68.98
Promotion of Agricultural Mechanisation	120.00	240.00	317.00
Infrastructure Development for Agriculture Marketing through PASIC	50.00	50.00	50.00
Group Insurance for Agricultural Labourers	50.00	50.00	—
Promotion of Post Harvest Technologies	15.00	—	20.00
Training and Capacity Building to Develop Human Resources	0.56	0.19	0.74
Introduction of e-Governance	8.63	20.00	22.32
Scheme for Monitoring and Evaluation	4.93	2.00	3.77
Soil Resources Management and Inputs Quality Control	17.88	20.15	28.90
HORTICULTURE			
Development of Horticulture Crops	207.27	332.39	292.94
AGRICULTURE RESEARCH AND EDUCATION			
Agricultural College and Krishi Vigyan Kendra	772.88	831.41	711.58
MARKETING AND QUALITY CONTROL			
Development of Infrastructure for Agriculture Marketing	21.00	57.88	290.89
Purchase and Distribution of Lands to Landless Rural SC People	—	—	100.00
Total	1673.67	2027.05	2326.34

Source: Department of Planning and Research, Puducherry.

TABLE 4.22

Sector-wise Expenditure on Schemes

(Rs. in lakh)

Sector	*Expenditure*				
	2000-01	*2001-02*	*2002-03*	*2003-04*	*2004-05*
Agriculture	1501.67	1571.72	1673.67	2027.05	2326.34
Animal Husbandry	810.61	817.13	856.81	965.88	1212.45
Dairy Development	6.31	59.72	13.50	95.16	80.00
Fisheries	296.18	415.29	322.20	557.18	841.39
Forestry and Wildlife	104.63	117.98	91.00	119.71	124.83

Source: Department of Planning and Research, Puducherry.

Among various sectors, agriculture has incurred the major share of expenditure followed by animal husbandry, fisheries, forestry and wild life. All the sectors have shown an increase in the expenditure over the years, among which agriculture sector has a major share in expenditure. It increased from Rs. 1501.67 lakh in 2000-01 to Rs. 2326.34 lakh in 2004-05. The expenditure pattern indicates the positive trend towards promoting growth through different agricultural schemes. A mechanism need to be developed with farmers' participation for continuous assessment of the progress and feedback for further improvement of the schemes.

4.1.15 Agricultural Finance

A. Capital Formation

Credit is one of the essential requirements for the agricultural development. Both formal and informal financial institutions are serving the farmers. In Puducherry the major source of finance is through informal institutions, mainly the processing unit operators, that is, rice mill owners. It is a traditional system with higher interest rate with speedy supply of short-term credit even on short notice. As a result, farmers are forced to sell either partially or full amount of production to meet the loan outstanding. The procedures involved in getting credit from formal institutions are time consuming, demands documentation and depends upon the value of the assets owned by the applicants. To overcome the difficulties, Kisan Credit Card has been introduced.

Kisan Credit Card provides adequate and timely support from the banking system to the farmers for their cultivation needs including purchase of all inputs in a flexible and cost effective manner. A model Kisan Credit Card Scheme was introduced in the year 1998 for implementation by all the rural financial institutions in the country. Under the Scheme, banks provided the Kisan Credit Cards to the farmers who are eligible for sanction of production loans (Table 4.23).

TABLE 4.23

Kisan Credit Cards issued up to March 2001

Agencies	*No. of Cards Issued*
Commercial Banks	4169
Cooperatives	799
Total	4968

Source: http://www.India stat.com

The procedures to get the card by the small and marginal farmers are cumbersome with practical constraints. Since timely credit is one of the major problems for the farming community, this scheme could be extensively promoted for wider use for the benefit of small and marginal farming communities, making the procedure simpler. Also it is essential to reduce the interest rate with flexible repayment modes. Special efforts need to be made to include women farmers to get access to Kisan Credit Card facility. In addition considering the risk factor to small and marginal farmers, suitable crop insurance systems need to be developed.

Table 4.24 shows the sector-wise target and achievement under annual credit plan. Achievement in agriculture sector was 112 per cent but it declined to 99 per cent. As per the data in the agricultural sector it is quite impressive on achieving the target, but it is still worth to note that farmers resort to other informal financial sources to meet their immediate requirements.

TABLE 4.24

Sector-wise Target and Achievement under Annual Credit Plan

(Rs. in crore)

Year	*Agriculture*			*Non-farm Sector*			*Trade/Service*		
	Target	*Achievement*	*% of Achievement*	*Target*	*Achievement*	*% of Achievement*	*Target*	*Achievement*	*% of Achievement*
2000-01	39.38	47.93	112	55.16	29.45	53	32.97	24.95	75
2001-02	39.36	33.96	86	54.63	44.36	81	44.75	44.03	98
2002-03	41.88	48.43	116	57.89	48.09	83	54.65	64.09	117
2003-04	33.18	32.92	99	46.59	30.96	66	57.23	44.69	78

Source: Annual Credit Plans, Puducherry.

TABLE 4.25

Comparison of Agricultural Credit to Gross Credit

(Rs. in crore)

Year	*Total Agricultural Credit*	*Gross Credit*	*% of Agriculture Credit to Gross Credit*
1992-93	47.95	232.64	21
1993-94	64.07	311.37	21
1994-95	55.24	336.79	16
1999-2000	68.43	734.90	9
2000-01	76.68	832.40	9
2001-02	89.61	1003.18	9
2002-03	114.70	1206.63	10

Source: Annual Credit Plans, Puducherry.

Table 4.25 shows reduction in the percentage of agricultural credit to total credit over the years and it was 21 per cent in 1993 and declined to 9 per cent in 2001-02. Then it increased marginally to 10 per cent in 2002-03. This declining trend reflects the importance given to agricultural credit. This situation as indicated above forced the farming community to look for other credit options with higher interest rate. The annual credit plan should be prepared considering the proposed changes in the cropping system and credit requirement.

4.1.16 Marketing of Agro Products

Apart from technology and credit, market plays an important role in augmenting the growth of agriculture. In the state of Puducherry, government promotes two kinds of market support—one is regulated market for paddy and uzhavar sandhai for direct retail marketing by the farmers.

Regulated market: There are five regulated markets at Thattanchavadi, Madagadipet, Kanniakoil, Koonichampet, and Karaikal. The government procures with an incentive at the rate of Rs.50 per quintal over the Minimum Support Price. In addition, the private traders in Puducherry as well as from Tamil Nadu are procuring paddy from the farmers. As such the problem of marketing of paddy does not exist. The Karaikal marketing committee operated five rural godowns for storing and providing produce pledge loans to the farmers. There are number of rice mills in Union Territory to provide necessary processing facilities to the farmers.

Uzhavar Sandhai (Farmers' market): The Uzhavar Sandhai programme is being implemented in Puducherry region for promotion of direct marketing facilities in respect of perishable commodities like vegetables, fruits, and flowers between the producer and the consumer. Public have given encouraging response so as to make arrangements for expanding this programme to a few more sub-urban centres in this region. As on date nearly 900 farmers have been identified as beneficiaries to trade in the uzhavar sandhais. The Puducherry Uzhavar Sandhai started with 70 stalls but due to the increase in the average number of farmers as well as consumers, the committee has constructed another 43 stalls.

Processing industry: In case of paddy in the context of post-harvesting, dehusking is the only practice followed. Considering the large area under paddy cultivation, the post-harvest processing with numerous value additions like rice bran oil, husk based products, etc., can be promoted. This could generate both employment opportunities and additional income to the farm families.

4.2 Allied Sector

i. Animal Husbandry

Generally animal population decreased during the period 1982–2003 in all categories except ducks and poultry units. Buffaloes' population decreased much more rapidly compared to cattle population. It might be due to the lack of much-improved breeds in buffalo compared to cattle and also the dry period of buffalo is five months compared to two months in cattle. Between sheep and goat, sheep population declined more than goat population. Due to reduction of all livestock categories the overall population also reduced. Reduction in the area under grazing and dependence of balanced feed from outside the region might have contributed to the decline. Since there are no feed preparation units at Puducherry, maize needs to be promoted in the region to reduce the feed cost. In the case of poultry sector it is slowly picking up. Scientific poultry, dairy and goat farming with suitable strong backward linkages need greater focus (Table 4.26).

TABLE 4.26

Livestock Census

(in numbers)

Category	*Year*		
	1982	*1992*	*2003*
Cattle	93526	92720	78095
Buffaloes	9042	7152	3887
Sheep	9030	3994	2589
Goat	52531	44016	47539
Total Livestock	176825	157761	158305
Ducks	9262	4857	34957
Other Poultry	246	1034	2402
Total Poultry	165126	123198	244475

Source: Directorate of Economics and Statistics, Puducherry.

Table 4.27 shows that milk production was 27,000 tonnes in 1992-93 and increased to 38180 tonnes in the year 2002-03. Egg production was 110 lakh in 1992-93 but it decreased to 77 lakh in 1996-97 and subsequently increased to 97.32 lakh in 2002-03.

TABLE 4.27

Milk and Egg Production

Year	*Milk (000 tonnes)*	*Egg (Nos in lakh)*
1992-93	27	110
2000-01	36	95
2002-03	38.18	97.32

Source: Animal Husbandry Department, Puducherry.

4.2.1 Infrastructure in Animal Husbandry

There is not much variation in infrastructure facility between the year 1997 and 2003 (Table 4.28). Due to the high number of decentralised production by the small and marginal farmers and agricultural labourers there is a need to increase number of hospitals and key village units.

TABLE 4.28

Veterinary Facilities

Description	*Year*	
	1997	*2003*
Veterinary Hospital	2	2
Mobile Veterinary	4	3
Veterinary Dispensary	14	15
Artificial Insemination Centre	3	3
Key Village Unit	52	61

Source: Animal Husbandry Department, Puducherry.

From the farmers perspective both crop cultivation and livestock are integrated but there is a need to promote and strengthen forward and backward linkages like vermicomposting, biogas, etc., for efficient utilisation of farm resources. Also, since paddy is the major crop cultivated in the region, there is a need to introduce preservation and value addition techniques like silage making for better utilisation of resources.

4.2.2 Fisheries Potential and Utilisation

Fisheries are well developed in Puducherry. All the four regions of the territory have maritime and posses rich fishery resources. Coastal length of Puducherry Union Territory is less when compared to all other states and union territories except Daman and Diu. Similarly the continental shelf is also only 1000 sq.km. as compared to all other coastal states. The proportion of number of landing centres (28) and number of fishing villages (50) is 1: 1.6. The total marine and inland population was 51,923 and 3,595 respectively, during 2005. Out of these 9,750 and 622 are active fishermen of marine and inland, respectively. There were 27 marine fishing village and 23 inland fishing villages in the UT. There is considerable scope for promoting intensive utilisation of resources with improved technologies in fisheries sector (Table 4.29).

TABLE 4.29

Fisheries Statistics across the Regions—2005

(in numbers)

Details	*Type*	*Puducherry*	*Karaikal*	*Mahe*	*Yanam*	*Total*
Fishermen Population	Marine	24135	11934	6000	9854	51923
	Inland	3059	536	0	0	3595
Active Fishermen	Marine	6226	2297	707	520	9750
	Inland	551	71	0	0	622
Fishing Village	Marine	15	10	1	1	27
	Inland	13	3	0	7	23

Source: Department of Fisheries and Fisherman Welfare, Puducherry.

TABLE 4.30

Fishing Crafts—2005

(in numbers)

Union Territory	*Traditional Crafts*	*Motorised Traditional Crafts*	*Mechanised Boats*	*Total*
Puducherry	5743	1376	491	7610

Source: Department of fisheries and Fisherman Welfare, Puducherry.

Table 4.30 shows that most of the fishermen still use tradition crafts compared to mechanised boats. The availability of fish seed increased during 1994 to 2000 (Table 4.31). There are no fish feed producing industries. This indicates the potential for the production of fish seed as well as fish feed since the production is at increasing rate.

TABLE 4.31

Fish Seed Availability

(million fry)

Year	*Fish Seed Availability*
1994-95	9.0
1999-2000	16.3
2000-01	15.1

Source: Department of Fisheries and Fisherman Welfare, Puducherry.

The contribution of marine fish is greater than that of inland fish. The production of inland and marine fish in the year 1980-1982 was 1238.9 MT and 14680.3 MT, respectively. It increased to 5550.0 MT and 31500 MT, respectively, in the year 2004-05. Production of total inland fish is increasing at a higher rate in Puducherry and Karaikal regions compared to Mahe and Yanam. Since Mahe constituted an urban area there is no area reported in inland fish production. In the case of marine fisheries also, the production increase is at higher rate in Puducherry and Karaikal than in Mahe and Yanam (Table 4.32).

TABLE 4.32

Marine and Inland Fish Production

(in million tonnes)

Sector/Year	*1980-1982*	*1989-1991*	*1998-2000*	*2004-05*
Inland	1238.9	2952.3	4222.7	5550.0
Marine	14680.3	31564.1	38721.7	31500

Source: Fisheries Directory and Information Book, Ocean life and medicine expo 2004.

To improve the socio-economic status of the poor fishermen families, various development schemes are being implemented to generate employment opportunities. The schemes implemented are as follows:

- Development of fresh water aquaculture;
- Development of brackish water aquaculture;
- Development of marine fisheries through mechanisation;
- Assistance to small-scale fisheries;
- Quick transport facilities to fisherman for transport of fish;
- Reimbursement of sales tax on oil processed for mechanisation fishing boats.

4.3 Agriculture and Rural Development

Government of Puducherry has introduced a number of schemes aimed at poverty alleviation and to provide employment opportunities to the rural people, especially agricultural labourers in the lean season. Some of the major programmes with credit linkage being implemented in the Union Territory of Puducherry are:

- Swarnajayanti Gram Swarozgar Yojana (SGSY)
- Prime Minister Rozgar Yojana (PMRY)
- Swarna Jayanti Shaharia Rozgar Yojana (SJSRY)
- Puducherry Adi-Dravidar Development Corporation for SC/ST (PADCO)
- Fish Farmers' Development Programme (FFDP)
- Women Development Programme
- KVIC-Margin Money scheme, etc.

TABLE 4.33

Target and Achievement of Development Programmes

Programme	*2001-02*		*2003-04*	
	Target	*Achievement*	*Target*	*Achievement*
SGSY: Revolving fund	349	321	400	400
SGSY: Economic assistance	67	41	65	76
PMRY (updated)	550	477	750	567
PADCO	650	668	650	657
SJSRY	565	257	625	360
BC and minority	500	529	700	859
Women Welfare	600	332	600	287
REGP-KVIC/KVIB	**	**	9	57

Source: Potential linked credit plan, Puducherry.

Differential response was seen for the different development schemes among the people. In schemes like PMRY, SJSRY, and Women Welfare, the target has not been achieved over the period of three years (Table 4.33). It was due to low participation by the people. In other schemes like BC and minority, PADCO the achievment is more than the targeted level. The response of the people is the main reason for the success. The reasons for the poor response to the schemes need to be studied and the lessons learnt are to be internalised and incorporated in subsequent project designing.

4.3.1 Food Security Status

Puducherry has less number of people under the category of below poverty line in rural areas (20.55 per cent) than urban (22.11 per cent) areas. Compared to the all India statistics (26.10 per cent) proportion of people living below poverty line is slightly lower (21.67 per cent). Ratio between population and food production indicates the deficiency ratio of food (Table 4.34). This ratio is increasing, which indicates clearly that the union territory is facing food insecurity. This is the direct implication of reduction in food production compared to the population growth.

TABLE 4.34

Food Deficit Ratio

Year	*Food Production Per Capita (in grams)*	*Food Deficit Ratio*
1980-81	4756432.98	6.307
1990-91	2401338.09	12.493
2000-01	2069663.62	14.495

4.3.2 Agricultural Research and Extension

The Royal Commission on Agriculture (1925) brought out the need for the research component in agricultural development. It is crucial to enhance the production and capacity of the farming communities to tune with the dynamic changes. The state has established its own agricultural college at Karaikal in 1987 and upgraded it as a research institute in 1997. A veterinary college and research institute has also been established in Puducherry to develop site-specific, need-based technologies to the farming community. The agricultural college and research institutes are slowly developing their capacity and catering to the needs of agricultural research and extension in the state.

Agricultural Extension Department is functioning with the aim of making available all the agricultural inputs, and high efficiency technologies required for scientific farming. It aims to provide all the technical needs to protect soil and crop health in order to increase the productivity. Apart from the traditional extension system, the state has taken efforts to use the developments in modern ICT sector for better delivery and provide need-based contents through Uzhavar Udaviyagam (Farmers' help centre).

During the Tenth Five-year Plan, Uzhavar Udhaviyagam, which is a village-based modern Information and Communication Technology supported help centre for farmers, was introduced as part of agricultural extension in the state for transferring knowledge and skills to the farmers. It is a one stop place for the farmers to learn/get latest technological know-how, weather details, schemes operated by the department, market forecast etc. So far 33 centres have been functioning and networked through a wide area network. In each of the centres local Farmers' Advisory Council have been formed which constantly interact with the Uzhavar Udaviyagams. Since it is functioning at the village level it could be effectively used as 'multipurpose centre' for other purposes apart from acting as a resource and input providing centre.

The other important aspect of agricultural extension is the involvement of private sector. Agro-based companies, the concepts of agri-clinics, farmers associations, etc., are emerging as extension agencies which could be identified and promoted.

4.4 Summary

In the context of globalisation and free trade, as India is one the signatories in Agreement on Agriculture under the WTO, Puducherry agriculture needs to gradually shift to 'demand driven–market oriented' production rather than 'production driven' agriculture to capitalise the available means of production namely soil and water, labour, enabling policies for industries etc.

Agriculture is the primary livelihood for majority of the population but the growth has been negative over the years. The declining area under cultivation, stagnant or declining productivity of the major crops, mounting constraints such as land degradation, poor soil fertility, overexploitation of water resources, intensive use of land and very high quantity of chemical fertiliser and pesticide usage, etc., are the major issues which need to be addressed to improve the growth in agriculture. In order to bring sustainable utilisation of the resources at the farm and village level the 'bio-village' concept (Box 4.1) is proposed.

BOX 4.1

Bio-village for Sustainable Development: Bio-village is an approach, which strengthens the capacity of the rural community to blend sustainable natural resource management with livelihood security through economically feasible, socially acceptable, ecologically viable, and gender sensitive interventions. It addresses concurrently the twin concerns of sustainable development namely, degradation of the natural resource base and persistence of rural poverty. The former is addressed through integrated resource management systems of both the biophysical resources (land, water and natural vegetation) and the human resources to which the rural households have access individually (farm households) and communally (Common Property Resources). Bio-village helps in strengthening the forward-backward linkages within the rural economy.

The bio-village concept could be implemented through Uzavar Udhaviyagams located in the village supported by Department of Agriculture in close collaboration with local farmer groups. Village specific plans could be drawn taking in to the consideration available natural and human resources. Through the Uzavar Udhaviyagams, horizontal network among bio-villages could be developed for sharing experiences and knowledge among the farming communities.

The net area cultivated is decreasing over the years affecting the total production. Given the situation vertical increase in production alone would be possible. Heavy application of chemical fertilisers has depleted the soil fertility, caused nutrient imbalances and micronutrient deficiencies, impeded drainage and increased the soil salinity. However, currently the production level is maintained except in paddy through increase in the productivity by using modern technologies coupled with high cropping intensity. Since paddy is the major crop it is essential to enhance the productivity to meet the needs of the growing population and to overcome the food insecure situation. It is essential to promote the utilisation of balanced application of nutrients, soil test crop response based application, integrated water and pest management, crop rotation with one pulse crop and post-harvest value addition. Though the government is promoting System of Rice Intensification (SRI) method, it needs to be intensified along with the above suggested terms.

Another reason for declining agricultural growth is timely unavailability of labour. Thus, increase in number of simple farm tools and implements suitable to the small and marginal farmers, would help in improving the agricultural activity in their farms.

Another important area, which needs attention, is irrigation. Number of tubewells has increased drastically and this has resulted in overexploitation of groundwater, leading to seawater intrusion and salinisation of soil. There is a need to promote farm based rainwater harvesting facilities wherever possible, coupled with the practice of water saving irrigation technologies like drip and sprinkler methods. Also, it is essential to renovate the common water storage systems to augment the ground water table. At present only in the major tanks the rehabilitation work has been initiated. It needs to be done at the village level and the annual renovation activity needs to be institutionalised at the village level through local *panchayat* and involving Uzhavar Udhaviyagams. The annual renovation activity could be linked with Rural Employment Guarantee Programme.

Crop diversification strategy needs to be comprehensive incorporating components like market linkages, necessary extension service and with the promotion of necessary infrastructural facilities.

Apart from agriculture, animal husbandry constitutes major proportion of the farmers' annual income. It is essential to promote integrated dairy farming with maximum forward and backward linkages to ensure sustainability. Goat farming has a better scope if it is combined with provision of adequate fodder sources and stall fed method of rearing.

Considering the pro-industry policies of the state, a number of integrated post-harvest value addition promoting zones could be identified to generate local employment as well as to ensure and enhance the profit to the farmers. Since the state has more area under paddy and considerable area under coconut there is a need to develop integrated processing facilities to diversify the value addition activities.

The role and the involvement of women in agriculture are increasing. Hence it is essential to give special focus to women. Similar to the project on Tamil Nadu Women in Agriculture (TANWA) it is essential to give special emphasis to mobilise women and make them technically empowered.

Given the predominant mono-cropping situation, it is necessary to promote crop diversification to conserve water and maintain soil fertility. Considering the geographic location horticultural crops, especially vegetable and flower cultivation could be promoted.

Area under wasteland is expanding every year and so wasteland development programme could be introduced for the benefit of the rural poor.

Inland crab and aquaculture rice-fish farming can be promoted to give additional income to the farmers. There is scope for production in this area as the Union Territory is endowed with good water resources.

Uzavar Sandhai is an upcoming marketing strategy for the benefit of small and marginal farmers. In order to strengthen it, it is necessary to improve infrastructure facilities to enable the farmers to reach the market. Even though the number of transport vehicles for agriculture has increased, farmers are forced to pay more to transport their produce to the market. For each commune/village, separate vehicle facilities should be provided to collect the produce from the fields and transport to the market at affordable cost. Apart from providing market facilities it is essential to fix and implement the Minimum Support Price for all the products throughout the year. Considering the greater percentage of small and marginal farmers, new approaches like group farming could be promoted with appropriate backward and forward linkages.

Finally it is essential to create awareness on the agricultural issues related to WTO and globalisation such as quality literacy and trade literacy to the existing state extension systems.

Chapter 5

Infrastructure Development

5.1 Introduction

To build on its earlier achievements in the field of industrial growth, Puducherry must focus its attention on considerably upgrading its infrastructure base in order to attract both domestic and foreign investments. A major reason why many industries located themselves in the Union Territory was the good infrastructure base that existed, particularly industrial estates, good roads, reliable power supply, and adequate water. Over the last few years, however, many of these have become inadequate for accelerated growth of the economy. The government should be a major player in trying to revamp the infrastructure base both through public sector investments and by encouraging more private sector participation in infrastructure development.

5.2 Industrial Estates

Industrial estates were to be the pillar of industrial policy in the Union Territory. At present there are six industrial estates in Puducherry, and an electronic estate in Thirubuvanai ready for plot allotment. In addition to these industrial estates, there are a number of industrial areas that are home to many industries. Industrial estates in particular were meant to provide a good infrastructural base to industries located within them. Besides good roads, assured water and power supply, was to be the norm. Puducherry Industrial Promotion Development and Investment Corporation (PIPDIC), moreover, has leased plots at concessional rates to industries and is in charge of continual maintenance of the estates.

Over time, however, the infrastructure situation in industrial estates has deteriorated significantly. The road conditions in many of the industrial estates are dismal despite the fact that industrialists often pay a monthly service charge for the upkeep of the estates. Power cuts are much more frequent than they once were and often occur without notice resulting in large losses to industries who depend on uninterrupted power supply. Serious efforts need to be made, therefore, to revamp these industrial estates so that they provide the necessary infrastructure. PIPDIC not only needs to invest sufficiently in improving the basic road infrastructure within these industrial estates but needs to work much more closely with departments such as the Electricity Department to ensure that power supply is continuous. As power tariffs are still much lower in the Union Territory than in the neighbouring states, that incentive remains very much in place. But cheaper tariffs are no substitute for good power supply. Other common facilities that need to be developed are sewage and effluent disposal facilities, security and banking. Much more effort also needs to be undertaken to bring industries aboard. Industries should be more actively involved in the planning of industrial estates and in decisions that affect them within the estates.

5.3 Power

Many of the problems within industrial estates are problems of industry in general. Power has become a major issue within the Union Territory. Industrialists are increasingly concerned with sudden cuts in power supply. While many industries (especially larger industries) have their own captive generation, the costs of this captive generation are substantially higher than the power bought from the Electricity Department.

The process of getting a power connection gets delayed in the Union Territory. As a result, while these industries have been ready for production, they have been either unable to commence or once again have had to depend on captive generation. The same problem exists with regard to obtaining additional power supply. Although many industries have expressed interest in expanding their operations in the Union Territory, they have been unable to get the necessary power.

Efforts, therefore, need to be made to improve the efficiency of power supply. Table 5.1 highlights the progress of electrification in Puducherry.

Region-wise progress in electrification is shown in Table 5.2(a) and (b). Region-wise electricity purchased and sold for 2002-03 is shown in Table 5.3.

TABLE 5.1

Progress in Electrification

Sl. No.	Items	Unit	As on 31st March				
			1999	2000	2001	2002	2003
1.	H.T. Lines	Km.	938.042	962.916	989.159	1016.928	1033.995
2.	L.T. Lines	Km.	3421.238	3487.200	3561.905	3651.671	3736.320
3.	Transformers	No.	1269	1312	1354	1408	1480
4.	Installed Capacity of Transformers	MVA	211.380	218.121	224.996	239.913	254.013
5.	Towns Electrified	No.	11	11	6**	6	6
6.	Villages and Hamlets Electrified	No.	263	263	263	263	263
7.	Domestic Connections						
	i) Light, Fan and Small Power	No.	128030	135538	143169	151038	158985
	ii) Hut Services	No.	29374	30547	—	32984	33871
8.	Commercial Connections	No.	25746	26766	27988	29311	30517
9.	Agricultural Connections	No.	10218	10267	10318	10362	10418
10.	Industrial Connections						
	i) H.T	No.	240	265	286	307	337
	ii) L.T	No.	4324	4445	4562	4712	4888
11.	Street Lights	No.	32152	32939	34179	35207	36656
12.	Maximum Demand*	MVA	239.584	255.348	267.494	303.87	332.071

Note: All towns and villages have already been electrified.
* Maximum demand related to the demand of a particular year. ** as per 2001 Census.
Source: Electricity Department, Puducherry.

TABLE 5.2(A)

Region-wise Progress in Electrification as on March 31, 2002

No.	Items	Unit	Puducherry	Karaikal	Mahe	Yanam	Total
1.	H.T. Lines	Km.	714.227	247.298	29.896	25.507	1016.928
2.	L.T. Lines	Km.	2676.606	670.067	233.452	71.546	3651.671
3.	Transformers	No.	1101	210	59	38	1408
4.	Installed Capacity of Transformers	MVA	199.607	273.11	74.20	55.75	602.667
5.	Towns Electrified	No.	3	1	1	1	6
6.	Villages and Hamlets Electrified	No.	163	100	-	-	263
7.	Domestic Connections						
	i) Light, Fan and Small Power	No.	113906	26487	6464	4181	151038
	ii) Hut Services	No.	23744	7458	440	1342	32984
8.	Commercial Connections	No.	21161	5022	2245	883	29311
9.	Agricultural Connections	No.	9672	674	3	13	10362
10.	Industrial Connections						
	i) H.T	No.	236	45	2	24	307
	ii) L.T	No.	3753	680	143	136	4712
11.	Street Lights	No.	23211	8230	2415	1351	35207
12.	Maximum Demand	MVA	211.934	77.723	3.460	10.170	303.287

Source: Electricity Department, Puducherry.

TABLE 5.2(B)

Region-wise Progress in Electrification as on March 31, 2003

No.	Items	Unit	Puducherry	Karaikal	Mahe	Yanam	Total
1.	H.T. Lines	Km.	723.436	254.486	30.101	25.972	1033.995
2.	L.T. Lines	Km.	2736.851	681.976	236.877	80.616	3736.320
3.	Transformers	No.	1159	220	61	40	1480
4.	Installed Capacity of Transformers	MVA	211.477	29.141	7.620	5.775	254.013
5.	Towns Eectrified	No.	3	1	1	1	6
6.	Villages and Hamlets Electrified	No.	163	100	-	-	263
7.	Domestic Connections						
	i) Light, Fan and Small Power	No.	119742	27887	6610	4746	158985
	ii) Hut Services	No.	24368	7714	447	1342	33871
8.	Commercial Connections	No.	22044	5230	2317	926	30517
9.	Agricultural Connections	No.	9704	698	3	13	10418
10.	Industrial Connections						
	i) H.T	No.	260	49	2	26	337
	ii) L.T	No.	3894	706	144	144	4888
11.	Street Lights	No.	24390	8343	2491	1432	36656
12.	Maximum Demand	MVA	275.368	40.824	5.109	10.770	332.071

Note: All towns and villages have already been electrified.

Source: Electricity Department, Puducherry.

TABLE 5.3

Region-wise Electricity Purchased and Sold, 2002-03

No.	Items	Unit	Puducherry	Karaikal	Mahe	Yanam	Total
1.	Electricity Purchased	Lakh of KWH	13860.26	4308.04	252.50	613.54	19034.34
2.	Electricity Sold		11642.37	3588.33	206.69	426.17	15863.56
2.1	Domestic Heat, Small Power Light and Fans	"	1829.90	324.88	76.76	63.73	2295.27
2.2	Hut Services	"	106.73	33.79	1.96	5.88	148.36
2.3	Commercial Light and Fans	"	556.03	89.94	34.30	27.37	707.64
2.4	Industrial Low and Medium Voltage	"	555.89	72.90	6.81	29.46	665.06
2.5	Industrial High Voltage	"	7071.71	2943.28	74.68	263.35	10353.02
2.6	Public Lighting	"	83.06	25.05	11.89	4.26	124.26
2.7	Irrigation	"	912.18	63.42	0.29	0.39	976.28
2.8	Public Water Works and Sewage Pumping	"	152.82	35.07	--	14.19	202.08
2.9	Export to Western Region	"	36.20	--	--	1.70	37.90
2.10	Unscheduled Interchange Sale of Power	"	337.85	--	--	15.84	353.69
3.	Per Capita Consumption	MVA	1583.99	2102.87	561.30	1358.90	5607.06

Source: Electricity Department, Puducherry.

The major physical achievements made under the Power sector in the Union Territory of Puducherry for the three years upto 2002-03 are:

1. Puducherry is directly connected to the Neyveli Lignite Corporation Thermal Station-II and is drawing power at 230 KV level through two separate 230 KV feeders at 230/110 KV Villianur and 230/110 KV Bahour Sub-Stations. These two Sub-Stations were earlier operating radially (individually) and are now interlinked by the 230 KV Villianur–Bahour line. The transmission lines were brought under the closed loop operation in

August 2003 for system reliability and improvement in voltage condition. Consequent to the tie-up, the interruption at 230 KV level had largely reduced. In addition, the voltage profile in the entire power system in Puducherry region had also improved substantially.

2. Under the Unified Load Despatch and Communication (ULDC) Project, a System Control Centre has been established at Puducherry. This ensures better control over the availability and allocation of power from various Central Generating Stations.
3. Four additional 16 MVA power transformers were energised, one each at Thethampakkam, Bahour, Eripakkam and Kurumbaper 110/22 KV Sub-Stations.
4. To improve the system voltage and to meet the growing demand in Thirubuvanai and its surrounding areas, an additional 16 MVA power transformer was energised at Thirubuvanai 110/22 KV Sub-Station. To provide reliable power supply in Karaikal region, an additional 16 MVA power transformer was energised at Sorakudi 110/11 KV Sub-Station. Besides, to meet the growing demand of this region, a new 110/11 KV Sub-Station with 2 numbers of 16 MVA power transformers was energised at Pillaitheruvasal.
5. In order to improve the voltage profile and to minimise the line losses, 11 and 22 KV Shunt Capacitor Banks totaling to 21.6 MVAR had been erected and commissioned in various 110 KV Sub-Stations.
6. Under normal development schemes, 236 numbers of distribution transformers were energised and 198 numbers of distribution transformers were enhanced to higher capacities. Further, 68,094 km of High Tension (HT) Lines, and 285.714 km of Low Tension (LT) lines were energised, while 26.686 km of HT lines and 113.775 km of LT lines were strengthened.
7. With the erection/strengthening of the above HT/LT lines, 71 numbers of HT industrial services, 515 numbers of LT industrial services, 26664 numbers of domestic services, 4117 numbers of commercial services, 2737 numbers of one hut one bulb (OHOB) services and 4826 numbers of street lights were energised.
8. Under 20 Point Programme, 176 numbers of agricultural pumpsets were energised.
9. Under Special Component Plan, 1083 numbers of OHOB services were effected to scheduled caste people and 760 numbers of street lights were energised in the scheduled caste area.
10. Further to the above, 11 numbers of 11 KV distribution transformers were energised and 13 numbers of 11 KV distribution transformers were enhanced to higher capacities. 10.660 km of HT under ground cables and 92.461 km of LT under ground cables were also laid and 3481 numbers of LT over head services and 313 numbers of LT over head street lights were converted into under ground cable system.

5.4 Transport

5.4.1 Roads

The transport network, both within and connecting the Union Territory, is critical for industrial growth. Puducherry is well-connected by national and state highways, especially after the completion of the East Coast Road which makes it easily accessible from Chennai and smaller towns such as Cuddalore and Chidambaram. The quality of roads, however, barring the East Coast Road is not very good. While the deterioration is perhaps largely due to the increase in vehicular traffic, efforts will have to be made to maintain these roads in good condition.

TABLE 5.4

Length of Roads Maintained by PWD

(in Kilometres)

Year	*Surfaced Roads*	*Unsurfaced Roads*	*Grand Total*
1990	505	1	506
1991	476	1	477
1992	535	1	536
1993	530	6	536
1994	551	8	559
1995	555	5	560
1996	557	3	560
1997	581	9	590
1998	598	-	598
1999	601	-	601
2000	603	-	603
2001	608	-	608

Source: Local Administration Department, Puducherry.

The condition of roads is of concern within the Union Territory itself. Traffic congestion has become so bad within Puducherry town especially, that the roads have taken a real battering. Quality control is paramount and this will depend, to a great extent, on regulation of traffic movement. As on March 2001, the length of the roads maintained by the Public Works Department is 608 km. in total, Puducherry having 394 km., Karaikal 165 km., Mahe 22 km., and Yanam 27 km (Table 5.4 and Table 5.5). The length of roads maintained by Municipalities across regions is given in Table 5.6.

5.4.2 Rail

The rail network in Puducherry is in the process of being upgraded. At present, Puducherry is connected by broad gauge line. Plans are also in the offing to connect Yanam with Kakinada, and Karaikal with Nagapattinam.

The advantage of having a good rail connection to Puducherry is that it makes it possible for industries to use this link for transporting their goods to and from

TABLE 5.5

Length of Roads Maintained by PWD

No.	Items/Details	Unit	2004-05 Region-wise				
			Puducherry	*Karaikal*	*Mahe*	*Yanam*	*State*
I	Roads						
	Length of Roads (PWD)	Kms					
	(a) National Highways		41,628	20,400	1,988		64,016
	(b) State Highways		35,247				35,247
	(c) Other PWD Roads		290,600	144,767	19,931	26,445	481,743
	(d) Major Dist. Roads		25,557				25,557
	Total		393,032	165,167	21,919	26,445	606,563
II	Transport						
	No. of Motor Vehicles Registered	Nos	29,406	4,067	403	363	34239

Source: Local Administration Department, Puducherry.

TABLE 5.6

Length of Roads Maintained by Municipalities

(in Kms.)

Year/Region	*Surfaced Roads*				*Unsurfaced Roads*			
	Cement Concrete	*Black Topped*	*Water Bound Macadam*	*Total*	*Motorable*	*Non-Motorable*	*Total*	*Grand Total (5+8)*
As on 31st March 2002								
Puducherry	3.451	225.130	9.600	238.181	—	0.744	0.744	238.925
Oulgaret	5.029	162.869	12.587	180.485	2.086	18.247	20.333	200.818
Karaikal	2.74	93.519	25.236	121.495	—	—	—	121.495
Mahe	—	76.284	—	76.284	0.788	—	0.788	77.072
Yanam	14.258	11.695	6.123	32.076	0.363	—	0.363	32.439
Total	25.478	569.497	53.546	648.521	3.237	18.991	22.228	670.749
As on 31st March 2003								
Puducherry	10.678	221.253	7.850	239.781	—	1.580	1.580	241.361
Oulgaret	8.620	167.820	16.360	192.800	1.660	15.260	16.920	209.720
Karaikal	3.240	104.507	26.204	133.951	—	—	—	133.951
Mahe	0.034	85.963	0.035	86.032	—	—	—	86.032
Yanam	18.289	8.572	6.535	33.396	—	0.398	0.398	33.794
Total	40.861	588.115	56.984	685.960	1.660	17.238	18.898	704.858

Source: Local Administration Department, Puducherry.

Puducherry. As Chennai is now well connected with the East Coast Road, the rail link will be more useful within the Union Territory, and between Puducherry and smaller towns which are not connected by good quality roads.

5.5 Port

Puducherry has an old port located near the Light House and a new port near Ariyankuppam. A cargo quay 150 metres long has been constructed in order to avoid the multiple handling of cargo. The handling capacity of the port has also been increased significantly to around 1000 to 1500 tonnes per day. The port is also equipped with cargo handling equipment like launchers, cranes, tractors and trailers. At present, however, the port is not being used much by industry. Besides, for molasses, few goods are currently being transported through the port despite the modernisation of the port facility. There are a number of reasons for this. Container facilities are still limited at the port. Moreover, the Port Authority is not actively seeking business by offering industry incentives to use its facilities. Efforts will have to be stepped up so as to activate the port and encourage industry to utilise it. While Puducherry cannot compete with large ports in Chennai and Tuticorin, a medium-size port itself will help industry considerably. Although plans to privatise the port have fallen through in the past, initiative has been taken to involve private parties. Table 5.7 highlights the value of the seaborne foreign trade handled by the port.

TABLE 5.7

Value of Seaborne Foreign Trade

(Rs. in thousands)

No.	*Years*	*Imports*	*Exports*	*Total*
1.	1990-91	2259.88	-	2259.88
2.	1991-92	2985.03	-	2985.03
3.	1992-93	2497.71	-	2497.71
4.	1993-94	1189.2	-	1189.2
5.	1994-95	1798.43	-	1798.43
6.	1995-96	4347.40	-	4347.40
7.	1996-97	Nil	-	Nil
8.	1997-98	2011.72	-	2011.72
9.	1998-99	178810.9	-	178810.9
10.	1999-2000	Nil	-	Nil
11.	2000-01	Nil	130138.6	130138.6

Source: Government of Puducherry, Industries Department.

5.6 Airport

Puducherry has a medium-sized airport, which has become operational since June 14, 2006. The closure of the airport for the last 15 years was largely due to the fact that no serious background work was done *vis-à-vis* possible demand. From the perspective of industrial growth, a well-functioning airport could encourage entrepreneurs to invest in Puducherry.

According to an MoU signed by the AAI with the Puducherry administration, the runway extension work is underway to enable medium sized aircrafts to operate. Flights to Puducherry operated by Vayudoot were stopped in 1991 due to 'poor patronage'.

5.7 Telecommunications

If Puducherry is keen about promoting its IT industry, telecommunication facilities should be top notch. While Puducherry has been upgrading its telecommunication facilities in the recent past, it is still no match for nearby centres such as Chennai, Bangalore, and Hyderabad. The government needs to prioritise attention to telecommunications and promote investment in that field in the future. The possibility of allowing private actors to enter the telecommunication market needs to be actively pursued. Table 5.8 gives region-wise progress of the Telecom sector in Puducherry between 1999 and 2003.

Table 5.9 indicates region-wise distribution of post offices during the period 2001 to 2003.

5.8 Water Resources

Another critical input for industries is water. Puducherry has taken pride in having excellent quality and sufficient quantity of water. The tide, however, is turning due mostly to over-exploitation but also to salinisation in the coastal belt. As it is the government's policy to promote sustainable industrialisation, the government must be proactive not only in encouraging industries which are less water dependent (to the extent possible) but also in ensuring that industries pay adequately for the quantity they utilise and treat the effluent water as well.

The industrial policy already offers small-scale industries financial incentives for adopting pollution control machinery. Moreover, industries with ISO certification are being recognised and promoted. This should go some way in ensuring that water quality (amongst other things) is maintained in the long-run. It

TABLE 5.8

Number of Telephones, Exchanges and Public Call Offices (1999-2003)

(in Nos.)

S. No.	*Region/Item*	*1999*	*2000*	*2001*	*2002*	*2003*
1.	Puducherry:					
	Telephone Connections	39,339	48,429	70,750	76,760	77,497
	Telephone Exchanges	16	15	20	22	22
	Public Call Offices	526	657	1,240	1,562	1,964
2.	Karaikal:					
	Telephone Connections	5,773	7,788	14,431	15,815	17,536
	Telephone Exchanges	1	1	9	9	9
	Public Call Offices	74	302	387	361	592
3.	Mahe:					
	Telephone Connections	4,652	5,536	5,804	5,958	6,091
	Telephone Exchanges	1	1	1	1	1
	Public Call Offices	46	52	68	90	91
4.	Yanam:					
	Telephone Connections	841	850	1,745	2,161	2,226
	Telephone Exchanges	1	1	1	1	1
	Public Call Offices	28	28	36	37	40
5.	Union Territory:					
	Telephone Connections	50,605	62,603	92,730	100,694	103,350
	Telephone Exchanges	19	18	31	33	33
	Public Call Offices	674	1,039	1,731	2050	2,687

Source: Department of Posts, Puducherry.

TABLE 5.9

Number of Post Offices Region-wise (2001-2003)

(in Nos.)

S. No.	*Region/Item*	*2001*	*2002*	*2003*
1.	Puducherry:			
	Rural Post Offices	36	36	37
	Urban Post Offices	32	32	32
2.	Karaikal:			
	Rural Post Offices	21	21	21
	Urban Post Offices	7	7	7
3.	Mahe:			
	Rural Post Offices	0	0	0
	Urban Post Offices	4	4	4
4.	Yanam:			
	Rural Post Offices	0	0	0
	Urban Post Offices	1	1	1
5.	State:			
	Rural Post Offices	57	57	58
	Urban Post Offices	44	44	44

Note: The entire Mahe and Yanam regions are treated as Urban areas.
Source: Department of Posts, Puducherry.

should also help in ensuring that water is not an input constraint for industrial growth.

5.9 Export Processing Zone/ Special Economic Zone

The Puducherry government has proposed to set-up an Export Processing Zone in Puducherry. Land of the order of 102.63 acres has already been allocated in Sedarapet village for this purpose. An Export Processing Zone will go a long way in promoting industrial exports from Puducherry given the incentives in place of 100 per cent export units. The government must ensure, however, that the infrastructural facilities in this zone are top notch and do not deteriorate as in the other industrial estates.

Special Economic Zones (SEZs) are being set-up under export policy 2000, with the view to provide internationally competitive and hassle free environment for export promotion. SEZ will be a duty-free enclave to be treated as foreign territory for trade operations, duties and tariffs.

SEZ is proposed to be set up at Sedarapet-Karasur Revenue villages in about 1000 acres by PIPDIC. Activities intended to be promoted in the zone are:

- Zone I: Automobile and auto parts—300 acres
- Zone II: Information Technology (including services, electronics, hardware and bioinformatics)—275 acres
- Zone III: Machinery and Equipments (on the anvil)—300 acres.

To facilitate the process, the Government of Puducherry have already notified SEZ policy. An SPV, a subsidiary of PIPDIC, has been formed which will have a strategic private investor having maximum participation/stake. The strategic partner will conceptualise, design, finance, build, operate and market the SEZ.

5.10 Information Technology Policy

Information Technology (IT), the most important development of the century, holds the key to rapid progress in the coming years, contributing to better governance and improved productivity, which will increase the growth of the economy and quality of life of the citizens.

Puducherry has limited physical resources like land, water, power, and raw materials. The environmental factors have also restricted the growth of major industries in the region in spite of attractive financial incentives offered by the Government. Puducherry is endowed with skilled and educated manpower, and around 1000 well trained IT professionals at various levels come out every year, and hence, it is ideally suited for the development in the area of IT.

The Government of Puducherry has been encouraging the use of IT in the government departments and educational institutions during the last decade. Some of the important departments like Accounts and Treasuries, Civil Supplies, Transport, Electricity etc., have already been computerised for facilitating the transactions with the public. Incentives offered by the government have already attracted a sizeable number of computer hardware manufacturers. A Software Technology Park is being set up by the PIPDIC in Puducherry and an Electronic Industrial Estate is also coming up. In addition, IT has penetrated other areas such as banking, shopping, etc. An IT SEZ is also being planned.

To make the UT a forerunner in the field of IT, a comprehensive IT Policy has been prepared which will act as a blue print for planning and implementation.

5.11 Summary

Puducherry with limited physical resources like land, water, power, and raw materials should focus its attention on providing infrastructure. There is a need to significantly improve its accessibility—road, rail, port, airport etc.—and also upgrade its present infrastructure base (industrial estates, power, social infrastructure), in order to attract investments in all sectors. State should provide world-class infrastructure for accelerated growth of industries with slant on exports. Tapping public-private partnerships mode for its infrastructure projects should be given top priority.

References

Electricity Department, Puducherry.

Local Administration Department, Puducherry.

Government of Puducherry, Industries Department.

Government of Puducherry (2003). *Pondicherry Vision 2020*. Madras School of Economics.

Department of Posts, Puducherry.

Chapter 6

Social Sector

6.1 Education

The historical evidence of systematic learning and education in the Puducherry region dates as back as 8th century A.D. Till the arrival of the missionaries and the French, the available evidence discloses the prevalence of traditional Sanskrit learning. From the beginning of 18th century, initiatives for modern education in Puducherry were attempted by the foreign missionaries (*Gazetteer of India*, Puducherry II volume). In 1703, Jesuits opened few schools for the children of the *colons* (settlers). Then they opened a college also in Puducherry. In 1738, Ursulines came to Puducherry at the invitation of Dumas to run some schools for girls.

With the advent of Puducherry coming under the control of the French in 1816, the emphasis was focused on education and Jesuits were encouraged to run schools and colleges. For the benefit of the natives, two free schools were opened by the arête of February 1, 1827, one at Puducherry and another at Karaikal. Reading, writing and arithmetic [three Rs] through French and Tamil medium were taught in the schools. Another school for depressed class was opened in 1828. In 1826, on invitation the Sisters of the Congregation of St. Joseph De Cluny from Bourbon started a school exclusively for girls for primary and upper primary education [ibid. p.1224].

A landmark in modern education in Puducherry was the Royal Ordinance of September 30, 1843, which promised to provide the same kind of education as in France with a view to bringing about the cultural assimilation of the local population through French Education [ibid. p.1225].

The education system was biased in favour of the French language. Nevertheless proficiency in any one of the three regional languages namely, Tamil, Hindi or Telugu was a precondition for appointment in administrative position since 1843. In the post-1843 period, there was a rapid increase in the number of schools in all the regions by the various Congregations of Sisters and Missionaries. Local *zamindars* also founded some schools. In order to study the unbridled growth of schools, both public and private schools, and the state of affairs of educational institutions, the French Government commissioned a study in 1879 to assess the status of the French and English education in primary and secondary schools. Following the report, an attempt was made to enable primary and upper primary teachers to qualify themselves.

In the year 1900, there were more private schools than public schools. By 1920 this trend was reversed due to the improvement in the system of school inspection. Even the enrolment of girls showed a marginal increase during the period. In the thirties, under the stewardship of Governor Grocicchia, new schools were established and more primary schools were started. Thus, education was given an impetus from the beginning of the French arrival. Their influence was at once liberal and deep. While they respected the manners and customs of the local people, they endeavoured to impart the benefit of their knowledge to their subject.

6.1.1 Growth of Literacy

After the merger with India, literacy rate has displayed a consistent growth from 37.43 per cent in 1961 to 81.49 per cent in the 2001 census. The difference between male and female literacy has narrowed remarkably from more than 20 per cent in the 1981 census to around 10 per cent in the 2001 census. Across the regions, Mahe has reported very high literacy rate from the beginning of the merger. This could be attributed to the higher priority for education in the adjoining region of Kerala. On the contrary, Yanam registered a very low literacy level among regions from the beginning of merger. The same reason could be assigned to this lower literacy rate as Andhra Pradesh literacy level is very low among the south Indian states

This exhibits that Karaikal and Puducherry regions have similar, with asymptotical variation, literacy level among the men and women. The other regions show huge difference in the literacy level though the gender difference is relatively marginal. This indicates that literacy level is influenced by the regional culture.

Table 6.1 presents the literacy level across regions in the Union Territory of Puducherry. Across rural and urban set up, there remains a difference of around 15 per cent. Though there is a decline, it is insignificant. Across gender in the rural and urban areas, it is deplorable. In the rural areas, the difference between male and female is around 25 per cent while it is around 17 per cent in the urban areas. This trend could be noticed in the Puducherry and Karaikal regions. This manifests that there is a noticeable gender bias in education in the rural areas in these two regions. This huge difference also indicates that impetus should be given in promoting education in the rural areas in general and women in rural areas particularly. A socially inclusive policy would enlist the participation of all the population in the development process

Figures 6.1 and 6.2 indicate that Puducherry and Karaikal regions have been reporting a consistent growth over the consecutive census periods from 1981 onwards and there is a convergence emerging in the literacy level in all the regions in the 2001 census though Mahe region has an edge over other regions.

FIGURE 6.1

Literacy Level across Regions

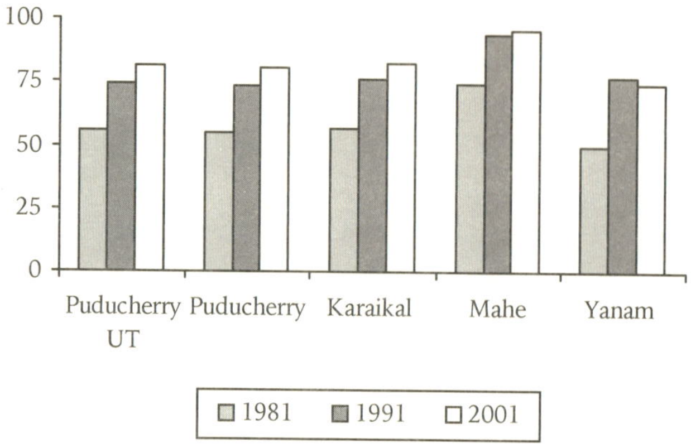

FIGURE 6.2

Literacy Level Over the Period

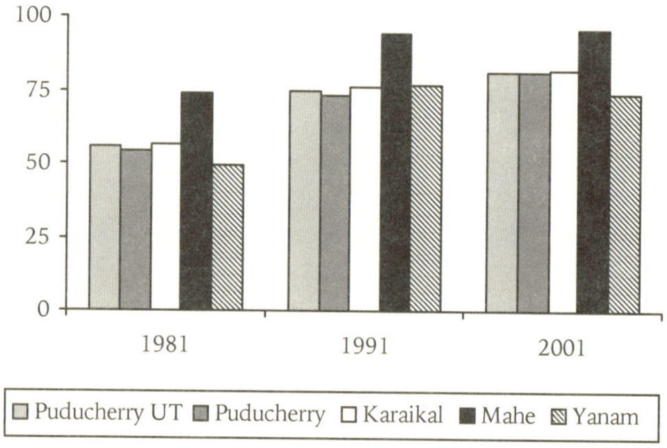

TABLE 6.1

Literacy Rates - 1981-2001

UT/Region	*1981*			*1991*			*2001*		
	Total	*Male*	*Female*	*Total*	*Male*	*Female*	*Total*	*Male*	*Female*
Puducherry UT	55.85	65.84	45.71	74.74	83.68	65.63	81.49	88.89	74.13
Puducherry	54.69	65.06	43.97	73.35	82.75	63.60	80.90	88.72	73.04
Karaikal	56.43	67.09	46.00	75.78	85.05	66.65	82.24	89.69	74.99
Mahe	74.11	78.02	70.70	94.10	96.91	91.73	95.78	97.59	94.23
Yanam	49.57	55.90	43.08	76.86	82.38	71.19	74.09	79.11	69.07

Source: Census 1981, 1991, 2001.

6.1.2 *Growth Rate of Students, Teachers and Institutions*

Simple annual growth rates (constant rates) have been computed for the period 1980-81 to 2002-03. It has been calculated for students, teachers and institutions across regions in government as well as private schools.

The growth rate of students across different level of schools in Puducherry as presented in Table 6.2 indicates that the growth rate at the pre-primary and higher secondary levels has been remarkably higher over the last two decades. This manifests the increasing interest in quality education among the children and parents. The negative growth rate in primary and middle schools indicates the preference of the students in continuing the school education. This also suggests that all the schools should be upgraded to higher secondary level to reduce the drop outs. Though it may be difficult to run higher secondary schools in remote isolated villages, it should not be a problem to run higher secondary schools as most of the regions in Puducherry come under urban area and high density of population. The higher growth rate among the girls in all levels of schools indicates the convergence in gender equity. The perceptible growth in the pre-primary or nursery education shows the interest in the English education and higher level of primary enrolment in the schools.

TABLE 6.2

Growth Rate of Students by Level of Education 1980-81 to 2002-03

Level of Education	*Boys*	*Girls*	*Total*
Pre-primary	8.90*	8.02*	8.48*
Primary	-0.53	0.50	-0.04
Middle	-1.63*	0.04	-0.84***
High	3.01*	4.50*	3.70*
Higher Secondary	7.93*	10.21*	8.85*
Arts and Science College	-1.16*	5.59*	2.08*

Note: * indicates significant at 1 per cent level;
** indicates 5 per cent level;
*** indicates 10 per cent level significance; No sign implies not significant.

Source: *Statistical Abstract of Puducherry-* Various Issues from 1980-81 to 2002-03.

Similar to the enrolment, the growth of teachers also underscores the narrowing down of gender gap in the teaching community. This inspires the girl children to enrol in the schools and vice versa. Interestingly, the growth rate of male teachers has been negative in the pre-primary, primary and middle schools (Table 6.3). This also shows that the maternal touch in the initial stage of school education to children reduces the drop out rates in the schools and group behaviour among the kids.

Conversely, the growth of educational institutions in the government sector has shown a dip in the pre-primary, primary and middle schools whereas in the higher secondary schools it has displayed an amazing growth rate. This could be attributed to the upgradation of middle and high schools into higher secondary schools. On the contrary, in the private sector there has been steady growth rate at all levels of school institutions (Table 6.4). This also elucidates the preference of children to high quality education. This throws a challenge to the government schools to face the competition. The department of education has also undertaken many proactive initiatives to face the challenge from the private institutions.

TABLE 6.3

Growth of Teachers by Levels of Schools

Level of Education	*Male*	*Female*	*Total*
Pre-primary	N.A.	8.60*	8.45*
Primary	-1.33*	3.50*	0.81**
Middle	-1.52*	2.04*	0.17
High	0.78*	5.33*	2.84*
Higher Secondary	7.12*	10.70*	8.58*

Note: * indicates significant at 1 per cent level;
** indicates 5 per cent level;
*** indicates 10 per cent level significance; No sign implies not significant.

Source: *Statistical Abstract of Puducherry-* Various Issues from 1980-81 to 2002-03.

TABLE 6.4

Growth of Institutions by Levels of Schools

Level of Education	*Government*	*Private*	*Total*
Pre-primary	-0.39	8.05*	5.32*
Primary	-0.30*	3.75*	0.30
Middle	-1.04*	6.24*	1.05*
High	1.21*	10.58*	3.83*
Higher Secondary	7.32*	8.60*	7.74*
Arts and Science College	-3.69**	0.00	-3.83*

Note: * indicates significant at 1 per cent level;
** indicates 5 per cent level;
*** indicates 10 per cent level significance; No sign implies not significant.

Source: *Statistical Abstract of Puducherry-* Various Issues from 1980-81 to 2002-03.

Table 6.5 presents the growth rates of students, teachers and institutions in Puducherry region. It explicates that there is a negative growth rate in the government pre-primary, primary and middle schools. All the other type of schools and colleges reported a significant growth in both government and private sectors. The same trend could be noticed in the number of students enrolled, teachers and institutions. Discussion with officials concerned in the Directorates of Planning, Economics and Statistics and Education transpired that most of the pre-primary, primary and middle schools have been upgraded to secondary level and higher secondary level with huge capital outlay for education. The facilities in middle schools have been improved to become

TABLE 6.5

Growth Rates of Students, Teachers and Institutions in Government and Private Schools in Puducherry Region

Type of Schools	*Government Schools*			*Private Schools*		
	Student	*Teacher*	*Institution*	*Student*	*Teacher*	*Institution*
Simple Annual Growth Rate with Constant						
Pre-primary	-2.17*	-0.96*	-0.76*	10.00*	8.24*	7.73*
Primary	-0.66**	-0.62**	-0.43*	1.27**	7.23*	5.01*
Middle	-2.19*	-2.26*	-1.56*	1.96**	5.58*	4.76*
Secondary	2.36*	1.39*	1.89*	11.72*	9.67*	12.41*
Higher Secondary	8.31*	7.83*	7.02*	7.72*	8.32*	7.13*
Total School	1.13*	1.02*	0.03**	7.22*	7.99*	6.74*
Arts and Science College	6.24*	2.57*	3.90*	0	0	0
Total	1.30*	1.11*	0.07*	6.90*	5.90*	6.60*

Note: * indicates significant at 1 per cent level; ** indicates 5 per cent level; *** indicates 10 per cent level significance; No star implies not significant.
Source: *Statistical Abstract of Puducherry*- Various Issues from 1980-81 to 2002-03.

secondary or higher secondary schools. In the private sector, the growth rate is noticeably higher in the secondary and higher secondary levels. Since most of the children, rather parents, prefer to study in secondary or higher secondary schools to have continuity in their education, the growth of secondary and higher secondary schools tends to be higher. Hence, it is inferred that the government and private sectors have to ensure continuity in their learning and education through starting or upgrading more and more secondary and higher secondary schools with adequate infrastructure.

The growth rates of number of students, teachers and institutions under different categories of schools in government and private sectors in Karaikal region are presented in Table 6.6. It exhibits a mixed trend up to the secondary level with government schools. The private sector is present only in primary and secondary levels. In line with the Puducherry district the upgradation of primary, middle and secondary schools also happens in regular intervals. At the secondary level, growth rate of students is negative in the government schools. On the contrary, the growth rate of students at the secondary level in the private sector has recorded a significant positive growth rate. This indicates that the private sector is putting up a tough challenge to government schools. It also manifests that parents want to provide better quality education to their wards at the secondary level, which is an important milestone in the education of children.

Table 6.7 presents the growth rate of students, teachers and institutions in the Mahe region. The secondary schools reported a negative growth in the region. This could be attributed to the upgradation of

TABLE 6.6

Growth Rates of Students, Teachers and Institutions in Government and Private schools in Karaikal Region

Type of Schools	*Government*			*Private*		
	Students	*Teachers*	*Institutions*	*Students*	*Teachers*	*Institution*
Simple Annual Growth Rate with Constant						
Pre-primary	0.12***	-5.09*	0	0	0	10.38*
Primary	-0.16	-1.63*	-0.61	9.44*	10.2*	4.21*
Middle	0.22	-0.51	-0.4	0	0	0
Secondary	-0.22	0.48	-0.79**	5.49*	0	5.31*
Higher Secondary	7.33*	9.65*	8.88*	0	0	0
Total School	0.24*	0.59*	0.76	9.64*	11.42*	7.99*
Arts and Science College	0	4.78*	1.09***	0	0	0
Total	0.24*	0.75*	0.82*	9.64*	11.41*	7.99*

Note: * indicates significant at 1 per cent level; ** indicates 5 per cent level; *** indicates 10 per cent level significance; No sign implies not significant.
Source: *Statistical Abstract of Puducherry*- Various Issues from 1980-81 to 2002-03.

TABLE 6.7

Growth Rates of Students, Teachers and Institutions in Government and Private Schools in Mahe Region

Type of Schools	*Government*			*Private*		
	Students	*Teachers*	*Institutions*	*Students*	*Teachers*	*Institution*
Simple Annual Growth Rate with Constant						
Pre-primary	0	0	0	0	0	0
Primary	1.19	1.88*	1.04*	0	0	0
Middle	-2.56*	-0.77	0.36***	0	0	0
Secondary	-4.78*	-3.88*	-4.47*	0	0	0
Higher Secondary	0	0	0	0	0	0
Total School	0.88**	1.93*	1*	12.74*	18.21*	11.32*
Arts and Science College	0	2.85*	0	0	0	0
Total	1.09**	2.07*	0.94*	12.74*	18.21*	11.32*

Note: * indicates significant at 1 per cent level; ** indicates 5 per cent level; *** indicates 10 per cent level significance; No sign implies not significant.
Source: Statistical Abstract of Puducherry- Various Issues from 1980-81 to 2002-03.

secondary schools into higher secondary school after 1991-92. Higher secondary system was introduced in Mahe in 1991-92 only. Private schools exist only up to middle school level. Since it is a small region with 9 square km area, private sector does not find much opportunity at higher level. In addition the efficiency of government schools in producing results and quality education also challenges the entry of private sector in Mahe region.

Similar to Mahe, Yanam region also introduced higher secondary system only in 1991-92. The growth rates presented in Table 6.8 explain that middle schools have recorded negative growth. This does not mean that middle schools have been closed down, rather most of the middle schools have been converted into secondary schools. Due to this, the secondary schools have not shown any negative growth rate after introducing the higher secondary school system in 1991-92. In addition private schools are entering into only primary and middle schools. In Yanam, the growth rates have been very low in all type of schools. This indicates the slow change or improvement in the education system here. Even the private sector does not attach much importance to education in the region.

Thus, the analysis of growth rates indicates that there is a noticeable decline in the primary, middle and preprimary schools in the government sector. This could be attributed to the upgradation of some of the middle and primary schools to secondary and higher secondary schools, competition from private sector and preference of parents to higher secondary schools to have continuum in their learning. These trends are prevalent in all the regions.

TABLE 6.8

Growth Rates of Students, Teachers and Institutions in Government Schools in Yanam Region

Type of Schools	*Students*	*Teachers*	*Institutions*
Simple Annual Growth Rate with Constant			
Pre-primary	0	0	0
Primary	2.12*	2.35*	1.14*
Middle	-2.10	-6.99*	0.72
Secondary	2.68**	2.58*	3.78*
Higher Secondary	0	0	0
Total School	2.09*	2.53*	1.89*
Arts and Science College	-6.48*	-0.96	-4.68*
Total	2.37*	1.87*	1.37*

Note: * indicates significant at 1 per cent level;
** indicates 5 per cent level;
*** indicates 10 per cent level significance; No sign implies not significant.
Source: Statistical Abstract of Puducherry- Various Issues from 1980-81 to 2002-03.

6.1.3 Student-Teacher Ratio

Student-teacher ratio has been computed for all the regions from 1980-81 to 2000-01 across all type of schools in both government and private schools. This analysis would bring out the personal attention given by the teachers to the students. The quality of education could be improved substantially by bringing down the student teacher ratio.

At the overall level, though the ratio has been declining over the period at all levels of schools (Figure 6.3), it is notably higher in the case of high schools and higher secondary schools (Table 6.9). However, it is still higher than the effective ratio of around 20 in all levels of schools. This suggests that there is still a burgeoning need to increase the number of teachers, particularly female teachers to improve the effective educational system and to face the challenges posed by the private schools in the Union Territory.

TABLE 6.9

Student-Teacher Ratio in the UT

Years	*Primary*	*Middle*	*High School*	*Higher Secondary*
1980-81	26.73	30.78	28.88	30.42
1981-82	29.15	32.01	27.62	27.17
1982-83	26.91	29.18	24.96	26.49
1983-84	28.40	29.23	24.23	28.26
1984-85	28.46	30.08	26.65	33.07
1985-86	28.66	31.83	25.21	32.59
1986-87	29.70	31.08	26.83	33.74
1987-88	28.54	27.95	26.13	33.40
1988-89	27.69	28.00	27.77	27.43
1989-90	26.53	29.00	29.99	27.52
1990-91	26.32	28.03	29.91	30.20
1991-92	26.69	28.11	31.72	28.51
1992-93	27.61	29.93	31.67	30.88
1993-94	24.72	29.90	29.99	29.34
1994-95	24.25	28.05	29.66	36.85
1995-96	23.77	26.44	31.91	31.82
1996-97	22.94	26.27	28.83	29.30
1997-98	22.26	24.74	30.72	30.10
1998-99	21.75	25.60	30.94	30.19
1999-2000	22.04	24.49	30.10	29.90
2000-01	25.02	26.12	28.42	28.73
2001-02	23.48	23.06	27.36	28.14
2002-03	22.15	22.76	26.83	28.00

Source: Statistical Abstract of Puducherry- Various Issues from 1980-81 to 2002-03.

Table 6.10 presents the student teacher ratio in both government and private schools for Puducherry region. It exhibits that there is a consistent but slow decline in the ratio at the government schools, though the ratio tends to increase at the higher secondary schools (Figure 6.4). This indicates that in spite of the increase in enrolment, the appointment of more teachers keeps the ratio within the optimum level. On the contrary, there has been a noticeable decline in the ratio at primary and middle schools run by private managements (Figure 6.5). This indicates the higher attention given to the children at the personal level by the teacher. The ratio is considerably low at the primary and middle level at the private schools in comparison with government schools. This could also be one of the reasons for more parents putting their children in the private schools at the primary and middle school levels. To face the challenge, the government has to reduce the ratio to at least 20:1 level at the primary and middle school level.

The student-teacher ratios for Karaikal region have been illustrated in Table 6.11. It shows that there has been a consistent decline in the ratio at the government schools. In the case of secondary schools the government sector has reported a positive growth in the ratio over the years (Figure 6.6). On the other hand in the private sector, the ratio in all the schools displayed a decline over the period (Figure 6.7). This could be one of the parameter for the quality of the education in the private schools, for the lower student-teacher ratio indicates the personal attention given to the students by the teachers.

Table 6.12 presents the student-teacher ratios for all type of schools in the Mahe region. Interestingly, the ratio in the government schools tends to be lower than the private schools in the region. This could be one of the reasons for the sluggish growth in the private sector in

FIGURE 6.3

Student-Teacher Ratio in the Puducherry

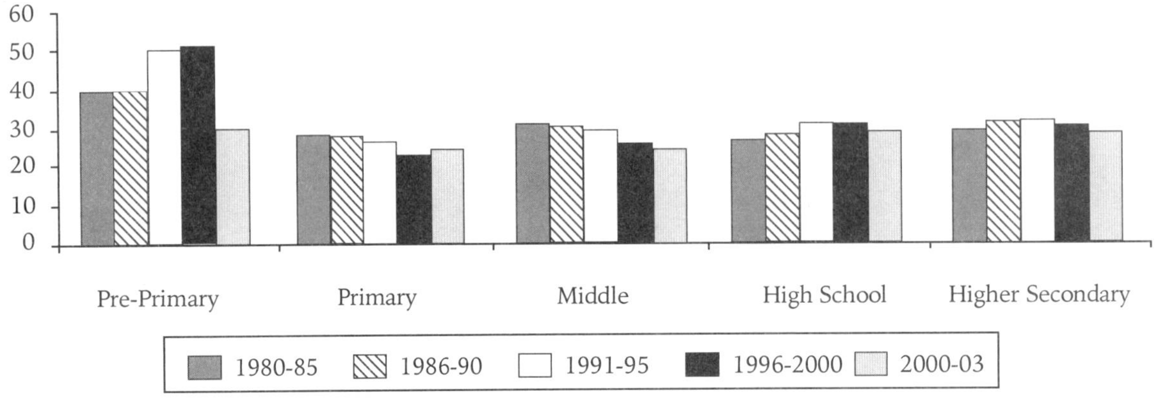

TABLE 6.10

Student-Teacher Ratio across Schools in Puducherry Region

	Primary	*Middle*	*Secondary*	*Higher Secondary*	*Total*	*Arts and Science College*	*Total*
				Government Schools			
1980-81 to 1984-85	28.27	30.21	28.26	26.04	28.65	10.70	27.65
1985-86 to 1989-90	28.68	28.18	26.94	26.49	27.73	11.33	26.81
1990-91 to 1994-95	30.83	30.26	29.44	27.67	29.59	13.78	28.58
1995-96 to 1999-2000	27.22	29.66	32.90	26.84	28.83	18.44	28.13
2000-01 to 2002-03	25.83	27.58	28.63	24.93	26.62	18.51	26.00
1980-81 to 2002-03	28.28	29.33	29.22	26.57	28.40	14.23	27.54
				Private Schools			
1980-81 to 1984-85	30.96	32.99	21.78	38.84	32.49	4.37	24.87
1985-86 to 1989-90	23.56	35.11	30.28	42.35	33.79	5.11	28.17
1990-91 to 1994-95	13.07	25.63	35.06	40.59	31.21	NA	29.58
1995-96 to 1999-2000	12.21	19.86	30.68	36.18	29.72	NA	29.72
2000-01 to 2002-03	14.54	17.39	26.73	32.65	27.06	NA	27.00
1980-81 to 2002-03	19.25	26.96	29.09	38.60	31.18	NA	27.94

Source: Statistical Abstract of Puducherry- Various Issues from 1980-81 to 2002-03.

FIGURE 6.4

Student-Teacher Ratio in the Puducherry Region—Government School

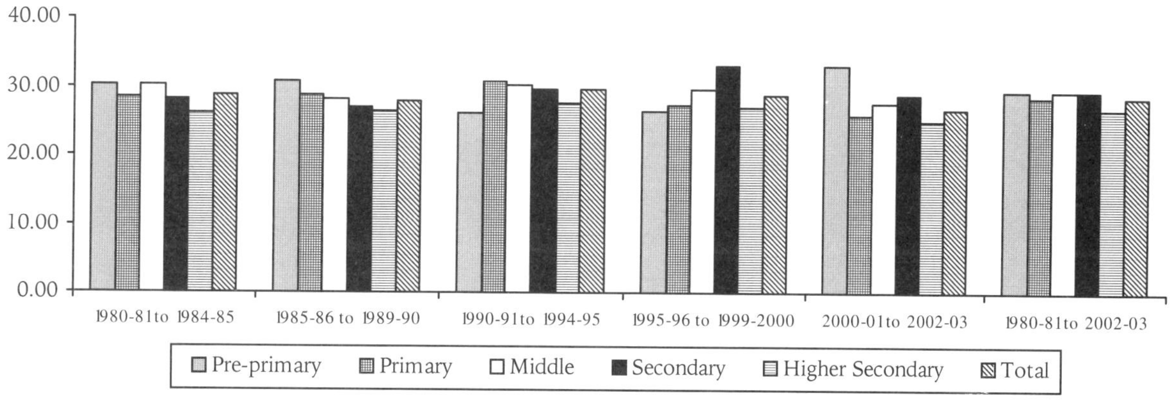

FIGURE 6.5

Student-Teacher Ratio in the Puducherry Region—Private School

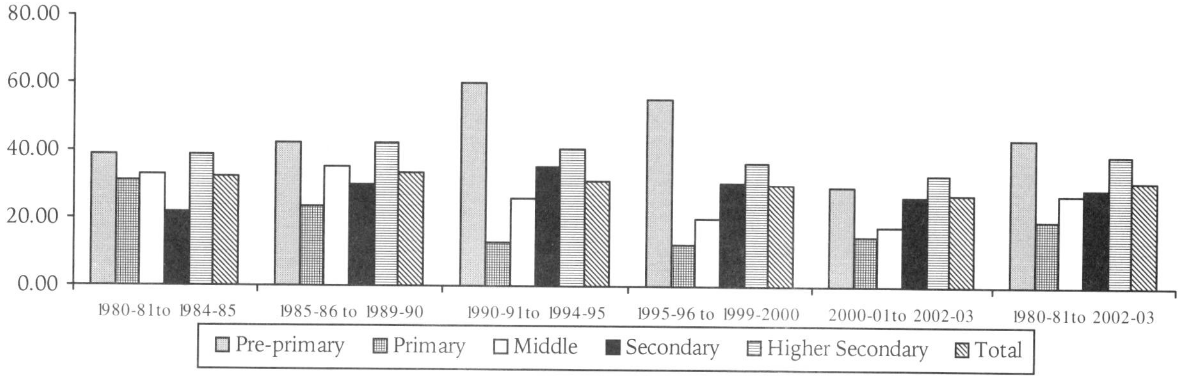

TABLE 6.11

Student-Teacher Ratio across Schools in Karaikal

	Primary	*Middle*	*Secondary*	*Higher Secondary*	*Total*	*Arts and Science College*	*Total*
				Government Schools			
1980-81 to 1984-85	24.75	28.54	20.62	20.52	24.39	7.26	22.93
1985-86 to 1989-90	26.49	30.85	21.82	18.73	25.90	7.80	24.34
1990-91 to 1994-95	24.63	27.72	26.81	22.52	25.77	9.41	24.37
1995-96 to 1999-2000	20.89	29.69	24.60	24.43	24.39	13.91	23.47
2000-01 to 2002-03	20.25	28.62	27.42	23.95	24.70	15.15	23.59
Total	23.68	29.12	23.98	21.86	25.06	10.32	23.75
				Private Schools			
1980-81 to 1984-85	20.36	NA	32.14	NA	33.02	NA	33.02
1985-86 to 1989-90	36.67	NA	32.53	NA	33.61	NA	48.09
1990-91 to 1994-95	19.26	32.94	33.69	NA	29.11	NA	29.11
1995-96 to 1999-2000	19.62	15.54	31.89	34.75	28.49	NA	28.52
2000-01 to 2002-03	26.04	16.72	28.79	37.68	27.29	NA	27.29
Total	24.25	NA	32.07	NA	30.57	NA	33.72

Source: *Statistical Abstract of Puducherry-* Various Issues from 1980-81 to 2002-03.

FIGURE 6.6

Student-Teacher Ratio in Karaikal Region—Government School

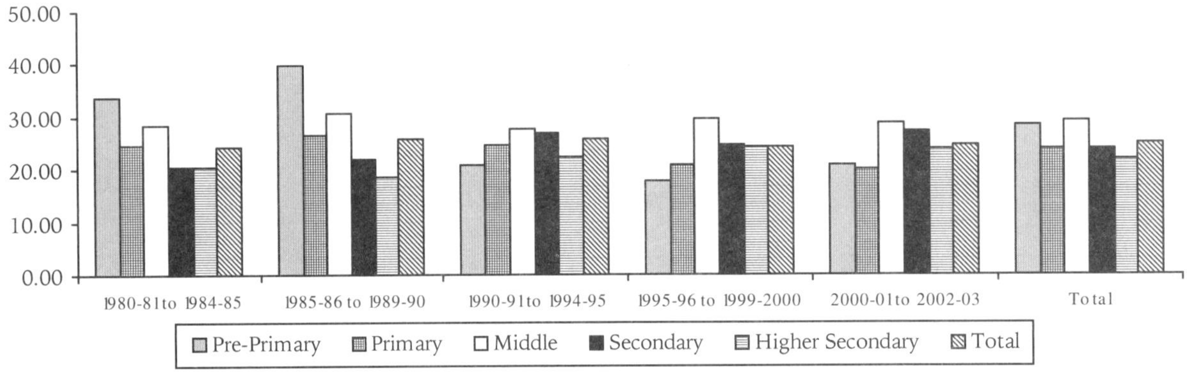

FIGURE 6.7

Student-Teacher Ratio in Karaikal Region—Private School

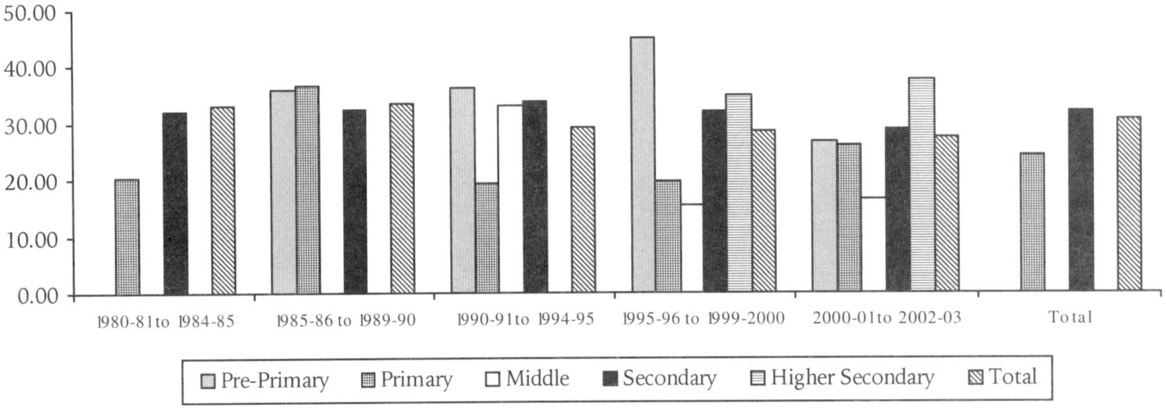

TABLE 6.12

Student-Teacher Ratio across Schools in Mahe

	Primary	*Middle*	*Secondary*	*Higher Secondary*	*Total*	*Arts and Science College*	*Total*
				Government Schools			
1980-81 to 1984-85	28.67	33.42	30.75	NA	30.52	11.94	27.87
1985-86 to 1989-90	42.71	32.14	31.88	NA	34.23	12.00	30.77
1990-91 to 1994-95	37.59	28.90	30.04	NA	31.16	16.29	28.58
1995-96 to 1999-2000	27.84	25.04	27.79	27.49	27.45	13.60	25.15
2000-01 to 2002-03	25.98	22.63	22.25	23.10	23.52	11.85	22.02
Total	33.13	28.93	29.09	NA	29.88	13.25	27.30
				Private Schools			
1980-81 to 1984-85	NA	NA	NA	NA	80.08	NA	80.08
1985-86 to 1989-90	110.80	NA	NA	NA	72.75	NA	72.75
1990-91 to 1994-95	29.43	NA	NA	NA	35.45	NA	35.45
1995-96 to 1999-2000	24.52	18.72	NA	NA	26.46	NA	26.46
2000-01 to 2002-03	29.45	24.89	26.34	NA	27.09	NA	27.09
Total	NA	NA	NA	NA	50.21	NA	50.21

Source: Statistical Abstract of Puducherry- Various Issues from 1980-81 to 2002-03.

FIGURE 6.8

Student-Teacher Ratio in Mahe: Government Schools

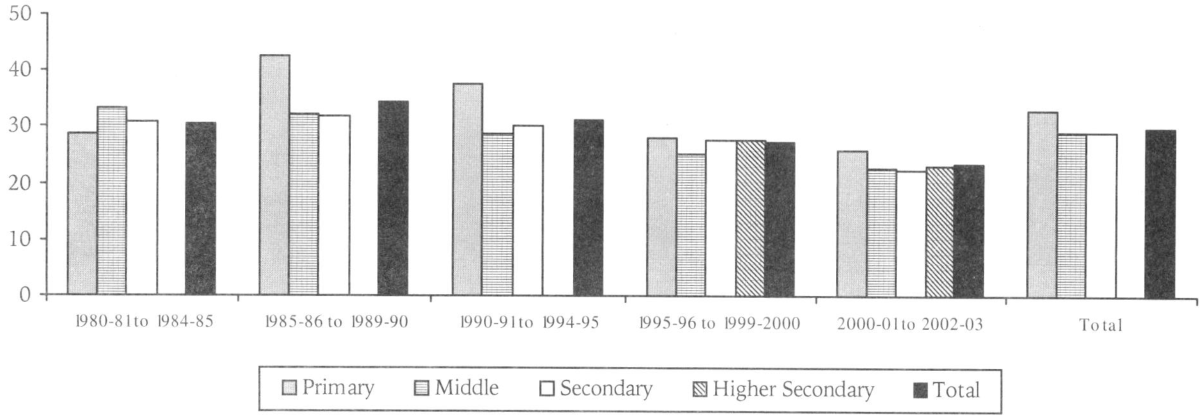

the Mahe region (Figure 6.8). Private schools are found largely at the primary level only. This transpires that the lower student-teacher ratio at the government schools would arrest the proliferation of the private schools. Since regular in-service trainings and orientation courses are given to the government school teachers, the lower ratio would undoubtedly enhance the quality of education.

The student-teacher ratios remain considerably higher in Yanam region in all type of schools at the government sector (Figure 6.9). The ratios are higher in comparison with the other regions in the Union Territory of Puducherry. This has reflected in the growth of private schools in the nineties. Table 6.13 presents the ratio of Yanam region, the higher secondary system was introduced in the mid-nineties. Still some of the higher secondary schools are part of the Arts and Science College.

Thus, the analysis of student-teacher ratios across the regions discloses that the ratios tend to be relatively higher in government schools than private schools. This indicates that there is a need to appoint more teachers to improve the quality of education. The increase in the

TABLE 6.13

Student-Teacher Ratio across Schools in Yanam

	Primary	*Middle*	*Secondary*	*Higher Secondary*	*Total*	*Arts and Science College*	*Total*
				Government Schools			
1980-81 to 1984-85	39.36	32.63	40.55	NA	39.28	16.30	34.05
1985-86 to 1989-90	49.84	38.17	24.37	NA	35.70	12.57	29.53
1990-91 to 1994-95	47.03	98.17	33.60	NA	41.96	9.85	33.99
1995-96 to 1999-2000	39.14	53.20	32.36	11.69	32.98	7.17	29.14
2000-01 to 2002-03	45.02	57.53	31.36	NA	33.46	9.02	30.32
Total	44.00	55.80	32.54	NA	36.96	11.15	31.50
				Private Schools			
1980-81 to 1984-85	NA	NA	NA	NA	NA	NA	NA
1985-86 to 1989-90	NA	NA	NA	NA	32.66	NA	32.66
1990-91 to 1994-95	NA	NA	NA	NA	14.50	NA	14.50
1995-96 to 1999-2000	NA	10.96	21.61	NA	19.14	NA	19.14
2000-01 to 2002-03	NA	13.60	19.52	NA	21.73	NA	21.73
Total	NA	NA	NA	NA	NA	NA	NA

Source: Statistical Abstract of Puducherry- Various Issues from 1980-81 to 2002-03.

FIGURE 6.9

Student-Teacher Ratio in Yanam Region: Government Schools

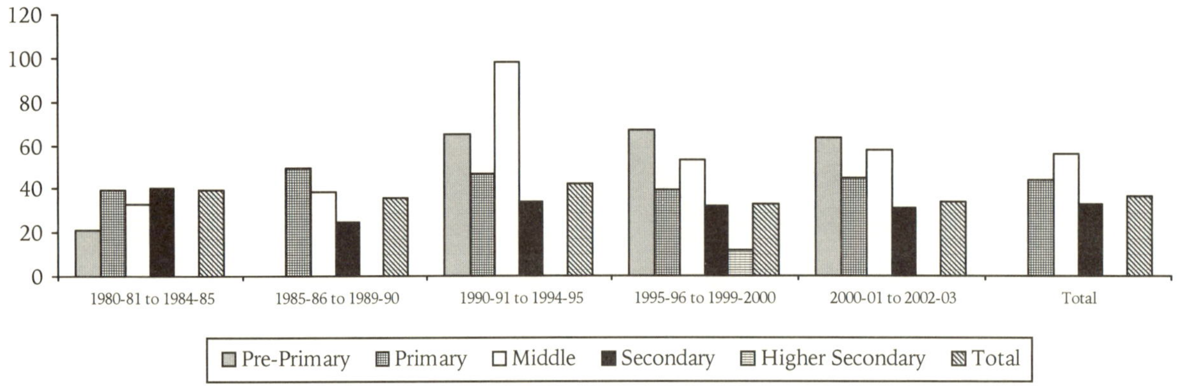

number of teachers would mean that personal attention of teachers will be there on the students.

Similar to student-teacher ratios, student-institution ratios and teacher-institution ratios have been computed to understand relative size and strength of different types of institutions. This shows that the teacher-institution ratio tends to go up over the period at the higher secondary level. This convergence at the higher secondary levels manifests the preference of parents for continuity in learning and education to their children in one atmosphere till the higher secondary level. This also suggests that there is a need for large number of higher secondary schools to avert the drop outs due to involuntary shift over to different schools.

6.1.4 Drop outs, Completion and Repetition

The effectiveness of education in Puducherry across regions and across caste groups has been assessed with the help of drop outs, repetition and completion at three levels like primary, middle and secondary school level. Table 6.14 elucidates the drop outs, repetition and completion across social groups at the primary level. It discloses that the drop out rates in Puducherry as a whole has been around 15 per cent. It is higher among the boys than the girls. Across social groups, it tends to be high among the BC boys and girls. Among the BCs, the drop out rate is higher among the girls. This indicates that the gender stereotyping remains to be high among the BCs. Across the regions, the drop out rate is deplorably higher in Yanam. Around one-third of the students drop out from the schools at the primary level itself. The drop out rate is noticeably higher among the BCs. Here too, the proportion of drop out of girls is higher than the boys. This could be due to the higher proportion of girls getting enrolled in the schools from even BPL families. They may not be able to pursue after a certain level. The IQ of the BCs in general is production-oriented. Hence they may not find it attractive to spend more time and resources in education. Puducherry and Karaikal regions have displayed an average of 10 per cent drop outs across caste groups. Mahe region has showcased a very low drop out rate due to its geographical proximity to Kerala. This also indicates that the drop out rate across caste group is visible only in the economically underdeveloped regions. The repetition rate and drop out rates seem to match in most of the regions indicating the major cause for drop out as repetition. Realising this, the repetition up to the 5th standard has been stopped. This would help to improve the enrolment and the completion of the primary level.

At the upper primary level also, the drop out rate appears to be high. Table 6.15 presents the drop outs, completion and repetition at the upper primary level. This also exhibits around 10 per cent drop out in the UT as a whole. Here the drop out rate of girls is marginally higher in the SC category. Interestingly the drop out rate is high in others' category. Across the regions while Yanam displays around 20 per cent drop out rate, it is around 2 per cent in the Mahe region. In all the regions, the 'other category' boys apparently drop out more than the girls in the same category at the upper primary level. This indicates that while the SCs and BCs drop out more at the primary level, others' category people drop out more at the upper primary level. Repetition seems to be perceptibly higher among the SC category boys and girls. However the drop out among the SC boys and girls at this level is lower than the other category people. This indicates the drive of the lower social category people to swim against the current.

TABLE 6.14

Rates of Drop Outs, Completion and Repetition across Communities and Regions at the Primary Level in 2002-03

Types	*SC*			*BC*			*Others*			*Total*		
	Boys	*Girls*	*Total*	*Boys*	*Girls*	*Total*	*Boys*	*Girls*	*Total*	*Boys*	*Girls*	*Total*
						Puducherry						
Drop Out	11.3	9.53	10.43	12.75	8.95	10.76	17.81	10.12	13.44	12.75	9.16	10.87
Completion	73.34	78.59	76.06	76.87	80.95	79	72.47	78.22	75.74	75.8	80.22	78.12
Repetition	15.27	11.89	13.51	10.38	10.11	10.24	9.72	11.66	10.82	11.45	10.61	11.01
						Karaikal						
Drop Out	11.07	6.84	9.11	13.06	10.47	11.88	17.16	11.57	13.73	13.22	9.88	11.57
Completion	74.11	73.5	73.86	75.19	81.29	77.97	72.19	79.1	76.43	74.39	78.76	76.54
Repetition	14.76	19.66	17.03	11.75	8.24	10.15	10.65	9.33	9.84	12.4	11.36	11.88
						Mahe						
Drop Out	0	0	0	1.89	1.58	1.74	8.82	8.2	8.53	3.26	2.85	3.06
Completion	0	0	0	95.83	95.63	95.74	79.41	85.21	82.17	92.58	93.67	93.11
Repetition	0	0	0	2.27	2.27	2.51	11.76	6.56	9.3	4.15	3.48	3.83
						Yanam						
Drop Out	39.39	18.52	30	38.52	53.1	50.76	20.41	10.53	16.09	34.31	32.6	33.51
Completion	49.39	69.26	78.33	56.33	55	55.63	66.73	74.74	73.23	68.88	64.25	62.47
Repetition	21.21	22.22	21.67	35.25	31.9	33.61	42.86	44.74	43.68	34.8	33.15	33.03
						Union Territory						
Drop Out	15.46	8.72	12.39	16.56	18.53	18.79	16.05	10.11	12.95	15.89	13.62	14.75
Completion	65.63	73.78	76.08	76.06	78.22	77.09	72.7	79.32	76.89	77.91	79.23	77.56
Repetition	12.81	13.44	13.05	14.91	13.13	14.13	18.75	18.07	18.41	15.7	14.65	14.94

Source: School Education Department, Puducherry.

TABLE 6.15

Rates of Drop Outs, Completion and Repetition across Communities across Regions at the Upper Primary Level in 2002-03

Types	*SC*			*BC*			*Others*			*Total*		
	Boys	*Girls*	*Total*	*Boys*	*Girls*	*Total*	*Boys*	*Girls*	*Total*	*Boys*	*Girls*	*Total*
					Puducherry							
Drop Out	14.75	12.05	13.42	10.58	11.56	11.04	9.22	13.9	11.65	11.36	11.85	11.59
Completion	49.78	50.51	50.14	62.7	68.52	65.44	63.4	72.73	68.24	60.04	64.85	62.34
Repetition	35.48	37.44	36.15	26.72	19.92	23.52	27.38	13.37	20.11	28.6	23.3	26.06
					Karaikal							
Drop Out	12.73	11.11	11.86	10.25	9.22	9.69	28.65	4.08	17.77	14.72	8.93	11.69
Completion	45.45	53.57	49.79	58.16	68	63.53	49.73	75.83	60.84	53.23	65.3	59.56
Repetition	41.82	35.32	38.35	31.59	22.78	26.78	21.62	21.09	21.39	32.05	25.77	28.76
					Mahe							
Drop Out	0	0	0	1.74	1.92	1.82	7.69	6.45	6.82	1.88	2.26	2.09
Completion	0	0	0	64.21	79.12	70.79	84.62	87.1	86.36	65.06	79.9	71.8
Repetition	14.71	34.88	25.97	2.94	31.71	23.28	13.51	20.34	17.71	10.48	28.8	22.15
					Yanam							
Drop Out	20.59	26.56	22.08	26.47	18.29	20.69	16.22	15.23	15.63	20.95	18.48	19.38
Completion	64.71	41.36	51.95	70.59	50	56.03	70.27	64.41	66.67	68.57	52.72	58.48
Repetition	14.71	34.88	25.97	2.94	31.71	23.28	13.51	20.34	17.71	10.48	28.8	22.15
					Union Territory							
Drop Out	12.02	12.43	11.84	12.26	10.25	10.81	15.45	9.92	12.97	12.23	10.38	11.19
Completion	53.31	48.65	50.63	63.92	66.41	63.95	67.01	75.02	70.53	61.73	65.69	63.05
Repetition	23	26.91	25.12	23.83	23.34	25.24	17.55	15.31	16.51	26.05	23.93	25.78

Source: School Education Department document.

The drop out rates, completion and repetition at the secondary level are illustrated in Table 6.16. It also shows that the drop out rate remains at 13 per cent at the secondary level too. Surprisingly, the drop out rate at this level is very high among the other category students. In the case of repetition it tends to be higher among the SCs and BCs. This transpires two things vividly. Firstly, the proportion of students at the secondary level is very high in the other category. Secondly, the higher repetition rate and lower drop out rates among the SCs and BCs proclaims the determination and perseverance of these pupils to pursue their education even with humiliations and aspersions. In other words, relatively well-to-do people or people with some push from some corners only reach up to the secondary level from the SCs and BCs categories. This external pressure compels them to continue their education even with repetition. Across the regions, the drop out rate of girls tends to be perceptibly higher in the Yanam region in all the social groups. The drop out of girls is higher in all the regions in the others category. This could be increasingly attributed to the biological developments in the girls and the society preventing the girls from going out for studies in majority of the villages even now.

Thus it indicates that the drop out rates and its social background vary at different levels of education. The repetition and drop outs are interlinked. The higher repetition at the primary level can precipitate a large scale drop outs and cause huge educational waste. Hence, consideration of automatic promotion at the primary level would see the children through one milestone in time and this would motivate them to take adequate effort to pass other milestones through perseverance and determination.

6.1.5 Children with Special Needs in Schools

A large number of children with one or other physical challenge attends the schools. The children with orthopaedic handicap, visual impairment, hearing impaired, speech impaired and mentally challenged people are also attending schools. All the children are able to reach up to secondary levels. Even some of the mentally challenged children are able to come up to the secondary level.

TABLE 6.16

Rates of Drop Outs, Completion and Repetition across Communities across Regions at the Secondary Level in 2002-03

Types	*SC*			*BC*			*Others*			*Total*		
	Boys	*Girls*	*Total*	*Boys*	*Girls*	*Total*	*Boys*	*Girls*	*Total*	*Boys*	*Girls*	*Total*
						Puducherry						
Drop Out	17.25	13.84	15.56	13.65	13.69	13.67	12.98	20.16	16.89	14.51	14.16	14.33
Completion	44.9	43.63	44.27	55.3	63.61	59.46	53.85	61.29	57.89	52.63	58.61	55.62
Repetition	37.85	42.52	40.16	31.05	22.71	26.87	33.17	18.55	25.22	32.86	27.24	30.05
						Karaikal						
Drop Out	10.09	6.38	8.37	7.56	4.05	5.57	32.37	1.94	19.42	15.43	4.06	9.75
Completion	50.46	68.09	58.62	63.56	75.76	70.44	49.64	81.55	63.22	56.45	75.46	65.96
Repetition	39.45	25.53	33	28.89	20.27	23.99	17.99	16.5	17.36	28.12	20.49	24.31
						Mahe						
Drop Out	0	0	0	1.44	1.5	1.47	3.33	6.82	5.41	1.51	1.9	1.71
Completion	0	0	0	73	84.96	78.5	90	86.36	87.84	74.02	85.15	79.59
Repetition	0	0	0	25.56	13.53	20	6.67	6.82	6.76	24.47	12.95	18.71
						Yanam						
Drop Out	16.67	36.96	30	17.39	31.51	28.13	16.67	32.65	27.4	16.9	33.33	25.12
Completion	66.67	43.48	51.43	43.48	27.4	31.25	70.83	48.98	56.16	60.56	38.1	49.33
Repetition	16.67	19.57	18.57	39.13	41.1	43.63	20.5	18.37	16.44	22.54	28.57	25.56
						Union Territory						
Drop Out	11	14.3	13.48	10.01	12.69	12.21	16.34	15.39	17.28	12.09	13.36	13.62
Completion	54.01	51.73	51.44	58.84	62.91	59.91	66.08	69.55	66.28	60.92	64.33	61.44
Repetition	23.49	21.91	22.93	31.16	24.4	28.63	19.85	15.06	16.45	27	22.31	25.04

Source: School Education Department document, 2002-03.

The children with special needs across regions and schools are presented in Table 6.17. The number of children with special needs like OH and visual impairment tends to be higher across regions. They are also able to come up to the secondary level. The majority of the mentally challenged students are able to complete only primary or upper primary level. The hearing impaired also remains to be high. The speech impaired tends to be very low. This indicates the nature of physical challenges children have and the special needs of the children in the schools. This also necessitates the school administration to ensure adequate facilities to the children with special needs.

Thus, the educational infrastructure and manpower have to be developed substantially to cater to the needs of students with special needs, students from socially marginalised groups and geographically constrained areas.

6.1.6 Educational Infrastructure

The substantial educational infrastructure has been developed in all the regions in the UT. Even the incentive schemes to students are also praiseworthy. The education department has been making efforts to achieve universalisation of primary education through sincere implementation of Sarva Shiksha Abhiyan (SSA), centrally sponsored schemes and in-service trainings to the teachers through DIET and SRC. The concerted effort of the government and department has made education as one of the top performing sectors in the UT.

The educational facilities available within the rural habitations are presented in Table 6.18. It shows that the number of rural inhabitations has declined by 50 per cent due to declaration of Mahe and Yanam regions as totally urban areas, and some of the rural areas in Puducherry and Karaikal regions are also included in the urban areas due to agglomerations. Thus it is sufficiently clear that the number of rural inhabitations having primary schools and upper primary schools has increased persistently though the facilities within one kilometre has not shown any significant change.

As discussed earlier, the primary school has not made noteworthy progress in both rural and urban areas. Upper primary schools have shown noticeable growth in the rural areas. As established elsewhere in the chapter, the

TABLE 6.17

Details of the Children with Special Needs in the Schools across Regions and Schools

Block	*Stage*	*OH*		*MR*		*VI*		*HI*		*SI*	
		M	*F*	*M*	*F*	*M*	*F*	*M*	*F*	*M*	*F*
						Puducherry					
I	P	67	33	29	16	35	36	16	12	1	1
	UP	61	53	5	3	40	13	7	10	1	1
	SEC	53	43	0	0	13	7	5	2	0	0
II	P	19	12	13	12	15	7	8	2	0	0
	UP	17	8	3	1	10	5	9	6	6	0
	SEC	19	17	0	0	11	8	6	6	4	0
III	P	19	15	22	17	18	11	13	6	0	0
	UP	27	6	2	2	20	7	5	5	0	0
	SEC	24	14	7	6	5	2	0	1	0	0
		306	201	81	57	167	96	69	50	12	2
						Karaikal					
I	P	52	20	35	18	13	18	11	14	0	0
	UP	41	12	3	1	14	4	1	6	0	0
	SEC	22	14	0	0	3	0	5	0	0	0
	Total	115	46	38	19	30	22	17	20	0	0
						Mahe					
I	P	3	2	6	3	3	2	1	1	0	0
	UP	2	2	0	0	3	0	2	0	0	0
	SEC	2	1	0	0	0	0	0	0	0	0
	Total	7	5	6	3	6	2	3	1	0	0
						Yanam					
I	P	9	8	5	7	1	4	5	4	0	0
	UP	6	4	2	1	3	4	3	3	0	0
	SEC	0	1	0	0	0	1	0	0	0	0
	Total	15	13	7	8	4	9	8	7	0	0
						Union Territory					
	P	169	90	110	73	85	78	54	39	1	1
	UP	154	85	15	8	90	33	27	30	7	1
	SEC	120	90	7	6	32	18	16	10	4	0
	Total	443	256	132	87	207	129	97	79	12	2

Note: OH: Orthopaedically Handicapped; MR: Mentally Retarded; VI: Visually Impaired; HI: Hearing Impaired; SI: Speech Impaired
P: Primary school; UP: Upper Primary; SEC: Secondary

Source: School Education Department document.

TABLE 6.18

Educational Facilities within Rural Habitations

Particulars	*1993*	*2002*
1) Total Number of Inhabitations	379	187
2) Number of Habitations having Primary Schools		
i) Within the habitation		
ii) Within 1 Km	197350	162172
3) Number of Habitations having Upper Primary Schools		
i) Within the habitation		
ii) Within 3 Km	74352	71164

Source: Seventh All India School Education Survey, Directorate of School Education, Puducherry.

secondary and higher secondary schools have displayed momentous growth due to upgradation of the lower level schools (Table 6.19). This manifests the noticeable growth in infrastructure development in school education system.

The status of building structures of schools as presented in Table 6.20 shows that there has been a remarkable progress from 1993 to 2002. More than 90 per cent of the primary and secondary schools have *pucca* buildings. At the higher secondary level, it is cent per cent in 2002. This is true in both rural and urban areas. Interestingly as the educational level goes up from

TABLE 6.19

Distribution of Schools

Type of Schools	*Rural*			*Urban*			*Total*		
	1993	*2002*	*Growth*	*1993*	*2002*	*Growth*	*1993*	*2002*	*Growth*
Total	280	313	11.79	302	342	13.25	582	655	12.54
Primary Schools	185	170	-8.11	150	149	-0.67	335	319	-4.78
Upper Primary	52	74	42.31	65	59	-9.23	117	133	13.68
Secondary	30	51	70.00	58	79	36.21	88	130	47.73
Higher Secondary	13	18	38.46	29	55	89.66	42	73	73.81

Source: Seventh·All India School Education Survey, Directorate of School Education, Puducherry, 2005.

primary to higher secondary, the proportion of *kutcha* buildings dwindle to become nil at the higher secondary level.

TABLE 6.20

Status of the Building Structures of the Schools

(in percentage)

Type of Schools	*1993*		*2002*	
	Total	*Rural*	*Total*	*Rural*
Primary Schools				
Without Building	0.00	0.00	0.31	0.00
With *Kutcha* Building	27.46	29.19	7.21	5.88
With Partly/*Pucca* Building	72.54	70.81	92.48	94.12
Upper Primary Schools				
Without Building	0.00	0.00	0.75	0.00
With *Kutcha* Building	17.95	17.31	8.27	5.41
With Partly/*Pucca* Building	82.05	82.69	90.98	94.59
Secondary Schools				
Without Building	0.00	0.00	0.00	0.00
With *Kutcha* Building	11.36	20.00	2.31	3.92
With Partly/*Pucca* Building	88.64	80.00	97.69	96.08
Higher Secondary Schools				
Without Building	0.00	0.00	0.00	0.00
With *Kutcha* Building	14.29	15.38	0.00	0.00
With Partly/*Pucca* Building	85.71	84.62	100	100

Source: Seventh All India School Education Survey, Directorate of School Education, Puducherry, 2005.

The status of primary schools with number of teachers transpires that there is hardly any discrimination in providing infrastructure to rural and urban areas in Puducherry. The number of one teacher schools has come down to 2 per cent (Table 6.21). Majority of the primary schools have more than five teachers. This indicates the importance given to primary education in Puducherry.

TABLE 6.21

Primary Schools with Number of Teachers

(in percentage)

Number of Teachers	*1993*		*2002*	
	Total	*Rural*	*Total*	*Rural*
Zero	0.00	0.00	0.00	0.00
One	5.67	7.03	2.20	2.35
Two	22.09	28.11	19.12	28.23
Three	7.46	10.81	7.52	7.65
Four	11.05	10.81	9.09	10.00
Five and above	53.73	43.24	61.13	50.59

Source: Seventh All India School Education Survey, Directorate of School Education, Puducherry, 2005.

The infrastructure position of the schools (Table 6.22) explicates that majority of the primary schools have the basic amenities like electricity, toilet and drinking water facilities. This could be attributed to the initiatives of SSA. In the case of basic amenities, all type of schools are blessed with adequate infrastructure. In the case of library, lab and teacher room, the need for improvement is highly felt. Even in other facilities it is still less than the desirable level. Hence, a big push is required to develop adequate infrastructure at the government schools to face the challenge posed by the private schools.

Though more than 90 per cent of the schools have own buildings (Table 6.23), still around 20 per cent of the classrooms are thatched. This needs immediate attention of officials concerned.

TABLE 6.22

Infrastructure Facilities Available at Schools

Level of Schools	Number of Schools	Number of Schools having							
		Library	Laboratory	Teacher Room	Electricity	Toilet	Drinking Water	Compound Wall	Play-ground
Primary	247	0	0	3	199	191	204	130	115
Middle	71	22	2	4	67	64	69	49	32
Secondary	66	39	33	34	64	60	64	53	40
Higher Secondary	424	101	75	81	370	355	376	269	217
Total	808	162	110	122	700	670	713	501	404

Source: Seventh All India School Education Survey, Directorate of School Education, Puducherry, 2005.

TABLE 6.23

Ownership Status of School Buildings

Schools	Number of Schools	Ownership Status	
		Own	Rented
Primary	247	237	10
Middle	71	66	5
Secondary	66	65	1
Higher Secondary	424	408	16
Total	808	776	32

Source: Seventh All India School Education Survey, Directorate of School Education, Puducherry, 2005.

Thus, the educational infrastructure created in the UT is impressive and it started paying off in all the other sectors too. Nevertheless there are still some areas of concern left to take education to all, equally.

6.1.7 Innovative Methods to Reach Higher Standards in Government Schools

Puducherry government has been providing education as one of the thrust sectors from the beginning of its formation. It has undertaken concerted effort to achieve this through sincerely implementing SSA, adult education programmes, teacher education, art education and vocational education programme. In addition, mid-day meal programme in Puducherry is one of the replicable success models.

1. Sarva Shiksha Abhiyan

Sarva Shiksha Abhiyan (SSA) is a major intervention towards achieving the long cherished goal of universalisation of elementary education (UEE) through a time-bound integrated approach in partnership with the states. It is an attempt to recognise the need for improving the performance of the school system and to provide community owned quality elementary education in mission mode.

The 'SSA Union Territory of Puducherry Mission Authority' came into existence in the form of a registered society in February 2002 to implement ambitious scheme in the UT. The Mission Authority has a General Body with the Chief Minister as the president, Education Minister as the vice president and 41 ex-officio and nominated members. The Executive Committee consists of the Chief Secretary as the Chairperson, the Secretary to Government (Education) as the vice chairperson, and 18 ex-officio and nominated members. Director of Education is the Member Secretary of the mission authority. The SSA Project was launched in the UT on November 14, 2002.

Various innovative activities have been undertaken. Under computer education, supply of computers to all high schools in Puducherry and computer aided learning (CAL) programme in high schools and government primary schools attached with high schools have been undertaken. In 2004-05, computers have been provided to 67 high schools in the UT. Azim Premji Foundation, Bangalore supplies the educational CD free of cost to the schools. Software on 'Computer Based Assessment' has been developed by SSA Puducherry in association with Azim Premji Foundation. The computer-based assessment is conducted to the children of II-VIII classes to assess the learning achievement of children under implementation of CAL Programme.

Through girl's education initiatives, guidance and counselling for the girls in schools, vocational skill development for the empowerment of girl children, supply of sewing machines and supply of sports materials have been done.

Under special focus on SC children, night school centre in schools in SC populated area, special coaching classes for slow learners among SC children and coaching classes for the SC children to attend entrance examination conducted by Navodaya Vidyalaya have been envisaged. At present, 207 night schools are functioning in the UT (85 in Puducherry, 84 in Karaikal, 20 in Yanam, and 18 in Mahe).

Under Early Childhood Care and Education (ECCE), play materials to primary schools having LKG and UKG classes, CDs on nursery rhymes for kids, and alternative schools for out of school children and enrolment of drop outs have been introduced. In this aspect, NGOs were also involved to organise night schools. Assessment camp and conferences/workshops under inclusive education for disabled children have been organised. A total of 2074 out of school children were identified through a Household Survey conducted during 2002 under SSA. In 2004-05, a survey was initiated through Village Education Committee and it identified an additional 500 out of school children. Out of the 500, 289 were enrolled in the alternative schools established in 38 government schools and 7 NGOs. These children were tied up with 'Friends in Learning' of the same locality who motivate and take care of the educational needs of the out of school children. They are entitled to breakfast scheme, noon meal scheme, evening bread and milk scheme, free supply of text books and notebooks, and free supply of uniforms, *chappals*, dictionary, stationary, school bag and cycle (IX standard).

A sum of Rs.275.55 lakh was made available in the year 2004-05 for the construction of 166 additional class rooms under civil works in SSA. In the post-Kumbakonam tragedy, it has become necessary to convert all the thatched sheds into *pucca* classrooms in short notice. The transfer of funds to PWD for construction of classrooms has been made with the approval of MHRD.

Vocational Skill Development Programmes are being implemented in 109 schools in Puducherry and Yanam. The girl children studying in classes VI and VII are given training by technical teachers in various crafts like clay/paper pulp toys, dolls, embroidery materials, wire bags, mats, etc., and also in visual and performing arts. During 2003-04 all the technical teachers in Puducherry district were given a three-day training in the vocational skill development activities like drawing, craft, sewing and music. The programme was carried out in 54 schools in 2004. In the year 2005-06 vocational skill development programme were implemented in 35 schools in Karaikal and 6 schools in Yanam.

Counselling services have been introduced for the girls in VI and VII standard by the women teachers of the respective schools. A five-day training programme was organised for 73 women teachers in Puducherry, 32 in Karaikal, and 7 in Yanam on guidance and counseling. They were designated as 'Guidance and Counseling Assistants'. A programme on counseling to Tsunami victims was designed. The counseling assistants carried out the counseling services in Puducherry and Karaikal districts. SSA along with WHO and JIPMER organised a one-day training programme for the teachers working in schools situated in Tsunami hit areas on 'Psycho Social support Programme for the Tsunami Victims' highlighting various aspects of social support and rehabilitation measures. A book titled *All about Tsunami* both in English and Tamil has been prepared by SSA to educate the students, parents and the public.

2. Adult Education Scheme

Adult Education Scheme seeks to eradicate illiteracy in the UT through the Centre based approach evolved in 1979 and followed by Government of India guidelines. It functions under different nomenclature such as:

a) Farmer's Functional Literacy Project.

b) Rural Functional Literacy Project.

c) State Adult Education Programme, and

d) Mass Functional Literacy Programme till 1988.

With the emergence of National Literacy Mission (Government of India) this Centre-based approach has been switched over to campaign mode as per guidelines of Government of India, under the title of 'Operation Arivozhi' based on the Ernakulam (Kerala) Total Literacy Campaign Model. Puducherry had been declared as a Total Literate State in the year 1991.

During the year 1988, Government of India introduced a new scheme of continuing education to the neo-literates, those who had completed the basic education during the Total Literacy Campaign under the title of 'Puduvai Arivozhi Iyakkam' society targeting one lakh neo-literates. A total of 172 Continuing Education Centres and 28 Nodal Continuing Education Centres have been established. For the first three years 100 per cent central grant was given. Fourth year onwards, 50:50 basis matching grant was given by the Centre.

Out of the target of one lakh neo-literates, 83071 have been enrolled so far (39904 males and 43167 females). The centres are functioning from 6 pm to 8 pm in government primary, middle, high school and *anganwadi* centres. Eight primary school teachers have been drafted from schools to supervise the centres. The training programmes for field functionaries have been organised every year with coordination of State Resource Centre, Chennai. The centres have been provided with the following materials to benefit the neo-literates:

a) library books,

b) daily newspapers and magazines (weekly and monthly),

c) *Yettram* (monthly magazine) published by the State Resource Centre, Chennai.

d) *Puduvai Seithigal* published by the Information and Publicity Department, Puducherry,

e) Carrom board and bicycle.

The centres are engaged by *Preraks* and paid Rs.700 to 1200 per month as honorarium. The Deputy Director (Adult Education) and project officer is supervising all the centres in Puducherry, Karaikal and Yanam.

3. Teacher Education

Two organisations take care of the in-service educational needs of the teachers, namely State Training Centre (STC) and District Institute of Education and Training (DIET).

I State Training Centre (STC)

The large scale in-service education of teachers in the UT became highly essential after the establishment of the 'Centre for Continuing Education' in the year 1982-83. STC became a miniature of 'State Council of Educational Research and Training' (SCERT). After the establishment of DIET in 1994-95, the STC has been providing training programmes for all categories of teachers at secondary and higher secondary level. STC has been catering to the in-service education needs of teachers and providing them the resource support. The STC is also entrusted with the selection and deputation of various categories of teachers for the in-service training programmes organised by various central and state agencies outside the UT (Table 6.24).

TABLE 6.24

Training Programmes Conducted by STC

Year	*No. of Programmes*	*Participants*	*Region*
1998-99	13	336	All
1999-2000	21	663	All
2000-01	22	659	All
2001-02	20	645	All
2002-03	13	417	All

Source: School Education Department document, 2002-03.

Constituents of STC

1) District Centre for English: It offers 10 day courses and one year correspondence courses in teaching of English at secondary level to the in-service teachers under the auspices of Central Institute of English and Foreign Languages, Hyderabad. The participants of the 10-day courses are provided with a book kit containing a Longman's Dictionary and a Grammar Book worth Rs.700.

2) Guidance and Counselling Bureau: It offers career guidance and counseling courses for career teachers in schools.

3) Environment Education Cell: It conducts awareness programmes on various aspects of environment to teachers and students. National Green Corps is implemented through the Cell.

II District Institute of Education and Training (DIET)

DIET comes under a Centrally Sponsored Scheme of 'Restructuring and Reorganisation of Teacher Education' which was approved in 1987. This scheme receives 100 per cent Central grant and academic support from the NCERT and NIEPA, New Delhi. DIET's mission is to provide academic and resource support for quality improvement in the area of elementary education with special reference to Universalisation of Elementary Education.

DIET Puducherry was established during 1994-95 and is registered as society to facilitate functional autonomy with responsibility and accountability. DIET provides academic and resource support to elementary education in the UT.

Main Functions

1) Pre-service and in-service training to teachers at primary level.

2) Resource support (Guidance, Development of materials, AIDS, Evaluation tools, etc.).

3) Action Research.

Branches of DIET

1) Pre-service Teacher Education

2) Work Experience

3) District Resource Unit
4) In-service Programmes, Field Interaction and Coordination
5) Curriculum Material development and Evaluation
6) Education Technology
7) Planning Management.

Table 6.25 provides details of various programmes organised since 1998-99.

TABLE 6.25

Training Programmes Conducted by DIET

Year	*No. of Programmes*	*Participants*	*Region*
1998-99	21	839	All
1999-2000	37	1357	All
2000-01	15	693	All
2001-02	22	1163	All
2002-03	30	1215	All

Source: School Education Department document, 2002-03.

4. Art Education

In addition to the art education provided to children in schools, the UT has Jawahar Bal Bhavans and Jawahar Mini Bal Bhavans to provide intensive coaching and training to children in various kinds of arts. There are four Jawahar Bal Bhavans, one each in Puducherry, Karaikal, Mahe and Yanam. The Jawahar Mini Bal Bhavans are situated in rural areas. There are 7 Mini Bal Bhavans in Puducherry, 2 in Karaikal, 2 in Mahe, and 1 in Yanam regions. Children attend the Bal Bhavans after the school hours in the evening and during the school holidays. Sixteen different arts are taught to the children.

Free 'Arangetram in Bharat Natyam' is organised in all the Bal Bhavans of Puducherry. Establishment of creativity clubs in schools, organising of art exhibitions and release of art catalogues are some of the activities of the Bal Bhavans. The children of Bal Bhavans in Puducherry have attended the International Children's Assembly at Mongolia and Norway.

5. Vocational Education

Vocational education was introduced in the higher secondary schools during 1978-79 in the UT. Out of the 42 government higher secondary schools, 19 higher secondary schools offer 44 vocational courses in the disciplines of agriculture, health and para-medicals, engineering technology, home science, business and commerce in classes XI and XII. The vocational courses are handled by the vocational instructors. Total number of students enrolled in various vocational courses in classes XI and XII during 2002-03 is 1794.

6. Mid-day Meals Scheme

The Mid-day Meals Scheme is being implemented in Puducherry right from the French Regime i.e., from the year 1930. At present it is being implemented to the students studying from I to XII standard in 464 government/government aided private schools besides the children of Balwadis. Nearly 1.26 lakh students are covered under the scheme. The mid-day meals are being prepared in 11 central kitchens and 114 school canteen centres in the UT. The mid-day meals include 130-160 grams of cooked rice, *sambar* with vegetable *porial* besides two boiled eggs weekly. There are 316 part time cooks/ assistant cooks engaged for the preparation of mid-day meals besides 177 part time meal carriers for the distribution of the cooked food. All the central kitchens are equipped with modern/hygienic cooking vessels.

The Government of India has allotted free rice under National Programme for Nutritional Support to primary education at the rate of 100 grams per student/school working day for the students studying from I to V standard in government and government aided schools. During the year 2004-05, Government of India allotted 8795.37 quintals per month through the Food Corporation of India under the National Programme for Nutritional Support to Primary Education popularly known as Mid-day Meals Scheme. However, the government of Puducherry prescribed 130 grams of rice per student/school day and the additional quantity of rice required over and above the allotment made by the Government of India are met from the state funds by procuring the same in the cooperative institutions as per the rates approved by the government. The Government of India provided an amount of Rs.59.92 lakh as grant-in-aid under CSS for National Programme of Nutritional support to Primary Education.

The implementation of the Mid-day Meals Scheme has reduced the drop out rate to 11.32 per cent at the primary level and 7.65 per cent at the upper primary level in 2004-2005. Further it is also proposed to involve mothers of the students in the distribution of mid-day meals in all the schools in order to have a strict vigil over the implementation. The mid-day meal also provides food security to the poor children. It plays a role in school attendance, punctuality and attentiveness in the class rooms, eliminating drop outs and also fostering social equity.

As a result of all the infrastructure development, manpower development, innovative initiatives and incentives to education, the results in the public examination is quite satisfactory in Puducherry, Karaikal and Mahe regions compared to Yanam. Across government and private schools, private schools have produced better results. Hence, there is a compulsion for the department of education to deliver results (Table 6.26).

6.1.8 Summary

Education and health sectors have been making noteworthy achievements in the state. The importance for education was prioritised from the date of French arrival. The literacy rate is very close to the Kerala level. It has grown with strides in the last three decades. The growth of enrolment of students, teachers and institutions in both government and private schools are indicative of the sustained proactive efforts of the government. The student-teacher ratio has been reaching the optimum level of around 20. The student-teacher ratio tends to be low in private schools. This indicates the quality of education through personal attention to the students. The drop out rates tend to be high among the SCs and BCs at the primary and upper primary level. At the secondary level, the drop out rate is high among the girls and upper caste students. This manifests that the upper caste students are invariably able to come up to the secondary level but in the case of SCs and BCs it is up to the primary and upper primary level. Those who cross this milestone are able to pursue their education to higher levels. Thus, proactive measures have to be taken up to arrest the drop out of students from SC and BC categories at the primary and upper primary level. The major reason for this is undoubtedly the repetition or retention. Similarly, the children with special needs have to be taken care at the school level.

6.2 Higher Education

6.2.1 Status of Higher Education

Directorate of Collegiate and Technical Education was bifurcated from the erstwhile Directorate of Education to set-up a separate establishment for dealing with matters pertaining to higher education. The teacher-student ratio stands as 1:16 in Arts and Science colleges, 1:14 in engineering, Technical and other Professional colleges, 1:3 in MBBS, 1:14 in Teacher Training College. On the whole it is 1:10 in higher education.

In the government sector every new initiative has to be approved by MHRD. Fee structure is fixed and no tuition fee is charged in government colleges. New courses like Foreign Trade, Applied Microbiology and Computer Science courses have been introduced to counter the competition from private sector.

Table 6.27 indicates that the proportion of people having higher education has been improving in a slow pace in the subsequent census from 1981. Still it is less than one per cent of the population in the rural areas. In

TABLE 6.26

Results in Public Examination

Schools	Secondary (SSLC)				Higher Secondary			
	Puducherry	*Karaikal*	*Mahe*	*Yanam*	*Puducherry*	*Karaikal*	*Mahe*	*Yanam*
			Government Schools					
1998-99	61.99	59.77	96.35	30.60	84.09	72.40	66.08	27.50
1999-2000	68.90	65.00	96.50	544.40	86.08	84.44	58.57	51.04
2000-01	66.60	67.50	95.05	62.00	83.49	84.17	47.47	45.40
2001-02	65.80	69.10	95.00	48.08	83.56	82.00	53.44	19.87
2002-03	71.78	67.05	93.56	52.56	63.76	62.88	52.69	30.16
			Private Schools					
1998-99		97.35	NA	NA		100	NA	NA
1999-2000	94.30	99.10	NA	NA	94.50	96.60	NA	NA
2000-01	92.10	98.10	NA	NA	92.20	88.10	NA	NA
2001-02	95.00	97.00	NA	NA	97.00	92.40	NA	NA
2002-03	96.72	97.98	NA	NA	89.54	93.10	NA	NA

Source: School Education Department document, 2002-03.

TABLE 6.27

Proportion of Population Attending Higher Education

Age Group	1981			1991			2001		
	Male	*Female*	*Total*	*Male*	*Female*	*Total*	*Male*	*Female*	*Total*
					Rural				
All Ages	0.10	0.01	0.05	0.24	0.07	0.16	0.59	0.63	0.61
15 - 19	0.06	0.02	0.04	0.29	0.16	0.22	1.34	1.32	1.33
20 - 24	0.72	0.05	0.40	1.38	0.44	0.91	2.64	4.14	3.42
25 - 29	0.24	0.01	0.12	0.63	0.07	0.35	1.62	0.64	1.16
30 - 34	0.03	0.02	0.03	0.11	0.01	0.07	0.36	0.01	0.21
35 +	0.01	0.00	0.00	0.03	0.00	0.01	0.08	0.00	0.00
					Urban				
All Ages	0.28	0.10	0.19	0.62	0.36	0.49	1.51	1.32	1.42
15 - 19	0.16	0.18	0.17	0.74	0.68	0.71	3.42	2.36	2.87
20 - 24	1.98	0.64	1.29	3.66	2.21	2.92	8.44	8.21	8.32
					Total				
All Ages	0.19	0.06	0.12	0.48	0.26	0.37	1.27	1.15	1.21
15 - 19	0.11	0.10	0.11	0.58	0.50	0.54	2.91	2.09	2.49
20 - 24	1.39	0.38	0.89	2.88	1.61	2.23	7.07	7.20	7.14
25 - 29	0.24	0.01	0.12	0.63	0.07	0.35	1.62	0.64	1.16
30 - 34	0.03	0.02	0.03	0.11	0.01	0.07	0.36	0.01	0.21
35 +	0.01	0.00	0.00	0.03	0.00	0.01	0.08	0.00	0.00

Source: Census Handbook, Socio Cultural Tables, Puducherry.

the urban areas, most of the students attending the graduate and above education is from the below 24-age category. Very negligible proportion attends the higher educational courses from the above 24-age category. Overall, more than one per cent of the population is attending the higher educational courses and the difference between the gender has also narrowed down. In the 20-24 age category, more than seven per cent attend higher educational courses indicating the preference to higher education among the youth.

6.2.2 *Student-Teacher Ratio in Higher Educational Institutions*

In the case of students, the proportion of girls in higher education in general is very low. In the Arts and Science colleges, the proportion of girls is higher than boys in the nineties though it is relatively less in the eighties. This could be attributed to the preference of boys to job-oriented professional courses. In engineering colleges, there has been a manifold increase in the number of students. Girl students' representation has also improved substantially. Similar trend is noticed in Law colleges and Polytechnic Institutes.

The student-teacher ratio is quite low in comparison with other states. Table 6.28 presents the student-teacher ratio in Puducherry as a whole. It indicates that the ratio tends to be very low in Arts and Science colleges and medical colleges. The medical colleges are not mere teaching colleges but also provide medical services to the people in the region and to the adjacent states. Very low student-teacher ratio in Arts and Science colleges explicates the under-utilisation of resources in the colleges. The increase in the ratio of girl student-teacher ratio in the nineties indicates the perceptibly higher enrolment of girls in Arts and Science colleges. This has been observed in other studies at the national level and Tamil Nadu state level too. In the Law colleges the ratio has been very high consistently. This indicates the higher preference to law courses in Puducherry. In the Polytechnic courses, the ratio has been increasing steadily. This elucidates the optimum utilisation of resources. Interestingly, the female student-teacher ratio has been declining. It indicates that there has been considerable increase in the number of women teachers. On the whole there has been noticeable increase in the enrolment of girls and recruitment of women teachers in all the higher educational courses.

TABLE 6.28

Student-Teacher Ratio in Higher Educational Institutions

	Arts, Science and Commerce College	*Medical College*	*Law College*	*Polytechnic Institutes*
1980-81	7.99	4.75	32.86	5.57
1981-82	8.29	4.15	26.44	6.58
1982-83	8.48	4.25	20.82	6.74
1983-84	7.85	3.51	35.44	7.69
1984-85	7.89	3.50	39.67	7.69
1985-86	7.83	4.14	29.46	11.78
1986-87	8.33	5.66	32.00	12.07
1987-88	8.82	4.35	35.82	11.57
1988-89	9.42	4.55	26.57	13.08
1989-90	9.29	4.62	20.53	9.25
1990-91	11.92	4.90	23.19	13.25
1991-92	9.46	10.00	27.87	13.03
1992-93	10.64	10.75	24.37	15.12
1993-94	13.53	5.32	33.81	14.61
1994-95	14.90	5.82	31.67	11.64
1995-96	15.32	4.13	29.26	16.12
1996-97	15.87	3.30	28.79	15.43
1997-98	15.82	5.08	36.80	15.05
1998-99	NA	3.17	36.07	18.32
1999-2000	NA	2.29	30.33	22.43
2000-01	0.69	2.79	34.53	21.40

Note: * Data Not Available.

Source: Statistical Abstract of Puducherry- Various Issues.

6.2.3 IT Education

IT policy for education is aimed at creating an Intelligent Society to raise IT literacy *per se* and to generate human resources with advanced skills and expertise in IT. The government has taken initiatives to mobilise the support of private sector training institutes, academic institutions, software companies, and vendors of software and hardware to help evolving several initiatives to produce high quality professionals. The major highlights of the IT policy for education are:

1) Courses on IT to be introduced in all branches of study starting from higher secondary level.
2) Specific courses to be launched to provide project management and software marketing skills.
3) Computers and Internet access to be made available in all degree level institutions. The quality of IT training offered by private institutes is to be monitored and enhanced through an accreditation programme.
4) Schemes to be worked out to enable students, teachers and schools to buy computers under attractive financial packages, such as easy instalment bank loans at lower interests, participation by manufacturing industries etc.
5) Digital libraries to be set-up in public libraries and academic institutions.

IT education has been promoted in the rural schools. Ten computers are given to each school at the ratio of one computer to four students. There is a plan to start Centre for Advanced Studies in Information Technology (CASIT). HCL, WIPRO and Pragati are having their hardware units in Puducherry. But Puducherry does not have enough qualified IT manpower to be absorbed in these units. Though these units are getting a lot of benefits from the state, they are not able to create employment opportunities in the state and absorb local people. Hence, there is a need for developing adequate manpower locally.

Scaling up initiative has been going on in all the major IT companies. In the private sector, some institutions have come up with high-end IT education. Nevertheless the employment generated in the UT is absorbed by the external candidates. Now the private institutions of higher education are proliferating in the state.

Puducherry has the tradition of producing highly competent professionals in the medical field. This brand value for Puducherry, *inter alia* has encouraged the private sector to start three medical colleges. Similarly the engineering field and management subjects also attracted increasing patronage from external students. Higher education through Puducherry Central University also has attracted large numbers of foreign students. Thus, higher education has got huge potential in Puducherry. This also facilitates the educational tourism earnings. In the nineties higher educational institutions have proliferated in all the regions in Puducherry. The permission to start institutions of higher education like medical colleges, engineering colleges, management schools and other professional courses is granted immediately.

6.2.4 Higher Education in the New Millennium

With a view to enhance the prospects of higher education for students belonging to economically backward sections, the Government of Puducherry introduced a scheme of financial assistance called 'Perunthalaivar Kamarajar Financial Assistance' to the students studying medical, engineering, B.Ed and D.T.Ed., courses. Under the scheme students sponsored by CENTAC are provided financial assistance to the extent of

60 per cent of the tuition fees charged by the unaided private institutions.

So far, during the year 2003-04 and 2004-05, Government of Puducherry has reimbursed an amount of Rs.3 crore to 1648 students studying in various professional courses.

In proof of the steps, taken by the Government of Puducherry to make Puducherry, a centre of excellence in education, the National Assessment and Accreditation Council, Bangalore accredited three government colleges. University Grants Commission accorded autonomous status to the Bharathidasan Government College for Women, Puducherry during the year 2004-05.

Keeping in mind the need for job oriented courses, the government introduced the three year degree courses, namely B.Sc. Microbiology in Indira Gandhi College of Arts and Science, Kadirkamam during the academic year 2004-05.

Sensing the prospects of a jump in the demand for teachers up to higher secondary level on account of various schemes like Universalisation of Education introduced by Central and state governments, the government of Puducherry has taken steps to start a D.T.Ed., college in Karaikal and increased the intake capacity of students from 60 to 100 in the B.Ed. course at Perunthalaivar Kamarajar College of Education, Karaikal.

6.2.5 Higher Educational Institutions in Puducherry

Apart from its French connection and image as a popular tourist destination, Puducherry is known for its educational institutions which are recognised as centres of academic excellence, both within the country and abroad.

Among these, the Jawaharlal Nehru Institute of Postgraduate Medical Education and Research (JIPMER), stands tall. Recognised as one of the three best medical colleges in the country, JIPMER's fame has spread among the medical fraternity all over the world. The institute plans to offer elective subject training for foreign medical graduates in response to request from them.

The college offers quality education in three streams both at the undergraduate and postgraduate level and full-time research in six subjects.

a. Pondicherry University

Another institute of higher education, which has acquired a name in a short span of time, is the Pondicherry University. It has the distinction of one of the earliest Central universities to offer choice based credit system that allows students to choose their combination of subjects according to their ability and career plan.

The university has emphasised new intra-disciplinary courses in its curriculum. It has introduced MBA in Banking Technology during the academic year 2004-05, with support from the University Grants Commission, the Department of Commerce and the Department of Information Technology.

In medicine education, besides JIPMER there is a Government dental college and the Vector Control Research Center offering research programme in paramedical science. They are affiliated to the Pondicherry University. The government is all set to start a medical college shortly.

b. Private Participation

Under the private sector, three medical colleges have come up during the last few years. The Puducherry Engineering College is the only Government institution. It offers 26 courses including M.Phil and Ph.D. There are two private engineering colleges.

Academicians say that for students aspiring to pursue higher education, Puducherry is an irresistible destination. The low cost of living and peaceful environs could make it a hot spot for higher education.

6.2.5 Summary

The higher education is highly privatised and the UT has been making concerted effort to attract more educational tourism and developing huge human resource potential locally to take advantage of the emerging industrialisation and information technology. In the higher education, there has been a steady increase in the enrolment of girls and entry of women teachers. This could be noticed in the reduction of student-teacher ratio, particularly the women student-teacher ratio. The IT education has been picking up in the state through the university courses and other higher educational private institutions. Private sector participation in the higher educational institutions has been phenomenally high. The democratisation of access to higher education has to be aimed at through selective targeting in the fees and other facilities to the genuinely deserving people.

6.3 Health Services

6.3.1 Introduction

World Health Organisation defines health as "a state of complete physical, mental and social well-being, and does not consist only of the absence of disease or infirmity." Public health is an approach to medicine that is concerned with the health of the community as a whole. The mission of public health is to ensure good health of the people. In the set of eight Millennium Development Goals of the United Nation, three are directly related to health i.e., to reduce child mortality, to improve maternal health, and to combat HIV/AIDS, malaria and other diseases. Health is also an important contributor to achieve several other goals related to the overall development of the state.

The policy towards health care in the state of Puducherry is primarily driven by the ideology to:

- Ensure availability, accessibility and acceptability for the population.
- Ensure quality in health care by monitoring and effective supervision.
- Ensure effective health care provision.
- Ensure effective implementation of preventive health care.

6.3.1.1 Brief History

Historically the region has been a place well known in the literature about sages who had profound knowledge of Siddha system of medicine and practices. In the literature it is said that few renowned personalities were accredited with the knowledge of reading the pulse of the patients, so making it evident that the practice of Siddha system of medicine was popular in the region during the eighteenth century.

The first hospital was built in 1690, the second hospital called Hospital Franco Martha in 1705 and in 1736 another hospital came up. All these hospitals catered to the needs of the whites alone. The local people were not allowed to avail the treatment rendered in these hospitals. In those days to assist the European doctors some Indians were trained, two of them reached higher ranks before retiring.

In 1832, a hospital was opened at the initiative of the then Governor to render free medical service to the local people. In 1841 initiatives were made to commence the construction of the Leprosarium in Puducherry. In 1853 two hospitals came into being. One was the military hospital with 40 beds and the other was the present general hospital then known as 'Hospital Colonial' with a capacity of 100 beds. This hospital had a maternity ward, a ward each for orphans, convicts and mental patients. The sisters of the Christian congregation helped to run the hospital.

In 1863, the administration constituted a health council to look into the working of hospitals and deal with all matters connected with public health. In 1867 a 'commission *sanitaire*' was constituted to take measures to prevent the spread of contagious disease, to improve the hygienic conditions of the establishment and to take all preventive measures to fight epidemics. In 1872 a council was formed exclusively that played an important role in maintaining public health. This council was consulted in matters relating to improvement of sanitation, preventive measures for various diseases, animal diseases, and cleanliness in public places. After 1925 the general hospital got many facilities like microbiology lab and bacteriological lab. In 1937 a separate maternity hospital came to be established. In 1948 a leprosy clinic was opened in the general hospital.

In 1956, when the French Puducherry was attached to the Indian administration, the status of health services was, one doctor for a population of 5,500, one nurse for 7,800 and one mid-wife for 4,300 persons. All doctors were in government service, in 6 hospitals and 32 dispensaries. The ratio of bed per 1,000 population was 3 in the Union Territory. In 1966, a re-designated directorate of health and family planning services started functioning.

6.3.2 Trends in Indicators of Health

The range of health indicators remains a vital source to assess the status of health, which interlinks key areas that influence the health outcomes. The vital indicators—the birth rate, death rate and infant mortality rate assess the status of health at a generic level. There are various indicators that could form the index of health in a state. The indicators of birth, death and infant mortality rates for the regions in Puducherry show a wide range of variation in rural and urban areas. Table 6.29 represents the five years' average. In the interpretation, figures for specific years have been used to indicate the fluctuations and differences.

There is a decrease from 28.7 per cent in 1981 to 9.66 per cent in 2003 in the birth rate in rural Puducherry region, but since 2001 there is an increasing trend in the birth rate i.e., from 5.1 to 9.66, an increase of 47.20 per cent within a span of three years, whereas in urban Puducherry, there is 5.8 per cent increase between 1981 and 2003. There are disparities between consecutive years of increases and decreases in the birth rate. The reason attributed to it is the influx of outside population to avail the delivery facilities; moreover, the incidences of home deliveries have decreased considerably and the institutional deliveries are nearing cent per cent. The fluctuation in the birth rate in the urban areas could be

TABLE 6.29

Birth, Death and Infant Mortality Rates

	1981-1986	*1986-1991*	*1991-1996*	*1996-2001*	*2001*	*2002*	*2003*
				Puducherry UT			
Rural							
B/R	27.1	23.92	15.35	6.94	5.17	6.92	8.19
D/R	6.6	5.70	5.98	4.39	5.51	5.89	6.16
I/R	23.4	13.58	12.90	8.40	2.14	6.11	9.09
Urban							
B/R	57.2	59.97	52.84	50.24	62.87	64.54	63.31
D/R	13.9	14.52	12.39	9.83	11.26	11.32	11.33
I/R	51.1	44.75	39.84	32.07	30.6	27.31	28.78
				Puducherry			
Rural							
B/R	28.0	26.88	15.73	6.82	5.1	7.34	9.66
D/R	6.6	5.90	5.93	4.26	5.55	6.03	6.17
I/R	25.3	14.57	12.14	11.38	0.85	7.01	10.94
Urban							
B/R	57.5	59.06	54.28	48.38	64.72	66.63	64.44
D/R	12.9	14.84	13.22	10.60	11.91	11.89	11.75
I/R	58.7	50.16	45.52	37.32	34.6	29.51	31.88
				Karaikal			
Rural							
B/R	26.2	17.40	14.48	8.93	7.17	5.92	4.67
D/R	7.2	5.48	6.17	4.73	5.4	5.56	6.15
I/R	22.7	13.13	9.14	3.37	4.33	3.45	NA
Urban							
B/R	50.3	62.59	58.36	58.85	80.37	81.35	82.81
D/R	10.1	14.27	11.48	8.69	12.18	12.83	12.59
I/R	23.0	23.64	21.49	10.35	18.84	24.19	22.33
				*Mahe **			
Rural							
B/R	21.2	20.08	-	-	-	-	-
D/R	4.8	4.57	-	-	-	-	-
I/R	1.4	1.37	-	-	-	-	-
Urban							
B/R	113.5	95.25	42.81	19.86	34.96	35.24	37.99
D/R	13.9	13.98	8.85	6.20	5.5	5.45	6.98
I/R	13.1	8.18	5.06	2.25	-	-	-
				Yanam			
Urban							
B/R	32.1	40.30	29.14	30.41	24.14	25.37	28.57
D/R	6.3	6.46	4.49	4.77	5.37	5.48	6.42
I/R	30.7	18.38	6.47	5.81	2.63	2.47	4.32

Note: * Mahe has been declared as an Urban area; B/R-birth rate; D/R-death rate; I/R-infant mortality rate.

Source: Local Administration Department

justified with the unpredictable influx of outside population. In Karaikal, the birth rate in urban area is higher than that of Puducherry and the trend is on the rise. Contrary to that of rural Puducherry, in rural Karaikal though there is a decrease in the birth rate. It has not shown any increase in the recent years rather a systematic decrease. A similar trend of decrease in the rural area and an increase in the urban area in the birth rate prevail in Puducherry as a whole, including the regions of Mahe and Yanam.

In the death and infant mortality rates though there are quantitative disparities between the urban and rural areas in the districts and the state as a whole; there is a decreasing trend in the rates over the years. This progressive trend is attributed to the efficiency of the health care system of the state.

The health service performance of Puducherry state is progressive when compared with indicators of the nation. Owing to the discontinuity of the districts in the state and contiguity with the neighbouring states, the difference between the regions poses challenges on the administration in functioning.

6.3.2.1 Sample Registration System

The sample registration system (SRS) is a large-scale demographic survey for providing reliable annual estimate of birth, death and other indicators at the national and sub-national level. In the case of Puducherry there are a total of 40 sample units with equal division in the urban and rural areas. The population covered in the sample are 36,000 with 23,000 in rural area and 13,000 in urban area.

TABLE 6.30

Birth Rate, Death Rate and IMR

Indicators		*1991*	*2001*	*2002*
Birth Rate	India	29.5	25.4	25.0
	Puducherry	19.2	17.9	17.9
Death Rate	India	9.8	8.4	8.1
	Puducherry	6.6	7.0	6.7
Infant Mortality rate	India	80.0	66.0	63.0
	Puducherry	-	22.0	22.0

Source: Directorate of Census Operations, Puducherry.

The basic indicators of birth, death and infant mortality rates of Puducherry state are progressive when compared with that of India (Table 6.30).

6.3.2.2 Still Birth Rate

According to the records available in the Department of Health and Family Welfare Service, within the state, Mahe has registered zero still birth rates in the year 2000, though its rate during 1980 was 4.5, comparatively very minimal. The district of Yanam has also shown a steep decrease in still birth rate in the past 20 years. The districts of Puducherry and Karaikal have an increase in the still birth rate at 10 per cent and 2 per cent respectively. The state as a whole saw a gradual decrease from 23.3 in 1980-81 to 17.1 in 1989-90 and from then onwards there was a gradual increase to 25.9 in 2000-2001.

6.3.3 Incidence of Diseases

The biggest challenge in the current health scenario is the control of communicable deceases. Major threat in the yesteryears was cholera and malaria, which got controlled in large scale. Due to improvement of the monitoring system and health facilities, other deceases are being detected and provided treatment—of them are tuberculosis and AIDS, the latter poses challenges. The high prevalence of sexually-transmitted diseases (STD) in India in general makes it vulnerable to AIDS threat. Treatment of patients in the hospitals and dispensaries (both in-patients and out-patients) over the period from 1980 to 2001 in absolute number has increased, though the rate had been proportionately on the decline with the population of the state.

The number of people per thousand population visiting the government hospital in Puducherry has been decreasing over the years from 830 in 1980 to 575 in 2001. This implies a considerable decline in the treatment of patients in the government hospital in spite of the influx of the patients from outside the Puducherry state availing the facilities, which is inclusive in the enumeration. There are two views on the decrease in the proportion of patients being treated, though the actual number has been on the increase. One is the general health status of the population in the Puducherry have improved thereby proportionately reducing the numbers. The second is the establishment of the private health facilities in the state. The facilities that are available with the government medical institutions are sophisticated and could be compared with the private medical institutions in the state.

The increase in incidences of diarrhoea and dysentery/ acute Gastro-enteritis and influenza/respiratory diseases over the period of years is a source of concern. (Table 6.31).

6.3.3.1 Cause Specific Death Rate

The cause specific death rate in this section was calculated for one lakh population to the deaths occurred under specific causes to the total population. The interpretations are made from the available data from 1980 to 1999 and their estimated population projections. In the following interpretations an attempt is being made to capture the distinct variations occurred in the particular year.

TABLE 6.31

Cases Treated in Hospitals and Dispensaries

Diseases	*1980-1985*	*1985-1990*	*1990-1995*	*1995-2000*	*2000-01*
Cholera	2	2	0	0	
Malaria	463	301	698	242	137
Diarrhoea and Dysentery	94102	2163	3491	29722	138948
Acute Gastroenteritis	9187	4403	6756	5272	
Influenza	14578	727	305	7518	47213
Respiratory Diseases	0	59	130	6490	
Tuberculosis	5675	4418	4899	12934	31184
Sexually Transmitted Diseases	2392	5650	850	2185	14231
Leprosy	0	0	149	670	997
AIDS	0	0	2	3	785
Other Diseases	4602560	4373320	4789770	4456656	5366021
Total	4728959	4391043	4807050	4521692	5599516

Source: Statistical Abstracts, Puducherry.

TABLE 6.32

Cause Specific Death Rates in the Regions

	1980	*1981*	*1990*	*1991*	*1999*
			Puducherry		
Cholera Rate	0.00	0.45	0.00	0.33	0.00
Plague Rate	0.00	0.23	0.00	0.00	0.00
Malaria	0.00	0.00	0.00	0.49	0.42
Fever	83.77	76.05	23.92	24.66	7.35
Diarrhoea and Dysentery	66.12	44.10	23.92	28.44	5.93
Respiratory Diseases	47.06	123.98	6.79	11.34	10.74
Tuberculosis	0.00	0.00	0.00	0.00	35.32
Leprosy	0.00	0.00	0.00	0.00	0.85
Tetanus	0.00	0.00	0.00	0.00	2.26
Cancer	0.00	0.00	0.00	0.00	20.77
Aneamia	0.00	0.00	0.00	0.00	8.62
Heart Disease	0.00	0.00	0.00	0.00	97.92
Jaundice	0.00	0.00	0.00	0.00	5.51
Suicide	0.00	0.00	0.00	0.00	51.71
Homicide	0.00	0.00	0.00	0.00	0.99
Others	975.63	959.23	973.65	956.54	663.67
			Karaikal		
Fever	34.41	45.83	18.89	10.29	0.00
Diarrhoea and Dysentery	18.41	54.16	57.38	56.97	7.26
Respiratory Diseases	103.24	62.49	11.20	14.41	5.44
Maternal Deaths	0.80	0.83	0.70	1.37	1.21
Tuberculosis	0.00	0.00	0.00	0.00	33.27
Tetanus	0.00	0.00	0.00	0.00	7.86
Cancer	0.00	0.00	0.00	0.00	8.47
Aneamia	0.00	0.00	0.00	0.00	7.86
Heart Disease	0.00	0.00	0.00	0.00	88.91
Jaundice	0.00	0.00	0.00	0.00	11.49
Suicide	0.00	0.00	0.00	0.00	31.45
Others	701.07	671.61	903.40	805.75	547.98

Contd. ...

...contd. ...

	1980	1981	1990	1991	1999
			Mahe		
Fever	0.00	0.00	0.00	11.96	52.60
Respiratory Diseases	0.00	0.00	21.27	26.91	38.76
Maternal Deaths	0.00	0.00	0.00	0.00	2.77
Tuberculosis	0.00	0.00	0.00	0.00	52.60
Cancer	0.00	0.00	0.00	0.00	22.15
Aneamia	0.00	0.00	0.00	0.00	5.54
Heart Disease	0.00	0.00	0.00	0.00	91.36
Suicide	0.00	0.00	0.00	0.00	19.38
Others	782.17	805.97	866.10	813.23	418.03
			Yanam		
Fever	67.59	8.60	5.17	9.85	10.38
Diarrhoea and Dysentery	9.66	25.79	10.33	19.71	6.92
Respiratory Diseases	0.00	25.79	10.33	9.85	6.92
Maternal Deaths	9.66	0.00	0.00	0.00	0.00
Tuberculosis	0.00	0.00	0.00	0.00	31.13
Cancer	0.00	0.00	0.00	0.00	17.30
Heart Disease	0.00	0.00	0.00	0.00	72.65
Suicide	0.00	0.00	0.00	0.00	17.30
Others	386.25	447.08	418.50	384.29	307.88
			Puducherry Total		
Cholera Rate	0	0.33	0.00	0.25	0.00
Plague Rate	0	0.17	0.00	0.00	0.00
Malaria	0	0.00	0.00	0.37	0.32
Fever	68.91	65.18	21.54	21.17	7.89
Diarrhoea and Dysentery	51.77	43.67	28.67	32.19	5.97
Respiratory Diseases	55.84	104.06	8.28	12.50	10.98
Maternal Deaths	3.06	1.16	6.75	5.32	2.13
Tuberculosis	0.00	0.00	0.00	0.00	35.50
Leprosy	0.00	0.00	0.00	0.00	0.64
Tetanus	0.00	0.00	0.00	0.00	3.09
Cancer	0.00	0.00	0.00	0.00	18.55
Aneamia	0.00	0.00	0.00	0.00	8.10
Heart Disease	0.00	0.00	0.00	0.00	95.30
Jaundice	0.00	0.00	0.00	0.00	6.18
Suicide	0.00	0.00	0.00	0.00	45.84
Homicide	0.00	0.00	0.00	0.00	0.75
Others	897.55	885.07	942.65	909.03	622.86

Source: Calculated from the Annual Reports, Department of Health and Family Welfare Services.

The death rate due to diarrhoea and dysentery in Karaikal had been relatively higher than the other regions of the state over the period of 1980 and 1999. Death rate due to respiratory deceases and tuberculosis have shown deviation from the normal in Mahe. It had been fluctuating. The cause specific death rates in many of the recorded years have remained higher than the regions. Deaths caused due to tetanus had been high in the Puducherry region, but in 1999 Karaikal has reported the highest amongst the other regions. In Mahe the incidences of death due to cancer has shown an increase over the period than other regions. Amongst the deaths on specific causes, death occurred during 1999 due to heart ailment had been high in the state, followed by tuberculosis (Table 6.32).

In Puducherry region deaths due to cholera had been minimal and since 1991 no cholera deaths have been reported till 1999. Death due to small pox had been reported only in 1984 with the rate of 4.3 and the death due to plague had been reported only in the year 1981 with the rate of 0.23. In regard to deaths due to malaria, the reported deaths are only from the year 1991, with a rate of 0.49 and it rose up to 1.91 in 1997, and declined to 0.42 in 1999. Death due to fever was reported at the rate of 83.77 in 1980 and it reduced drastically to 7.35 in 1999. The rates of deaths due to other than cancer were on the decreasing trend. Cancer deaths since 1992, with the rate 13.39 had risen up to 20.77 in 1999. Amongst the causes for death in the region during the year 1999, death due to heart ailments (97.92) is more followed by tuberculosis (35.32) and then cancer (20.77).

In Karaikal all the deaths due to various causes had been on the decreasing trend since 1980. Amongst all, the deaths due to heart related ailments are maximum with 88.91, followed by tuberculosis 33.27 during the year 1999.

In Mahe death due to cholera has been reported only once in 1992 and at the rate of 18.84 per lakh population. Death rate due to fever in this region had been on the increase which has reached up to 52.60 in 1999, whereas the rate was 6.81 in 1983. Though in 1983 deaths due to respiratory disease were 68.13, it came down to 5.75 in 1994 but had increased up to 38.76 in 1999. Deaths due to anaemia have been fluctuating since 1991; the rate that was 2.8 in 1998 had risen to 5.54 in 1999. Amongst the death due to various reasons, in 1999, also in the region deaths due to heart ailment have high (91.36) incidences followed by tuberculosis and fever (52.6), respiratory decease (38.76), and cancer (22.15).

In Yanam region, death due to malaria had been reported only in the year 1989 with the rate of 5.43. During 1999, amongst the causes for the deaths within the region, deaths due to heart ailments have been in high (72.65) incidence followed by tuberculosis (31.13), which is in an increasing trend since 1980 and then cancer (17.30).

The information on cause specific death reveals that a few cases like dysentery and diarrhoea, tuberculosis, cancer, anaemia, heart diseases and heart attack are in considerable numbers. Another aspect, which needs immediate attention, is the increasing rate of suicide during these three years. A thorough situation analysis could help us to know the factors behind them and propose activities which could reduce the rate and eliminate the problems over period of time.

6.3.4 *Health Infrastructure*

Despite the disparities on the health indicators within the regions in Puducherry state, there are strong acceptances on a good health delivery system. Department of Health and Family Welfare Services has two directorates, one is health and family welfare services, and from 1999 onwards a separate directorate came into existence for Indian system of medicine and homeopathy, which was bifurcated from the former.

The status of the health delivery system in the Puducherry has been widely appreciated. The health delivery structures that were functioning during the French Puducherry made a good precedence for the current heath infrastructure. There are eight hospitals in the state of Puducherry, of which four are general hospitals one each in the four regions. The remaining four hospitals of maternity hospital, chest diseases hospital, leprosy hospital and ESI hospital are situated in the region of Puducherry.

In Puducherry region till 2001 there are five hospitals, two community health centres that fall under the urban area, to support the delivery system. There are 27 PHC, 35 sub-centres in the rural area, and 16 sub-centres in the urban area. There are eleven PHCs (5 urban, 6 rural) that function round the clock with nurses working in three shifts; four PHCs (3 urban, 1 rural) working in two shifts and eleven PHCs (3 urban, 8 rural) working from 8 am to 2 pm. In Karaikal region there is one general hospital, one CHC and two PHCs in the urban region. In the rural Karaikal there are 9 PHCs and 17 sub-centres to cater to the health of the population of the region. In Mahe region there is one general hospital, one CHC, one PHC and three sub-centres, all falling under the urban category. The only PHC in this region functions from 8 am to 2 pm. Yanam region has one general hospital and four sub-centres in the urban category (Table 6.33).

With a general norm of one PHC for 30,000 population stipulated by the Union Government, Puducherry has been catering to a range of 10,000 to 60,000 population, within a reach of one to three kilometres. Higher the population, the delivery system is congregated and lesser the population the delivery mechanism is dispersed.

TABLE 6.33

Number of Hospitals

	State			Puducherry			Karaikal			Mahe			Yanam		
	1981	*1991*	*2001*	*1981*	*1991*	*2001*	*1981*	*1991*	*2001*	*1981*	*1991*	*2001*	*1981*	*1991*	*2001*
Hospitals (urban)	8	8	8	5	5	5	1	1	1	1	1	1	1	1	1
Chest Clinics	1	1	3	1	1	1	-	-	1	-	-	1			
Community Health Centre	-	4	4	-	2	2	-	1	1	-	1	1			
PHC	12	26	39	7	19	27	4	6	11	1	1	1			
Subsidiary Health (urban)	4	4	-	4	3	-	-	1	-						
Subsidiary Health (rural)	24	11	-	16	6	-	7	4	-	1	1	-			
Sub-centre (urban)	-	17	23	-	12	16	-	1	-	-	2	3	-	2	4
Sub-centre (rural)	48	62	52	29	44	35	16	17	17	3	1	-			
Medical Depot (urban)	3	-	-	1	-	-							2	-	-
Medical Depot (rural)	16	-	-	14	-	-	2	-	-						
ESI Urban Dispensaries	3	7	10	3	6	8					1	1	-	-	1
ESI Rural Dispensaries	4	4	2	2	3	1	1	1	1	1	-	-			

Source: Directorate of Economics and Statistics.

The facilities available in proportion to the population of the state are an indicator of the status of available health facilities.

The facilities in respect to the population in this section are calculated from the three population figures from the census data and the respective years' specific data pertaining to the facilities (Table 6.34). In Puducherry region the bed-population ratio for the year 1981 was 1:410. This had risen gradually to 1:423 in 1991 and to 1:505 in 2001. The condition in Karaikal is perhaps better than that of Puducherry, with a ratio of 1:381 in 1981, and again in 2001 to 1:392. The provisions of more beds in Mahe lead to the bed population ratio to remain a near constant for two decades. The condition in Yanam is alarming with a steep rise in the pressure of bed population ratio with 1:291 in 1981; 1:406 in 1991, and 1:627 in 2001. With the recent expansion of the hospital in the Mahe, the pressure has been reduced to some extent.

Though the demand for medical personnel is on the rise, the policy refrains from creation of new posts. Therefore, the state is managing with the available manpower in the health sector. The following table represents the number of medical personnel in government health system on a five-year average from 1980 to 2000 (Table 6.35).

The population covered by one doctor in government was 2628 and in 1991 it improved to 1779. In 2001 the population covered by one doctor rose to 2000. This is calculated from the respective years' population figures from the census data. And still the claim is that they are able to provide better service compared to the neighbouring states, the type of service rendered attracts patients also from far off places in the neighbouring states.

6.3.5 Preventive and Curative Health Facilities

6.3.5.1 Family Welfare Programmes

In regard to the birth control, the state has been on a progressive front. The number of women undergoing tubectomy in the reproductive age groups 15-44 has been increasing over the years.

Number of men undergoing vasectomy showed fluctuation from 1980-81 to 1988-89. Since then there was a gradual decrease. When compared with the number of tubectomy cases, vasectomy cases are very less. During 2003-04 the number of vasectomy operations is just 21 whereas tubectomy is 12,524. Details of both permanent and temporary family planning methods are shown in Table 6.36.

It is claimed that Puducherry is the first state to establish telemedicine in the country. A year ago, the general hospital was connected with other four hospitals in the Puducherry region itself to facilitate interaction through video conferencing to enhance the quality of service provided. In 2005, the connectivity was up-linked through satellite with the support of ISRO, with the hospitals in Mahe, Yanam and Karaikal. The connectivity can be further extended with the hospital facilities available in the rural areas.

TABLE 6.34

Number of Beds in Hospitals

Region / Year	1980-1985	1985-1990	1990-1995	1995-2000	2000-01
			Puducherry Total		
Hospital Beds	1458	1674	1766	1776	1759
CHC Beds	0	78	126	124	120
PHC Beds	119	89	131	184	192
Subsidiary Health Beds	85	76	43	1	-
Sub-centre Beds	0	0	0	0	75
			Puducherry		
Hospital Beds	1020	1189	1267	1267	1241
CHC Beds	0	51	66	64	60
PHC Beds	69	41	85	111	104
Subsidiary Health Beds	56	56	24	1	-
Sub-centre Beds	0	0	0	0	51
			Karaikal		
Hospital Beds	276	290	320	325	326
CHC Beds	0	0	30	30	30
PHC Beds	28	44	46	71	79
Subsidiary Health Beds	29	21	18	0	-
Sub-centre Beds	0	0	0	0	17
			Mahe		
Hospital Beds	115	124	129	134	142
CHC Beds	15	15	30	30	30
PHC Beds	22	11	0	3	9
Subsidiary Health Bbeds	0	0	1	0	-
Sub-centre Beds	0	0	0	0	3
			Yanam		
Hospital Beds	46	50	50	50	50
CHC Beds	0	0	0	0	0
PHC Beds	0	0	0	0	0
Subsidiary Health Beds	0	0	0	0	0
Sub-centre Beds	0	0	0	0	4

Source: Statistical Abstract.

All the PHCs in the state of Puducherry provide medical facilities of insulin, anti-rabies vaccine and anti-snake venom free of cost to the public, it is claimed that this facility is provided only in Puducherry.

6.3.5.2 Control of Communicable Diseases

Leprosy: The National Leprosy Control Programme, which had been in operation, was redesigned as Nation Leprosy Eradication Programme since 1983, and with the introduction of Multi Drug Therapy (MDT) since 1989, the prevalence rate has come down encouragingly. The 24 survey education training centres and two urban leprosy centres are providing adequate services to the leprosy patients in all the four regions.

The data collected from the Department of Health and Family Welfare Service indicates the prevalence rate of leprosy had come down from 12.8 per thousand population in the mid-eighties to 3.2 in 1991. The intensified remedial activities in the state had helped to maintain the prevalence rate to 3.43 per ten thousand population in 2001 and after this drastically reduced to 0.85/10000 in 2004.

6.3.5.3 National Anti-Malaria Programme

National Anti-Malaria Programme was taken over by this administration from the Government of Tamil Nadu in March 1975. Modified plan of operation for malaria control was implemented from April 1, 1997. With regard

TABLE 6.35

Number of Medical Personnel in Government

Items	*1980-1985*	*1985-1990*	*1990-1995*	*1995-2000*	*2000-01*
Doctors	267	397	477	487	487
Pharmacist	162	183	159	167	168
Bio-chemists	3	4	4	5.2	6
Nursing Tutors	4	6	7	7	7
Staff Nurses	361	508	669	704	748
Head Nurses	48	64	72	70	87
Assistant Dental Surgeons	4	5	3	7.4	9
Senior Laboratory Technicians	65	75	81	83	85
Darkroom Assistants	9	11	11	11	11
Laboratory Technicians Grade-11	6	7	6	6	6
BCG Technicians	8	8	7	8	8
Laboratory Assistants Grade-I	12	13	12	13	
Health Visitors	17	20	25	25	25
Maternity Assistants	173	189	182	209	216
Nursing Orderlies	111	141	149	162	174
Radiographers	18	22	24	24	24
Health Inspectors	31	28	29	29	29
Filarial Inspectors	14	21	22	22	22
Laboratory Assistants Grade-II	21	20	21	21	21
Health Assistants (qcl)	23	51	77	31	77
Health Workers (Malaria)	43	26	0	46	
Public Health Nurses	21	14	13	17	17
Para Medical Workers	26	26	26	26	26

Source: Statistical abstract.

dissection is done to study the presence of vector. Early case detection and prompt treatment is carried out through active and passive surveillance very effectively and effected a declining trend in the number of positive cases reported. Constant checking of breeding places like unused wells, water storage tanks, casuarina pits in coastal villages are carried out by anti-larval teams. The health assistants and health inspectors regularly supervise the fieldwork. Apart from treating the positive cases in Puducherry the system also caters to the patients from the neighbouring states.

Tuberculosis (TB): The national TB Control Programme is underway in the state of Puducherry since 1964. Over the years the figures of the number of TB cases detected had shown progressive improvement.

It is interesting to note that both in case of sputum positive case detection and TB cases (all varieties), there is a gradual decline during the recent years (Table 6.37).

6.3.5.4 Sexually Transmitted Diseases (STD)

In 1980 there were two STD clinics, one each at government hospitals at Puducherry and Karaikal. In 2003-04 few more STD clinics were added including one at JIPMER. The treatment is now available in 43 PHCs and four CHCs using the syndromic approach. The number of STD cases (6524) since 1980 had been on the decreasing trend up to (521) 1993-94 and then since 1997

TABLE 6.36

Birth Control Statistics

Items	*1980-1985*	*1985-1990*	*1990-1995*	*1995-2000*	*2000-01*	*2001-02*	*2002-03*	*2003-04*
Number of Male Operated (Vasectomy)	136	162	34	30	17	18	16	21
Number of Females Operated (Tubectomy)	5114	6349	8257	10000	11362	12793	12273	12524
Number of IUD Insertions	2603	3762	4123	3898	4553	4137	4075	3737
Number of Regular Users of Oral Pills	343	1143	964	2996	1340	1588	1791	1758
Number of Regular Users of Condoms	2401	8994	10531	8891	9761	11315	11547	10526

Source: Annual Reports, Department of Health and Family Welfare Services.

to the facilities available the state has two malaria clinics (one in Puducherry and another in Karaikal), 5 hospitals, 4 CHCs, 39 PHCs, and 75 sub-centres with 77 health workers carrying out the surveillance quite effectively. Laboratory facilities are available in the office of the Assistant Director (Malaria), district hospitals, CHCs, and in designated PHCs. The blood smears are sent for cross checking to the Regional Director (Health and Family Welfare), Chennai regularly. No missed positive case is reported in recent years. Daily mosquito collection and

TABLE 6.37

Number of TB Cases

Year	*No. of Sputum Positive Cases Detected*	*No. of TB Cases (all varieties) Detected*
2001-02	1511	3342
2002-03	1477	3369
2003-04	1041	2182

Source: Department of Health and Family Welfare Services.

the STD cases had increased. This is attributed to the increase in the facilities of detection since the introduction of Puducherry AIDS Cell in 1992.

6.3.5.5 Acquired Immune Deficiency Syndrome (AIDS)

The National AIDS Control Programme was started in Puducherry in May 1986. Since 1986 up to 1993-94, 24 people died of AIDS/AIDS-related complexities. There were three AIDS Surveillance Centres, including one in JIPMER. In 1994 Puducherry AIDS Society was registered. The society implements the entire programme under the guidance of National AIDS Control Organisation. In 1988 the cases detected with HIV positive were 39, of which 13 cases were from the adjoining Tamil Nadu. In 1991 the cases detected rose to 180 with 56 cases from Tamil Nadu. The outreach programmes of the society in Puducherry have induced the awareness on AIDS. This is reflected in the detection of positive cases, 877 in 2000-01 and 837 in 2002-03.

Puducherry AIDS Control Society is implementing all the programmes under the guidance of National AIDS Control Organisation. In addition, AIDS Prevention and Control Project (APAC), is also implemented since 2001, mainly to curtail sexual transmission of HIV through targeted intervention. In addition, training and awareness generating activities and surveys are also undertaken.

Blindness: The National Programme for Control of Blindness had been functioning since 1976 nationwide. The district Mobile Ophthalmic Unit was established in Puducherry during 1988-89. The unit visits all CHCs and PHCs. Ophthalmic technicians posted in the centres provide comprehensive eye care. Under the programme, cataract operations are conducted.

TABLE 6.38

Number of Cataract Operations

Year	*Cataract Operation*
1997-98	4232
1998-99	5033
1999-2000	6297
2000-01	6372
2001-02	7374
2002-03	7397
2003-04	9969

Source: Annual Reports, Department of Health and Family Welfare Services.

Table 6.38 gives details of cataract operations in Puducherry since 1997-98.

6.3.5.6 Immunisation

The state is keen on promoting the vaccine for the preventable diseases like neo-natal tetanus, whooping cough, polio, measles, etc. There was 100 per cent immunisation of pregnant women with tetanus toxoid. About 94.7 per cent of children below 1 year were immunised against measles. Most of the children in the age group of 10 and 16 years were immunised against tetanus. During the year 2004, hepatitis 'B' vaccination was launched as a pilot project in Puducherry, Mahe and Yanam regions. In this programme children in the group of 0-1 year were immunised against hepatitis 'B'.

The programme for total eradication of polio has been implemented through Polio Immunisation Programme since 1995, as a result of which no case of polio was reported from 1999 onwards. Acute flaccid paralysis surveillance is being implemented to rule out polio disease from other allied conditions like traumatic neuritis, transverse myelitis and GB syndrome.

In the case of Tetanus Prevention Immunisation, the data from 1994-95 to 2003-04 shows that in the case of pregnant women even though year-wise fluctuation is there, the status is more or less stable. The same trend is observed in the cases of TT prevention immunisation for children below 10 years and 16 years as well (Table 6.39).

6.3.5.7 Preventive Measures

The relationship between water, sanitation and health status, is volatile and vulnerable. The World Bank has estimated that more than 30 million life years are wasted annually due to water-related diseases. It is estimated that 80 per cent of all diseases and sicknesses are water-borne and water-related.

In Puducherry state, 89 per cent of the households have 'tap' as source for drinking water, where as 50 per cent of the households have no latrine according to the 2001 census figures. This leaves half of the population in a relatively hazardous situation susceptible to infection and diseases.

The health department in order to control the water borne diseases undertakes chlorination twice a month in all the overhead tanks that distribute water through the taps. Also, the laboratory makes periodical checks on the sample collected from the tanks. There are *dais* who are trained in scientific midwifery. There are community health guides who serve as a link between the community and the health care delivery system. There are multipurpose health workers and health supervisors to serve the rural population.

TABLE 6.39

Distribution of Tetanus Prevention Immunisation in the State

Tetanus	*1994-95*	*1995-96*	*1996-97*	*1997-98*	*1998-99*	*1999-2000*	*2000-01*	*2001-02*	*2002-03*	*2003-04*
T.T. (Pregnant Women)	19092	17624	19265	16625	19308	19519	19517	19764	19294	19410
T.T. (10 yrs)	20914	18060	19470	18093	19745	28502	21146	21238	21303	20548
T.T. (16 yrs)	17040	16806	16385	12530	19615	25527	19306	19572	21057	20286

Source: Department of Health and Family Welfare Services.

6.3.6 Private Hospitals and Clinics

Apart from the government hospitals, dispensaries and public health centres, the nursing homes, clinics and hospital run privately by individuals cater substantially to the health needs of the population. There are 24 private hospitals and nursing homes in the Puducherry region, three in Karaikal, one in Mahe, and four in Yanam. Thc overall decrease in the patients' visit to government hospitals in Puducherry is attributed to the increase in private hospitals and private medical practitioners in the state.

The Indian Medical Association is a national body of representative voluntary organisation of doctors of modern scientific system of medicine. The Puducherry chapter has 326 doctors who have registered themselves with the association. Among the registered members 28 are from JIPMER, 5 demised and 24 of them have left Puducherry. 57 members do not undertake any private practice in Puducherry. The remaining 269 undertake private practices. Of this, 73 are attached with the Department of Health and Family Welfare, and 58 with four medical colleges in the region. About 138 doctors exclusively undertake private practice in the Puducherry region alone.

In an estimate by the head of the Puducherry chapter of IMA in 2001-2003, the strength of IMA Puducherry chapter was 102, and in the beginning of 2003 it rose up to 107 and now it has a registered strength of 326. Still it is believed that there would be an estimated 25 per cent who are not 'not registered' with the IMA.

In the wake of private-state partnership, there are seven private medical colleges that have been providing support to the PHCs of the state. Each of the colleges has with them two PHCs each, where they provide three staff including a doctor.

6.3.7 Indian System of Medicines and Homeopathy

Under this category there are six *ayurveda* units and four *siddha* units in Puducherry. Puducherry region had all three treatment facilities, *ayurveda, siddha* and homeopathy. Over a period of five years from 1999-2000, there was 17.5 per cent increase in the patients availing this treatment in Puducherry. Karaikal has *ayurveda* and *siddha* clinics. Mahe has *ayurveda* and homeopathy clinics. Yanam has only one *ayurveda* clinic. There is an increase in the number of patients availing the Indian system of medicine in the state as a whole.

6.3.8 Academic and Research Institutions

There are seven medical colleges in the state, six at Puducherry and one at Karaikal. All of them have already started functioning partially.

A medical school called Cole de Medicine de Puducherry was established by the French Government in 1823. In November 1956 when Puducherry was merged with India, the Government of India took over the medical college in the wake of the *de facto* transfer of Puducherry. It was called Dhanvanthari Medical College then. The college was upgraded as a Regional Centre and named as Jawaharlal Institute of Postgraduate Medical Education and Research (JIPMER) on July 13, 1964. JIPMER has a tertiary care referral hospital under the direct administrative control of Directorate General of Health Services (DGHS), Ministry of Health and Family Welfare, Government of India. The average occupancy rate in the hospital is 106.9 per cent, which has 912 beds to provide inpatient services. There are 497 doctors and 578 nurses in the hospital.

Vector Control Research Centre (VCRC) that was established in 1975 under the support of ICMR, has been active in Puducherry. It has produced 591 original research articles, 30 unpublished reports. It had developed nine vector control products and has registered seven patents. It has developed and transferred nine strategies for disease vector control. It has developed four disease prediction models and has developed plans for mosquito control. It has set-up reference cells at VCRC linking research with operational activities.

6.3.9 Pharmaceuticals and Pharmacies

The Government Pharmacy in Puducherry is a very old institution. It had four functional units, sales section, manufacturing unit, stores and hospital equipment workshop, until 1993-94. Then it was reduced to three functional units of administrative/accounts section, stores section and hospital equipment workshop. There is a drug inspector under the food and drug administration who controls the wholesale and retail medical shops in the state. A private body, Puducherry Druggist Association is functioning in the Puducherry region. This body registers the private wholesale and retail outlets as its members. There are 268 pharmaceutical shops in Puducherry region, of which 42 are wholesale units and 226 are retail units.

6.3.10 State Expenditure and Budget Outlay

In the Tenth Plan for 2002-2007, the outlay for medical and public health stood at 8.58 per cent of the grand total outlay of 1,90,649 lakh and 17.7 per cent of the total outlay under the social services was 92,440 lakh, whereas under the Ninth Plan for 1997-2002, the outlay for social service was 52,150 lakh.

TABLE 6.40

Expenditure on Health

(in lakh)

	1980-1985	1985-1990	1990-1995	1995-2000	2000-01
Medical	404.01	1145.13	2198.04	4936.97	7806.22
Family Planning, Health Sanitation and Water Supply	182.40	277.96	509.94	1004.57	1732.23

Source: Statistical abstracts, Directorate of Economics and Statistics.

The expenditure on the medical and health related issues have been increasing over the years (Table 6.40).

6.3.11 Summary

The health indicators in Puducherry have been progressive when compared with the national indicators. But within the state, region-wise variations prevail. The urban Karaikal region has the highest birth and death rates within the state, where as the IMR is highest in the Puducherry urban region. But the decrease of death and infant mortality rates could be related to the better health care facilities available in the state. The sudden increase in the still birth rate needs special attention. The decrease in the number of visitors for treatment could be linked to the improvement in the health status of the state's population and the increasing private sector health facilities in the state. The issue of cause specific deaths in the case of a few diseases requires immediate attention to promote intensive curative and preventive measures.

In the recent release of the Directorate of Health and Family Welfare, the doctor and nurse population ratio is not comfortable. Currently Puducherry is able to manage the medical and surgical facilities in the medical institutions of the state. The region-wise disparities in terms of the facilities and provisions need to be addressed. The state has passed orders to register all the private practitioners, private hospitals and nursing homes, which would be underway to make a new policy on health that includes the private sector as well.

Under the health services provided by the state in the allopathic treatment, there is a decline in the patients availing the services. The private health services have contributed substantially in balancing the health services provided in the state. There is a steep increase in availing services under the homeopathy treatment, which is still limited in the state. The Indian system of medicine and homeopathy could be boosted, to reach more population by adding the facilities in the dispensaries and PHCs with simultaneous awareness creation on the facilities available.

Lack of good drainage system and good drinking water facilities are other possible causes contributing to water-borne diseases. In Puducherry open drains are prevalent. Closing these drains with a cover could avert the spread of diseases. In rural areas there are reported leaks and tapping of water from the public water supply systems. Due to poor maintenance of distribution pipes and sanitation facilities, incidences of contamination and subsequent infections were reported. Regular IEC activities addressing these issues could reduce/avert such cases.

Innovative methods like telemedicine can be strengthened further and could be expanded with the ICT supported Village Knowledge Centres facilitated by government, NGOs and Community Based Organisations in different localities of the state. Even though the increase in AIDS cases is not alarming, it is still a crucial area to promote intensive and extensive awareness and must be supported with medical services to prevent the man-made disaster.

The Department of Health and Family Welfare and the Department of Women and Child Welfare look into the issue of maternal health, through the PHCs and ICDS centres respectively. The recorded maternal deaths in Puducherry state though minimal, there are significant signs of the rise in the recent years. In Puducherry, the outreach facilities are proximately minimal than other parts of the country. To ensure a progressive achievement in maternal health, a comprehensive approach with community participation involving local women groups could enhance the system.

To meet the health concerns in the Millennium Development Goals, further enhancement of training to the Village health guides and trained *dais* need to be promoted. An effective maternal health care would automatically reduce the child mortality. In providing such a comprehensive safety net of medical care, through a system of effective extension mechanism, all the three goals, which are directly related to health, could be addressed.

6.4 Social Security

6.4.1 Introduction

Social security is a programme of public provision (as through social assistance or insurance) for the economic security and social welfare of the individual and his or her family. Generally the society is divided in to several subsections based on the economic and social conditions. In this context the state designs and implements programmes to provide for the basic economic security and welfare of individuals and their dependents. These supports help the beneficiaries to meet their basic needs. The programmes classified under the term 'social security' is the result of government legislation to ensure a social order for the welfare of the people of the state.

Matters relating to social security are listed in the Directive Principles of State Policy and the subjects are in the Concurrent List. The following social security issues are mentioned in the Concurrent List (List III in the Seventh Schedule of the Constitution of India):

- Item No. 23: Social security and insurance, employment and unemployment.
- Item No. 24: Welfare of labour including conditions of work, provident funds, employers' liability, workmen's compensation, invalid and old age pension and maternity benefits.

Part IV Directive Principles of State Policy ensures in Article 41, right to work, education and public assistance in certain cases. The state shall, within the limits of its economic capacity and development, make effective provision for securing the right to work, to education and to public assistance in cases of unemployment, old age, sickness and disablement, and in other cases of undeserved want. Article 42 makes provision for just and humane conditions of work and maternity relief.

Social security represents a system of support to individuals who are in need by the state as an agent of the society. The concept of social security is addressed through a series of public measures against the economic and social distress that otherwise is caused by the stoppage or substantial reduction of earnings resulting from sickness, maternity, employment injury, occupational diseases, unemployment, invalidity, old age and death (Planning Commission, 2001). This section deals with the different schemes covered under the social security of the socially and economically disadvantaged sections of the society in Puducherry. Lack of region-wise and gender segregated data on certain aspects is a major drawback, the availability of which could have helped to make region-wise comparative analysis.

Social security measures are of protective and promotional in kind. Under the category of protective in kind, the social security schemes can be divided into two, namely, organised and unorganised sector.

6.4.2 Protective Social Security

The Gazetteer of Puducherry on labour welfare gives an account of how the unorganised workers attained the status of becoming 'organised' in availing various welfare measures. After the merger of French-India with the Indian Government, many of the constitutional acts were appended in the legislation. Thereby, various protective measures of social security have become statutory in Puducherry.

6.4.2.1 Organised Sector

The social security laws in India provide for financing of the social security programmes by contributions paid by workers and employers and in some cases supplemented by contributions/grants from the government. The important contributory schemes include the employees' state insurance facility, the provident fund, pension and deposit linked insurance schemes.

The ESI scheme was introduced in Puducherry in 1966 and the scheme is being operated in all the four regions. The expenditure on ESI scheme is being shared in the ratio of 7:1 between the ESI Corporation and the Government under the terms of an agreement under Section 58(3) of the ESI Act. The Union Territory has one local office, which comes under the control of Regional

Office, ESI Corporation, Chennai. The Corporation has recently set-up a second local office at Puducherry.

In 1995, there were 1315 working factories in the state of Puducherry where 33,549 persons were employed and in the year 2001 the factories rose to 1870 with 53,589 employees. These employees are covered under the employees' provident fund schemes. Employees' Provident Fund Organisation is responsible in administering three social security schemes. Under the EPF scheme there are nine categories under which the members could make partial withdrawals in the form of advances. On death of the members while in service, the family is benefited by the employees deposit linked insurance scheme. Under the pension scheme there are eight categories of pension under which the beneficiaries are covered. A comprehensive picture for Puducherry state is not available, since there is no separate regional office of Puducherry. For better understanding of the situation it is essential to get a complete and comprehensive picture covering all four regions of Puducherry.

Employees' State Insurance Act, 1948 is applicable to few categories of establishment with stipulated number of employees. Until 1995, the scheme had the ceiling of the salary drawn by the employees which was Rs. 3000 and in 1997 it was increased to Rs.6500 and from 2004 onwards to Rs. 7500. The scheme encompasses benefits like medical benefits, which is rendered by the way of treatment in the hospital run by the corporation and as well referred to the other government hospitals. Other benefits are in the form of cash given under sickness benefit, disablement benefit, dependant benefit and maternity benefit. The regional office of the Puducherry state was established during 2001 on bifurcation from the Tamil Nadu.

Table 6.41 reveals a gradual increase in the number of employees benefiting from the scheme. The employees and employers who are registering in the corporation have been increasing. When there was hike in the ceiling of the employees' salary to be covered under the ESI schemes, there was decrease in the number of employees. It is stated that to evade the employers contribution to the corporation, the employers would increase the salary of the employees above the given ceiling. This also attributes to the fluctuation in number of the registered employees.

Insured persons or the family units are the one who fall under the category of dependants who are receiving benefits at the time of employee's death. With regard to the infrastructure facilities 11 full time ESI dispensaries, one part-time dispensary and one ESI hospital are

TABLE 6.41

ESI: Region-wise Details

Region	*1994-95*	*1995-96*	*1996-97*	*1997-98*	*1998-99*	*1999-2000*	*2000-01*	*2001-02*	*2002-03*	*2003-04*
					Puducherry					
No. of Employees	22650	18350	24950	33550	38750	36250	49900	49800	45500	44800
I/P Family Members	24100	19800	26350	35050	40200	37700	51350	51250	51100	50350
					Karaikal					
No. of Employees	950	550	700	900	1000	900	2400	2500	2400	3750
I/P Family Members	1000	600	800	900	1050	950	2450	2550	2700	4200
					Mahe					
No. of Employees	800	800	1050	650	650	700	1000	1200	900	900
I/P Family Members	850	800	1150	700	750	700	1000	1250	950	1000
					Yanam					
No. of Employees	750	2300	1650	1700	1700	3000	2900	2750	2750	2950
I/P Family Members	750	2300	1850	1850	1700	3000	2900	3000	3000	3150
					Puducherry state					
No. of Employees	25150	22000	28350	36800	42100	40850	56200	56250	51550	52400
I/P Family Members	26700	23500	30150	38500	43700	42350	57700	58050	57750	58700
Employers						870	990	1300	1556	1668

Source: Various issues of *Statistical Brochure*, ESIC, New Delhi.

functioning in the Union Territory of Puducherry. The beneficiaries have been on the rise over a period of ten years. The officials are sceptical on the reach of the ESI act, as there are employers to evade their contribution to the ESI.

6.4.2.2 Unorganised Sector

The unorganised sector comprises mainly workers who have not been able to organise themselves in pursuit of common objectives on account of constraints like casual nature of employment, ignorance and illiteracy, small and scattered size of establishments and position of power enjoyed by employers because of the nature of industry etc (Planning Commission, 2001). The Government of Puducherry has formed a society, The Puducherry Unorganised Labourer's Welfare Society and registered in 2001 under the Societies Registration Act, 1860. In the unorganised sector there is plethora of problems to be addressed. Workers in the age group of 18-60 are eligible to enrol in the Puducherry Unorganised Labourer's Welfare Society. The benefits entitled for its members are monetary benefits at time of death or partial/total permanent disability due to accident, at times of maternity and funeral grants. The society is yet to start functioning in Mahe.

Table 6.42 shows the number of members who received benefits since the establishment of the above society. Though in the year of establishment the beneficiaries were minimal, in the subsequent year there was a substantial increase in the beneficiaries under the society. Among the enrolled 18 per cent of them are women workers engaged in twelve categories of work.

TABLE 6.42

Benefits Received by Society Members

Schemes	*2001-02*	*2002-03*	*2003-04*	*2004-05*
Maternity Benefits	3	44	69	70
Incentives for SSLC Exams		40	32	Na
Incentives for HS Exams		12	14	Na
Funeral Assistance	2	7	22	14
Groups Insurance Death Benefit	1	7	17	11
Scholarship under LIC Groups Insurance Scheme		62	116	Na

Source: Department of Labour, Government of Puducherry.

Another major effort made was the establishment of the Puducherry Building and Other Construction Workers Welfare Board which started functioning in 2003, where a variety of construction workers get themselves registered but the enrolment of membership could be lesser if we compare with the total labour force of the state.

TABLE 6.43

Membership Status of the Puducherry Building and Other Construction Workers Welfare Board (2005)

Category	*Puducherry*	*Karaikal*	*Yanam*	*Total*
Male	1885	822	103	2718
Female	833	50		883
Total	2718	872	103	3693

Source: Labour Department, Government of Puducherry.

The formation of an exclusive board for the welfare of the construction workers is a recent effort by the labour department of the state. Awareness generation, promotion of gender specific schemes and encouraging the active participation of women labour could enhance the membership in future, which could bring women workers in to the fold of the welfare board (Table 6.43).

Amongst these members the majority are from the Puducherry region followed by Karaikal and then Yanam, workers from Mahe have not yet been enrolled in this board (which needs to initiate mobilisation of the unorganised labour force). The data further reveals around 24 per cent of the members are women construction workers.

Pension and other supports for the aged, widows, destitute and the disabled.

The old age dependency ratio represents the number of persons in the age group 60 years and above per 100 persons. This indicator is a useful measure to calculate the elderly population in the total population. Information gathered from the Statistical Abstract and the records of Department of Women and Child Welfare, indicates that the old age dependency ratio has decreased marginally from about 11.83 per cent in 1981 to 11.81 per cent in 1991, and has increased to 12.86 per cent in 2001 (with 14.41 for females which is higher than 11.53 for the males). An increase in the old age dependency ratio implies that an increasing number of elderly people depend more on the population in the working age group for support. With regard to the number of beneficiaries (Table 6.44) in the category of old age pensioners there is a steep increase during the period 1995 to 2000 and a little increase for the next three years. In the case of widow pensioners there was a marginal increase between 1995 to 2000, the number increased significantly in the next three years. Pension for the disabled persons was introduced after 2000 and is providing benefits to the needy population in the state.

TABLE 6.44

Beneficiaries of the Pension Scheme

Scheme	*1990-1995*	*1995-2000*	*2002-03*
Old Age Pension	10947	41359	42488
Widow Pension	8146	10726	43995
Disabled Pension	-	-	10411

Source: Statistical Abstract and Dept. of Women and Child Welfare, Government of Puducherry.

The other schemes covered for the old age people is the funeral expenses of pensioners, financial assistance for medical expenses of pensioner, free supply of clothing item to the poor.

The government provided educational allowance to widows' children, in the year 1990-91 to 754 persons, then the beneficiaries decreased rapidly. With duplication of the similar schemes by the education department that had higher allowance, the children benefiting from this scheme has decreased. Now the department has requested the government for a hike in the educational allowance.

Grant of marriage allowance towards marriage of daughters of widows is another scheme. In the year 1990-1991, there were 99 beneficiaries under the scheme which increased to 121 during 2000-01 and subsequently to 199 during 2002-03. The monetary value of the allowance was Rs. 1000 till 1998-99, which was increased to Rs. 5000 and in 2002-03 the assistance was further hiked to Rs. 10,000. Beneficiaries of Widow Remarriage had been very minimal, not exceeding 4 during 2000-01 and nil in 2001-2002 (Table 6.45).

TABLE 6.45

Details of Support Extended to Widows

Schemes	*1990-91*	*2000-01*	*2001-02*	*2002-03*
Grants of Educational Allowance to Widow's Children	754	Nil	4	7
Grants of Marriage Allowances Towards Marriage of Daughters of Destitute and Deserted	99	121	159	199
Widow's Remarriage		4	4	Nil
Total		125	163	206

Source: Directorate of Social Welfare, Puducherry and Dept. of Women and Child Development, Puducherry.

The state extends financial support to the physically disabled persons based on the disability status. A person with 40 per cent disability will get Rs.300 the next category 40 per cent to 74 per cent will get Rs.500 and above 74 per cent gets Rs.1000 per month. The financial assistance to the disabled persons is distributed through the local *anganwadis*. The details of the different categories of disabled population and their percentage-wise distribution are given in Tables 6.46 and 6.47.

TABLE 6.46

Region-wise Benefits to the Disabled

Region	*2003-04*	*2004-05*
Puducherry	12434	14277
Karaikal	2001	2180
Mahe	297	575
Yanam	437	378
Total	15169	17410

Source: Department of Social Welfare, Government of Puducherry.

TABLE 6.47

Disabled Population

(in per cent)

Region	*Total*	*In Seeing*	*In Speech*	*In hearing*	*In Movement*	*Mental*
Puducherry	19151	39.24	6.86	9.22	35.73	8.94
Karaikal	5389	47.86	6.62	7.77	30.25	7.5
Mahe	685	32.41	12.55	8.47	27.59	18.98
Yanam	632	52.22	9.65	5.38	26.58	6.17
Puducherry UT	25857	41.17	7.03	8.81	34.15	8.84

Source: Census 2001.

Among the four categories, majority of the disabled population are visually handicapped followed by physical disability, speech and hearing, and mentally retarded are more or less in the same percentage level. Immediate special attention is needed to focus on the preventive measures for the visually handicapped.

Conducting the vocational training programme for the disabled persons like courses on TV mechanic, AC mechanic, tailoring etc., is another other major programme for the disabled. The programmes are conducted by the Puducherry Women Development and Handicapped Persons' Corporation. The Social Welfare department extends the funding support. The trained persons are linked with the local banks for financial support, for each loanee the Social Welfare department provides subsidy. The other services are prevention and early detection of disabled. Social Welfare department is also supporting the disabled students to get spectacles, hearing aid, providing tuition facilities, meeting the medical expenses, books, notes, etc., through the education department. Apart from these, in the lower grade government positions (Grade C and D), 1 per cent reservation is provided in direct recruitment for visually, orthopaedically and hearing handicapped.

The government has shown commitment to support the disabled through several schemes over a period of time. Table 6.48 provides details of the support provided and the number of beneficiaries from 1999 to 2005.

It is important to correlate the birth rate of the disabled children with the general birth rate of the state to understand the seriousness of the problem and also to promote preventive measures to reduce the rate of disabled persons in the future.

The state is implementing a scheme to promote Voluntary Action for Persons with Disabilities through NGOs. This has been in practice since 1999 and the amount spent is relatively little (1999-2000: 1.44 lakh, 2000-01: 6.59 lakh, 2001-02: 5.85 lakh, 2002-03: 6.13 lakh, 2003-04: 7.75 lakh). The other scheme supports the voluntary organisations to take care of the welfare of the women, old persons, mentally retarded and physically challenged persons. Eight voluntary organisations are taking this support from the government and each one is getting Rs.25,000 per year. This aspect needs to be strengthened with the support of NGOs with genuine social commitment and experience in the field.

6.4.2.3 Other Social Welfare Programmes

To support the socially and economically vulnerable groups, the government has formulated several programmes aimed at promoting the social safety net of these vulnerable group members. For each of the programme the department has stipulated conditions like annual income, age, residence status, disability, occupational and marital status, etc.

The general trend of support extended to different sections of the vulnerable groups in communities is gradually increasing. Substantial amount has been spent and the number of beneficiaries is increasing. It is worth noting that the government is adding new welfare schemes every year. Insurance schemes for the disabled other than the government servants and payment of ex gratia for funeral expenses of the disabled are the programmes recently added in the list. Apart from the above indicated general schemes, the state has introduced occupational specific schemes recently for supporting some of the service castes like washermen and barber to buy the required equipments to do the job. The washer

TABLE 6.48

Beneficiaries of Various Schemes for the Disabled

Schemes	*1999-2000*	*2000-01*	*2001-02*	*2002-03*	*2003-04*	*2004-05*
Financial Assistance	797	3100	10190	13764	15169	16686
Scholarship	244	221	137	321	266	293
Prosthetic Appliances			60	72	31	34
Marriage Incentives	17	11	21	28	32	35
Fuel Subsidy		50	56	56	56	62
Unemployment Allowance	209	259	285	322	195	215
State Award	33	12	9	10	8	9
Insurance		265	265	326	326	359
Motorised Invalid Carriage					40	44
Eye Donation		5	3	1	1	1
Transport Allowance			759	465	1108	1219
Reimbursement of Maintenance Cost of Tricycle	8	8	8	8	11	12
Free Rice				10190	13764	15140
Insurance Scheme for the Disabled Other than the Government Servants						6127
Payment of Ex gratia for Funeral Expenses of the Disabled						360
Issue of Multiple Identity Card			3100	2900	475	500

Source: Department of Social Welfare, Government of Puducherry.

men were supplied ironing table/mobile cart at the cost of around Rs.7000 per person to support the professionally self-employed members of the communities.

6.4.3 Promotional Social Security

The Labour department is running labour welfare centres for the women folks hailing from labour families. There are eleven centres. Seven welfare centres function in Puducherry region, three at urban locations and four at rural locations. Two are in Karaikal and one each in Mahe and Yanam. For children in the age group of 3 to 5 years from the labour family, the labour department is running child welfare centres. There are seven child welfare centres in Puducherry region.

In order to assist the people of schedule castes, a separate department 'Adi-Dravidar Welfare' has been functioning in Puducherry state. The department administers several schemes related to shelter, livelihoods, health, etc. Since there is no ST population in the state, no special programme has been developed for the scheduled tribe. The department has listed about 27 schemes exclusively for the benefit of SCs in Puducherry, which also includes the centrally sponsored schemes.

Table 6.49 shows a steady increase to support the scheduled castes through different schemes with different objectives.

TABLE 6.49

Beneficiaries of Economic Development Schemes: SCs

Schemes	*2002-03*	*2003-04*	*2004-05*	*2005-06*
No. of Free House Sites *Pattas*			230	
Infrastructural Facilities	13	24	20	22
Grant of Subsidy for Construction of House	335	840	750	700
Burial Ground Pathway Scheme		1		
Funeral Rites Scheme	948	972	1072	600
Distribution of Free *Dhotis* and *Sarees* of Poor SC	129766	144360	151311	151300
Financial Assistance to SC People for Performing Marriage	445	454	461	580
Financial Assistance to Pregnant and Lactating Women	500	853	905	800
Financial Assistance to SC Patients Suffering from Prolonged Disease	0	04	39	100
Financial Assistance to Inter-caste Marriage	24	32	25	25
Financial Assistance to the Victims of Atrocities belonging to SC			9	
Mahatma Gandhi Memorial Award to Clean Houses		805	1000	1000

Source: Adi-Dravidar welfare dept, Government of Puducherry.

Education is one of the major aspects, which could promote the community to equip and empower and also assist the community to become aware of the development opportunities. It also helps in getting access to the programmes and utilise them effectively. The state is also motivating and supporting the students towards attaining education through several schemes. The data given in Table 6.50 provides the details of the number of students benefited under each of the programme.

The trend with regard to different programmes and the coverage is positively going on to achieve benefits to large number of students. But a detailed analysis needs to be

TABLE 6.50

Beneficiaries of Educational Development Schemes: SCs

Schemes	*1999-2000*	*2000-01*	*2001-02*	*2002-03*	*2003-04*	*2004-05*
Award of Pre-matric Scholarship to Students	10297	9735	11809	11977	10517	12460
Award of Retention Scholarship to SC Girl Students	3500	3500	5774	6063	5994	6354
Award of Opportunity Cost to the Parents of Girl Students	4829	4758	5249	9599	7610	7290
Award of Post-Matric Scholarship to Students	1604	1514	1448	3239	2276	1601
Award of Ad hoc Merit Grant to Students	135	135	232	236	358	295
Ambedkar Memorial Award to Students	6	5	4	5	6	4
Stipend to SC Trainees in Technical Training Institutes	292	292	295	289	252	214
Pre-matric Scholarship to the Students whose Parents are Engaged in Unclean Occupation	186	620	999	1039	1910	1721
Supplemental Maintenance Allowance to SC Students	16	16	9	32	26	18

Source: Adi-Dravidar welfare dept, Government of Puducherry.

done to find out whether the programme would be sufficient enough to meet the needs of the community.

6.4.4 Women and Child Welfare Programmes

Separate department for Women and Child Development was formed during the year 1996 by the Social Welfare Department with a view to focus more attention on women and child development exclusively. The Department of Women and Child Development provides nutrition/health support to the children, and pregnant and lactating mothers. Old age people and widows are being given financial assistance, free rice, and clothing.

The nutritional and pre-school support has been extended to the children through *anganwadis* and *balwadis*. For girl children a special scheme Balika Samridhi Yojana is being implemented. Several women welfare schemes are being implemented to extend support for various requirements like educational allowance to children of widows, grant of marriage allowances to the widow's daughters, grant of incentive for widow's re-marriage, reimbursement of tuition fees for the typewriting/ shorthand courses for the children of widows. Admission of destitute women in the service home for destitute women, admission of working women in the hostel for working women, national maternity benefit scheme, supply of utensils and sewing machines to Mathar Sangams and national family benefit scheme.

TABLE 6.51

Details of Region-wise Distribution of *Anganwadis* and *Balwadis*

Institution/ Regions	*2000-01*	*2001-02*	*2002-03*	*2003-04*	*2004-05*	*2005-06*
Anganwadis						
Puducherry	517	517	517	517	517	517
Karaikal	140	140	140	140	140	140
Mahe	12	12	12	12	12	12
Yanam	8	8	8	8	8	8
Total	677	677	677	677	677	677
Balwadis						
Puducherry	142	135	136	NA*	NA	NA
Karaikal	28	26	26	NA	NA	NA
Mahe	11	10	10	NA	NA	NA
Yanam	10	10	9	NA	NA	NA
Total	191	181	181			

Note: * Not Available.
Source: Dept. of Women and Child Development, Puducherry.

The Centrally sponsored Integrated Child Development Services Scheme (ICDS) was launched in Puducherry during 1978. There are 677 *anganwadis* in the state and had remained the same from 1990 to 2001 with 517 in Puducherry, 140 in Karaikal, 12 in Mahe and 8 in Yanam region. The number of *balwadis* in the state was 232 in 1990 and then it reduced to 191 in the year 2001. From 1998-99 onwards these centres are being assisted by the special nutritional programme. The nutritional support given for child is of supplementary nature with 300 calories and 10 gram protein, and the lactating and pregnant mother is provided 500 calories and 20 gm protein. These centres also monitor babies' weight and pregnant mothers suffering from anaemia. The severely malnourished babies are given extra care and nutritional support, and the mothers are supplied with iron tablets. The pregnant women are supported to meet the nutritional requirement with a grant of Rs.200 per month.

The Below Poverty Line families are now supported to marry their daughters of above 18 years with a sum of Rs.15,000. Similarly in the case of widows' daughters, Rs.24,000 is given to support their marriage. The financial support for widows' remarriage is Rs.15,000. The other provision available is, if the parents of two girl children decide to adopt family planning, the department would deposit Rs.7,500 for each girl. After 18 years, the girl would get a sum of Rs.45,000.

Schemes like Kulavilakku is granting Rs. 500 for the pregnant women and Aravanaippu granting Rs. 500 each to the mothers of the girl child for six months. A similar scheme sponsored by the Central government has been successful, where the number of beneficiaries have been on the rise. These two schemes were introduced from 2001-02.

Total number of the *anganwadis* and *balwadis* remain the same for the last five years in all four regions. It is essential to find out the need and accordingly decisions could be made with regard to establishing new centres. The reason is that in the state of Puducherry apart from *anganwadis* there are other facilities like crèche, nursery schools which attract the children better. Hence, none of the *anganwadis* is full to its strength. In many places the strength is less than 50 per cent of the capacity. Three years ago the *balwadis* were merged with the education department and attached to the local government schools where LKG, UKG classes are conducted.

Lack of proper building is the main drawback. The amount allotted is not sufficient to rent a good building. The poor quality of the environment is being considered as one of the main reasons for not attracting more students to *anganwadis* especially in the urban areas. With regard to the development of human resource it is essential to appoint qualified teachers, and organising regularly skill development training programmes for both *anganwadi* teachers and the supervisors with the support of the suitable training institutions. Planning for human resource development needs to be done to improve the present situation.

Moreover *anganwadis* are being used as the village level implementing agency for several government welfare schemes like implementing relief measures to natural calamities, schemes for physically handicapped, distribution of free *dhoti* and *sarees* to the BPL families etc. The teachers are spending considerable amount of time on these activities. Hence they lack the focus on the jobs given to them. Another issue focused on the need to prepare multilingual training materials for the *anganwadi* teachers.

To improve the conditions, services and performances, it is proposed to convert the *anganwadis* to the nurseries which could attract more number of children. As a first step it is proposed to convert 100 *anganwadis* to nurseries with pre-school education. ICDS could create greater impact in the society, provided it is implemented well with real spirit and skill.

TABLE 6.52

Funds Released and Expenditure under Integrated Child Development Scheme

(Rs. in lakh)

Year	*Released*	*Spent*
1997-98	105.55	148.12
1998-99	151.82	181.27
1999-2000	181.58	142.31
2000-01	154.85	173.75
2001-02	159.85	183.81
2002-03	241.05	232.35
2003-04	205.54	218.90
2004-05	236.89	230.59

Source: Department of Women and Child Development, Puducherry.

Table 6.52 indicates that every year the amount spent is more than what has been released by the Central government. It also shows the gradual increase of fund every year by the Central government to meet the requirements of the project activities. The state government contributes the extra amount spent in each year.

6.4.4.1 Children in Need of Care and Protection

Government of Puducherry is implementing a Centrally sponsored programme for 'Children in need of Care and Protection' for the children in distress through voluntary organisations to address the issues related to the disabled and the most vulnerable persons. This programme aims to take care of the destitute, neglected, abandoned, and vulnerable children who are exposed to various kinds of abuse and exploitation. Around 20 homes/orphanages are functioning in the state and are getting the financial support of Rs.250 per month per child. The fund is disbursed to the concerned organisations in two equal installments. The total grant released per year is Rs.27.17 lakh.

6.4.4.2 Noon Meal Scheme for School Students

The government has introduced noon meal scheme to ensure nutritionally balanced food to children in schools. The scheme is implemented at elementary and high school levels. The data indicates the downward trend in terms of schools implementing the scheme and students benefiting out it. The table shows that more or less one-fourth of the students are from SC communities (Table 6.53).

TABLE 6.53

Coverage under Noon Meal Scheme

Year	*Total Schools*	*Total Students*	*SC*
2001-02	411	62349	-
2002-03	411	62349	24046
2003-04	366	-	13803
2004-05	337	53221	13438

Source: Indiastat.com

The trend indicates that the number of schools providing this facility is declining, as also the number of students enjoying the benefits. To make the scheme more attractive the government has recently introduced the new method called 'community kitchen'. In this new method the food for each commune is prepared at one place and distributed to the schools located in the entire area. The centralised kitchen helps to maintain uniformity in the quality.

6.4.4.3 Social Welfare Homes

The Social Welfare department run homes for the orthopaedically handicapped, service homes, observation homes and special schools, beggar homes, special schools for blind and mute, homes for blind, homes for aged and infirm, hostels for working women, crèches, hostels for BC students and homes for mentally retarded.

The data in Table 6.54 reveals that there could be better performance by these institutions meant for the most vulnerable sections in the society. A detailed study

TABLE 6.54

Social Welfare Homes

Homes		*1990-91*	*1991-92*	*1992-93*	*1993-94*	*1994-95*	*1995-96*	*1996-97*	*1997-98*	*1998-99*	*1999-2000*	*2000-01*	*2001-02*	*2002-03*
Home for Orthopaedically Handicapped	Instn.	2	2	2	2	2	2	2	2	2	2	2	2	2
	Inmate	122	141	155	168	170	180	185	170	165	258	158	130	106
Service Home	Instn.	1	1	1	1	1	1	1	1	1	1	1	-	-
	Inmate	53	47	55	52	3	26	21	17	25	14	11	-	-
Observations Home and Special School	Instn.	1	1	1	1	1	1	1	1	1	1	1	1	1
	Inmate	110	120	130	140	150	114	115	124	100	150	150	80	77
Beggar Home	Instn.	1	1	1	1	1	1	1	1	1	1	1	1	1
	Inmate	31	37	56	40	21	25	17	17	18	25	25	20	22
Special School for Blind and Mute	Instn.	1	1	1	1	1	1	1	1	2	1	2	2	2
	Inmate	160	170	180	190	194	190	145	165	147	180	180	215	188
Home for Blind	Instn.	1	1	1	1	1	1	1	2	1	1	1	1	1
	Inmate	15	17	17	18	22	25	16	26	17	18	18	18	19
Home for Aged and Infirm	Instn.	1	1	1	1	1	1	1	1	1	1	1	2	2
	Inmate	20	21	22	23	20	25	23	23	22	25	25	50	49
Hostel for Working Women	Instn.	1	2	2	2	2	1	2	2	2	1	1	-	2
	Inmate	40	54	58	58	55	28	23	54	65	31	36	-	65
Crèches	Instn.	8	8	8	8	8	8	7	7	7	7	7	-	7
	Inmate	130	140	140	135	125	160	140	140	140	140	140	-	136
Hostel for BC Students	Instn.								3	3	5	3	5	5
	Inmate								45	73	125	75	140	148
Home for Mentally Retarded	Instn.								1	1	1	1	1	1
	Inmate								30	22	25	25	19	20

Source: Statistical Abstract, Directorate of Economic and Statistics.

on the prevailing conditions, performance and the impact could help to design and plan to improve the situation in future.

6.4.4.5 Puducherry Women's Commission

The state has constituted a women's commission to address some of the social evils that prevail due to the gendered hierarchical social system. The Commission conducts awareness campaigns on women's rights and against domestic violence. It also conducts meetings and interactive sessions with women in rural and urban areas on AIDS control, reproductive health, dowry, women illiteracy and female child abuse etc. The Commission also organises counselling programmes for the victims and extends legal support to overcome the problem.

6.4.5 Women Self Help Groups

The scheme Indira Mahila Yojana (IMY) was launched in the year 1996-97. The earlier programme that targeted the poor families was IRDP and since 1990, Swarnajayanthi Gram Swarozgar Yojana (SGSY) replaced it. This programme facilitated the poor families (below poverty line) to undertake self-employment through formation of Self Help Groups (SHGs). The formation of SHGs under SGSY replaced the erstwhile DWACRA groups.

As per the rules, the group would get the support of revolving fund of Rs.25,000 after six months based on its performance assessment in collaboration with the local bank. The revolving fund has the component Rs.10000 as subsidy the remaining amount being the loan. After the repayment of loan, based on the groups' performance, financial assistance is provided for income generating activities and for livelihood promotion with maximum of

TABLE 6.55

Details of SHGs Formed

Year	*Number of SHGs Formed*	*Number of Groups Availing Loans*	*Amount of Subsidy Released (in lakh)*
1999-2000	16	-	-
2000-01	150	3	2.94
2001-02	386	30	30.50
2002-03	110	56	55.34
2003-04	148	38	40.50
2004-05	160	72	81.87
2005-06	262	64	71.98
Total	1232	263	283.13

Source: Annual Credit Plans, Puducherry.

Rs.1.25 lakh as subsidy. If the group is able to repay the loan and successful in its income generation activity, it is considered as 'matured group' and will not be eligible for any future support from DRDA.

The number of groups formed in 2001-02 and 2005-06 is high compared to other years. A deeper analysis would help us to know the reasons for this variation. It is worth to design a plan to ensure a steady growth in the number of groups formed through mobilisation of especially the BPL families under the SHG framework to improve the situation (Table 6.55).

Table 6.56 reveals that substantial numbers of qualified SHGs are yet to be graded both at I and II levels. Similarly there is no proportionate release of loans to the subsidy released by the banks. These issues need further analysis and would lead to the facilitation of prompt loan disbursement by the banks to promote successful income generation and micro enterprise activities managed by the members of SHGs.

Apart from this, the Women Development Corporation is promoting women SHGs in rural and urban areas in collaboration with a local NGO. Numerous NGOs in the state are involved in mobilising the rural women and men in forming SHGs. Around 71 NGOs (48 in Puducherry, 18 in Karaikal, 1 in Mahe, and 4 in Yanam) have been formally collaborating with the government for implementing different development programmes.

6.5 Summary

Under protective system of social security, the public and private undertakings enrol their employees under the EPF and ESI. They avail of the benefits under the respective organisations. The unorganised sector in Puducherry has two divisions, one is a society and the other is a welfare board. These two divisions have started functioning only recently. Awareness generation among the unorganised labour force and the promotion of relevant schemes could enhance the outreach.

The promotional social security is being undertaken by Social Welfare department, Adi-Dravidar Welfare department and the department of Women and Child Development in Puducherry. A mechanism in documenting the social security details of the organised sector in the state could enhance the policymakers to address the issues in an efficient manner. The recently bifurcated ESI and the segregation of Puducherry EPF details in the Regional office in Chennai would project a clear/complete picture of the status in state of Puducherry.

The recently finalised draft social security legislation for workers in unorganised sector when enacted should further the status of the workers in the state. Now it is able to support them with two agencies (welfare board and society) through the centrally sponsored schemes. The proposed legislation seeks to create a participatory structure that builds on already existing civil society, government and semi-government organisations. Representation from the grassroots level self help groups, farm labourers forum would enhance the suitability and the quality of schemes designed, and the implementation. Such endemic provision in the structures would also accelerate the enrolment of workers in future.

The institutional arrangements developed for the unorganised sector in the form of registered societies need to be strengthened with more number of labourers mobilised and to address several of the genuine issues related to their life. It is also suggested to design a plan and strategy to generate awareness among the labourers about the existence of these institutions.

The SGSY programme introduced since 1999 is to elevate people from below poverty line. The surveys of 1997 reveals 63,232 families are below poverty line. Since the introduction of SGSY, as on date there are about 1000 SHGs in the state promoted by government and NGOs. The programme outreach has to be more vibrant. Moreover from the BPL surveys it is understood that the

TABLE 6.56

Details of SHGs Graded

Year	*SHGs in Operation*	*SHGs Eligible for I Grading*	*SHGs Completed I Grading*	*Yet to be Graded*	*Subsidy Released by DRDA (lakh)*	*Credit Released by Bank (lakh)*	*SHGs Eligible for II Grading*	*SHGs Completed II Grading*	*Yet to be Graded*	*Subsidy Released by DRDA (lakh)*	*Credit Released by DRDA (lakh)*
2005-06	1232	1078	910	169	861	843	710	342	380	290	272

Source: Annual Credit Plans, Puducherry.

families under the BPL category are on the rise. Being a small state, focus on bringing down the BPL list should be the main agenda.

In the case of the disabled persons, prevention should get priority with comprehensive package of support activities to promote the disabled to become more and more independent with sustainable livelihood options.

It is essential to ensure sufficient representation and participation of women and female children in the different schemes implemented by different departments. Women are in a disadvantageous position with several constraints, hence it is suggested to promote and ensure gender mainstreaming in the project activities and also the development of gender database for better analysis and planning in the future.

Skill and capacity building schemes for the target population should receive more attention. More than achieving the set target the quality and approach of the programme is more important. It is suggested to involve the appropriate technical institutions, NGOs, with proven experiences and strengths in the particular area. The other effective mode could be successful entrepreneurs sharing their experience and training the others through a horizontal transfer of knowledge.

Human resource development as an essential aspect needs to be taken care of to improve the quality and strengthen the programmes related to Integrated Child Development Schemes. This has been strongly felt by the supervisor and the *anganwadi* teachers of the different regions of Puducherry. The same is applicable to other social welfare homes meant for different purposes.

The schemes should ultimately help the target groups to become more independent in life. The skill and entrepreneurship development schemes with financial support and linkages with banks should really take them to the level of managing any profit making sustainable livelihoods in course of time.

The self help group formula is working well to mobilise the women in the BPL families. But the percentage of the mobilised is not very impressive when compared with the state's total BPL families. In this regard NGOs' support could be very useful to mobilise the women as members of SHGs and enable the department to improve the outreach of the programme.

References

Government of Puducherry, *Annual Statistical Abstract*, Directorate of Economics and Statistics, Puducherry.

Government of Puducherry, *Status of Primary Education—2002-03*, Directorate of School Education, Puducherry.

Government of Puducherry (2005). Seventh All India School Education Survey, Directorate of School Education, Puducherry.

Government of India, Socio-cultural Tables, *Census Handbook*, Census Department, Government of India, New Delhi.

Chapter 7

Tourism

Tourism has both growth and employment benefits. Direct spin-offs include the growth of hotels, restaurants and leisure centres. Indirect benefits will come in the form of hospitality services, retailing and transportation. Tourism is also a major foreign exchange earner. The major types of tourism include leisure/adventure tourism, medical tourism, educational tourism, and religious tourism. Karaikal attracts a large number of religious tourists to Thirunallar Saneeswara (Saturn) temple. It is considered as a mini-Thirupathi. Similarly, Puducherry also attracts considerable religious tourists to Auroville and other temples.

7.1 Structure and Functions of Tourism Department

Puducherry Tourism Development Corporation has four units to enable the tourism industry attract more tourists. They comprise of festivals and fairs, advertisement, constructions and budget. The festival and fair unit organises festivals like yoga festival, summer festival with cultural programmes, food festival, mangani festival in Thirunallar-Karaikal, people's festival in Yanam and Mahe. These are exclusively organised to attract tourists. In addition, there are a number of religious festivals attracting large number of tourists from the neighbouring states. Every year fairs and exhibitions are also conducted to encourage trade. They include shopping fair, vintage car race, sand image-making fair and air show by IAF. Around 1000 people visit per day during the fairs and festivals. Around Rs.32 crore was earned during the festivals and fairs through charges for the shops and stalls last year. Around 40 hotels are in the list of the tourism department to enable the tourists in the range of Rs.100 to Rs.5000.

Under the constructions unit, the tourism department receives fund from Central schemes around one crore and a matching grant from the state government. It is spent on both buildings and non-buildings. This section has taken up the works of Kanakan lake picnic spot development, Karaikal beach development, Oussudu lake picnic spot-cum-jogging track building and Mahe water sports complex, which is attracting a good number of local tourists now. Heritage building project in the old French settlements around the Beach road area with the help of INTACH is undertaken on a 50:50 basis in the private buildings. Financial incentives to attract private capital investments are extended to the private promoters at the rate of 20 per cent subsidy to a maximum of Rs.20 lakh. PTDC has spent Rs.68 lakh this year for construction on development of tourism destinations. The heritage building development, Antics and Hero shops, and *La Café* buildings comprise the additional works of the section.

The advertisement section looks after the media relations, marketing and publicity. The major modes of advertisement include television, AIR, Radio Mirchi, newspapers, foreign magazines and websites. From 1999 onwards, Mc Cann Erikson India Ltd., and TBWA/ Anthem, Chennai took care of the publicity. In 2005-06, other companies are invited. J.Waltair Thombson, Chennai was shortlisted and retained.

All these units with the leadership of assistant directors work in perfect coordination with the budget unit.

Puducherry's tourism vision for the next 20 years includes the following:

1) Identifying potential new tourist sites within the Union Territory and developing them within a framework of eco-tourism,

2) Upgrading hotel infrastructure to acceptable service standards,

3) Improving physical infrastructure,
4) Introducing courses in tourism related topics so as to improve the quality of trained personnel,
5) Establishing a strong promotional base for the tourist industry, and
6) Promoting private sector participation in tourism-related activities, and in the operation and maintenance of tourist and heritage sites.

This vision signals an attempt to entice the entrepreneur to invest in Puducherry and consequently to develop the attractiveness of Puducherry as a tourist destination. The Puducherry government facilitates this by providing attractive incentives to private actors. The upgradation of physical and service infrastructure will require significant investment from the private sector. The government's responsibility should be more of a facilitator. In addition to facilitation, the government should ensure that the environment is protected and that environmental standards are not dispensed with.

These concerted efforts to promote tourism have paid off with increasing arrival of foreign and domestic tourists. The weekend tourists' flow remains to be quite encouraging though official figures are not readily available. Occupancy rate is reasonably higher in the hotels during the weekend, and during fairs and festivals.

7.2 Domestic and Foreign Tourists

From the beginning of the formation of tourism department in 1992, data has been maintained on the number of domestic and foreign tourist arrival. The domestic and foreign tourists arrived from 1992 is presented in Table 7.1. This manifests the vast potential for tourism development in Puducherry. It exhibits that while the domestic tourist arrival has nearly doubled over the period, the foreign tourist arrival has increased by 2.5 times. This indicates the constant patronage of foreign tourists to Puducherry tourism. The consistent increase in the number also emphasises the need for developing the tourism infrastructure to facilitate the visitors. The low cost facilities with attractive tourist destinations would entice the foreign tourists to visit Puducherry regularly, and patronage the economy.

The advertisement and publicity section in the tourism department has been taking innovative initiatives through wide publicity and propaganda to entice both the foreign and domestic tourists. Mass media and information technology have been widely used. The department has been showcasing the low cost facilities available, tourist destinations, and the fairs and festivals being conducted during the important tourist arrival months. Innovative tourism products and services have been designed and developed year after year.

TABLE 7.1

Domestic and Foreign Tourist Arrivals

Sl. No.	*Years*	*Domestic Tourists*	*Foreign Tourists*
1.	1992	311570	10744
2.	1993	305415	10940
3.	1994	324105	11029
4.	1995	336090	11697
5.	1996	372870	12118
6.	1997	401040	20774
7.	1998	406990	18501
8.	1999	449429	22983
9.	2000	527274	23878
10.	2001	476804	22115
11.	2002	480522	20094
12.	2003	500139	25559
13.	2004	558445	32053

Note: The above table does not cover the 'Day Visitors', which comes to a minimum 50000-60000 per day (commercial/shopping/weekend visit/students).

Source: Department of Tourism, Government of Puducherry.

7.2.1 Regional Variations

There are perceptible regional variations in the number of tourists arrived across regions due to the inadequate infrastructure facilities. Hence, regional tourism councils have been set-up to undertake tourism promotional activities in the respective regions. After setting up of these councils, regular investments are made on providing new tourism products and services in all the regions.

Water sports are being organised in the backwaters of river Chunnambar at Puducherry, Arasallar at Karaikal, Mahe river at Mahe, and river Gowdami at Yanam. Tourist homes and guesthouses have been upgraded with more rooms and modern facilities in all the regions like Karaikal, Mahe and Yanam. Though there are perceptible variations across regions in the tourist infrastructure, tourist products and number of tourists, conscious initiatives are being undertaken to reduce the regional variations through deliberate intervention on integrated development of tourism.

7.3 Coverage of Hotels and Other Facilities

The development of tourism in Puducherry has enabled the growth of shops, commercial establishments and hotels. Table 7.2 explicates that there has been a threefold increase in the number of shops, commercial establishments and hotels. Equally the number of workers and in turn their families depending on the tourism industry also increased exponentially. The increase in the number of shops and commercial establishments may indicate the increase in the number of day visitors from the neighbouring states for shopping due to the low sales tax and excise duties in the UT. The addition of new shops and other commercial establishments after the introduction of Uniform Floor Rate insinuates the dependence of these commercial units to the tourism industry. This indicates that nearly 16 per cent of the population is depending on the tourism industry indirectly in the Puducherry. Hence tourism in the UT has to be looked at not only from the economic point of view but also from the social importance of the sector to the people.

The cost of accommodation in Puducherry varies from Rs.100 to Rs.10,000. Puducherry has many hotels with all facilities. Table 7.3 presents the number of rooms and

TABLE 7.2

Employment in Shops and Commercial Establishments

Year	*Shops*		*Commercial Establishment*		*Cinema Theatres, Hotels and Restaurants*		*Total Establishment*	
	Numbers	*Persons Employed*	*Numbers*	*Persons Employed*	*Numbers*	*Persons Employed*	*Numbers*	*Persons Employed*
1980	5077	6603	544	2045	755	3171	6376	11819
1981	6581	7609	520	2087	760	3507	7861	13203
1982	6984	8837	585	2307	824	4207	8393	15351
1983	7640	8654	668	2499	868	3953	9176	15106
1984	7959	8832	729	2639	935	4082	9653	15533
1985	8565	9237	800	2771	988	4161	10353	16169
1986	9149	9439	870	2876	1029	4369	11048	16684
1987	9851	9790	927	2974	1066	4455	11844	17219
1988	10388	9502	954	3018	1073	4482	12415	17002
1989	12072	11829	985	3087	1298	4764	14355	19680
1990	12724	12234	1030	3257	1395	4989	15149	20480
1991	13436	13038	1082	3554	1440	5214	15958	21806
1992	13629	13492	1116	3637	1479	5356	16224	22485
1993	13850	13927	1413	3911	1532	5600	16793	22348
1994	11477	14413	1447	4087	1306	4959	14225	22956
1995	11477	14413	1447	4087	1306	4959	14225	22956
1996	12775	15664	1578	5261	1347	5863	15700	26788
1997	12977	16346	1621	5434	1369	6247	15967	28027
1998	13368	17581	1749	5690	1370	5966	16487	29237
1999	14122	17507	1822	5953	1432	6001	17377	31463
2000	15163	20435	1928	6237	1484	6233	18575	32901
2001	15769	22813	1935	6448	1539	6290	19243	35551
2002	15860	22395	2017	6663	1673	6478	19550	35536
2003	16407	24140	2104	7892	1594	6688	20105	38720

Source: Abstract of Statistics, Puducherry, Various Issues.

TABLE 7.3

Rooms and Beds Available to Tourists as on 31 May 2005

Puducherry Region	*No. of Rooms in Government Accommodation*	*No. of Beds in Government Accommodation*	*No. of Rooms in Private Accommodation*	*No. of Beds in Private Accommodation*
Classified Hotels	21	42	251	435
Unclassified Hotels	106	160	1914	3490
Dormitory Accommodation	17	108	64	299
Total	144	310	2229	4224

Source: Department of Tourism, Government of Puducherry.

beds available in both government and private sectors as on May 2005. This indicates that both government and private sector cater to the needs of all categories of tourists. This explicates the importance given to tourism in the UT. Particularly, private sector is increasingly encouraged to participate in the tourism development with incentives.

7.3.1 Private Sector Participation

Under the scheme 'Grant of Incentive to the Tourism Industry', private entrepreneurs have been encouraged with huge incentives to start tourist resorts, hotels, etc.

7.3.2 Tourist Infrastructure

In terms of hotel accommodation, good restaurants, roads, transport and communication systems, and availability of financial services like commercial banks and foreign exchange dealers, Puducherry is relatively well provided with the requirements of different categories of tourists.

There are a host of boutique shops in tourist locations offering a choice of products and services to the tourists. Various handicrafts and artifacts which are made of metals, stones and wood, textile products, curio items like brass/bronze sculptures, images of deities and terra cotta images are sold.

For the leisure/adventure tourists, there are a variety of attractions at the Chunnambar Water Sports Complex, providing options like tree house, island with restaurants and relaxation facilities, rowing boats and pedal boats (Kayaks), bar and room accommodation too. There is a newly set-up amusement park in Puducherry, which is more likely to be an attraction for the local citizens and the domestic tourists. In Karaikal and Yanam also, the amusement parks for children are being developed.

The airport is rejuvenated by extending the runway in Puducherry airport in order to operate private airlines. In Karaikal also, action towards development of airport is initiated through preparing a techno-economic feasibility report. Approach roads to all the regions like Yanam, Mahe and Karaikal are being developed with the collaboration of concerned state governments to facilitate the tourists to avail the facilities in the regions.

7.4 Locations of Heritage Areas, Parks and Beaches

7.4.1 Beaches

Puducherry has a lovely beach, 1.5 kms long, where one can relax, sunbathe, swim or take a stroll along the promenade. The beach has historical connections too. The sands have witnessed some of the fierce Anglo-French battles.

7.4.2 Boat House

Facilities for boating are available at the boat house on the river Chunnambar, 8 kms from Puducherry. The backwaters and the lush greenery on both sides of the river provide an ideal setting for boating. Boats are available for hire on all days of the week. Garden umbrellas, chairs and teapoys can also be hired on nominal rent at the boat house. The same facilities are also available in the Karaikal region.

7.4.3 Sri Aurobindo Ashram

Sri Aurobindo Ashram is situated at the eastern part of Puducherry. It is the *samadhi* of Shri Aurobindo and the Mother. It is not only a quiet place of retreat but also a vibrant centre of life. It comprises of almost 1500 members who live here and practice *sadhna* for the evolution of another kind and form of life, which will move towards a higher spiritual consciousness.

7.4.4 Auroville

Auroville, about 10 kms north of Puducherry, is an international city, which was built and started in 1968 by Mother with an idea to experiment in international living. The residents live in and around 15 different communes and speak 55 different languages. The purpose of Auroville is to realise the human unity. It is an exciting project for understanding the environmental needs for spiritual growth. On completion, it is expected to accommodate 50,000 residents. Matrimandir, the meditation hall is still under construction and is in the centre of 800 hectares land of Auroville. It is in the form of a golden globe, which is a worth-seeing architectural structure. Auroville is a community of around 1500 people from 30 countries. They are involved in all round development of 13 surrounding villages.

7.4.5 Monuments

There are a host of monuments in Puducherry, which have a history behind them. The various monuments are: Park Monument, Arikamedu, statues of Mahatma Gandhi and Dupleix, French War Memorial, 19th century Light House, Puducherry Museum, Bharathi and Bharathidasan Memorial Museums, Ananda Ranga Pillai Mansion, etc.

7.4.6 Religious Monuments

Puducherry consists of Hindus, Christians and Muslims. Puducherry has various temples, churches and mosques, which have a historical background. In and around Puducherry there are more than 350 temples, both big and small. Some were built by Chola Kings between the 10th and 12th centuries. Various churches and mosques of historical importance are also the places of interest for the tourist.

BOX 7.1

Aayi Mandapam: Definitely Puducherry's most famous and most viewed monument, the Aayi Mandapam at the centre of the Government Park has the distinction of having been built to honour a courtesan, who lived in the 16th century. The story told is that when the French Emperor, Napolean III, sent his chief engineer, Mon. Lamairesse to Puducherry to find new sources of fresh water, the engineer built a canal from a tank that he discovered lying about 5 kilometres west of the town. The tank was Aayikulam, in honour of Aayi, a courtesan.The name piqued the Emperor's interest. When he was told the story behind the naming of the tank, he was even amazed. The tank was named after Aayi, because she built it herself, in place of the palatial residence she lived in. Krishna Deva Raya, King of the Vijayanagar Empire had been fooled by the palace's looks to believe it was a temple, and he knelt to pay obeisance to it. When told that the building housed not a god, but a courtesan, he was humiliated and angered and ordered it razed, and that a tank should be built in its place. However, when Aayi appealed that she be allowed to raze her home herself and build the tank, she was given the permission to do so.When Napolean heard of his chief engineer's success with finding water and of the then Governor of Puducherry's request that he be rewarded, keeping the story of Aayi in mind, the Emperor remarked, "Be grateful to Aayi, she deserves a monument." Aayi's monument continues to offer comfort to travellers, and to sleepy tourists who loll or doze under its dome when the noon-time sun gets hot to allow them to wander.

7.4.7 Festivals

Puducherry is the land of various cultures and faiths, and has many festivals to its credit. The various festivals are: Masimagam, Villianur Car Festival, Veerampattinam Car Festival, Villianur Madha Car Festival, Ariyankkupam Madha Car Festival, All Souls' Day, International Yoga Festival, Pongal, Bastille Day, Mangani Festival, etc.

7.5 Promotional Policies

7.5.1 Puducherry Tourism and Transport Development Corporation

This is one of the constituents of the tourism department. It has the responsibility to run the bus service and caterings. It runs charted bus service within the UT and luxury buses to Nagercoil, Bangalore and Goa. It also takes up conducted tours for a day or two. It is a model in the transport sector though it does not mind profit or loss. Salaries of the staff come to 40 per cent of the PTTDC earnings and another 40 per cent goes for fuel and spare parts. With the other 20 per cent the capital cost, depreciation and other tax coverage have to be taken care of. Unless the fuel efficiency is increased, PTTDC would find it difficult to come out of the loss incurred every year. Bus fares are influenced by the fares in the neighbouring states due to geographical limitations. Even the authorities plead helplessness as they only have responsibility and not the authority to take necessary action. The number of workers per bus is nine, though it is considerably low in comparison with Kerala and West Bengal. Now PTTDC has taken a huge loan to modernise the transport sector from the state government to the tune of Rs.3.4 crore on share capital basis. Most of the senior positions in PTTDC are filled with in-charge officers. The in-charge positions create ambiguity in decision-making. It results in huge losses to the corporation. PTTDC has since been divided into two corporations.

7.5.2 Youth Hostels and Low Cost Catering Facilities

Most of the *La caffes* are running in loss due to heavy cost of the human resources. In addition, most of the *la caffes* are located in the government buildings and guesthouses for services. Hence it cannot be expected to generate profit. Some *La caffes* are closed now. Seagulls group is a three-star catering centre under the PTTDC. However, the services provided by the *La caffes* with hospitality at reasonable prices make an indelible impression on the tourists.

There are two guesthouses and one youth hostel to provide low cost accommodation facilities to the tourists.

7.5.3 Policies and Resources to Promote Tourism

Thus, the holistic development of tourism necessitates building up of proper road facilities, comfortable accommodation and transport facilities in addition to the tourist destinations. Since Puducherry has many tourist destinations to attract all type of tourists like religious, medical, educational and leisure seeking tourists, would facilitate the tourists to prefer Puducherry as the most favoured destination.

7.6 Future Plans

Plan schemes drawn up by the tourism authorities for implementation of tourism related projects during 2002-2003 as well as the 10th Five Year Plan periods (2002-2007) include the following:

1) Beach beautification at Puducherry.
2) Augmentation of facilities and beautification of Chunnambar Water Sports Complex.
3) Development of tourism infrastructure at Oussudu and Bahoor lake, and Aikamedu archaeological site.
4) Expansion of *Yatri Nivas* and tourism homes at Puducherry.
5) Providing additional furniture and other facilities for tourist homes and *Yatri Nivas*.
6) Establishing an amusement park.
7) Establishing a heritage village.
8) Setting up a recreation centre.
9) Additions and improvements to heritage buildings.
10) Provision of wayside amenities at select centres in Puducherry, Mahabalipuram, etc.

7.7 Summary

The establishment of a separate tourism development corporation and transport service has facilitated the tourism industry by providing innovative tourism products and services. The low cost accommodation through youth hostels, *yatri niwas* accommodation, government guest houses and low cost high quality food provided through the *La Caffes* and the Seagull restaurants encouraged the tourists to prefer Puducherry as the favoured destination. The JIPMER and multi-specialty private medical colleges bring in a lot of medical tourists to the state. The government has been encouraging increasingly the private sector to establish tourist resorts, parks and hotels with attractive incentives. All these things boosted up the number of tourists, both domestic and foreign, visiting the state. The concomitant impact is noticed in the number of people depending on the tourism industry. The government has been making huge investments on the development of innovative products and services to the tourists and showcasing it through increased advertisement budget.

Chapter 8

Public Sector Units/Corporations/ Boards Restructuring and Reforms

8.1 Introduction

Public sector undertakings in the Union Territory of Puducherry could be categorised as: (a) commercial purpose and (b) service purpose. While commercial PSUs were created with the objective of producing goods and services at competitive rates to serve the public better, service purpose organisations were for social cause.

8.2 Commercial PSUs

The objective, function and performance of ten commercial PSUs are as follows:

8.2.1 Puducherry Agro Service and Industries Corporation Limited (PASIC)

The Puducherry Agro Service and Industries Corporation Limited, commonly known as PASIC was incorporated in the year 1986 under the Companies Act, 1956 as No. 399 of 1986. The main objective of the corporation is supply of all agricultural inputs like fertilisers, seeds, organic manures, plant protection chemicals and equipments, horticultural planting materials, agricultural implements and tools, bio-fertilisers, soil amendments etc., to the farming community at a reasonable price under one roof at the right time. To cater to the needs of the farming community, there is a network of 40 agro depots in all the four regions. Because of the establishment of the network of agro depots, the requirement of agricultural inputs of the farmers is met within a radius of 5 kms.

PASIC serves to the farmers and the public by undertaking production and marketing activities. It produces Puducherry water with ISI 9001 mark, different grades of fertiliser mixtures, horticultural planting materials, garbage compost, biofertilisers and biopesticides. PASIC undertakes the purchase and marketing of agricultural inputs, fertilisers, different kinds of plant protection chemicals and equipments, certified and truthfully labeled seeds of different varieties. The different kinds of vegetables, fruits and eggs requirement of public schools, central kitchens, school canteens in Puducherry and Karaikal regions are taken care of. At present the annual turnover of business of PASIC is Rs.37 crore approximately. The PASIC's market share on fertiliser is 40 per cent, plant protection chemicals 45 per cent and seeds around 80 per cent.

It has a paid-up capital of about Rs.5.5 crore and operating profitability since inception.

8.2.2 Puducherry Co-operative Sugar Mills

The Puducherry Co-operative Sugar Mills was registered as Co-operative Society under the Puducherry Co-operative Societies Act, 1972 on 24.7.1976. The mill started its first crushing operations during 1984. The main activity of the mills is to produce and sell white crystal sugar. The mill is located in an area of 120 acres at Lingareddipalayam in Mannadipet Commune area. The mill crushes on an average 2.20 lakh million tonnes of cane and produces on an average 20000 MTs of sugar. The annual turnover of the mills is Rs.28.22 crore (2003-2004). The mill has also proposed to set-up a distillery unit within its premises. It has been making profits intermittently.

8.2.3 Puducherry Power Corporation

The Puducherry Power Corporation was incorporated during 1993 with the objective of generating 32.5 MW of electricity (22.9 MV) from gas turbine and 9.6 MW from steam turbine at Karaikal. The required gas is obtained from the gas wells at Narimanam in the Cauvery basin under an agreement with the Gas Authority of India.

The first and prestigious gas-based power plant was set up at T.R. Pattinam, Karaikal, to cater to the power demand of Karaikal region. The plant on Open Cycle (22.9 MW gas turbine) was synchronised during March 1999 and the Combined Cycle (9.6 MW Steam Turbine) was synchronised during October 1999. The plant was put into commercial operation with effect from January 2000. The entire power generated from the Karaikal Gas Power Plant is supplied to the electricity department, Karaikal. The plant is performing extremely well with highest plant load factor of 103.58 per cent during January 2003. The Government of Puducherry has proposed to expand the existing capacity of the power plant at Karaikal from 32.5 MW to 132.5 MW and Central Electricity Authority (CEA) has been appointed as the consultant for the project. It has a substantial paid-up capital of Rs.133 crore and has been making profits since its inception. During 2005-06 it has made a profit of Rs.889.41 lakh.

8.2.4 Puducherry Industrial Promotion Development and Investment Corporation Limited (PIPDIC)

The corporation was established during April 1974. This is the only corporation under the administration of the Government of Puducherry for the development of industries in the Union Territory. To cope with the increased industrial development and to facilitate the entrepreneurs to set-up their industrial units, the corporation is providing term loans and equity assistance on a selective basis. Besides this, the corporation has developed its own industrial estates/parks with all infrastructural facilities. PIPDIC at present has four industrial estates at Mettupalayam, Sedarapet, Kirumampakkam and Thirubuvanai. The industrial park at Thirubhuvanai was set-up in an area of about 52 acres at a project cost of about Rs.4.12 crore.

The Government of India, Ministry of Industries, Department of Industrial Policy and Promotion, New Delhi has accorded approval for the growth centre project at Polagam, Karaikal. The estimated project cost is Rs.31.00 crore. The growth centre has been inaugurated and the developed plots are available for allotment. Phase-I of Puducherry Technopolis at Kalapet has become operational. To ensure high speed data communication facility, a satellite earth station has been provided at a cost of Rs.5.50 crore through STPI under CIB scheme. To provide additional space, it is proposed to construct a multi-storeyed building in Phase-II.

The Ministry of Commerce and Industry have approved the proposal regarding setting up of a Special Economic Zone in Puducherry. PIPDIC has been nominated as the implementing agency for the project. An area of 351 hectares have been acquired at Sedarapet and Karasur revenue village, to set up the Special Economic Zone. The SEZ policy has been notified in the gazette as suggested by Government of India. It has substantial paid-up capital of Rs.40.4 crore and operating profitability. During 2005-06 the Corporation has made a profit of Rs.473 lakh.

8.2.5 Puducherry Distilleries

The Puducherry Distilleries Limited was incorporated in 1971 by taking over the erstwhile French Government Distillery which was in existence right from 1916. The company had to cross a severe hurdle when the Supreme Court passed orders for its closure by April 1997 since this distillery was located in the residential area. A new site was located and with the financial aid from the Government, a blending and bottling unit was established and commercial production was started during the month of July 1998. During 2003-04 the distillery has blended around 108.39 lakh litres, bottled 46.05 lakh litres and sold the arrack of 50.00 lakh litres. The turnover of the distillery is Rs.13.92 crore. It has paid-up capital of Rs.8.45 crore. During 2005-06 the distilleries has made a profit of Rs. 237.3 lakh.

8.2.6 Anglo French Textiles

Anglo French Textiles was taken over by the Government of Puducherry under the Anglo French Textiles Limited (Acquisition and transfer of Textile undertaking) Act, 1986 on 24.2.1985 and the Management of the Anglo French Textiles was vested with the Puducherry Textile Corporation Limited, a Government of Puducherry undertaking. A comprehensive modernisation programme at a cost of Rs.104 crore to be implemented in four phases spread over a period of 3.5 years has been approved by the government. The corporation has requested the Government of Puducherry to provide funds for Voluntary Retirement Scheme by way of grant-in-aid to the extent of Rs.25 crore under Tenth Plan to shed away the excess manpower strength. In this regard, the Government of Puducherry has implemented a new Voluntary Retirement Scheme with an enhanced VRS package. It is incurring losses continuously.

8.2.7 Puducherry Co-operative Spinning Mills Limited

The Puducherry Co-operative Spinning Mills Ltd., Puducherry was established during December 1979 and started its first phase commercial production during March 1984 and second phase in 1996. The mill has a capacity of 35,160 spindles. It is situated at Thirubhuvanai, Puducherry. It produces approximately Rs.26.30 lakh of yarn every year. The mill has been awarded ISO 9001-2000 quality certificate of its Quality Management System during March 2004 by SGS Yarsley International Certification Services, United Kingdom. The main activity of the mill is producing yarn from the cotton and selling of yarn to cooperative handloom societies on a priority basis. It is intermittently making profits.

8.2.8 Jayaprakash Narayan Co-operative Spinning Mills Limited, Karaikal

The Jayaprakash Narayan Co-operative Spinning Mills Ltd., Karaikal was registered during 1990 and started production during August 1995. The mill has a capacity of 18,144 spindles and is situated at Kezhamanai village, Karaikal.

8.2.9 Puducherry Tourism and Transport Development Corporation (PTTDC)

Puducherry Tourism Development Corporation Limited (PTDC) was incorporated during February 1986 to promote tourism in the Union Territory of Puducherry. With the introduction of transport service (March 1988) the Corporation was converted into Puducherry Tourism and Transport Development Corporation Limited (PTTDC) with effect from December 1992.

The Puducherry Tourism and Transport Development Corporation Limited on the transport side is operating buses in 47 routes in all the four regions. Through its interstate routes, PTTDC provides direct services to important tourist places in all the southern states of India. The Corporation has set up a prestigious *La Café* Puducherry at Beach Road in September 1989 to recreate the French ambience. Since then the Corporation started a chain of 11 Cafeterias in Puducherry, Karaikal, and Mahe. Four beautiful seaside restaurants under the name style Seagulls are functioning, two in Puducherry and one each in Karaikal and Yanam. There are four water sports centres in Puducherry, Karaikal, Mahe and Yanam equipped with reasonably good water sports equipments. These centres offer good entertainment and highlight Puducherry's natural resources. At Chunnambar, the Corporation also has an eco-friendly resort, which it started alongside water sport-facilities. It has a paid-up capital of about Rs.18 crore and incurring substantial annual loss. Scouting for a suitable joint venture partner may be considered. PTTDC has since been divided into two different corporations for Tourism and Transport.

8.2.10 Puducherry Agro Products, Food and Civil Supplies Corporation (PAPSCO)

PAPSCO was incorporated as a subsidiary corporation of PASIC which was later converted into a government-owned company during September 1995. The company commenced business from 1.2.1991. The main objective of this corporation is to supplement the efforts of the government towards strengthening the public distribution system and to undertake marketing intervention programme for containing the escalation of prices of essential commodities and also to safeguard the interest of farmers by procurement at remunerative prices not below the level of minimum support price during the peak season of the harvest. It also undertakes supply of essential commodities during emergencies like flood and cyclone. PAPSCO is also running fair price shops in Puducherry and Karaikal regions. Apart from this, Festival Bazaars are opened during festival seasons where essential items including vegetables, fruits, oil, grocery are sold at nominal prices thereby effectively curtailing unnecessary escalation of prices. Apart from the PDS activities, the corporation undertakes procurement of agricultural produce by offering remunerative price to the farming community keeping away the middlemen exploitation. The turnover of the corporation during 2003-04 was about Rs.22.56 crore. It has a paid-up capital of about 9 crore and incurring substantial annual loss till recently. However during 2005-06 the Corporation has made a turn around with a marginal profit of Rs. 17.4 lakh.

8.3 Service Enterprises/Corporations/Boards

Six corporations/boards were also created with share capital contribution/grants from both Central and state governments. The corporations were created to act as nodal agencies for implementing economic development schemes for various sections of the people. Boards were created for promoting social cause. Grants are also released to these corporations/boards under State Plan to meet the establishment charges. The objectives and functions of the corporations/boards are as under:

8.3.1 Puducherry Khadi and Village Industries Board

PKVIB was established during March 1981 under the act of the State Legislature called the PKVIB Act, 1980 to promote and develop programmes with special emphasis to create employment opportunity in rural areas. The Board is running 20 *khadi* spinning centres, 3 *khadi* weaving centres and 3 silk weaving centres. These centres are producing cloth and silk *sarees* for a value of Rs.25 lakh per year. These centres are producing cloth for a value of Rs.14 lakh per year. There are 7 *khadi bhandars* run by the Board through which goods worth around Rs.80 lakh is being sold every year. Apart from this, the Board is running 9 village industrial units namely, brush making, carpentry and blacksmith works, steel furniture, leather, laundry soap, toilet soap, hand made paper, *agarbathi* and readymade garment. The Board has played a key role in rendering assistance for self employment to rural artisans and institutions. It implements the loan schemes extended by the KIC and this has benefited the rural public.

8.3.2 Puducherry Adi-Dravidar Development Corporation Limited

Puducherry Adi-Dravidar Development Corporation Limited (PADCO Ltd.) was incorporated on 26 September 1986, under the Companies Act, with the main objective to uplift the economic conditions of the members of the Adi-Dravidar people in the Union Territory of Puducherry living below the poverty line. Later, based on the orders of the government, welfare schemes to the members of *safai karamcharis* are also undertaken. PADCO extends financial assistance through banks and imparts training to seek wage/self-employment. Apart from this, PADCO acts as the channelising agency for the NSFDC and NSKFDC.

Grant-in-aid for implementation of schemes is released by the state government in the form of subsidy, which is released to the targeted people by way of subsidy at the rate of 50 per cent of loan amount under loan-cum-subsidy scheme, and stipend/course fee under training scheme. Besides this, the state government releases managerial assistance for the salary to staff and other office establishment expenses of the corporation. The Central government provides SCA to the state government as an additive to the special component plan. The state government in turn releases the SCA to PADCO for implementing welfare schemes. SCA is utilised by the corporation towards the release of subsidy under loan schemes and stipend and course fees under the training schemes. It has a paid-up capital of Rs.3.11 crore during 2005-06 and over the years the losses as percentage of share capital has reduced substantially. During 2005-06 the corporation has incurred a loss of about 98.3 lakh.

8.3.3 Puducherry Corporation for Development of Women and Handicapped Persons Limited

The Puducherry Corporation for Development of Women and Handicapped Persons Limited was incorporated on 31.03.1993. The main objective of the corporation is to make every woman and handicapped person socially and economically independent. The corporation has been imparting training in various skills and also helping the women and handicapped persons to set-up their own trade or business. The grant-in-aid being released by the Government of Puducherry to the corporation is utilised for administrative expenses, loan schemes, releasing of subsidy, purchase of permanent assets, conducting of training programmes, running of working women's hostel at Puducherry, Karaikal and Mahe, running of day care centres at Puducherry and Karaikal, disbursement of stipend, etc.

Arrangement has been made for the formation of self help groups in various villages with a view to increase social awareness, development of leadership qualities and towards building up of self-confidence among women. Training on health, nutrition, legal awareness, self-confidence, accounts maintenance, leadership quality, human understanding etc., are being given to women of self help groups. After one year group loan will be sanctioned under this scheme. Under microcredit scheme, loan facilities are extended to poor women to run small business such as vegetable shops, flower shops and fruit shops etc. The corporation has also been nominated as the channelising agency of the National Handicapped Finance and Development Corporation for extending benefits to the handicapped persons. The corporation has also been nominated for giving training in ICDS functionaries under UDISHA scheme. From time to time exhibition and fairs are held both at national and state level to market the handicraft items produced by the women and handicapped persons. It has a paid-up capital of less than Rs.1 crore and incurring losses.

8.3.4 Puducherry Backward Classes and Minorities Development Corporation Limited

The Puducherry Backward Classes and Minorities Development Corporation was registered on 3.3.1999 with an authorised share capital of Rs.5 crore as the agency for bringing about development of backward classes and minorities in the Union Territory who form major chunk of the population. Besides implementing loan-cum-subsidy schemes jointly with banks and training schemes to the youths, out of the funds released from state government, this corporation also acts as the State Challenging Agency (SCA) for National Backward Classes and Finance Development Corporation (NBCFDC) and National Minorities Development and Finance Corporation (NMDFC), New Delhi for implementing their term loan/education loan schemes.

8.3.5 Puducherry Slum Clearance Board

The Puducherry Slum Clearance Board came into existence with effect from 1.12.1986, under the Provisions of the Slum Areas (improvement and Clearance) (Puducherry Amendment) Act, 1986. The board's activities are mainly funded by the Town and Country Planning Department, Puducherry under housing sector, for carrying out development works in the slum areas by a limited allocation every year, since the board has no resources of its own. The administrative charges levied on scheme works and deposit works, and interest earned on fixed deposits are the major revenue of the board, to meet out the expenditure on salaries, wages, establishment and maintenance items.

Funds were also released for the implementation of various scheme works (SUP, EIUS, VAMBAY and NSDP) to this board. By utilising the scheme funds received from the Town and Country Planning Department, the board has so far laid 1,07,230 metres of road in slum areas, the length of surface drain constructed is 74,090 metres and the board has constructed 47 bathrooms and 296 latrines to the benefit of slum dwellers. The board has constructed 419 nos. of temporary light roof sheds and they were allotted to the victims, whose huts were damaged in fire accidents. Under slum upgradation programme, 1796 nos. of developed plots were provided/allotted to the beneficiaries on monthly rental basis. Till 31.03.2004, the board has completed the construction of 1534 tenements and out of this, 1310 are allotted. Further 112 tenements are under construction.

Under the Perun Thalaivar Kamaraj Centenary Housing Scheme for Houseless Poor, the Government of Puducherry has proposed to grant financial assistance of Rs.40,000 to eligible *patta* owners of EWS for constructing/re-constructing their thatched houses with *pucca* houses with a plinth area of not less than 200 sq. ft. in Puducherry state. The financial assistance will be given to the beneficiaries in three instalments. The scheme has already commenced and it is in good progress. The aim of the scheme is to convert the huts into *pucca* houses with roof slab.

8.3.6 Puducherry Housing Board

The Puducherry Housing Board was constituted in the year 1975 by the government to provide housing facilities to the growing population in the Union Territory of Puducherry. The board acquires large chunks of land in the Union Territory of Puducherry and develops them into plots with basic infrastructural facilities. The plots are then allotted and sold to the public on reasonable rates. The board also constructs houses for HIG, MIG, LIG and EWS. In addition to the above, the board also undertakes deposit works from other departments.

The main source of funds of the board for taking up housing schemes are loans released by HUDCO in phased manner, seed capital from government etc. The expenditure before release of HUDCO loan and also the excess amount incurred over and above HUDCO loan have to be met, out of the board's funds. In order to make good of the shortfall between the work programme and anticipated revenue receipts, and with a view to achieve the targets of the board and meeting its running expenditure, the government is providing funds as seed capital to the board.

The constructed houses are allotted/sold to the public on outright sale/hire purchase instalment basis. The board is also implementing plotted development scheme for the benefit of the public. The board is also undertaking deposit works on behalf of several government departments. The board has so far constructed 5772 houses/flats, 80 shops, 164 offices/other buildings and developed 1847 plots. This includes the 49 MIG flats constructed at Suthandira Ponvizha Nagar, Puducherry during the year 2003-04.

Table 8.1 indicates that about one-half of the total Annual Plan outlay for PSUs/boards is earmarked for Anglo French Textiles and Puducherry Co-operative Sugar Mills.

8.4 Need and Policy Measures for Restructuring and Reforms

Sixteen PSUs of Puducherry account for Annual Plan revised outlays of about Rs.55 crore in 2004-05 with substantial amount earmarked for loss making ones. The few who generate surplus make only marginal profits. Substantial share capital and grants provided to the PSUs, earn negative returns of 8 per cent on share capital invested by the state (Table 2.13 in Chapter 2 and latest position indicated below the table).

In 1996, the Tamil Nadu government constituted Raghavan Committee to study and recommend reforms and restructuring of state PSUs. A similar exercise needs to be taken up in Puducherry for state PSUs. They could be broadly classified into four categories as under:

Category 1: Economic purpose as PSU justified and making profits consistently. Prime examples are PASIC, PIPDIC, etc. They should be encouraged to gradually become self-reliant.

Category 2: Economic purpose as PSU justified and incurring losses.

In the case of PAPSCO, there is social purpose also. On the other hand, PTDC with commercial prospects would do better as joint venture.

Category 3: Economic purpose as PSU not justified but making profits. Puducherry Power Corporation is one such example for privatisation.

Category 4: Economic purpose as PSU not justified and incurring losses.

All state-controlled sugar, distillery and textile mills come under this category.

Restructuring could be on the lines of internal measures (productivity and efficiency-oriented) and external measures (privatisation in terms of divestment, displacement and delegation). Reforms and restructuring could be in terms of making category 1 units self-reliant. Productivity and efficiency measures for category 2 units to improve cost-benefit ratio only in case it also envisages social purpose; otherwise convert it as joint venture or public-private partnership, if it has commercial prospects. Privatisation of category 3 units, and either privatisation or close down of category 4 units may be considered.

8.5 Summary

Puducherry government needs to have a hard look on most of its PSUs in an era of privatisation and public-private partnership. It would do well to set up, similar to Raghavan Committee constituted a decade back in Tamil Nadu, PSU reforms and restructuring committee to pave the way for various options of disinvestments, spin-offs as joint ventures, mergers and phased closed down of PSUs.

TABLE 8.1

Annual Plan Outlays of PSUs/Boards

Sl. No.	*Name of the Public Sector Undertakings/Boards*	*Annual Plan 2003-04*	*Annual Plan 2004-05*		*Annual Plan 2005-06*
		Actuals	*Approved Outlay*	*Revised Outlay*	*Proposed Outlay*
1.	Puducherry Agro Service Industries Corporation	50.00	70.00	70.00	70.00
2.	Puducherry Co-Operative Sugar Mill	845.00	665.00	925.00	1110.00
3.	Puducherry Power Corporation	0.00	0.00	0.00	0.00
4.	Puducherry Khadi and Village Industries Board	250.00	300.00	300.00	500.00
5.	Puducherry Industrial Promotion Development and Investment Corporation	122.00	150.00	0.00	150.00
6.	Puducherry Distilleries	0.00	0.00	0.00	0.00
7.	Anglo French Textiles	1764.00	1537.00	1537.00	1400.00
8.	Puducherry Co-Operative Spinning Mills	75.00	75.00	75.00	200.00
9.	Jayaprakash Narayan Co-Operative Spinning Mills Ltd., Karaikal	75.00	75.00	75.00	200.00
10.	Puducherry Tourism and Transport Development Corporation	200.00	595.00	595.00	205.00
11.	Puducherry Agro Products, Foods and Civil Supplies Corporation	110.00	90.00	340.00	340.00
12.	Puducherry Adi-Dravidar Corporation	71.00	121.00	121.00	100.00
13.	Puducherry Corporation for Development of Women and Handicapped Persons	349.10	172.28	470.88	471.00
14.	Puducherry Backward Classes and Minorities Corporation	81.75	81.75	85.00	85.00
15.	Slum Clearance Board	348.89	153.00	800.00	900.00
16.	Housing Board	75.00	75.00	75.00	75.00
	Total	4416.74	4160.03	5468.88	5806.00

Source: Government of Puducherry, Annual Plan Documents.

References

Government of Puducherry. *Annual Plan Documents.*

Government of Puducherry (2003). *Pondicherry Vision 2020.* Madras School of Economics.

Chapter 9

Financial Services

9.1 Introduction

Real sector that drives the economy needs a vibrant financial sector for its healthy and accelerated growth. In this era of economic liberalisation, financial institutions and markets have in effect become the most important commodity as their rise and expansion lead to economic growth. On the other hand, a fragile financial sector can deepen the real economy crisis with consequent heavy social costs.

Global and national trends in financial sector now increasingly relies on the concept and practice of universal banking, securitisation process, innovative financing of not only infrastructure but also informal sector and small and medium enterprises, important role for private sector in banking and non-banking financial activities and public-private sector partnership even in development of schemes and infrastructure projects. It has also opened the channel for tapping of institutional and financial market funds by the Government and its bodies through special vehicles and appropriate financial structuring for its economic development and infrastructure schemes.

The financial sector provides the conduit for the household savings to be channelised towards productive activities. Its main function lies in enabling financial resource to be allocated for different types of business and agricultural activities. In the Union Territory of Puducherry, banks comprise the major segment of the financial sector. Scheduled Commercial Banks (SCB) consisting of public and private sector banks provide the bulk of the short-term capital requirements to business and agriculture. State cooperative banks, urban cooperative banks along with the non-banking financial companies provide financial services. The long-term capital requirements of the state are provided by the Development Financial Institutions, PIPDIC, and by private corporations (invariably with the head office outside UT) who have invested in the Union Territory. Interbank call money markets do not exist here, so all treasury operations of SCBs are undertaken by their respective head offices outside Puducherry. Moreover, most of the top 20 industrial units in Puducherry have their headquarters and bank credit sanctions outside the UT, accounting for, to some extent the UT's low credit-deposit ratio.

9.2 Overview

Puducherry economy has been growing at a fast rate in the period 1993-94 to 2000-01. While the total GSDP grew at the rate of 12.8 per cent, the service sector in Puducherry grew at the CAGR of 10.44 per cent between 1993-94 and 1998-99. The financial sector comprising banking and finance, which was 8 per cent of the service sector at the beginning of economic liberalism in 1991-92, presently forms 12 per cent. As in the other states, the banking sector provides the bulk of credit requirements in the Union Territory of Puducherry also. The SCBs and Cooperative banks that operate throughout the state have thrived in the post-economic liberalisation era in Puducherry, particularly in terms of deposit mobilisation. In fact, a recent study by the Department of Economics and Statistics, Puducherry indicates the growth rate of GSDP in 2002-03 over previous year of 8.62 per cent, 6.64 per cent and 6.27 in banking, service sector and overall respectively.

SCBs as per the Second Schedule of the RBI Act 1934, consist of commercial banks, regional rural banks (RRBs) and other scheduled commercial banks, urban cooperative banks (UCB) and state cooperative banks (SCB). Nationalised banks including the State Bank of India (SBI) and its associates are the major bank entities. In Puducherry there are three associate banks operating out of the seven associate banks of the SBI. Puducherry being largely urban and semi-urban in nature does not have any RRBs. There are no foreign banks operating in the Union Territory of Puducherry.

Cooperative credit institutions largely serve the rural sector. In terms of reach and volume of operations, cooperative credit institutions occupy an important position by providing almost 70 per cent of rural credit. Urban cooperative banks aim at mobilising savings from middle and lower income urban groups, and purvey credit to the weaker sections. In Puducherry the cooperative banks are of two-tier structure, so there are no District Co-operative banks as in the three-tier structure. Fifty-three primary agricultural credit societies (PACS) are affiliated members of the Puducherry state cooperative banks. Rural cooperative institutions account for 30 per cent of rural deposits and 44 per cent of outstanding loans, and advances of the banking sector for agriculture and rural development as per RBI report on currency and finance of 1999-2000.

9.3 Role and Growth of Banking Sector

In Puducherry, 34 SCBs with 108 branches are in operation. Of the 34 banks, 21 are in the public sector and all of the rest belong to old private sector except one new private bank. With nationalisation of banks, erstwhile private banks had to assume the role of catalysts for economic growth through branch expansion spreading to unbanked areas and providing credit to neglected sectors of agriculture and small industries. In the Union Territory of Puducherry the lead bank is the Indian Bank. Access to banking facilities is a significant criterion for evaluating the efficiency of the banking sector. Average population per bank in Union Territory of Puducherry was rather high during 1969 (31,000 per branch) compared to 1996. Population per bank fell to 13,000 in 1996 and has remained more or less constant till 2001 fluctuating between 12,000 and 13,000. At present, population per branch in Puducherry (12,000) is below the national average (15,000). The states and Union Territories, which have the lowest population per branch, are Goa, and Chandigarh (5,000), and Lakshadweep (8,000) followed by Himachal Pradesh and Punjab at 9,000. In all 108 numbers of bank branches of SCBs are functioning in the UT of Puducherry out of which 41 are in rural areas, 17 in semi-urban and 50 in urban areas.

In 1969 there were only 12 branches of SCBs in Puducherry, which rose to 59 in 1980, 69 in 1990 and 84 in 2000, and further to 108 in 2003 (Table 9.1). As information technology is being rapidly introduced at different levels of the banking sector, it is possible that Internet related banking facility as well as ATMs would spread rapidly to provide easier access to banking facility in the Union Territory of Puducherry.

TABLE 9.1

No. of Branches of Scheduled Commercial and Cooperative Banks

	Types of Scheduled Banks	*1980*	*1990*	*2000*	*2003*
1.	SBI and its Associates	12	13	15	86
2.	Nationalised Banks	37	45	51	
3.	Public Sector Banks (1+2)	49	58	66	
4.	Other Scheduled Banks	10	11	18	22
5.	All Scheduled Banks (3+4)	59	69	84	108

Source: Various issues of *Report on Currency and Finance* and *RBI Bulletin*.

9.4 Credit-Deposit Trends

The credit offtake in the nineties around 40 per cent or less has been relatively modest. The credit-deposit ratio, has recently picked up to cross 50 per cent. The growth of deposits is largely because of the large pension and other payments received from France by the French citizens. The rising deposits without balancing growth in credit offtake can be to some extent explained by the above factor. The other important factor being, most of the top 20 industrial units in Puducherry have their headquarters and bank credit sanctions outside the UT.

The earlier credit-deposit ratio trend of much less than 50 per cent prior to 2000-01, touched nearly 50 per cent in 2000-01 (49 per cent). Further it increased to 52 per cent in 2002-03 and 53 per cent in 2003-04 as shown in Table 9.2.

TABLE 9.2

Credit-Deposit Ratio

Year	*Credit*	*Deposit*	*CD Ratio (per cent)*
2000-01	832	1683	49
2001-02	1207	2328	52
2003-04	1334	2512	53

Source: Government of Puducherry, *Annual Plan Documents*.

The rank of Puducherry in CD ratio was 16th in 1991 and is 17th in 2001. Neighbouring Tamil Nadu has the second highest credit-deposit ratio (more than 100 per cent) in the country after Chandigarh.

The performance indicators of the credit delivery system given in Table 9.3 indicates that on most of the fronts the banking sector as on 31 March 2004 has been a vital force in assisting the real sector of Puducherry.

The rate of increase of bank deposits is an accepted criterion for measuring the growth rate of financial resources of an economy. In Puducherry, the annual compound growth rate of bank deposits of SCBs was 9.64 per cent in the decade of the nineties, which is an indicator of the growth of the financial sector. The rate of growth of loans was 4.55 per cent in the same period indicating much lower level of fund usage, and this is again reflected in the marked decline in the CD ratio throughout the last decade. There has been no shortage of financial resources in the state.

TABLE 9.3

Performance Indicators of the Credit Delivery System—Key Banking Statistics: As on 31.03.2004

No.	*Particulars*	*Cooperatives*		*CBs*	*Total*
		PSCB	*PCCLDB*		
1.	No. of Banks	1	1	32	34
2.	No. of Branches				
	i. Rural	12	-	29	41
	ii. Semi-Urban	2	1	14	17
	iii. Urban	6	1(HO)	43	50
	Total	20	2	86	108
3.	No. of Staff per Branch/Society	12.6	NA	NA	NA
4.	No. of Loan Accounts	NA	2600	70000	72600
5.	No. of Loan Accounts per Branch/Society	NA	1300	833	NA
6.	Average Population per Branch	48717	487172	11330	9106
7.	Average Number of Villages Covered per Branch	13.2	132	3.0	2.4
8.	Total Deposits as on 31 March 2004 (Rs.in lakh)	16581	367.74	234187	251135.74
9.	Average Deposit per Branch (Rs. lakh)	829.05	183.87	2723.10	2347.15
10.	Growth in Deposits				
	A. 2004 over 2003 (%)	10.9	61.5	7.6	7.9
	B. 2003 over 2002 (%)	11.5	16.7	15.6	15.3
	C 2002 over 2001 (%)	24.6	75.8	19.6	19.9
11.	Total Loans Outstanding as on 31 March 2004 (Rs. in lakh)	9561.38	873.68	123002.62	133437.68
12.	% Increase in Loan Outstanding				
	A. 2004 over 2003 (%)	0.03	-3.2	20.7	10.4
	B. 2003 over 2002 (%)	28.5	15.9	20.8	21.4
	C 2002 over 2001 (%)	19.0	9.3	10.5	11.2
13.	Loan Outstanding per Account (Rs. lakh)		0.34	1.76	
14.	Loan Outstanding per Branch (Rs. in lakh)	478.07	437.00	1430.26	1247.08
15.	Loan Outstanding per Ha i. ST ii. MT/LT	NA	NA	NA	NA
16.	% of Agri. Advances to Total Adv.	10	100	9	10
17.	CD Ratio	58	232	52	53
18.	Percentage of Recovery to Demand				
	As on 30.06.2000	78.0	34.7	53.6	55.4
	As on 30.06.2001	69.7	27.8	58.5	52.0
	As on 30.06.2002	69.5	64	64	65.8
	As on 30.06.2003	79.7	60.4	68.0	69.4
	As on 30.06.2004	79.2	63.6	70.7	71.7
19.	% of Overdues to Loans	12.6	28.9	NA	-
20.	% of Net NPAs to Total Assets	19.0	35.6	NA	-
21.	Brief Information on the Performance of Credit Institutions				

Note: NA - Not Available; MT - Medium; LT - Long Term; HO - Head Office.

Source: RBI Banking Statistics Document.

Since 1996-97 there has been a steady upsurge in term deposits while savings and current deposits have stagnated. As the majority of the banks are in the public sector they are perceived to have little or no risk. Despite the recent reduction in the interest rate, households continue to repose faith in banks for safeguarding their savings particularly after failure of many NBFCs. Puducherry has been no exception. In 1990-91 the total current deposits in the state of SCBs was Rs.36.82 crore which fell to Rs.2.66 crore in 1991-92 at the height of the boom, more or less in the same way as in the rest of the country. It rose in 1992-93 to Rs.59.8 crore and grew to Rs.166 crore in 1999-2000. Other southern states also followed the same trend. Interestingly, the term deposits in all the states continue to grow at a steady rate throughout the last decade followed by the savings deposits.

9.5 Sector-Wise Distribution of Loans and Advances by SCBS

The pattern of sector-wise loans outstanding to different sectors of the economy in the Union Territory of Puducherry by SCBs appears to be changing in the last decade in response to the development in the economy. There is a marked decline in credit offtake by agricultural/ farm sector while disbursal has been growing in the manufacturing, trade and finance sectors. The growth in the credit disbursal to industry has risen due to the growth of the industrial activity in the Union Territory of Puducherry. Consequently as more industrial units were set-up, the agricultural land has been converted to industrial use. With greater urbanisation (66.5 per cent), the profile of Puducherry has changed remarkably. The nineties also witnessed a remarkable growth in the services sector.

In 1990, 15.85 per cent of the total outstanding loans went to agriculture, but a decade later it came down to 9.15 per cent, although in absolute value it rose from Rs. 29.42 crore in 1990 to Rs.49.50 crore in 1999-2000. On the other hand, loans to industries have nearly tripled over the decade from Rs.91.56 crore to Rs. 227.40 crore (Table 9.4). The service sector (excluding trade and finance) has risen by almost four times whereas trade and finance sector rose by six times.

The manufacturing industries sector was booming in the last decade and this trend is likely to remain in the future. It is also necessary to identify areas of the growth for the future. As per our discussions with local officials the government has identified tourism as a major source of revenue and this sector is also already growing rapidly. This expansion is perhaps due to the proactive policy of the Union Territory government. The credit offtake exhibited by the loans disbursed by SCBs to the service sector especially after 1997-98 are indicative of the likely trend in the future.

Loans received by the trade and finance, and other sectors have shot up from 34.8 per cent in 1990-91 to 48.8 per cent ten years later. The thrust area of growth in Puducherry is the services sector, and credit disbursal figures of the past decade bear witness to it. This also reiterates the view that the momentum of growth is inherent in the tertiary sector, already experiencing a growth rate of almost 20 per cent in the last decade. Deliberate policy to support the rural sector through NABARD's refinance strategy and targeting of self help groups will reduce hardships for those associated with agriculture and allied activities.

TABLE 9.4

Sector-wise Distribution of Loans at Constant Prices

(Rs. in crore)

	1990-91	*1991-92*	*1992-93*	*1993-94*	*1994-95*	*1995-96*	*1996-97*	*1997-98*	*1998-99*	*1999-2000*
Agriculture	29.42 (15.9)	28.93 (14.0)	28.1 (12.7)	32.29 (12.2)	36.13 (11.7)	47.4 (12.8)	97 (21.7)	116.6 (24.8)	48.1 (10.2)	49.5 (9.2)
Industry	91.56 (49.3)	113.5 (55.0)	115.1 (52.1)	126.6 (47.9)	150.2 (48.7)	186 (50.0)	205.8 (46.1)	193.9 (41.2)	194.5 (41.1)	227.4 (42.1)
Trade and Finance	16.18 (8.7)	18.2 (8.8)	22.1 (10.0)	28.61 (10.8)	36.7 (11.9)	37.3 (10.0)	47.5 (10.7)	63.4 (13.5)	67.6 (14.3)	73.5 (13.6)
Others	48.49 (26.1)	45.71 (22.2)	55.6 (25.2)	76.4 (28.9)	85.2 (27.6)	101.2 (27.2)	95.8 (21.5)	96.9 (20.6)	162.7 (34.4)	190.4 (35.2)
Total	185.7 (100)	206.3 (100)	220.9 (100)	263.9 (100)	308.2 (100)	371.9 (100)	446.1 (100)	470.8 (100)	472.9 (100)	540.8 (100)

Note: Figures in brackets are percentages.

Source: Money and Banking CMIE, October 1998-2001.

9.6 Innovations in Financial Services

9.6.1 Housing Finance

Past experiences of the lead bank and other commercial banks reveal that banks which provide loans and advances to medium and small-scale industries often faced problems of poor recovery leading to mounting non-performing assets. Hence, banks have been facing increased amount of defaults and non-repayments of loans. Nationalised banks instructed their regional and local branches to diversify their customer base and business focus.

The increasing pressure on banks to raise efficiency level through reduced non-performing assets has forced managers to be far more cautious in their lending. Deposits are now being shifted to treasury bill investment for lower but safe return. The nationalised banks looking for new avenues of business found the housing sector loans to salary earners as an untapped avenue of lending and a rich potential market for growth in Puducherry. It is observed that banks in Puducherry are shifting their loans and advances into the housing sector. Puducherry is rapidly growing in its urban stature as more and more non-agricultural activities are undertaken. Banks are competing with housing finance companies to provide housing loans to salary earners. This scheme was introduced in November 2001 and it has helped many banks do good business in Puducherry.

Banks are offering housing loan within the range of 10 per cent to 8 per cent of interest to all types of salary earners working in both the government and private sectors. This is a much lower interest rate than the range of 14 per cent to 16 per cent charged by housing finance companies. The procedures with regard to documentation for granting loans has been simplified and lead time for loan processing has been reduced. So far Rs.8 crore housing loans have been disbursed since the inception of the scheme in 2001. The annual size of their business is expected to be Rs.40 to 50 crore. The shift of business focus is expected to raise profits for the nationalised banks and usher greater profitability and efficiency.

9.6.2 Information Technology

The financial sector reform of the nineties, and the opening up of the economy and integration with global markets have facilitated faster automation of bank procedures through computerisation. This has led to reducing operational costs enhancing quality of customer service in the medium term. The technology adoption and absorption has so far revolved around two basic themes: retail banking and corporate banking. The former has leaned more on basic technology infrastructure. The challenge for Indian banks is the principle of 'all banks to all people' and 'banking at the nearest bank'. High level of customer service, timelines, efficiency, and risk management can be enhanced if infrastructure is upgraded effectively. However, interbank connectivity through public switching telephone network (PSTN) and network communication, through VSAT is an essential step to achieve this goal. The two major areas where retail banking can grow rapidly at the customer interface level are the Automatic Teller Machine (ATM) and the credit card.

Banks under increasing pressure to improve their profit performance through efficient credit disbursal and lower cost of operation are now closing uneconomic branches and investing in Automatic Teller Machines (ATMs) to provide teller service at a much lower cost. The annual maintenance cost per unit of ATM is in the range of Rs.10,000 to Rs.30,000 apart from the initial installation cost. A minimum 10,000 card holders per ATM will make this investment profitable. Since ATMs serve both the purpose of payout and receipt of cash, it can reduce the operational costs substantially. The installation of ATMs needs to be accompanied by a parallel programme of familiarising customers about the convenience of 24 hours access to cash and cheque deposit facility. Any time and anywhere banking has to be popularised for its success.

Credit cards which have gained considerable popularity in metropolitan cities are accepted at only a limited number of retail showrooms and three star hotels in Puducherry. It is visualised that credit cards will become a major instrument of bank transactions. The Indian Bank, being a lead bank in Puducherry is offering overdraft facility through credit cards.

9.7 State Cooperative Banks

Cooperative credit institutions occupy an important position in the financial system of the economy in terms of their reach, volume of operations and the purpose they serve. The organisational structure of cooperative credit institutions is given in Figure 9.1. Rural cooperative banks play a pivotal role in the rural credit delivery system. This section surveys the Urban Co-operative Bank and State Co-operative Bank which are the two types of Cooperative banks operating in the Union Territory of Puducherry providing up to 5 per cent of the total bank credit in the region.

FIGURE 9.1

Organisational Structure of the Cooperative Credit Institutions/Cooperative Banks

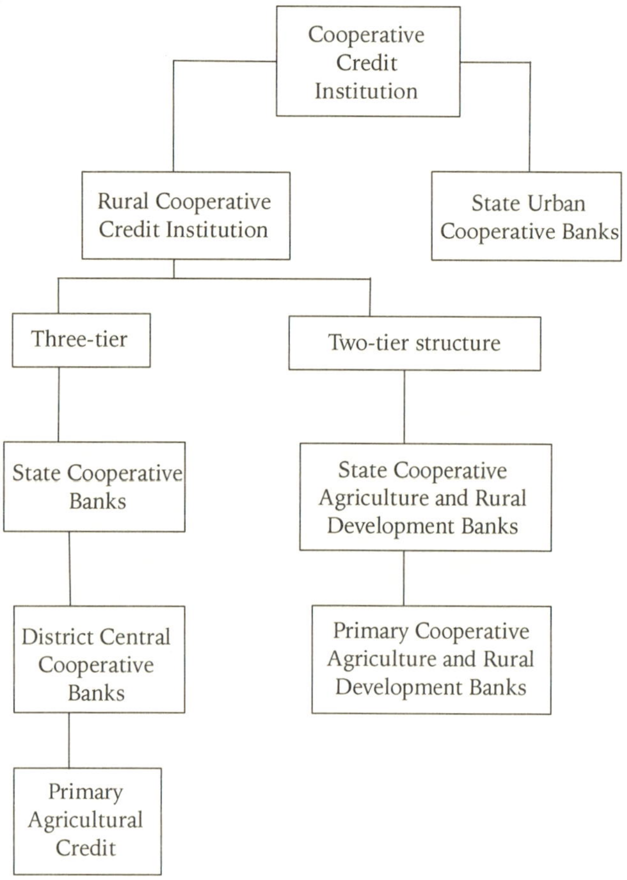

BOX 9.1

Mangalam—A Village with Cent Per cent Bank

Connectivity: Mangalam village in Puducherry has achieved the distinction of being the first village where every house has a bank account. The 100 per cent banking connectivity of the village was taken up by the Indian Bank, the lead bank in the Union Territory, after the Reserve Bank of India selected Puducherry for the National Pilot Project for Financial Inclusion (NPPFI). The NPPFI is as per RBI's decision to make available a basic banking 'no frills' account either with nil or very minimum balance as well as charges that would make such accounts accessible to a vast section of population. At a function held in Mangalam, account books and general credit cards were handed over to the villagers.

In the Union Territory of Puducherry the cooperative banks are organised on the two-tier structure. The primary credit societies are members of the State Cooperative Bank of Puducherry; there are no district cooperative banks in Puducherry. The Puducherry State Cooperative Bank started functioning in October 1958 and was registered under the Co-operative Society Act, 1904. It received license from RBI in 1994 and the scheduled status in 1995 coming under the purview of the Banking Regulation Act, 1949. It is statutorily inspected by the NABARD. The bank started operations with a share capital of Rs.0.06 crore and working capital of Rs.0.117 crore, which have now grown to Rs.4.63 crore and Rs.142 crore respectively. The major contribution of the share capital is from the affiliated societies and the state government; the working capital consists of reserves, deposits and loans from the state government and NABARD. The bank is managed by the administrator appointed under the Puducherry Cooperative Societies Act, 1972. The present administrator of the bank is the Registrar of Co-operative Societies, Puducherry.

At present there are 19 branches of the Puducherry State Co-operative Bank, of which four are in the outlying region of the city. There are 53 primary credit societies, whose activities range from agriculture to spinning, weaving, sugar mills, and fisheries. The bank provides various types of loans:

- Seasonal agricultural operations,
- Working capital loans to Weavers Co-operative Society,
- Loans for farm and non-farm sectors,
- Cash credit limits to Co-operative Societies including the Co-operative Sugar Mills,
- Spinning Mills, and
- Conversion of short-term agricultural loans given on account of natural calamities into medium-term loans.

The bank also issued a term loan to Co-operative Spinning Mill at Karaikal under consortium arrangement to the extent of Rs.470 lakh. The total loans outstanding as on 31st March 2001 amounted to Rs.6,251.98 lakh. Table 9.5 gives the sectoral deployment of advances from 31st March 1997 to 31st March 2001.

As there was no significant growth of outstanding loans and advances in the past three years several new schemes to diversify business opportunities for the bank were initiated, such as (a) house mortgage loan, (b) agricultural jewel loan to agriculturists with lower rate of interest at 13 per cent p.a. (c) personal computer loan to individuals, and (d) loans to the public on government servant surety. These new schemes have turned out to be popular and thus broadened the scope of issuing more loans in the future. The bank has further framed subsidiary rules for providing a) cash credit to businessman, (b) cash credit to agriculturists and has also

TABLE 9.5

Loans and Advances

(Rs. in lakh)

	Particulars	1996-97	1997-98	1998-99	1999-2000	2000-01
1.	ST Loan (Agr 1)	850.81	935.61	991.51	692.40	619.98
2.	MT Loan (Agr 1)	77.68	64.96	65.35	40.77	32.52
3.	ST Loan (Others)	44.92	43.66	148.20	39.44	40.00
4.	MT Loan (Others)	805.93	772.14	696.71	857.09	1045.52
5.	LT Loan (Others)	476.30	459.34	324.95	207.45	198.52
6.	CC (Weavers)	497.61	706.17	787.66	792.01	865.67
7.	CC (Consumers)	248.96	139.59	132.59	89.00	87.68
8.	CC (Others+O.D)	206.15	185.06	219.55	220.09	277.68
9.	Salary Earners Socs.	682.54	558.90	933.25	983.84	837.98
10.	Transport Loans	59.07	55.81	33.53	25.79	19.35
11.	Jewel Loans	526.66	570.04	477.75	379.35	379.48
12.	NFS (SSI Units Loans)	35.68	37.32	38.85	38.27	34.50
13.	Loan on Deposits	260.21	107.22	137.23	119.29	185.10
14.	Sugar Mills	416.84	881.20	910.14	1457.08	1321.96
15.	Spinning Mills	344.10	280.70	35.86	151.87	305.98
	Total	5533.46	5798.09	5933.13	6,093.74	6,251.98

Source: Note on the Working of the Puducherry State Co-operative Bank Limited, March 2001.

taken steps for relaxing/amending various subsidiary rules for increasing outstanding loans.

Loans to agricultural activities both short-term and medium-term are on the decline while loans and advances for non-farm activities have increased for the bank from Rs.8.1 crore to Rs10.5 crore. The loans to salary earners have doubled in the span of 5 years of 1996-2001. The sugar mills have increased their cash credit offtake by three folds in the same time period. The sugar mill industry, despite downturn globally, seems to be picking up in the Union Territory of Puducherry in terms of its credit requirements. On the other hand, there is a sharp fall in the cash credit availed by the consumers' cooperative societies. A similar trend is also visible in loans to transport owners society and to members for purchase of jewellery.

The Puducherry State Cooperative Bank which has been in operation for more than four decades, has been through periods of uncertain business. We note that it has had negative earnings in the eighties and nineties. The recent surge of failures of cooperative banks highlights the need to restructure their regulatory guidelines keeping in view their intrinsic character. Their functioning and constraints in operation have been examined by a high power committee (HPC), a task force and an expert group to devise ways to improve their efficiency and make the credit delivery system more viable. The State Cooperative Bank of Puducherry notwithstanding its earlier records has become profitable in the last three years of its operations. However, profit as a percentage of working capital has been less than 2 per cent, while establishment expenses as percentage of working capital is more than 2 per cent,

TABLE 9.6

Key Banking Indicators

(Rs. in crore)

		1998-99	1999-2000	2000-01
1.	Deposit per Employee	0.3961	0.4980	0.5075
2.	Advance per Employee	0.2961	0.2874	0.2949
3.	Non-interest Income as Percentage to Total Income	1.46	1.60	1.21
4.	Establishment Expenses as Percentage to Total Expenses	24.19	25.54	22.75
5.	Profit as Percentage to Working Capital	1.1	0.78	1.08
6.	Establishment Expenses as Percentage to Working Capital	2.5	2.4	2.5
7.	Cost of Management as Percentage to Working Capital	3.3	3.2	3.1

Source: The Puducherry State Co-operative Bank Ltd 43rd Annual Report 2000-2001.

and cost of management as percentage of working capital is more than 3 per cent. These indicate that there is scope for increasing the efficiency of operations through more economic use of working capital (Table 9.6).

Table 9.7 indicates trend of deposits, loans and profits of state cooperative banks indicating satisfactory growth over the years.

9.8 Urban Cooperative Banks

Urban cooperative banks (UCBs), aim at mobilising savings from the middle and low-income urban groups and purvey credit towards the weaker sections. The major part of credit from UCBs is channelised towards priority sector segments. The Union Territory of Puducherry which consists of a sizeable urban and

TABLE 9.7

Trend and Pattern of Deposits, Loans and Profits of State Cooperative Banks (Rs. in crore) ^

Year	*Deposits*				*Total Deposits*	*Loans*	*P and L Credit Balance***	*Interest Recoverable (assets)- Interest Payable (liabilities)**
	Fixed	*Current*	*Saving*	*Others*				
1980	2.034 (65.55)	0.337 (10.86)	0.720 (23.21)	0.012 (0.38)	3.102 (100)	2.806	0.027 (0.81)	0.067 (2.01)
1985	1.864 (58.96)	0.429 (13.55)	0.869 (27.47)	0.0004 (0.01)	3.162 (100)	3.276	0.022 (0.42)	-0.003 (-0.06)
1990	9.080 (79.47)	0.757 (6.62)	1.589 (13.91)	0	11.426 (100)	9.810	0.255 (2.24)	0.120 (1.05)
1995	9.911 (72.52)	1.487 (10.88)	2.269 (16.60)	0	13.667 (100)	10.679	0.111 (0.94)	-0.001 (-0.01)
2000	15.125 (69.60)	2.503 (11.52)	4.104 (18.89)	0	21.733 (100)	11.609	0.220 (1.75)	5.36 (42.72)
2001	13.665 (63.77)	2.941 (13.73)	4.821 (22.50)	0	21.427 (100)	11.450	0.304 (2.44)	5.63 (45.24)

Note : ^ 1980-81 prices.

* Interest recoverable (assets) – interest payable (liabilities) as a percentage of loans to cooperative society and individuals (assets) in the *Abstract of Statistics*- Government of Puducherry (1980-81 series).

** Profit and loss credit balance as a percentage of loans to cooperative society.

Source: Table prepared from data in various issues of *Abstract of Statistics- Government of Puducherry* (1980-81 constant prices).

TABLE 9.8

Trend and Pattern of Deposits, Loans and Profits of Urban Cooperative Banks (Rs. in crore) ^

Year	*Deposits*				*Total Deposits*	*Loans*	*P and L Credit Balance***	*Interest Recoverable (assets)- Interest Payable (liabilities)**
	Fixed	*Current*	*Saving*	*Others*				
1980	0.321 (81.19)	0.004 (0.89)	0.071 (17.92)	0	0.395 (100)	0.356	0.003 (0.69)	0.005 (1.20)
1985	0.622 (76.88)	0.017 (2.15)	0.170 (20.98)	0	0.810 (100)	0.861	0.023 (2.59)	0.031 (3.51)
1990	0.750 (34.23)	0.051 (2.34)	0.483 (22.03)	0.907 (41.40)	2.191 (100)	1.505	0.073 (4.82)	-0.040 (-2.66)
1995	0.183 (21.23)	0.028 (3.30)	0.556 (64.40)	0.096 (11.08)	0.863 (100)	2.098	0.026 (1.25)	-0.005 (-0.26)
2000	5.834 (84.72)	0.156 (2.27)	0.896 (13.01)	0	6.887 (100)	4.879	0.119 (2.44)	-0.022 (-0.45)
2001	5.947 (83.60)	0.131 (1.83)	1.036 (14.57)	0	7.114 (100)	5.965	0.233 (3.90)	0.037 (0.63)

Note: ^ 1980-81 prices. ** Profit and loss credit balance as a percentage of loans (assets).

* Interest (assets) – interest (liabilities) as a percentage of loans (assets).

Figure in brackets are percentages of total.

Source: Table prepared from data in *Abstract of Statistics- Government of Puducherry* (1980-81 prices).

semi-urban population has UCBs operating within its territory.

The trend of various financial indicators of UCBs in the Union Territory of Puducherry is presented in Table 9.8 The deposit mobilised by UCBs was only Rs.0.39 crore in 1980 which went up to Rs.7.11 crore in 2001. The major part of deposits at present comes from fixed deposits, followed by saving deposits and current deposits. The share of fixed deposits in total deposits has increased over the years. The difference between interest recoverable and interest payable as a percentage of loans remains less than 1 per cent, is an indicator of weak returns earned by UCBs. There is an urgent need for the UCBs to improve the interest earning capacity and to identify other sources of income to improve their financial position.

The financial fragility of these banks could be partly traced to the increased competition among banks after reforms in the nineties, and to the interdependence between financial institution through inter-institution exposure and payment settlement channels. The UCBs appear to be exhibiting traits of weakness as they were found to be incurring losses in several years after 1995. Corrective steps need be taken to strengthen the cooperative credit delivery system in the urban areas of Puducherry. Those which are sick, may either be closed down or amalgamated with stronger ones.

9.9 Policy Initiatives of Rural Credit Disbursal

Major policy initiatives at the national level relating to cooperative credit institutions and rural credit system since 2000-01 include the launch of new trance of rural infrastructure development fund (RIDF), enhancement of KCC (Kisan Credit Card), formation of self help groups (SHG) and microcredit. Prudential and operational norms relating to UCBs have been changed significantly.

The concept of potential linked credit plan (PLP), introduced by NABARD can be used to judge credit requirements in Puducherry. The estimated credit flow in the UT of Puducherry during the Tenth Five Year Plan period (2002-2007) in terms of potential available and likely to be developed aggregate to Rs.1,193.30 crore. The estimated credit requirement is expected to increase from Rs.192.78 crore during 2002-03 to Rs.308.66 crore during 2006-07. The projected amount under the PLP for 2002-2003 is Rs.198.72 crore, which represents a 9.95 per cent increase above the PLP projection of 2001-02. A sizeable share amounting to 38.6 per cent has been allocated to non-farm sector followed by 'other priority sector' (25.9 per cent) and crop loans (20.4 per cent). Storage and market yard and minor irrigation accounted for 3.5 per cent and 3.3 per cent, respectively followed by dairy development (3.2 per cent), farm mechanisation (2.4 per cent) and fisheries (1.0 per cent). The share of remaining activities accounts for less than 1 per cent each.

However, the flow of ground level credit disbursement to non-farm sectors of 1997-98 during the Ninth Five Year Plan was 49.6 per cent. Term loans for minor irrigation, farm mechanisation, and dairy development attracted a higher allocation than proposed for the Tenth plan; the shares being 4.57 per cent, 5.57 per cent, and 4.6 per cent, respectively. The other activities including land development, plantation and agriculture, poultry and fisheries attracted less than 17 per cent of total disbursement

Of the six blocks in Puducherry, Reddiarpalayam block accounts for 35.2 per cent of the total PLP projection for the year 2002-03 followed by Karaikal (20.4 per cent), Villianur (17.3 per cent), Karaikalampakkam (16.5 per cent), Mahe (6.1 per cent), and Yanam (4.5 per cent).

The credit-deposit ratio of rural sector banks was 49.4 per cent at the end of March 2001. Efforts are on to raise it to 60 per cent. The recovery performance has been declining and stands at 52 per cent (June 2001) as against 60.3 per cent in 1996.

The Union Budget 2001-02, provided for an increase of the corpus of RIDF VII from Rs.4,500 crore during 2000-2001 to Rs.5,000 crore in 2001-02. To help the state, the rate of interest charged on RIDF lending has been reduced from 11.5 per cent to 10.5 per cent. The KCC scheme which turned out to be very successful, as its popularity among farmers indicates, has been further stimulated by banks being authorised to provide personal insurance package to the KCC holders up to a maximum of Rs.50,000. The premium burden is being shared by card issuing institutions. KCC scheme introduced in 1999 is popular among both farmers and issuing bankers. Farmers have the flexibility to avail of production credit, and also avoid procedural delays in getting credit sanctioned. At present 1,700 KCCs have been issued for the disbursal of loans and the card is valid for three years. Furthermore, to ensure that small and medium farmers are not denied access to KCC facility, NABARD in consultation with the RBI disposed with the floor limit of Rs.5,000 earlier suggested for coverage under the scheme. The loans dispersed under KCC scheme were also brought under the Rashtriya Krishi Bima Yojana of the general insurance corporations, and personal accident insurance cover of Rs.50,000 for death and Rs.25,000 for disability from 2001-02 would be provided to KCC holders.

9.10 Microfinance—Informal Credit Delivery System

The self help groups (SHGs), which constitute an informal credit delivery system, are now increasingly recognised as an effective mechanism for reaching a large number of unbanked sections of the rural poor. The SHGs have been formed to help banks in reducing transaction costs and risk, and also to improve recovery performance. The microfinance groups in UTP include SHG and CMG (Credit Management Groups). CMG organised by M.S.Swaminathan Research Foundation (MSSRF) participate in research-oriented farming, dairying, goat rearing, fisheries, and allied activities. The profile of microfinance existing in Puducherry is given in Table 9.9.

9.11 Role and Growth of Non-banking Financial Companies

Non-banking financial companies undertake a wide spectrum of financial activities ranging from hire purchase and leasing to pure investments. NBFCs are, in terms of Sections 45-I(f) and 45-I(c) of the RBI Act, 1934 as amended in 1997, involved in the principal business of receiving deposits and engaging themselves in lending, investments in securities, hire purchase finance or equipment leasing. There are broadly 8 types of NBFCs: (1) equipment leasing companies, (2) loan companies, (3) hire purchase companies, (4) investment companies, (5) mutual benefit companies (Nidhis), (6) miscellaneous non-banking companies (chit funds), (7) residuary finance companies, and (8) housing finance companies.

With such range of services, NBFCs cater to a wide range of customised demands for many types of loans. The salient characteristic of NBFCs is their non-formality. Further documentation for availing of loans is simple in contrast to that in relation to SCBs. The convenience of easy processing and timely loan sanctions draws proprietary and partnership enterprises towards them. A large number of companies depend on direct contract through agents who are sometimes family or community members. The NBFCs in Puducherry therefore, are rather popular among the small traders and businessmen, lorry and bus operators and middle-income groups, for jewellery purchase, commercial vehicles, consumer durables, etc.

9.12 Supervision of NBFCs

The supervisory framework for NBFCs is based on three criteria, namely, (a) the size of NBFC, (b) the type of activity performed, and (c) the acceptance or otherwise of public deposits. Towards this end, a four-pronged supervisory strategy comprising (a) on-site inspection based on CAMELS (capital, assets, management, earnings, liquidity, systems and procedures) methodology, (b) computerised off-site surveillance through periodic control returns, (c) an effective market intelligence network, and (d) a system of submission of exception reports by

TABLE 9.9

The Microfinance Profile in the UT

Total Number of Blocks in the UT	6
No. of Blocks where SHGs exist	6
Total Number of Blocks where SHGs are Credit-linked	3
No. of NGOs in the UT	50
No. of NGOs participating in Linkage Programme	3 (M.S.Swaminathan Research Foundation, CERD and Mangalam Society)
No. of Additional NGOs to be roped in during the year	2
Total No. of Bank Branches in the UT (Rural and Semi-Urban)	Com.Banks : 41 Coop. Banks: 14
Of which : No. of Branches Participating in Linkage Programme	Com.Banks : 17 Coop. Banks: Nil
No. of Additional Branches Proposed to be roped in	Com. Banks: 6 Coop. Banks: 7
No. of Government/Other Agencies Participating	3 (Women Development Corporation, Krishi Vigyan Kendra and PONLAIT)
No. of Government/Other Agencies likely to Participate	5 (District Rural Development Agency/BDO, Agriculture, Animal Husbandry, Fisheries and Social Welfare)

Source: Potential Linked Credit Plan, Union Territory of Puducherry, X[th] Five Year Plan Period with Block-wise Projections for 2002-03.

auditors of NBFCs, has been put in place. The regulation and supervision is comprehensive for companies accepting or holding public deposits to ensure protection of the interests of depositors.

The comprehensive regulatory structures evolved by RBI would mitigate the fragility of the operational environment. The entry norm of Rs.25 lakh as minimum net owned funds in chapter III (B), III (C), and V of the RBI Act in 1999 will streamline the NBFCs operations. However, small operators at the rural level will continue to thrive or go underground. This is because the rural people are not aware of conditions like certificate of registration that have to be complied with before any NBFC can accept deposits from the public.

In Puducherry although as per records 51 NBFCs were registered and operating, the primary survey revealed that only 31 were actually operational of which only 21 firms responded to the survey. These firms were operating as nidhis or mutual benefit funds. While 57 per cent of these were partnership firms, 19 per cent were private limited companies. Only 4.7 per cent were public limited, the rest were sole ownership enterprises. The client base of these NBFCs consists of mostly small traders, and businessmen, lorry and bus operators and the middle-income group. The NBFCs revealed that they had in all 61,794 customers, among them 87.5 per cent were depositors and only 12.5 per cent were borrowers. The balance is obviously skewed against the borrowers. Further failure of many NBFCs to honour their obligations to depositors has dampened the scene. Consequently, deposits are now overflowing to banks, particularly public sector banks and new technology savvy private sector banks.

9.13 Summary

Corrective steps need to be taken to improve its credit –deposit ratio significantly, in consultation with all stakeholders—industry, agriculture, service sector and scheduled banks. Active joint campaign and support by the government and scheduled banks for setting up of SMEs and SSSBEs would not only improve credit-deposit ratio but also provide significant employment opportunities. With dwindling agriculture sector base, all out emphasis on tiny sector and microfinance/SHGs would boost the rural economy.

References

Abstract of Statistics- Government of Puducherry (1980-81 constant prices).

Report on Currency and Finance (2002). RBI, March 2002.

Government of Puducherry, *Annual Plan Documents*.

Government of Puducherry (2003). *Puducherry Vision 2020*. Madras School of Economics.

Money and Banking CMIE, October 1998-2001.

Potential Linked Credit Plan, Union Territory of Puducherry, Xth Five Year Plan Period with Block-wise Projections for 2002-03.

RBI Banking Statistics Document.

RBI Bulletin, RBI.

The Puducherry State Co-operative Bank Ltd 43rd Annual Report 2000-2001.

Working of the Puducherry State Co-operative Bank Limited, March 2001.

Chapter 10

Governance

10.1 History of Local Self-Government during French Rule

Local self-government was introduced during the French rule in the year 1880 by a decree dated 12 March 1880. The whole system was devised on the same pattern as prevailed in France and other French colonies. The territory was originally divided into 10 communes, namely Puducherry, Oulgaret, Villianur, Bahour, Karaikal, Grand Aldee, Nedungadu, Chandernagore, Mahe, and Yanam. Subsequently, these establishments were divided into 17 communes, namely, Puducherry, Ariyankuppam, Mudaliarpettai, Ozukarai, Bahour, Nettapakkam, Villianur, Thirubuvanai, Karaikal, Thirunallar, Nedungadu, Kottucherry, Grand Aldee, Neravy, Chandarnagore, Yanam, and Mahe. Consequent on the merge of Chandarnagore with West Bengal, the number of communes has been reduced to 16. These 16 local areas (communes) were declared as municipalities and administered by mayors and the councils.

10.1.1 The Post-Merger Period

Those areas comprising the French establishments in India were merged *de facto* with the Indian Union on the 1 November 1954. At the time of merger, the subject of local administration was dealt with by the Bureau des Affairs Politiques and the municipal administration was covered by the decree of 12 March 1880. The local administration department was constituted only on 1 July 1963 to deal with all matters connected with local administration at the secretariat level. The inspectorate of municipal councils and local boards were formed in June 1967, to exercise control over the municipalities. Except a few changes, the municipal administration continued to carry on according to the French laws.

10.1.2 Re-organisation of Local Bodies in 1973

In Puducherry, the decree of 12 March 1880, which provided for a common structure of municipal administration for urban as well as rural areas, continued to be in force. The Panchayat Raj system was in vogue in other parts of the country and village administration has been carried out through people's representatives from the village level to the block level. Moreover, the old French laws had become so outdated that its replacement by a new law to meet the requirements of the changed circumstances was felt necessary. Moreover, the municipalities remained stagnant and the establishment charges had increased gradually to reach almost half of the income of the municipalities. Adequate funds were not left to meet even the essential as well as basic needs of the population. Further, much of the powers conferred on the municipalities by the various French laws ceased to have effect as these laws had been replaced by Indian laws. As a result, the municipal administration as conceived in the nineteenth century stood eroded, substantially. Hence, the system was replaced by the Pondicherry Village and Commune Panchayat Act, 1973 and the Pondicherry Municipalities Act, 1973 respectively, to govern village and town administration. Both these acts came into force from 26 January 1974. Commune Panchayat Act provides for a two-tier system of *panchayat* administration, one at the village level and the other at the commune level. The mayors and deputy mayors ceased to function with effect from that date. All the executive powers of the mayors stood transferred to the commissioners appointed under these acts.

Under the reorganised set-up, the inspectorate of local bodies was converted into a directorate headed by a director to deal with the administrative matters. He was conferred the ex-officio secretariat status with two deputy directors to deal with municipal administration and rural development, respectively.

10.2 Municipalities

Following the introduction of the Pondicherry Municipalities Act, 1973, four municipalities came into existence in Puducherry, Karaikal, Mahe, and Yanam towns. The jurisdiction of the Puducherry municipality extended to Puducherry and Mudaliarpettai commune which stood amalgamated to form a single municipality. The entities of Karaikal, Mahe and Yanam communes formed the municipalities of Karaikal, Mahe and Yanam. Under the new law, all functions excluding those which were assigned to the chairman, i.e., those which were hitherto exercised by the mayor appointed under the municipal decree came to be exercised by the commissioner. The mayors were also relieved of their day-to-day administrative responsibilities enabling them to be in greater contact with the public. Commissioners were appointed as the chief executive heads of the municipalities in different ranks according to the grade of the municipalities. The erstwhile Ozhukarai Commune *panchayat* was upgraded as a municipality with effect from the 14 January 1994 and thereby the number of municipalities in this Union Territory has increased to five and the Commune *Panchayat* became 10 in number.

10.2.1 Power and Functions of Municipal Authorities

The council, the chairman and councillors, and the commissioner are the trinity of the municipal authorities for running the municipal administration. They are clothed with adequate statutory powers to carry out their respective duties and responsibilities so as to run the municipal administration effectively. With regard to financial powers, the municipal council which is the governing body has been delegated with the financial powers equivalent to the head of the department in the government and the commissioner has been delegated with the financial powers equivalent to the head of office in the government, respectively.

The council being the governing body of the municipality is vested with the powers to issue directions to the commissioner who is the executive authority. The chairman, as the presiding officer of the municipal council represents the council in the day-to-day administration of the municipality and he is entitled to be kept continuously informed of the working of the executive authority. The commissioner has to consult the chairman in respect of all matters as such consultation would be conducive to the smooth working of the municipality. While the commissioner is to function under the general control of the council and to carry out all the lawful decisions and directions, and he is expected to discharge all the executive functions vested in him at his full discretion whenever the commissioner feels that a particular direction is against the law, he is entitled to make a reference to the government and seek orders. To sum up, the commissioner is the repository of all executive powers under the acts. No official correspondence between the municipality and the government shall be conducted except through the chairman.

Any measure which is likely to promote public safety, health, or the convenience of the inhabitants of the locality generally comes within the ambit of the functions of the council. Except in matters where it involves relaxation of any provision of law, rule and in respect of matters which may be subject to restriction and control by the government, no resolution of the municipal council would require the prior approval of the government. However, an authenticated copy of the minutes of the proceedings of the municipal council is to be forwarded by the chairman to the director within three days of the date of meeting. The municipal councils are empowered to levy taxes, which are compulsory. In some cases, the tax may be imposed with approval of the government. The municipal councils could frame their own budget within the limits of their own financial resources. The responsibility for the collection of taxes lies with the commissioner.

The municipalities are responsible for lighting of public streets, places and buildings, keeping them tidy and free from all encumbrances, controlling and stopping dangerous trades and practices, constructing and maintaining burial grounds, markets, slaughter houses, cattle sheds, etc. They are also responsible for water supply, drainage and sewerage, preparation of composted manure, providing relief for destitute and also in times of scarcity, for providing preventive and remedial measures during outbreak of epidemics, etc. The municipalities are also responsible for the registration of births, deaths and marriages.

As part of their optional duties, the municipalities also provide for laying new streets, establishment and maintenance of libraries, museums, lunatic asylums, houses for destitute and disabled persons, town-halls, municipal offices, shops, *dharmasalas*, rest houses, maintenance of parks, control of milk trade, control of dog menace within the municipal limits, etc.

10.2.2 Financial Resources

The municipal fund is constituted of the following sources of revenue:

- Tax revenue.
- Non-tax revenue
- Grants-in-aid and loan from the government.

The tax revenue consists of the income from property tax, entertainment tax, profession tax, advertisement tax, duty on transfer of properties and duty on toddy trees. All other items such as licence fee, bus stand parking fees, income from leasing of usufructs of trees, income from leasing of fishing rights, income from land properties, hire charges of vehicles, etc., constitute the non-tax revenue of the municipalities as well as some statutory grants. The government contributes every year to the funds of the municipalities by way of non-statutory grant for undertaking various developmental works so as to provide civic amenities. Loan is also given to the municipalities by the government for remunerative enterprises.

10.3 Commune *Panchayat*

Following the introduction of the Puducherry Village and Commune Panchayat Act, 1973, ten commune *panchayats*, came into existence in Puducherry and Karaikal regions, as follows:

Puducherry Region

- Ariankuppam Commune *Panchayat*
- Bahour Commune *Panchayat*
- Mannadipet Commune *Panchayat*
- Nettapakkam Commune *Panchayat*
- Villianur Commune *Panchayat*

Karaikal Region

- Kottucherry Commune *Panchayat*
- Nedungadu Commune *Panchayat*
- Neravy Commune *Panchayat*
- T.R. Pattinam Commune *Panchayat*
- Thirunallar Commune *Panchayat*

Under the new law all functions excluding those which were assigned to the chairman i.e., those which were hitherto exercised by the mayor appointed under the municipal decree came to be exercised by the commissioner. The mayors were also relieved of their day-today administrative responsibilities enabling them to be in greater contact with the public. Commissioners were appointed as the chief executive heads of the commune *panchayat*, in different ranks according to the grade of the commune *panchayat*.

10.3.1 Power and Functions of Commune Panchayat Authorities

The council, the chairman and councillors, and the commissioners are the trinity of the Commune Panchayat Authorities for running the commune *panchayat* administration. They are vested with adequate statutory powers to carry out their respective duties and responsibilities so as to run the commune *panchayat* administration effectively. With regard to financial powers, the commune *panchayat* council which is the governing body has been delegated with the adequate financial powers to run the administration of the commune *panchayat*. The commissioner has also been delegated with the adequate financial powers.

The council being the governing body of the Commune *panchayat* is vested with the powers to issue directions to the commissioner who is the chief executive authority of the commune *panchayat*. The chairman, as the presiding officer of the commune *panchayat* council represents the council in the day-to-day administration of the commune *panchayat* and he is entitled to be kept continuously informed of the working of the executive authority. The commissioner has to consult the chairman in respect of all matters on which such consultation would be conducive to the smooth working of the commune *panchayat*. While the commissioner is to function under the general control of the council and to carry out all the resolution of the commune *panchayat* council. Whenever the commissioner feels that a particular direction is against the law, he is entitled to make a reference to the government and seek its orders. To sum up, the commissioner is the commune *panchayat* and the government shall be conducted except through the chairman.

Any measure which is likely to promote public safety, health, or the convenience of the inhabitants of the locality generally comes within the ambit of the functions of the council except in matters where it involves relaxation of any provisions of law, rule and in respect of matters which may be subject to restriction and control by the government, no resolution of the commune *panchayat* council would require the prior approval of the government. However, an authenticated copy of the minutes of the proceedings of the commune *panchayat* councils is to be forwarded by the chairman, to the director within three days of the date of meeting. The commune *panchayat* councils are empowered to levy tax, which are compulsory. In some cases, the tax may be imposed with the approval of the government. The commune *panchayat* councils could frame their own budget within the limits of their own financial resources. The responsibility for the collection of taxes lies with the commissioner.

The functions and responsibilities of the commune *panchayat* are classified as mandatory, discretionary and agency functions. The construction and maintenance of commune *panchayat* roads, shops and markets, etc., execution of minor irrigation works and community development programme, taking preventive as well as remedial measures against epidemics are the main duties of the commune *panchayat*. The commune *panchayats* are also responsible for the registration of births, deaths and marriages.

10.3.2 Financial Resources

The commune *panchayat* fund constitutes tax revenue, non-tax revenue, statutory grants and non-statutory grants, and loans. The tax revenue consists of the income from the following taxes:

- Entertainment tax
- Tax on cinematography exhibition
- Any of the taxes and duties leviable by the village *panchayat*
- Part of local cess
- Local cess surcharge

All other items of income such as market fees, licence fees, income from ferries and fisheries, etc., constitute non-tax revenue.

The following statutory grants are paid by the government:

- Local cess surcharge matching grant
- Local roads maintenance grant.

The government contributes every year to the funds of the commune *panchayats* by way of non-statutory grants and loans for undertaking various developmental works and remunerative enterprises.

10.4 Village *Panchayats*

The Pondicherry Village and Commune Panchayats Act, 1973 provides for formation of village *panchayats*. There are 98 village *panchayats* in this Union Territory. There are 71 village *panchayats* in the Puducherry region and 27 village *panchayats* in Karaikal region. The administration of the village *panchayats* lies in the hands of the *panchayat* president, the members, and the executive authority. There will be a total of 815 village *panchayat* members.

10.4.1 Powers and Functions of Village Panchayat Authorities

The village *panchayat* will be responsible for the construction and maintenance of roads, burial grounds, drainage, sanitation, provision of public latrines, drinking water supply and other purposes and for taking measures to promote public hygiene. The village *panchayats* have got discretionary functions like planting of trees, provision of lights, opening and maintenance of public markets, public landing places, slaughter houses, reading rooms, control of fairs and festivals, parks, play grounds, etc.

The village *panchayats* are empowered to levy house tax, profession tax, duty on transfer of properties, duty on toddy trees, surcharge on cess on sugarcane, tax on agriculture lands for specific purposes, tax on fairs and festivals and tax on village product sold in the village. They are also empowered to levy and collect various fees for the use of poromboke or communal land, market, cart stand, supply of water, etc.

10.4.2 Financial Resources

The village *panchayat* fund is constituted with the following sources of revenue:

- Tax revenue
- Non-tax revenue
- Statutory grant

The tax revenue consists of the income from house tax, profession tax, duty on transfer of properties, duty on toddy trees, surcharge on cess on sugarcane, tax on agricultural land for a specific purposes, tax on fairs and festivals, tax on village produce sold in the village.

All other items of income such as fee for use of poromboke and communal lands, market fee, cart stand fee, etc., constitute non-tax revenue.

A statutory grant of 'house tax matching grant' is paid by the government on every rupee of house tax collected by the village *panchayat*, every year.

As the election to local bodies has not been conducted so far, there is no village *panchayat* or *Gram Sabha* in any of a commune *panchayats*, and consequently the special officers appointed by the government representing the commune *panchayat* council and as well as the chairman are exercising all the powers and performing the functions of village *panchayats*. The commissioners of the commune *panchayats* are exercising the powers and performing the functions of the executive authorities of the village *panchayat*.

10.5 Taxation and Finance

A. Taxation

The following are the taxes which are leviable by the municipalities, commune *panchayats,* and village *panchayats* as per the provisions of the Puducherry Municipalities Act and the Puducherry Village and Commune Panchayats Act:

Municipalities

- Property tax (compulsory tax)
- Profession tax
- Tax on advertisements
- Duty on transfer of property
- Tax on entertainment
- Duty on toddy trees (optional tax)
- Additional tax on buildings and lands
- Toll on animals and vehicles
- Any other tax which the legislature of the Union Territory has power to impose.

Commune *Panchayats*

- Local cess surcharge (optional tax)
- Entertainment tax (compulsory tax)
- Tax on cinematography exhibition
- House tax
- Profession tax
- Surcharge on cess on sugarcane
- Duty on transfer of property
- Duty on toddy trees
- Tax on agricultural land on specific purposes
- Tax on fairs and festivals
- Tax on village produce sold in village
- Any other tax as the government may by notification direct.

Village *Panchayats*

- House tax (compulsory tax)
- Profession tax
- Such other tax as the government may by notification direct
- Duty on transfer of property
- Duty on toddy trees
- Tax on agricultural land for a specific purpose
- Tax on fairs and festivals
- Tax on village produce sold in the village.

But at present the following taxes are levied by the local bodies:

Municipalities

- Property tax
- Profession tax
- Tax on advertisements
- Duty on transfer of property
- Tax on entertainment
- Duty on toddy trees.

Commune *Panchayats*

- Local cess and surcharge
- Entertainment tax
- Tax on cinematographic exhibition
- Village *panchayats*
- House tax
- Profession tax
- Surcharge on cess on sugarcane
- Duty on transfer of property
- Duty on toddy trees.

As there were no village *panchayats* in existence till recently, the commune *panchayats* were levying and collecting all the taxes which are leviable by the village *panchayats*. The following taxes which are levied by local bodies are collected by the government department noted against each and a collection charge of 3 per cent on the total collection is credited to the government account:

- Duty on transfer of property—Registration Department

- Local cess and surcharge—Revenue Department
- Duty on toddy trees—Excise Department.

As per the provisions of the Puducherry Village and Commune Panchayats Act, local cess is levied and collected by the government (i.e., Revenue Department) at the rate of 50 paise on every rupee of land revenue. Out of the total proceeds of local cess collected (i.e., after deducting the collection charge at 3 per cent) 20 per cent is credited to the *panchayat* equalisation fund, and out of the remaining 80 per cent, 75 per cent is credited to the village *panchayat* fund and the remaining 5 per cent is credited to the commune *panchayat*.

B. Finance

The municipal fund constitutes the following:

Own Funds:

- Tax revenue
- Non-tax revenue
- Grants-in-aid
- Loan

The commune *panchayat* funds constitutes the following:

Own Funds:

- Tax revenue
- Non-tax revenue
- Statutory grant
- Non-statutory grants-in-aid

10.6 Finance Commission

Following the constitutional amendments and amendments made in the Local Body Acts, a Finance Commission was constituted in the Union Territory on 12 March 1997 to review the financial position of the local bodies, and to make recommendations to the government to augment their financial positions on their own and as well through devolution by the Government. The commission started functioning with effect from 18 March 1997. As per the government order, the commission should furnish the report containing its recommendations to the Lieutenant Governor once in six months during its tenure of three years, from the date of its constitution. The Finance Commission in its three year tenure has submitted six 6-monthly reports. The second Finance Commission was constituted on 5 January 2004 for a period of one year.

10.7 Recent Trends

After a gap of 38 years the elections to the local bodies have been held in Puducherry, during June-July 2006, following High Court orders from the Madras High Court. The previous elections were held in 1968 under the French system of Commune Municipal Councils. Elections would be conducted for a total of 1138 local body posts, including those of municipal chairmen, 98 village *panchayat* presidents, 122 municipal councillors, 98 commune *panchayat* councillors and 815 village *panchayat* ward members, for 5 municipalities, 10 commune *panchayats* and 98 village *panchayats*.

Local administration department monitors the various schemes sponsored by the government and executed by the local bodies. In addition, it allots the grants to the local bodies from the resources earmarked by the Government of India under Five Year Pans. A separate engineering division has also been created in the department to assist the local bodies to execute various civil works in the commune *panchayats* in Puducherry and Karaikal regions.

The amendment of Article 40 of the Constitution to make the formation of PRIs a mandatory principle, and the 73rd and 74th Amendments making special provisions for the states to empower PRIs have brought democratic decentralisation by organising institutions of local self-governance in many states. Unfortunately Puducherry has not made any effective step towards passing Conformity Act for 73rd Amendment and conducting elections to the institutions of local self-governance. Being a small state with one MLA for small areas, the election of commune *panchayat* presidents and village *panchayat* presidents, it was felt, would impinge upon the power of the state legislature. Hence, the state legislature may be reluctant to share their power with another layer of power structure in the form of commune and village *panchayat* presidents. However two finance commissions have been constituted and reports were submitted but no effective step was taken to implement the recommendations. According to the second Finance Commission report, out of the 29 functions and responsibilities included in the Eleventh Schedule, few were partially implemented or transferred to the local bodies at the recommendation of the first Finance Commission.

10.8 Resource Mobilisation by Local Bodies

The inherent weakness of the local bodies, both rural and urban, remains to be in the resource mobilisation. The powers to tax and collect the tax lay with the Central and state governments. Only residual powers are transferred to the local bodies. PRIs in majority of the states depend increasingly on the Centre and states for their resources. Major chunk of their resources comes in the form of grants from the state through its commitment to transfer one-third of the own tax revenue to the local bodies, and from the Centre through the Finance Commission transfers and the Centrally Sponsored Schemes implemented through the PRIs. Thus, in most of the states it remains as democratic deconcentration rather than the democratic decentralisation as James Manor calls it. Without elected representatives in the local bodies, the funds earmarked by the Centre and state to the local bodies insinuate the deconcentration of the powers of the states and Centre.

10.9 Right to Information

Right to Information Act implemented with effect from October 2005 is a major step in bringing in transparency in the functioning of the government. While it provides the citizen the right of access to the government documents, this right of accessibility should not be misused. The government departments have released the Information Handbooks pertaining to each department and have also hosted the complete information on the website. The citizens can now have access to the various schemes that are implemented by the various government departments and by a click of button they will be able to obtain complete information about each and every scheme of the government. Under the Central Act, the State Information Commission has already been set-up since October 2005.

10.10 e-Governance

The IT policy for the government aims at bringing in electronic governance, thereby improving productivity and efficiency in the government services to the public. It will also help in quick decision making in government operations and providing better implementation of programmes and policies of the government. This will be achieved through the following strategies *inter alia*:-

1. Government to initiate action towards the standardisation of basic data, which ensures the manageability, portability and interoperability of systems across the departments.
2. A citizen's charter for effective and responsive administration in terms of time-bound service to the public to be framed and implemented in all the government departments.
3. Each department in the government to prepare a five-year IT plan with prioritisation of applications to create a visible impact on citizens at large, and should have its own web pages in the Internet comprising procedures to allow people to make complaints and suggestions electronically.
4. Two per cent of the budget to be earmarked for IT usage in the government for purchase of IT products, training and services.
5. Databases of relevant information to be created for each department and made available to other departments and the public wherever necessary.
6. All government departments to be networked by intranet for information exchange.
7. A vast majority of the government officials to be trained on the usage of IT on a continuous basis.

A number of initiatives have already been taken by the government to promote e-governance. The kiosks are available in some departments. Already 14 departments are networked as part of e-governance. E-mails and wireless communications are encouraged in the official communications. Alloting two per cent of the total outlay of the departments encourages office automation of departments. Computer training is given to all the clerical staff. Computerisation of accounts, medical, vital statistics, revenue and land records are reaching near total. IBM is retained as the major service provider for setting up e-governance network among the departments. It has been proposed to roll-on citizen centric services on e' mode.

10.11 Summary

The democratic decentralisation initiatives in the UT needs to be stepped up. The elections to the communes and *panchayats* have been conducted after a long gap. The Conformity Act for the 73rd and 74th Amendments Act has not been passed. Two Finance Commissions have been appointed and they have submitted their reports. The recommendations of these reports needs to be looked into with seriousness. The revenue and expenditure pattern in the communes manifest the huge potential available for generating more resources and spending on development activities. The e-governance initiatives have been commissioned with the help of the IBM company. Already some of the departments have been networked and automated. There is a provision for alloting two per cent of the budget of each department for office automation and e-governance initiatives. The right to information process has been initiated through the publication of citizens' charters and installation of kiosks in the department offices. Thus, the government has been increasingly proactive in the e-governance initiatives.